بسم الله الرحمن الرحيم

IN THE NAME OF ALLAH, THE MOST GRACIOUS, THE MOST MERCIFUL

Regards

Munir Nabi Khan

آپ کے دکھ درد کا ساتھی

Book Title: Medicinal Plants

A Holistic Guide to Herbal Wisdom

First Edition 2022

Author: **Munir Nabi Khan**

Director Dwakhana Hakim Ajmal Khan Pvt, Ltd.

155 Quid-e-Azam Industrial Estate, Lahore 54770, Pakistan

Impression: 1000

Price in Rs. This is a non-commercial publication.

Price in US $. This is a non-commercial publication.

All Rights Reserved.

Copyrights Author and Publisher

Published By

Ajmal publications, Lahore

Plot No. 155, Kot Lackhpat, Industrial Estate, Lahore, Pakistan

ISBN 978-1-80068-083-8

Medicinal Plants

Ajmal

Munir Nabi Khan

B Pharm (University of the Punjab), MSc (University of Lancaster, UK).

Director Dawakhana Hakim Ajmal Khan Pvt. Ltd.

155, Quaid-e-Azam Industrial Area, Lahore, Pakistan.

I would like to dedicate this book to my mother, Mehar Jehan Begum; there are not enough words to describe the inspirational role you continue to play in my life, persuading me to strive for excellence and never give up.

To my loving, supporting and caring wife, Anjum: my deepest gratitude. Your encouragement when times got rough is much appreciated and duly noted.

And

To my children

Tamkeen Nabi Khan

Moiz Nabi Khan

Momin Nabi Khan

Contents

Acknowledgement	i
Preface	v
Notes	vi
Traditional Systems of Medicine	vii
Alkaloids	1
Carbohydrates	77
Fixed Oils	105
Glycosides	131
Saponins	205
Gums and Mucilage	231
Resins	258
Tannins	297
Volatile Oils and Isoprenoids (Terpenoids)	329
Plants with anti-cancer Properties	429
Medicinal Plants in Holy Scriptures	449
Historical Facts of the Medicinal Plant	467
Index of Therapeutic Action	497
Bibliography	506
Index of Latin Binomials	509
Index of English Names	515
Index of Urdu Names	519
Index of Plant Family	523

Acknowledgements

I would like to express my gratitude to several people without whom writing this book would not have been possible. At the outset, I sincerely thank my brother and friend Dr Abdul Quadeer Khan (NI & BAR, HI), the pride of our nation, Mohsin-e-Pakistan (saviour of Pakistan), father of Pakistan's nuclear programme for writing the review for my book.

Professor Dr Mustayeen Ahmad Khan (Faculty of Pharmacy, University of Angers, France): I cannot express enough thanks for your continued support, encouragement and contribution towards accomplishing this book. I am forever indebted to you.

In memoriam, my Professor, my friend Dr Naim Anwar Muzaffer (TI), Father of Pharmacy in Pakistan, former Dean of Faculty of Pharmacy, University of Punjab, ex-member Pakistan Pharmacopoeia Committee, Drug Advisory Committee, member of the Board of Studies of Universities of Sindh, Balochistan, B.Z University, Gomal University and member of University Grants Commission, Islamabad. My profound thanks to his son Dr Muhammed Ali Muzaffer, Director, LCPS, Lahore, for allowing me to use all Medicinal Plant books and giving me access to his library, which helped my research for this project.

My respectful and affectionate thoughts are for Professor Dr Khan Usman Ghani (Late), Faculty of Pharmacy, University of Karachi, for the generous gift of his books on Medicinal Plants, Herbal Medicine and Analysis of Plants. When I told Usman Sahib that I plan to write a book, he was delighted and said, 'Munir Sahib, it will be my pleasure to write notes for your book.' May he rest in eternal peace.

I am also thankful to my Emeritus Professor Dr Philip Hodge (Department of Chemistry, The University of Manchester, UK), for his help and support.

I am deeply grateful to Mohtarma Sadia Rashid, daughter of Hakim Muhammed Saeed (Shaheed), President of the Hamdard Foundation, for presenting me the second edition of Hamdard Pharmacopoeia of Eastern Medicine.

I take pride in thanking Mohtarma Ummul Fazal, former Deputy Director, Central Council for research in the Unani medicine, Government of India, for providing many scientific books on the Standardization of Plants and a book on 'Mujahid-e-Tibb,' Hakim Abdul Razzack.

I cannot begin to express my thanks to my friend, classmate Professor Dr Muhammed Jamshaid, former Dean of Faculty of Pharmacy, University of the Punjab and Dean of Faculty of Pharmacy, University of Central Punjab; Dr Abu Shamsul Huq of New Jersey, USA, Prof Dr Abdul Rehman Memon (Late) of Faculty of Pharmacy, University of Sind, Jamshoro and Dr Syed Ibrahim Mohammed Ismail of Malaysia, for their help and constant encouragement.

My sincere thanks also goes to Meritorious Professor Dr Zafer Iqbal (TI), Department of Pharmacy, the University of Peshawar, for his valuable suggestions and ever-encouraging and motivating guidance.

I would like to extend my deepest gratitude to Professor Dr Hakim Abdul Hannan of Hamdard Laboratory, for his valuable book of 'Pharmacognosy and Materia Medica for Eastern Medicine.'

Professor Dr Waqar Yousuf Azami of the Sufi Khwaja Shamsuddin Azeemi family and for his continuous support and help.

I am grateful to Dr Saleem Khan (MD, MA and MHDO) of the U.K. for gifting me two of his scholarly books on Islamic Medicine.

I am thankful to Ms Angela Williams (founder of Bloomfield Hall Schools), Ms Jamila John (who has a Joint Honours degree from the University of London) and Ms Amna Shafqat (MA in the English Language and MA in Business education) for their help.

To many knowledgeable Hakims, Pharmacists and Scientists of Pakistan who helped and encouraged me, I am thankful to them all.

I am blessed and forever grateful to be surrounded by family members who supported me at different stages of this book. Jalil Nabi Khan, Tanvir Nabi Khan, Sabih Behzad, Ashima Shuja, Sumera Farid (Chemistry Teacher), Muhammed Ajmal Khan, Shariq Iqrar, Mahnoor Mohsin Khan, (final year student of Doctor of Pharmacy, University of Wisconsin-Madison, USA), Mahvasha Shahab and Mavra Nasir. Mrs Zeba Zia, for her encouragement that kept me in touch with the medicinal properties of plants.

DR. A. Q. KHAN
NI & BAR, HI

"Mountain View"
207, Hillside Road,
E-7, Islamabad
Pakistan
hkhan42@gmail.com

Date: 11.6.21

MEDICINAL PLANTS
Munir Nabi Khan
Review by Dr. A.Q. Khan NI & Bar, HI

I am extremely honoured to have been requested by my dear friend, Munir Nabi Khan, great grandson of Masihul Mulk (curer of the nation) Hakim Ajmal Khan, Quaid-e-Azam's dear friend and staunch supporter, to write this review.

The book is a marvel, an encyclopaedia of medicinal plants and Eastern Medicine. I belong to Bhopal State, a state governed by Orakzai Pathans. The Begums of Bhopal, who ruled Bhopal for hundreds of years, were enlightened and educated and promoted education and culture. Near our school – Jehangiria Model School – was Asfia College where hikmat (Eastern Medicine) was taught. Students from Afghanistan, Central Asia, Frontier, Baluchistan, etc. came there to study. It had excellent facilities and Unani and Ayurvedic medicines were taught too and hakims graduating from Bhopal were posted in villages with ample stocks of medicines and facilities, hostels, etc. There was a huge Unani Dawakhana in addition to the western Prince of Wales and Lady Duffen's Hospitals, the latter being exclusively for ladies. I sometimes went to the Unani Dawakhana and received excellent treatment from qualified and experienced hakims. Thousands of people benefitted from the Dawakhana.

The book by M.N. Khan is like a voluminous tafsir of the Holy Quran. It explains every medicinal plant, its Latin, English and Urdu names, properties, usage, availability and, above all and most importantly, with organic, chemical and compound diagrams (structural formulae diagrams). The author has consulted a large number of important, experienced professionals and important relevant literature in order to write this beautiful, voluminous, invaluable book, to be used as a reference work. Only those familiar with the subject can appreciate the hard, sustained work that went into its compilation.

May Almighty Allah shower His infinite blessings on brother Munir Nabi Khan, his family and collaborators in this fine work – Ameen.

Dr. A.Q. Khan
NI & Bar, HI

Preface

I desired to publish this book in 2020, but I could not do so due to the Coronavirus's impact. Coronavirus has been an unprecedented pandemic, with a significant impact on the lives of many millions of people around the world. It has led to drastic changes in how we live and interact with one another and we have, of course, sadly lost many lives globally, to this blight. It has, however, given me the opportunity to spend more time at home to work, to compile this book with the diligence it required.

There are a variety of plant classifications, namely: Alphabetical, Taxonomical, Morphological, Pharmacological and Chemical. In this book, plants are classified in Chemical categories – an approach similar to any Pharmacognosy book published by other European, American or Asian authors. In chemical classifications, the crude drugs are divided into different groups according to the chemical nature of their most important constituent present in the plant, to which the pharmacological/therapeutic activity of the drug is attributed.

Each classification type has its advantages and disadvantages. In Chemical classification, the main disadvantage is that plants of different origin are grouped under a similar chemical title. This type of classification makes no proper placement of medicinal herbs containing two different types of chemicals. The great advantages are the chemical constituents and the medicinal uses that are known, which have enabled me to adopt a similar approach.

The Indo-Pak subcontinent is rich in natural resources and is renowned for its traditional medicinal practices, some going back many hundreds of years. The main objective is to append many useful medicinal plants from Unani and Ayurvedic medicinal systems into chemical classifications. The selection of the plants is based on available books of Pharmacognosy, the plant's biologically active constituents, Herbal, Unani, Ayurvedic and Official Pharmacopeias. In addition to the scientific literature, research articles and most important biological activities of the constituents have also been used. The categorization and selection of plants that I have mentioned in my book have not been made before for many traditional medicinal plants. Hence, if there are any errors, I will be obliged if they are brought to my notice. I will gratefully acknowledge constructive and helpful suggestions for improving any future editions of this book.

Notes

There is substantial scientific literature that either proves or is in the process of establishing the efficacy of orthodox, folk or traditional uses of medicinal plants. However, this does not cover all the plants and claims. Some of the conventional benefits recorded by Hakims, Ayurveda, Homoeopaths, Folk healers and Herbalists reflected in this book may not be fit for the present time. It is conceivable that pharmacists, scientists and chemists may evaluate and then prove their medical treatment's efficacy with time. The ultimate aim of science is to promote discovery and uncover truths that may aid humanity.

The Holy Quran says that the believers have been sent for the betterment of mankind, that they will promote what is good and prevent what is wrong. (Al-I-Imran: 110).

Prophet Muhammad (PBUH) said, "It is also a charity to utter a good word." (Al-Bukhari and Muslim, Riyad as-Salihin 693 Book 1, Hadith 14).

> Note: Do not undertake any course of treatment without consultation of a qualified health adviser or physician.

Traditional Systems of Medicine

Unani System of Medicine

The Unani System of Medicine refers to Graeco-Arabic medicine, which is based on the teachings of the Greek physician Hippocrates and the Roman physicians Galen, which was developed into an elaborate medical system during the Middle Ages by Arabian and Persian physicians, such as Ali Raban Tabri (d. 870), Al-Dinawari (d. 895), Al-Razi (Rhazes, d. 925), Ibn Juljul (Gilgil, d. 994), Al-Zahrawi (Abulcassis, d. 1013), Ibn Sina (Avicenna, d. 1037), Ibn Zuhr (Avenzoar, d. 1162), Al-Ghafiqi (d. 1170), Ibn Baytar (d. 1248) and Ibn Nafis (Ebenefis, d. 1288).

Unani medicines became enriched by imbibing what was best in the contemporary systems of traditional medicines in Egypt, Syria, Iraq, Persia, India and other Middle Eastern countries. In the Indo-Pak subcontinent, the Unani System of Medicine was introduced by the Arabs and soon, it took firm roots. During the Delhi Sultanate period (1192-1526 AD), the Delhi Sultans provided patronage to the Unani System's scholars and even enrolled some state employees and court physicians. Between the 13th and the 19th centuries, Unani medicine had its hey-day in India. During the British rule, the Unani system suffered a setback due to the withdrawal of the state patronage but continued to be practised as the masses reposed faith in the system. It was mainly due to the Sharifi Family's efforts and Hakim Abdul Majeed's family in Delhi, the Azizi Family in Lucknow, the Tayyebi Family in Indore and the patronage of Nizam of Hyderabad that the Unani medicine survived during the British period.

In India, the concept of research in the Unani system of medicine was initially perceived, in the 1920s, by Masih-ul-Mulk Hakim Ajmal Khan (my great grandfather), a versatile genius. Hakim Ajmal Khan is considered as one of the 100 great Muslim leaders of the 20th century. He draws his ancestry from the famous Saint Khwaja Ubaidullah Ahrar (1404 - 1490) from Samarqand in Central Asia. Hakim Ajmal Khan (1868 - 1927) spotted Dr Salimuzzaman Siddiqui (1897 - 1994), a chemist, for the undertaking of chemical studies on some important medicinal plants used in Unani Medicine. Dr Siddiqui undertook the task visualized by Masih-ul-Mulk, and his discovery of a plant's medicinal properties, commonly known as Asrol (Pagal Booti), which led to sustained research that established the unique efficacy of this plant known worldwide as Rauwolfia serpentina of the Apocynaceae family. It is used for neurovascular and nervous disorders, such as hypertension and insanity, schizophrenia, hysteria, insomnia and psychosomatic conditions, etc.

Ayurvedic system of medicine[1]

The Ayurvedic Medicinal System is a system of traditional medicine native to the Indian subcontinent and practised in other parts of the world as a form of conventional medicine. The earliest literature on the Indian medical practice appeared during India's Vedic period. Ayurvedic treatment of disease consists of the healthful use of drugs, diets and certain practices. Medicinal preparation is invariably complex mixtures, based mostly on plant products. Around one thousand plants are used in various Ayurvedic preparations. Many Indian medicinal plants have come under scientific scrutiny since the middle of the nineteenth century, albeit in a periodic fashion. According to Ayurveda, all objects in the universe, including the human body, are composed of five basic elements: water, fire, earth, air and vacuum. There is a balanced condensation of these elements in different proportions to suit the needs and requirements of different structures and functions of the body matrix and its parts. The growth and development of the body matrix depend on its nutrition, i.e., food. The food, in turn, is composed of the above five elements, which replenish or nourish the like elements of the body after the action of bio-fire (Agni). The body tissues are structural, whereas humours are the physiological entities derived from different combinations and permutations of five basic elements. The treatment of a disease consists of avoiding causative factors responsible for their disequilibrium of the body matrix or any of its constituent parts through the use of Panchkarma procedures, medicines, suitable diet, activity and regimen for restoring the balance and strengthening the body mechanisms to prevent or minimize future occurrence of the disease. Normally treatment measures involve medicines, a specific diet and a prescribed activity routine. In one treatment approach, the three measures antagonize the disease by counteracting the disease's etiological factors and various manifestations. In the second approach, the same three medicines, diet and activity measures, are targeted to exert effects similar to the diseases process of etiological factors and manifestations. These two therapeutic approaches are known as Vipreeta and Vipreetarthkari treatments.

Homoeopathic System of Medicine

Homoeopathy, founded by a German physician Samuel Hahnemann in 1796, is based on the idea that 'like cures like'; substances that cause certain symptoms in a healthy person can also cure those same symptoms in someone who is sick. This so-called law of similar homoeopathy is named 'homeo' for similar 'pathy' designating disease. In this experiment, Hahnemann developed a method of 'potentizing' homoeopathic remedies by diluting them in a water-alcohol solution and then vigorously shaking the mixtures. The result convinced him that a high degree of dilution minimizes the

---

[1] This and the following paragraph are extracts from "Traditional Systems of Medicine" by Y.V. Jayalakhshmi and R.K. Singla (Article ID: WMC003299).

remedies' side effects and simultaneously enhances their medical efficacy. Most Homoeopathic remedies have undergone 'proving' or medical observations in which healthy individuals are given doses of undiluted homoeopathic substances. Mental, emotional, psychic and other patient details are most important; this leads the physician to understand better, that which remedy will best suit a particular set of symptoms.

Medicinal Plants
Plants containing Alkaloids

Medicinal Plants — Alkaloids

Note:

In nature, there are many compounds. Among them, many naturally occurring organic compounds such as glycosides, carbohydrates, flavonoids, saponins, resin, steroids and tannins seem to be quite remarkable and the most popular are alkaloids.

What makes them special? They are derived from amino acids and can be synthesized as secondary metabolites. These compounds play an important role in living organisms. Alkaloids are extremely important for human beings of all ages. They have shown strong biological effects on animals and human organisms in minimal doses. Alkaloids are present in a human's daily food and drinks and also as stimulant herbs. In the human diet, the plants which contain alkaloids are not only coffee seeds (caffeine), cacao seeds (theobromine and caffeine), tea leaves (theophylline and caffeine) but also tomatoes (tomatine) and potatoes (solanine). The most common alkaloid is caffeine, an ingredient of soft drinks like Coca-Cola, Pepsi-Cola and 7-Up, to improve their taste as energy drinks.

It is worth mentioning here that some alkaloids are also poisonous, like Tubocurarine. They show anti-inflammatory, anti-cancerous, analgesic, diuretic, local anaesthetic, antifungal and many other activities. Alkaloids are beneficial as diet ingredients, supplements, pharmaceuticals, medicine and other human life applications.

Tomatine ($C_{50}H_{83}NO_{21}$)   Solanine ($C_{45}H_{73}NO_{15}$)   Tubocurarine ($C_{37}H_{42}Cl_2N_2O_6$)

Alkaloids

Definition: Alkaloids are organic compounds derived from plants, with a primary character. Hence alkaloids from alkali contain a nitrogen-based heterocyclic ring within their molecules.

Properties of Alkaloids

Alkaloids are insoluble or sparingly soluble in water.

Alkaloid salts, formed in reaction with acids, are water-soluble.

Most alkaloids are crystalline solids, but a few are amorphous (coniine and nicotine), some are liquid (nicotine and pilocarpine) and some are volatile like nicotine.

Alkaloid salts are crystalline.

Most alkaloids are poisonous when injected.

The alkaloids usually possess a bitter taste.

Most alkaloids contain oxygen in their molecular structure. These compounds are usually colourless crystals. The basicity of alkaloids depends on the availability of a lone pair of electrons.

Some alkaloids are coloured, e.g., canadine. Some alkaloids are optically active.

Function in Plants: (i) They act as a protective shield against insects and herbivores due to their bitter taste and toxicity. (ii) They are a source of nitrogen. (iii) They sometimes act as growth regulators in certain metabolic systems. (iv) They may be utilized as sources of energy in case of deficiency in carbon dioxide assimilation.

Tests for Alkaloids

Most alkaloids form a precipitate from a neutral or slightly acidic solution.

Dragendorff's reagent: It is a potassium bismuth iodide solution. When added to the alkaloid solution, it gives an orange or orange-red precipitate.

Mayer's reagent: It is a potassium mercuric iodide solution. It gives a cream or pale yellow precipitates (except for the 'purine group),' when added to the alkaloid solution.

Wagner's reagent: It is an iodine and potassium iodide solution. When added to an alkaloid solution, it gives a brown or reddish-brown precipitate.

Hager's reagent: It is a saturated solution of picric acid. When added to an alkaloid solution, it gives a yellow precipitate.

Dragendorff's,	Mayer's,	Wagner's	Hager's
(Orange Red)	(Light Yellow)	(Reddish-Brown)	(Yellow)

Types of Alkaloids

True Alkaloids: They are derived from amino acids and have nitrogen in a heterocyclic ring, e.g., atropine.

Proto Alkaloids: This group of alkaloids has the nitrogen atom that originates from an amino group but is not present in a heterocyclic ring, e.g., ephedrine

Pseudo Alkaloids: These are not derived from amino acids but have nitrogen in a heterocyclic ring, e.g., caffeine.

False Alkaloids: These are the non-alkaloids that give a false-positive reaction with an alkaloidal regent.

Atropine ($C_{17}H_{23}NO_3$)   Ephedrine ($C_{10}H_{15}NO$)   Caffeine ($C_8H_{10}N_4O_2$)

Type of alkaloid	Precursor	Type of nitrogen
True alkaloids	Amino acids	Heterocyclic
Protoalkaloids	Amino acids	Non-heterocyclic
Pseudoalkaloids	Non-amino acids	Heterocyclic

Main Classes of Monomeric Alkaloids

1. Tropane Alkaloids

2. Quinoline Alkaloids

3. Isoquinoline Alkaloids

4. Purine Alkaloids

5. Terpenoid (Isoprenoid) Alkaloids

6. Pyridine and Pyrrolidine Alkaloids

7. Imidazole Alkaloids

8. Piperine Alkaloids

9. Indole Alkaloids

1. Tropane Alkaloids

The Tropane Alkaloids are among the first ones detected in nature, with a wide application for various remedies.

Tropane is a bicycle with pyrrolidine and piperidine rings sharing a common nitrogen atom and two carbon atoms. Nitrogen is the common structural element of all tropane alkaloids. The principal alkaloids of medicinal interest in this group are (-)-hyoscyamine and its more stable racemates, atropine and hyoscine. Tropane alkaloids occur naturally in Solanaceae, Convolvulaceae and the Erythroxylaceae families. The important plants containing tropane alkaloids are Atropa belladonna, Datura stramonium, Erythroxylon coca and Hyoscyamus niger.

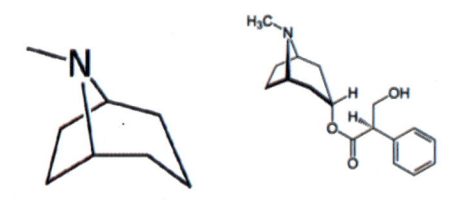

Tropane Alkaloids

Tropane Alkaloids are classified into:

1- Solanaceous Tropane Alkaloids

2- Erythroxylon (Coca) Tropane Alkaloids

2. Quinoline Alkaloids

In general, the alkaloids containing the 'quinoline' nucleus essentially include a series of alkaloids obtained exclusively from the Cinchona bark; the major members of this particular group are Quinine, quinidine, cinchonine and cinchonidine.

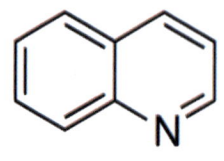

Quinoline

3. Isoquinoline Alkaloids

Isoquinoline is benzopyridine and is composed of a benzene ring fused into a pyridine ring. The difference between quinoline and isoquinoline is that in the former, the nitrogen atom is at position one, whereas, in the latter, it is at position two of the ring structure. In a broader sense, the term isoquinoline refers to isoquinoline derivatives. Isoquinoline alkaloids are a class of alkaloids containing a structural moiety of isoquinoline derivatives.

Isoquinoline

4. Purine Alkaloids

Purine is an aromatic organic compound that consists of a pyrimidine ring fused into an imidazole ring. Purine alkaloids are important since they pose strong effects on the central nervous system (CNS), as stimulants, for kidneys, as a diuretic, to promote circulation and smooth muscles to relax, including muscles of the respiratory tract.

Purine

5. Terpenoid (Isoprenoid) Alkaloids

Terpenoids are any large organic compounds class, including terpenes, diterpenes and sesquiterpenes. They have unsaturated molecules composed of linked isoprene units, generally having the formula (C_5H_8) n.

Isoprene Unit

6. Pyridine and Pyrrolidine Alkaloids

Pyridine contains an aromatic ring with one nitrogen atom as part of the heterocyclic structure with the chemical formula (C_5H_5N). It is structurally related to benzene, with one methine group (=CH–) replaced by a nitrogen atom. The nitrogen nucleus is unsaturated. Pyrrolidine is a cyclic amine whose five-membered ring contains four carbon atoms and one nitrogen atom, the pyrrolidine family's parent compound. An example of Pyridine alkaloid is Trigonella foenum-graecum (trigonelline) of the Fabaceae family. For a pyrrolidine alkaloid, an example is Nicotiana tobacco (nicotine) of the Solanaceae family.

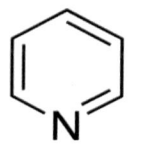

Pyridine

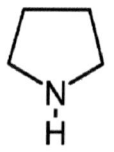

Pyrrolidine

7. Imidazole Alkaloids

Imidazole is a heterocyclic, aromatic organic compound with the formula $C_3N_2H_4$. Imidazole alkaloids are a class of alkaloids containing a structural moiety of imidazole. The ring system of imidazole is essential as it is present in the biological building blocks such as histidine and histamine.

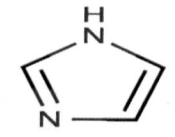

Imidazole

8. Piperine Alkaloids

Piperine is an alkaloid present in black pepper (Piper nigrum), which is one of the most widely used spices, in long pepper (Piper longum) and other Piper species, the plant belonging to the family Piperaceae. Piperine is an alkaloid responsible for black pepper and long pepper pungency. It is interesting that piperine is neither basic nor possesses any physiological activity, but it is considered an alkaloid.

Piperine

9. Indole Alkaloids

Indole alkaloids have a bicyclic structure, consisting of a six-membered benzene ring fused into a five-membered nitrogen-containing pyrrole ring. This pyrrole ring with a nitrogen atom gives rise to the indole alkaloids basic properties that make them particularly pharmacologically active. Indole alkaloids are a class of alkaloids containing a structural moiety of indole. These alkaloids are widely distributed in plants belonging to the Apocynaceae, Loganiaceae, Rubiaceae and Clavicipitaceae families. Plants containing indole alkaloids are Strychnos nux vomica (strychnine and brucine), Claviceps purpurea (Ergotamine and ergometrinine), Catharanthus roseus (vincristine and vinblastine), Rauwolfia serpentina (Reserpine, Ajmaline and Ajmalicine) and Physostigma venenosum (physostigmine).

Indole group

Fischer Indole Synthesis

Achillea millefolium

Biranjasif (Flowers and Leaves)

Latin Binomial	Achillea millefolium
Family	Compositae/Asteraceae
English Name	Yarrow
Urdu Name	Biranjasif

Medicinal Uses: The leaves and flowers of the herbaceous, perennial, flowering Achillea millefolium plant are mildly aromatic, diaphoretic, stimulative, vasodilator, anti-inflammatory and carminative in action. These are most useful in colds, obstructed sweat, fevers, in the commencement of menstrual bleeding and in pain.

Traditional Uses: In Unani and Ayurvedic medicinal systems, the plant can induce sweating and stop wound bleeding. Achillea millefolium is beneficial in reducing heavy menstrual complaints such as mild cramp-like discomfort in the gastrointestinal area and painful spasmodic inflammations. It is also helpful in treating mild skin and mucous membrane inflammations.

The plant's fresh leaves can be applied directly to an aching tooth to relieve pain. The leaves and flowers are useful as a diuretic and a cleansing tonic in kidney and urinary tract infections. It is also valuable as an emmenagogue and is a remedy for women in regulating the menstrual cycle, stabilizing mood swings and increasing appetite.

Traditional healers (Hakims and Ayurveda) of the Indo-Pak subcontinent used this plant as a bitter tonic to stimulate and harmonize the appetite, digestion and promote bile flow. As a blood tonic to optimize the flow, and to promote its circulation. Externally, poultices and fomentations of leaves and flowers are haemostatic vulneraries to stop bleeding.

Biological Uses: The oil of these flowers and the non-aqueous (methanol) extract of the plant showed antiviral, antitumor, antibacterial, anti-inflammatory, cytotoxic, antifungal, antiproliferative and antiseptic properties. The plant's hydroalcoholic and ethanolic fractions have antiulcer, antispermatogenic and hepatoprotective properties. Crude extracts of the aerial parts of Achillea millefolium have shown estrogenic activity.

The non-aqueous fraction of methanol and ethyl acetate of this flower have antityrosinase (tyrosinase is a copper-containing enzyme present in animal tissues) activity. However, the ethanolic and aqueous extracts are not adequate for this enzyme. The anti-diabetic effect of the hydroalcoholic fraction of the plant may be due to the presence of flavonoids.

Chemical Constituents: The presence of glycoalkaloids (betonicine and achillicine), flavonoids (apigenin, artemetin, luteolin and rutin) and volatile oils may alleviate symptoms of depression and anxiety.

The plant also contains constituents like tannins, other alkaloids, sterols, phenols, resins, terpenoids (achineine, betaine and choline) and sweet odour coumarin. The main components of the oil are cineole, germacrene and caryophyllene, etc.

The dark blue to green Yarrow oil is mainly derived from flowers. Polish Pharmacopoeia (part-IV) specifies requirements for oil content as 0.25 per cent. The European species of Achillea are rich in oxygenated compounds (more aroma) and contain a small amount of chamazulene (a hydrocarbon volatile oil).

Distribution: Achillea millefolium is native to Northern Hemisphere's temperate regions, Asia, Europe and America. The plant is common in Austria and New Zealand in wet and dry areas, such as roadside, grassland, fields, and near seasides.

(-) - Betonicine Achillein ($C_7H_{13}NO_3$)   Flavonoid Apigenin ($C_{15}H_{10}O_5$)

Aconitum napellus

Bichnag/Atees (Plant, Flowers and Tubes)

Latin Binomials	Aconitum napellus/Aconitum heterophyllum
Family	Ranunculaceae
English Name	Aconite
Urdu Names	Bichnag/Atees

Medicinal Uses: The plant's fresh leaves and dried tubers are useful, medicinally. The flowering, extremely toxic, herbaceous, perennial Aconitum napellus plant is antipyretic, stimulative, anodyne, atrabilious, anti-phlegmatic, sedative and diuretic in action. It is an effective agent for fevers that are due to inflammation. The root is valuable in the treatment of catarrh, tonsillitis and croup.

The Aconitum species are poisonous plants that have been useful in Western medicine for centuries. In the nineteenth century, these plants were part of official and folk medicine in the Slovenian territory. However, according to current ethnobotanical studies, folk use of Aconitum species is rarely reported in Europe.

Traditional Uses: A different species of the Aconitum plant, 'Aconitum heterophyllum,' is useful in Unani and Ayurvedic medicinal systems for diarrhoea, dysentery, bleeding piles and menorrhagia. The decoction of rhizomes is often taken along with ghee (clarified butter) to restore energy. The juice of the root added to milk, acts as an expectorant.

The powder added to water helps as an antidote in food poisoning, snakebite and treatment for fever, headache and stomach ache. The root is beneficial as an anaesthetic, analgesic, anti-inflammatory, antirheumatic, stimulant and vasodilator. In folk medicine, infusions or tinctures are helpful as a sedative and antineuralgic for sciatica and rheumatic pains.

In Central China, it is still used as a home medicine and in food. In far-western Nepal, the Aconitum tubes are beneficial as antipyretic and analgesic for gastritis and debility.

Biological Uses: The ethanolic extracts of the rhizome possess anti-inflammatory, antioxidant, analgesic, antipyretic and anti-cancer activities. The antimicrobial potential of the methanol fractions of Aconitum against gram-negative and gram-positive bacteria, indicated an irrelevant activity compared with the standards. However, all the methanolic fractions tested, presented an intense antifungal property.

Chemical Constituents: Aconitum napellus contains isoprenoid (diterpenoid) alkaloids, of which the most important is aconitine. The plant also has other alkaloids such as hypaconitine, neopelline, jesacontine and valuable biologically active compounds like glycosides, phenols, terpenoids, steroids, flavonoids, essential oils and resins.

Distribution: Aconitum napellus is grown in the hilly regions of Central Asia, Russia, Europe and the United Kingdom.

Note: All parts of the plant, especially the roots, contain toxins and should only be used under medical advice. Aconitine is the most dangerous of these toxins. Aconite poisoning is rare in North America. When it does occur, it is generally due to a confusion with an edible plant or unintentional ingestion by children.

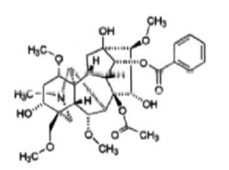

Aconitine ($C_{34}H_{47}NO_{11}$) 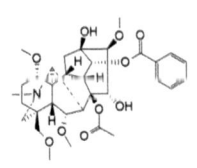   Hypaconitine ($C_{33}H_{45}NO_{10}$)

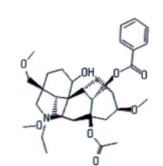

Neopelline (C$_{33}$H$_{45}$NO$_8$)

Adhatoda vasica

Arosa (Plant, Flowers and Leaf)

Latin Binomials	Adhatoda vasica/Justicia adhatoda
Family	Acanthaceae
English Names	Vasaka/Malabar-nut
Urdu Names	Bansa/Arosa

Medicinal Uses: All parts of the plant, from roots to leaves, are used for medicinal purposes. However, the leaves are of great importance. The leaves of the flowering Adhatoda vasica shrub are expectorant, antispasmodic, diuretic, germicidal in action and beneficial in paralysis. European herbalists have used this herb with success in typhus fever and diphtheria.

Traditional Uses: In Unani and Ayurvedic medicinal systems, the plant's leaves are a precious remedy for all bronchial and pulmonary diseases. The expectorant activity is due to the stimulation of the bronchial glands. The whole plant can be helpful in getting rid of intestinal parasites. The powdered herb, boiled with sesame oil, helps heal ear infections and arrests bleeding. Boiled leaves are suitable in treating rheumatic pain. They also have abortifacient properties. A decoction of its leaves helps treat scabies and other skin diseases. The juice of the plant (above the ground parts) is valuable in treating diarrhoea and dysentery. Its local use gives relief in pyorrhoea and bleeding gums. In the Ayurvedic medicinal system, the plant is also suitable for blood purification. It ensures lowering blood pressure and is a valuable tonic for the heart.

Biological Uses: The aqueous (decoction) and non-aqueous (ethanol) extracts of the plant possess antiulcer, antifungal, antibacterial, cholagogue and insecticidal activities. The ethanolic fractions have antioxidant and antilipidemic properties.

Chemical Constituents: The valuable alkaloids found in Adhatoda vasica leaves are the quinazoline alkaloids known as vasicine, betaine and an anti-inflammatory agent vasicinolone. The immense variety of pharmacological uses of Adhatoda vasica are due to its high concentration of alkaloids, flavonoids, triterpenoids, essential oils, resin and vitamin C. The leaves of the plant are also rich in volatile oils.

Distribution: The plant is a native to the Indo-Pak subcontinent, Bangladesh, Nepal and Assam. It has also grown in the Far East countries like Laos and Myanmar. This plant is abundant in Khyber Pakhtunkhwa (KPK), Pakistan and is famous for its unique medicinal importance.

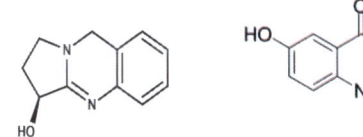

Vasicine ($C_{11}H_{12}N_2O$)   Vasicinolone ($C_{11}H_{10}N_2O_3$)

Areca catechu

Supari (Tree and Fresh and Dried Nuts)

Latin Binomial	Areca catechu
Family	Palmae/Arecaceae
English Name	Betel Nut

Urdu name   Supari/Chaliya

Medicinal Uses: The nut of a medium-sized Areca catechu tree is astringent, a stimulant herb that relieves hunger, abdominal discomfort and weariness.

Traditional Uses: In Unani and Ayurvedic medicinal systems, Areca catechu is useful as an astringent, stimulant, anthelmintic and to sweeten the breath. It kills intestinal parasites and other pathogens and has diuretic and laxative effects. The nut is valuable in stomatitis, bleeding gums, gingivitis, conjunctivitis, leucorrhoea, urinary disorders and diarrhoea. In Ayurvedic medicine, the nut's fine powder is useful externally as a dusting powder to treat wounds and to control bleeding. The decoction is helpful as a vaginal enema in the treatment of leucorrhoea. The juice of the root is valuable in treating various liver disease manifestations. It is a purgative and an ointment for nasal ulcers when combined with other ingredients. The rind is used as a laxative in constipation cases with flatulence and bloating and as a diuretic in treating oedema. The seeds are beneficial in treating leucoderma, leprosy, obesity and worms. The skin of the fruit is edible. Tannins from these plants are a valuable antidote for snake venom.

The nut of Areca catechu tree is very popular for chewing in many Asian countries, for example, Pakistan, India, Myanmar, the Philippines and Bangladesh.

Biological Uses: Aqueous extract (decoction) is effective in gram-negative and gram-positive bacteria. The non-aqueous extracts (hexane, ethyl acetate and methanol) possess antifungal, antiviral and antimalarial properties. The presence of arecoline alkaloids in the plant, significantly decreases sperm motility. An ethanol fraction of Areca has low antibacterial activity, whereas the methanol extract has potent antioxidant properties.

Chemical Constituents: The stimulant action of the Areca nut is due to the presence of arecoline, which is a nicotinic acid-based mild parasympathomimetic (stimulates nervous system) stimulant alkaloid. Other alkaloids present in nuts are arecaidine, guvacine and choline. The Areca nut also contains valuable phytochemicals like tannins, glycosides, flavonoids, gum, polyphenols and minerals like copper, calcium, phosphorus and iron. The plant is an equally good source of vitamin B_6, vitamin C and tannins.

Distribution: Areca catechu is cultivated in tropical India, Sri Lanka, Malaysia, South China, the East Indies, the Philippines Islands and East Africa, including Zanzibar and Tanzania.

Note: A study in the American Dental Association reports that Betel nut users are at a higher risk of oral sub-mucous fibrosis. This incurable condition can cause stiffness in the mouth and eventually, jaw movement loss.

Arecoline ($C_8H_{13}NO_2$) Arecaidine ($C_7H_{11}NO_2$)

Atropa belladonna

Anab-us-Saalab (Plant, Flowers and Leaves)

Latin Binomial	Atropa belladonna/Atropa acuminata
Family	Solanaceae
English Name	Belladonna/Deadly Nightshade
Urdu name	Luffah/Anub-us-Saa'lab

Medicinal Uses: The leaves, stem and root of this plant are useful, medicinally. The flowering, poisonous, perennial, herbaceous Atropa belladonna plant is narcotic, diuretic, sedative, mydriatic (herb induces dilation of the pupil) and antispasmodic in action. The herb is useful as an anaesthetic in febrile conditions, night sweats and coughs. It is valuable in treating eye diseases and as a pain-relieving lotion in treating neuralgia, gout, rheumatism and sciatica. Internally, the plant is also beneficial as a sedative.

Traditional Uses: Atropa belladonna has been used for centuries in traditional medicine for ailments ranging from headaches, ulcers and menstrual problems to inflammation and cardiovascular diseases. Externally, the leaves and roots (as a paste) are helpful as an antispasmodic, in relieving palpitation and as a diuretic. The whole plant has sedative and diuretic properties and is most commonly known for its uses in ophthalmology for pupil dilation. Atropa belladonna helps to bring relief from spasmodic asthma. For centuries, it has been beneficial in Unani and Ayurvedic medicinal systems as a pain reliever, muscle relaxant, anti-inflammatory and as a treatment for menstrual problems, peptic ulcers, histaminic reaction and motion sickness. In leucorrhoea, its suppository is helpful.

Biological Uses: Extracts of all parts of the plant have antioxidant properties. The aqueous extract of the plant has wound healing and anti-inflammatory activities. Anticholinergic effects of the plant have also been established. The methanolic extract obtained from the aerial parts of Atropa belladonna, has exhibited high acaricide activity (a pesticide that kills mites and ticks).

Chemical Constituents: The leaves and fruit contain tropane alkaloids: atropine, hyoscyamine, apoatropine, belladonine, cuscohygrine and scopolamine (hyoscine). These alkaloids are naturally occurring muscarinic antagonists. A muscarinic antagonist is used to treat peptic ulcers, nausea, vomiting, motion sickness, etc.

Distribution: Atropa belladonna is native to Europe (the United Kingdom, France and Germany), North Africa, Western Asia (Turkey and Iran) and South Asia (Pakistan and India).

Note: Belladonna is a highly poisonous plant and should always be administered under medical supervision. The causes of its accidental poisoning and death are well known. The risk of poisoning in children is significant because of possible confusion with other berries. In many countries, the plant Atropa belladonna has been declared a poisonous herb for internal use.

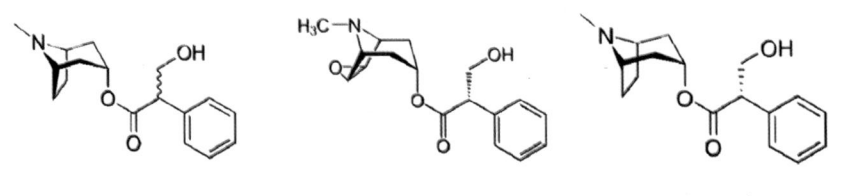

Atropine ($C_{17}H_{23}NO_3$) Scopolamine ($C_{17}H_{21}NO_4$) Hyoscyamine ($C_{17}H_{23}NO_3$)

Berberis aristata

Rasaut (Fresh and Dried Berries and Extract)

Latin Binomial	Berberis aristata
Family	Berberidaceae
English Name	Berberry
Urdu name	Rasout/Darhald/Zarishk

Medicinal Uses: The fruit and bark of the evergreen, flowering Berberis aristata shrub are antipyretic, cholagogue, antiperiodic and antidiarrhoeal in action. The plant is usually used to treat jaundice and liver complaints and regulate digestion. The berries (fruit) help produce an acid drink that helps ease diarrhoea and fevers. The fruit is most commonly taken by mouth for diabetes, for high cholesterol or other fats (lipids) in the blood (hyperlipidemia) and for high blood pressure. The berries are edible.

Traditional Uses: In Unani and Ayurvedic medicinal systems, the bark and stem are a tonic, diaphoretic, stomachic in action and beneficial in malarial fevers, diarrhoea, dysentery and acute diseases. The root is purgative and the root gum is a valuable blood purifier. The bark's decoction has helped treat haemorrhoids, eye, ear infections and gynaecological disorders. The traditional healers (Hakims and Ayurveda) of the Indo-Pak subcontinent use the root's extract in the treatment of jaundice, enlargement of spleen, spleen cancer and skin diseases.

Biological Uses: The plant's (root, bark and flowers) aqueous-alcohol extracts exhibit antipyretic, antibacterial, antimicrobial, antihyperglycaemic and antioxidant properties. The methanol fraction of the stem is very beneficial in colon cancer. The antidepressant, antimicrobial and anti-diabetic properties of the plant are also reported. One study shows when Berberis aristata is administered in high doses to cancer patients for a long time, the alkaloid present in Berberry, known as 'berberine,' kills cancer cells in tests conducted on humans.

Chemical Constituents: The plant contains an isoquinoline type of alkaloid, e.g., berberine, oxyberberine, berbamine, aromoline, karachine, palmatine and taxilamine. It also has some beneficial, biologically active compounds such as sterols, terpenoids, polyphenols, flavonoids, anthocyanins, vitamin C, resins and carotenoids. The plant's bark is a good source of fibre and minerals like zinc, magnesium, calcium, manganese, copper and potassium. The fruit of the plant is low in minerals.

Distribution: Berberis aristata is an evergreen shrub in temperate and subtropical regions of South Asia, Europe, China and North and South Americas. In Pakistan, the Berberis species belonging to this genus are found across most of the mountainous regions.

Note: Pregnant women should not take the plant's roots because of its stimulating effects on the uterus.

Dr Ibrahim Khan and Dr Zabta K. Shinwari *et al.* published a highly informative review of recent advances in phytopharmacological and ethnomedicinal uses of the plant Berberis genus.[2]

Berberine ($C_{20}H_{18}NO_4+$)   Oxyberbarine ($C_{20}H_{17}NO_5$)   Palmatine ($C_{21}H_{24}NO_4+$)

---

[2] Phytopharmacological and ethnomedicinal uses of the Genus Berberis (Berberidaceae): A review, Tropical Journal of Pharmaceutical Research September 2016; 15 (9): 2047-2057.

Camellia sinensis

Chayi (Flowers, Dried and Fresh Leaves)

Latin Binomial	Camellia sinensis
Family	Theaceae
English Name	Tea
Urdu Name	Chayi

Medicinal Uses: Tea is the most consumed drink globally, after water. The leaves of the evergreen, flowering Camellia sinensis shrub are aromatic, stimulant, diuretic, anti-diabetic and astringent in action.

There are three main varieties of Tea:- green, black and Oolong (semi-oxidized Chinese Tea). The difference between them is in their processing. Regardless of the colours of the Tea, all possess antioxidant properties.

Studies on humans and animals show that the antioxidants present in black and green Tea are highly beneficial to our health. Tea is also a natural diuretic, mainly because of its caffeine content. It contains tannins that can bind, to iron in certain foods, rendering it unavailable for absorption in the digestive tract.

Studies suggest that green Tea extract may boost metabolism and help burn fat. One study confirmed that the combination of green Tea and caffeine improved weight loss. However, a second study found that weight maintenance, following weight loss was not affected by green Tea. Some researchers speculate that green Tea substances are known as polyphenols; specifically, the catechins are responsible for the herb's fat-burning effect.

Traditional Uses: Traditional Chinese, Unani and Ayurvedic practitioners used Tea as a stimulant, diuretic, astringent and for improved heart health. Some herbalists also use Tea in flatulence, regulating body temperature, high blood sugar and improving mental processes. Camellia sinensis is considered a stimulant in Chinese folk medicine, which acts as a nervine or nerve sedative and frequently relieves headaches. It may also cause unpleasant nerve and digestive disturbances. Once recommended in China as a cancer cure, the infusion contains some tannin, suspected of being carcinogenic.

Externally, Camellia sinensis bags (Teabags) have been poulticed onto baggy or tired eyes and also used against sunburn.

Biological Uses: The aqueous and non-aqueous (methanol) extracts of leaves of green Tea exhibited anti-inflammatory, antioxidant, antimalarial, antihypertensive and anti-cancer properties. An alcoholic extract of black Tea is antibacterial and the aqueous extract possesses the hepatoprotective property. Hot water extract and tannin fraction of the whole plant exhibited antispasmodic activity.

Chemical Constituents: The leaves of the plant contain purine alkaloids, i.e., caffeine, theophylline and theobromine. The plant also has important constituents such as flavonoids, polyphenols, alkaloids, saponins, flavonols, tannins, essential oils and minerals like calcium, potassium, magnesium, iron, zinc and copper.

Distribution: Camellia sinensis is native to East and South Asia and probably originated around the meeting points of North Burma and Southwest China.

Note: Pakistan bought Tea worth around USD 571 million while the Russian Federation and the USA were closely tipped at USD 497 and USD 487 million, respectively, in 2019-2020.

Caffeine ($C_8H_{10}N_4O_2$)   Theophylline ($C_7H_8N_4O_2$)   Theobromine ($C_7H_8N_4O_2$)

Catharanthus roseus

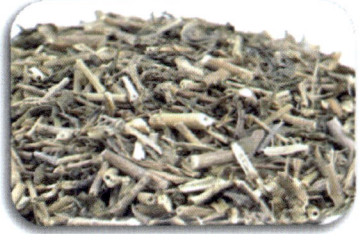

Sada Bahar (Flowers and Roots)

Latin Binomial	Catharanthus roseus/Vinca minor
Family	Apocynaceae
English Name	Cape Periwinkle/Periwinkle
Urdu Name	Sada-Bahar

Medicinal Uses: The leaves, flowers and roots of this herb are useful for medicinal purposes. The everblooming, perennial, flowering Catharanthus roseus herb is sedative, hypotensive, anti-diabetic and anti-leukemic.

Traditional Uses: The plant has long been useful in traditional medicine. In Unani and Ayurvedic medicinal systems, the extract of its roots and leaves, though poisonous, is helpful against several diseases, like diabetes and controls haemorrhage, malaria, muscle pain and depression. The decoction of leaves is also beneficial in managing heavy menstrual flow. An infusion of the flowers is a remedy in treating mild diabetes. Externally, the leaf extract has antiseptic properties.

In traditional Chinese medicine, extracts are valuable in Hodgkin's disease. In the West Indies, the plant is beneficial in treating high blood sugar and ulcers. Traditional healers (Albularyo) of the Philippines considered the root extract an effective remedy for diabetics. In Europe, related plant species are valued in suppressing the flow of milk. The plant is an excellent antioxidant and valuable in Hodgkin's disease (cancer of the lymphatic system).

Biological Uses: It has been reported that the plant's total alkaloids possess a limited antibacterial activity and a significant and sustained hypotensive action. The non-aqueous (ethanol) extract of the root possesses antioxidant and wound healing properties. The leaves fraction showed antibacterial activities and the ethanolic extracts of the whole plant exhibited anthelmintic properties. An extract (methanol) of the plant leaves also has an antiulcer effect.

Chemical Constituents: The indole alkaloids, vincristine and vinblastine, are prescribed in anti-cancer therapy, particularly in acute leukaemia (especially in children). The dried root is an industrial source of Ajmalicine, which increases the blood flow to the brain and peripheral parts of the body. Preparations of Ajmalicine are beneficial in treating the psychological and behavioural problems of senility, sensory issues, cranial traumas (damage to the scalp, skull and brain) and neurological complications. Ajmalicine and another indole alkaloid serpentine are prescribed in treating hypertension (see plant Rauwolfia serpentina, Page 65). Vinpocetine has various actions that would hypothetically benefit Alzheimer's disease. The ethanol fraction shows important biologically active constituents such as alkaloids, glycosides, terpenoids, flavonoids, phenols, tannins, saponins and phytosterols. The leaves and flowers contain waxy essential oils.

Distribution: It is native and endemic to Madagascar but grown elsewhere as an ornamental and medicinal plant, a source of the drugs vincristine and vinblastine used to treat cancer.

Note: When isolated from the plant, the alkaloids are highly toxic. Still, they have also been shown to reduce the numbers of white blood cells, leading to applications that have revolutionized conventional cancer therapy.

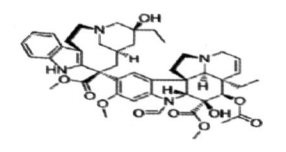

Vincristine ($C_{46}H_{56}N_4O_{10}$) 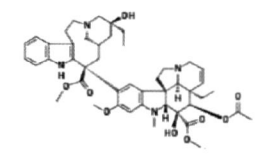   Vinblastine ($C_{46}H_{58}N_4O_9$)

Ajmaline ($C_{20}H_{26}N_2O_2$)

Cephaelis ipecacuanha

Arq-uz-zahab (Plant, Leaves and Roots)

Latin Binomial	Cephaelis ipecacuanha/Psychotria ipecacuanha
Family	Rubiaceae
English Name	Ipecacuanha/Indian Ipecac
Urdu name	Arq-uz-Zahab

Medicinal Uses: The root of the evergreen, flowering Cephaelis ipecacuanha plant is useful as an expectorant, stimulant, diaphoretic, emetic and amoebic dysentery treatment. The herb's effects on the body are entirely dependent on its dose. It stimulates the stomach, liver, intestine, aiding digestion and increasing appetite in minimal amounts. Simultaneously, it has diaphoretic and expectorant properties in slightly large quantities, which are suitable for cold, coughs and dysentery.

Traditional Uses: Cephaelis ipecacuanha's roots have a violently irritant action, stimulating the gastric and bronchial systems, lowering fevers and preventing cyst formation in amoebic dysentery. It is beneficial in syrup form in inducing vomiting in children who have ingested toxins. In small doses, roots are strongly expectorant and it is a common ingredient, in patent cough medicines. When applied to the skin, Ipecacuanha powder acts as a potent irritant. When inhaled, it causes sneezing and mild inflammation of the nasal mucous membrane.

Tylophora indica, of the Apocynaceae family, is one of the plant species known as Indian Ipecac. In the Ayurvedic medicinal system, this plant's root is beneficial in treating bronchitis, asthma, rhinitis, hay fever and allergy of the respiratory tract. It also has antispasmodic and antiprotozoal action. A decoction of the leaf is useful as an expectorant and the powdered form is effective against dysentery. It is applied externally on bites of venomous insects and scorpions.

Paradoxically, Ipecac is itself a poison as it promptly induces vomiting. The plant also shows some anti-cancer properties. The plant is now seldom used in the Unani system of medicine.

Biological Uses: The aqueous and non-aqueous extracts (methanol, ethanol, chloroform, etc.) of Cephaelis species, as well as their isolated compounds, possess diverse biological activities, including anti-inflammatory, antitumor, antimicrobial, larvicidal, antioxidant, gastrointestinal, antiulcer and hepatoprotective, with alkaloids and iridoids as the essential active principles.

Chemical Constituents: The isoquinoline alkaloids, emetine (isolated by P. G.Pelletier in 1817), cephaeline, psychotrine, protoemetine etc., have local irritant action. Emetine is more of an expectorant and less emetic as compared to cephaeline. The plant also contains valuable bioactive constituents such as other alkaloids, anthraquinone glycosides, terpenoids, saponins, pseudo tannins, resins and citric acid.

Distribution: Cephaelis ipecacuanha is indigenous to Brazil and found in Colombia, Cartagena, Nicaragua, Malaya, Burma, Panama and West Bengal. It is cultivated at Mungpoo (Darjeeling) in India, Nilgiris and Sikkim.

Note: The plant needs to be used with caution since an excess causes severe vomiting and diarrhoea. The quinoline alkaloid 'emetine' can have toxic effects on the heart, blood vessels, lungs and intestine.

Emetine ($C_{29}H_{40}N_2O_4$)   Cephaeline ($C_{28}H_{38}N_2O_4$)

Psychotrine ($C_{28}H_{36}N_2O_4$)

Cinchona officinalis

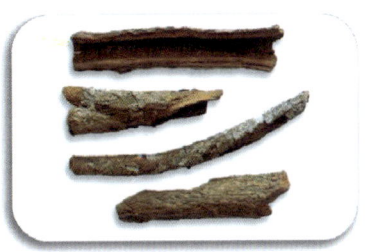

Cinchona (Tree, Barks and Flowers)

Latin Binomial	Cinchona officinalis/Cinchona calisaya
Family	Rubiaceae
English Name	Jesuit's bark/Cinchona Bark
Urdu Name	Alkina/Alkayna alnibah/Post Cinchona

Medicinal Uses: The bark of the evergreen, flowering Cinchona officinalis shrub or tree is antimalarial, antipyretic, an appetizer and analgesic in action. The bark has been useful for thousands of years and is deeply embedded in traditional knowledge as medicine. This is considered the most effective bark medicine in human history. It is an ingredient in various proprietary cold and influenza remedies.

Quinine, extracted from the tree's bark, is used as a bitter flavouring in tonic water and carbonated drinks. A shampoo containing Quinine with vitamin B, helps restore hair's vigour and strength. The bark extract, in large doses, may cause blindness and deafness preceded by violent noises in the ear.

Traditional Uses: This plant was first reported from Peru in 1630 as a traditional malaria treatment remedy. Cinchona bark is valuable in dyspepsia, gastric catarrh and cardiac depressant property. It is also beneficial in fever and also as an analgesic.

The traditional healers (Hakims and Ayurveda) of the Indo-Pak subcontinent prescribe a decoction of the bark and root to treat whooping cough, hay fever, enlargement of spleen, hemicranias (persistent unilateral headache) and other neuralgic affections. It is also suitable for smallpox, septic fevers, pneumonia, tonsillitis, catarrh, etc.

Galenical of Cinchona is beneficial as bitter tonics and stomachic. A decoction and acid infusion are used for gargling on account of the astringent action. The liquid extract is useful as a cure for drunkenness.

Biological Uses: The plant's aqueous and non-aqueous extracts (methanol and ethanol) exhibited antioxidant, antimalarial, anti-inflammatory and antimicrobial properties. It is reported that quinine is potent in inhibiting cell proliferation and inducing apoptotic cell death in the cancer cell line in a dose and time-dependent manner. It also reduces body weight, which may be due to alkaloid 'cinchonine.'

Chemical Constituents: The four most prevalent quinoline alkaloids in the bark are quinine, quinidine, cinchonine and cinchonidine. The plant also contains biologically active compounds like glycosides, terpenoids, tannins, bitter essential oils, flavonoids, phenolic compounds and resins.

Distribution: Cinchona is native to South America's highlands and was introduced in South Asia (Pakistan and India) in 1859. It is grown in Colombia, Peru and Bolivia.

Quinine ($C_{20}H_{24}N_2O_2$)   Cinchonine ($C_{19}H_{22}N_2O$)

Claviceps purpurea

Argot (In Rai Field)

Latin Binomial	Claviceps purpurea
Family	Clavicipitaceae/Hypocreaceae
English Name	Ergot
Urdu Name	Arghut

Medicinal Uses: Ergot is the dried sclerotium of fungus Claviceps purpurea, developing in the rye plant's ovary, Secale cereal (Rye in Urdu) of the Gramineae family.

The Claviceps purpurea, the plant's fungus, is an emmenagogue, haemostatic, menorrhagia, stimulant and is sedative in action. It is generally helpful as a muscle stimulant in menstrual disorders such as leucorrhoea, painful or low menstruation. It can be beneficial in stopping internal bleeding, with results against uterine haemorrhage. It is valuable as a sedative for delirium, asthma or hysteria and acts as a galactagogue (herbs that promote the mother's milk flow).

Ergot alkaloids are still a valuable resource for modern medicine. The broad spectrum of pharmacological activities includes modulation of blood pressure, migraine prevention and stimulating dopamine activity.

Traditional Uses: The traditional healers (Hakims and Ayurveda) of the Indo-Pak subcontinent used Ergot after childbirth to expel the placenta and contract the uterus. Historically, Ergot was used to speed up labour, but it was abandoned when it was observed that it had a connection between its use and an increased number of stillbirths.

Claviceps purpurea plant is not mentioned in any official, unofficial Unani and Ayurvedic pharmacopoeias.

Biological Uses: The plant non-aqueous extracts have anti-inflammatory, hypolipemic, immunomodulatory and antibacterial activities. The methanol extract of the plant appears to have oxytocic properties.

Chemical Constituents: The fungus of this plant contains water-soluble alkaloids like ergotamine, ergometrine, ergotaminine, ergosine and water-insoluble alkaloids ergocristine and ergocristinine.

Distribution: The most important Claviceps purpurea producers are Czechoslovakia, Hungary, Switzerland and Yugoslavia. It is also found in Asia, Africa, North and South America, Australia and New Zealand.

Note: The use of Ergot in large quantities may cause poisoning and can be fatal. Early poisoning symptoms include nausea, vomiting, muscle pain, weakness, numbness, itching and rapid or slow heartbeat. Ergot poisoning can progress to gangrene, vision problems, confusion, spasms, convulsions, unconsciousness and death.

Ergotamine ($C_{33}H_{35}N_5O_5$)   Ergocristine ($C_{35}H_{39}N_5O_5$)   Ergosine ($C_{30}H_{37}N_5O_5$)

Coffea Arabica

Kofi (Branch, Fresh and Roasted Beans)

Latin Binomial	Coffea arabica
Family	Rubiaceae
English Name	Coffee
Urdu Name	Qahua/Kafi

Medicinal Uses: Coffee is a commonly used beverage, but it can also be useful as a medicine. The beans of the small evergreen tree of Coffee arabica are stimulant, diuretic, anti-narcotic, vasoconstrictor and antiemetic in action. An extract from the seeds is useful as flavouring in ice cream. Coffee is often included in anti-migraine formulations since it has been proved to increase the analgesic's effectiveness. Coffee beans are safe to eat but should not be used excessively.

Traditional Uses: In traditional folk medicine, the Coffee beans are used as a brain stimulant, causing sleeplessness and as a useful narcotic poisoning. For this reason, it is perfect against snakebite in that it helps stop people from falling into a coma. It is a remedy for asthma, fever, flu, headache, jaundice, malaria, opium poisoning, migraine, sores and vertigo. Infusion of coffee seeds (roasted and grounded) is valuable as antiasthmatic, anthelmintic, aphrodisiac, antipyretic and anti-jaundice and easing childbirth. An enema made using coffee beans is an effective cleanser for the large bowel. Coffee can be valuable in heart disease and fluid retention and is helpful against drunkenness. It is effective in some cases of headaches or migraines. A decoction of Coffee leaves has blood purifying properties, improves blood circulation and haemorrhagic conjunctivitis.

Externally, pulverized Coffee is used in Japan as a body scrub and skin cleanser and internally, in heart failure, cardiac insufficiency and to prevent heart diseases. In Chinese traditional medicine, Coffee's flavour is bitter and acrid and considered warm. A European herbalist Dr Krishan Chopra (b 1949), has shown beneficial effects of regular coffee drinking to reduce the risk of diabetes mellitus and Parkinson's disease. Also, hepatic cirrhosis (reduce Alanine transaminase ALT and Aspartate transaminase AST levels), rectal cancer and cardiovascular diseases.

Biological Uses: The pharmacological benefits of Coffee beans include a wide range of anti-inflammatory, antiviral, antifungal, antioxidant, analgesic, antineoplastic (anticancer) and detoxifying activities. The hot aqueous extract of Coffee beans is antibacterial. The hydroalcoholic fraction of coffee silver-screen can be used for topical application because it has no irritant effects. The methanolic extracts of coffee beans appear to have better antioxidants than hexane fractions.

Chemical Constituents: Coffee beans are rich in purine alkaloids like caffeine, theophylline, trigonelline and phenolic compounds such as chlorogenic acids, diterpenoid alcohols and essential oils. The leaves contain more caffeine than the fruit and are used as a tea substitute.

Distribution: Coffea arabica tree is a native to Abyssinia (Ethiopia) and is cultivated throughout the tropics. Brazil is the leading exporter of coffee beans, followed by Vietnam, Colombia, Indonesia, Ethiopia and Honduras.

Note: Over 2.25 billion (approximately) cups of coffee are consumed daily and over **90 per cent of production occurs in developing countries.**

Theophylline ($C_7H_8N_4O_2$)   Trigonelline ($C_7H_7NO_2$)

Colchicum autumnale

Suranjan (Flowers and Bulbs)

Latin Binomial	Colchicum autumnale/Colchium luteum
Family	Liliaceae/Colchicaceae
English Name	Colchicum/Meadow Saffron/Autumn Crocus
Urdu Name	Suranjan-e-Shireen

Medicinal Uses: The bulbs (corms) of herbaceous, perennial, flowering Colchicum autumnale herb are emetic, alternative, antirheumatic, cathartic, antispasmodic and aperient in action. Colchicum preparations from bulbs are widely beneficial in relieving gout and rheumatic complaints. Seeds of Colchicum are analgesic and emetic. In modern herbals, it is still helpful in easing the pain and inflammation of acute gout and rheumatism, although the frequent use encourages more frequent attacks of the complaint. The corm and the seeds are beneficial in treating gout and rheumatic complaints, usually accompanied by an alkaline diuretic. Leukaemia is successfully treated with Colchicum autumnale. The plant has also been used with some success to treat Bechet's syndrome (a type of inflammatory disorder that affects multiple parts of the body).

Traditional Uses: In the Unani system of medicine, the bulbs or corms, roots and seeds of the plant are used for therapeutic purposes. In some Unani texts, it is mentioned that the Colchicum (Suranjan) plant and its extract may also ameliorate hepatitis, cirrhosis and may have potential in chemotherapeutic regimens. The plant is traditionally used by traditional healers of the Indo-Pak subcontinent for headache, joint pain, gout, rheumatism, worm infestation, piles, chronic ulcers and constipation.

A famous Unani medicine known as 'Majun-e-Suranjan,' is one of the most reputed poly-herbal preparations commonly used in managing arthritis. It is mentioned by all renowned Muslim authors in their books as a primordial medicine in arthritis[3]. Colchium autumnale is also beneficial in joint pains, skin-related problems, as an aphrodisiac, in liver and spleen disorders, in the Ayurvedic medicinal system.

Biological Uses: The phytochemicals present in the plant have antioxidant, antibacterial, antiviral, anti-allergenic, cardioprotective, neuroprotective and anti-cancer activities. The methanol fraction of all parts of the plant also exhibits anti-cancer effects.

Chemical Constituents: The plant contains tropane alkaloid colchicines, an amorphous, yellowish-white alkaloid, darkening on light exposure. The plant also contains valuable ingredients like demecolcine, also known as colcemid, other alkaloids, flavonoids, lignans, phenolic acids, sterols, resin (colchicoresin), fixed oil, glucose and starch.

Distribution: Colchicum autumnale is native to West Asia, Europe, parts of the Mediterranean coast, down the East African coast to South Africa and the Western Cape.

Note: Colchicum autumnale (In Urdu, Suranjan e Talkh) is the plant's bitter species. Its internal use is recommended only in severe pain attacks in skeletal parts, joints, etc. However, it finds its frequent use in external applications where its potential is regarded as superior to Colchicum autumnale (Suranjan-e-Shireen).

---

[3] Abu Sahl 'Isa ibn Yahya al-Masihi al-Jurjani (d.1010 A D) in his book 'al-māʾa fi-l-sanāʿa al-tabiʿiyyah,' he was the teacher of Ibn- Sena. Ibn-Sina (d 1037) in his book al-Qānūn fī al-Ṭibb and Ibn-al-Baiter (d. 1248) in his book Kitāb al-Jāmiʿ li-Mufradāt al-Adwiya wa-l-Aghdhiya.

Roghan-e-Suranjan, an oily preparation, contains Colchicum Luteum as one of the ingredients in a poly-herbal formulation.

Colchicine ($C_{22}H_{25}NO_6$)   Demecolcine ($C_{21}H_{25}NO_5$)

Conium maculatum

Qonyun/Shukran (Plants and Flowers)

Latin Binomial	Conium maculatum
Family	Umbelliferae/Apiaceae
English Name	Hemlock
Urdu name	Qonyun/Shukran

Medicinal Uses: The fruit, leaves and roots of the herbaceous, flowering Conium maculatum plant are useful, medicinally. The plant is sedative, hypnotic, antispasmodic and a local anaesthetic in action. The herb acts on the centres of motion and causes paralysis. Hence, it is used to remedy undue nervous motor excitability, e.g., teething, cramp, muscle spasms of the larynx and gullet. When inhaled, Hemlock is good in relieving coughs, bronchitis, whooping cough and asthma.

Traditional Uses: The plant is mentioned in Unani literature but seldom used in medicine. Conium maculatum is a traditional folk treatment for cancer and was formerly widely used internally, in minimal doses, to treat various complaints, including tumours, epilepsy, whooping cough, rabies and as an antidote in strychnine poisoning. It is still used externally, usually in ointments and oils, in treating mastitis, malignant tumours (especially breast cancer), anal fissures and haemorrhoids.

Biological Uses: The aqueous and non-aqueous extracts of leaves have antibacterial, anthelmintic, anti-inflammatory and insecticidal properties. The oil also possesses antibacterial and antiseptic activities. The plant has anti-cancer properties because of piperidine alkaloids. They can interact with the DNA and hinder cell proliferation and cell cycle. The teratogenic (herb may cause congenital disability) effects have also been reported.

Chemical Constituents: In flower buds, the primary alkaloid found is γ-coniceine. The plant contains piperidine alkaloids, coniine and a novel volatile alkaloid relating to coniine. The plant also has bioactive constituents such as flavonoids, coumarins, other alkaloids, steroids, terpenoids (mostly monoterpenes), essential and non-essential oils.

Distribution: Conium maculatum is native to Europe and North Africa. **It exists in some woodlands (and elsewhere) in most British Isles counties. It has become naturalized in Asia,**

Note: Hemlock has to be administered with care as narcotic poisoning may result from the internal application and overdose induces paralysis with loss of speech and depression of the respiratory function leading to death. All parts of the plant are highly toxic.

Coniine ($C_8H_{17}N$)

Conhydrine ($C_8H_{17}NO$)

Coptis teeta

Mamiran (Plant and Roots)

Latin Binomial	Coptis teeta/Coptis chinensis
Family	Ranunculaceae
English Name	Golden Thread Root
Urdu Name	Mamiran

Medicinal Uses: The root of the evergreen, perennial Coptis teeta plant is a detergent, carminative, diuretic in action and a tonic for the liver and it improves eyesight. The root is an aromatic, very bitter, a cooling herb that controls bacterial and viral infections, relaxes spasms, lowers fevers and stimulates circulation.

Traditional Uses: It is a local analgesic and anaesthetic and is useful in Chinese medicine as a general panacea with alterative, ophthalmic and pectoral activity. The root contains several compounds that effectively inhibit various bacteria and are a safe and effective treatment for many ailments, such as some forms of dysentery caused by bacteria. The root is harvested in autumn and can be used fresh or dried.

The Indo-Pak subcontinent's traditional healers use this plant to cure malaria, stomach pain, diarrhoea, loose motion and insect bites. Coptis teeta plant helps cure inflammation, eye diseases, skin diseases, stomach problems, jaundice, urinary disorders and cancer. The root is also recommended in inflammation, purging fire and detoxification. It is frequently valuable in treating bacillary dysentery, typhoid, cerebrospinal meningitis and whooping cough. In Unani and Ayurvedic medicinal systems, externally, a paste from the root in a suitable solvent, is applied to sores. The root is useful as an antibacterial and anti-inflammatory medicine in the traditional Chinese medicinal system.

Safuf Mamiran, Kuhl-al-Jawahir and Basliquin are some of the externally used Unani preparations containing Coptic teeta as one of the ingredients.

Biological Uses: The plant's aqueous and non-aqueous (methanol and ethanol) extracts possess antihypertensive, anti-diarrheal, anti-inflammatory, antibacterial, anti-arrhythmic antidepressant and antihyperlipidemic activities. The presence of berberine in the plant appears to have anti-trachoma and anti-cancer properties.

Chemical Constituents: The rhizomes are bitter due to several benzylisoquinoline alkaloids, e.g., berberine, coptisine, palmatine, etc. The plant also contains bioactive ingredients such as other alkaloids, flavonoids, phenolic acids, steroids, glycosides, resins and phenylpropanoids.

Distribution: Coptis teeta is native to Asia, China and North America.

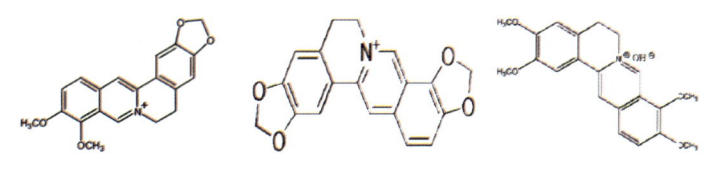

Berberine ($C_{20}H_{18}NO_4+$)   Coptisine ($C_{19}H_{14}NO_4+$)   Palmatine ($C_{21}H_{24}NO_4+$)

Datura stramonium

Dhaturah (Plant, Flower and Fruits)

Latin Binomial	Datura stramonium
Family	Solanaceae
English Name	Stramonium/Thorn Apple/Datura
Urdu Name	Dhaturah

Medicinal Uses: The whole plant has medicinal qualities, and the leaves and seeds are commonly used today. The flowering Datura stramonium plant is antispasmodic, anodyne, narcotic and anticatarrhal in action. The Datura plant acts as belladonna (Atropa belladonna), except it does not cause constipation.

An extract of the seeds helps, in pill form, to stop cough, spasmodic bronchial asthma, whooping cough and the bladder's spasm. In modern herbals, it is considered a better cough remedy than opium, but is used with extreme care as it can act as a narcotic poison in overdoses. When smoked with tobacco alone or with other herbs, it can ease asthma by relaxing the bronchiole spasms during an attack. The herb can relieve sciatica and rheumatism when used externally in an ointment form. European herbalists apply a warm pad of the leaf to the body's pain and swollen parts.

Traditional Uses: In Unani and Ayurvedic medicinal systems, the plant is very beneficial in asthma, persistent cough, seasickness, gastric ulcer, pain disorders and insomnia. The leaves, flowering tops and seeds are anodyne, antiasthmatic, antispasmodic, hallucinogenic, hypnotic and narcotic. An infusion of the leaves is valuable in treating venereal disease. The leaves have also been smoked as an antispasmodic in treating Parkinson's disease.

Traditional healers (Hakims and Ayurveda) of the Indo-Pak subcontinent also used a paste of the leaves to relieve headaches, burnt seeds to treat malaria and a decoction of flowers as a sedative. The leaves are beneficial as antispasmodic and fresh leaves with oil as an antidote for poisonous insect bites. The juice from the fruit is applied to the scalp to treat dandruff and falling hair.

Biological Uses: The plant's non-aqueous (methanol and ethanol) extracts exhibit antiasthmatic, anticholinergic, antimicrobial, anti-cancer and anti-inflammatory properties. The oil of the plant also possesses analgesic, antioxidant and anti-inflammatory activity. The secondary metabolites of Datura stramonium are highly effective against different diseases such as diabetes and viruses (antiviral), etc.

Chemical Constituents: The plant contains various tropane alkaloids, including atropine, hyoscyamine, littorine, valtropine, acetoxtropine and scopolamine. The Datura plant also has other essential biologically active compounds such as other alkaloids, glycosides, saponins, essential oils, tannins and terpenoids. The seed contains about seventeen per cent of a pale yellow oil, used as a massage oil.

Distribution: Datura stramonium is native to South and Central America but was spread widely to the Old World (Africa, Asia and Europe). The plant has become a cosmopolitan weed in the warm regions of North, Central and South America, Africa, Asia, Australia and New Zealand.

Note: Datura is a poisonous plant, so it should be taken only after consultation with experienced physicians.

Atropine (C$_{17}$H$_{23}$NO$_3$) Hyoscamine (C$_{17}$H$_{23}$NO$_3$)

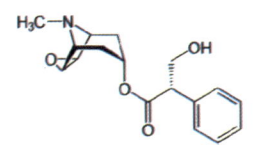

Scopolamine (C$_{17}$H$_{21}$NO$_4$)

Doronicum hookeri

Darunaj Aqrabi (Flowers and Rhizome)

Latin Binomial	Doronicum hookeri
Family	Compositae/Asteraceae
English Name	Leopards Bane
Urdu Name	Darunaj Aqrabi

Medicinal Uses: The roots of the flowering Doronicum hookeri plant are anti-phlegmatic, carminative, anti-inflammatory, exhilarant, digestive in action and a cardiac and nerve tonic. They are also valuable in paralysis, melancholia and palpitation.

Traditional Uses: In Unani and Ayurvedic medicinal systems, the roots are helpful as a cardiac tonic, nerve tonic, protective of the foetus and as an antidote. The roots are traditionally valuable as an exhilarant. They act as a stomachic and dissolve trapped gases, reduce pain, especially the pain related to the musculoskeletal system. It has antibacterial properties; thus, it helps treat ulcers and aids in early healing. The root is said to protect from the attack of the plague (epidemic). The root prevents giddiness caused during high-altitude ascents.

The traditional healers (Hakims and Ayurveda) also recommended the root of the plant in palpitation, paralysis, melancholia, nervous disorders and indigestion. The root of Doronicum hookeri forms many Unani poly-herbal general tonic medicinal preparations like 'Mufarreh Yaquti, Majun-e-Hamal and Labub-e-Kabir.'

Biological Uses: The root extract (methanol) shows antibacterial, hepatoprotective, anti-diabetic and antioxidant activity. The methanolic fraction of the root possesses higher phenolic content and higher free radical scavenging and reducing activities. Doronicum hookeri has shown promising *in-vitro* antifungal properties.

Chemical Constituents: The root contains pyrrolizine alkaloids, e.g., otosenine, floridanine and doronine. The alkaloid otosenine is believed to have cardiovascular properties. The plant also has valuable bioactive constituents such as saponins, flavonoids, flavonol, coumarins, sesquiterpenes, phenolic compounds and tannins. The bark of the plant is aromatic.

Distribution: The plant is distributed in the Himalayas in Sikkim, Nepal, Bhutan and Tibet, at an altitude of 12,000 to 14,000 feet.

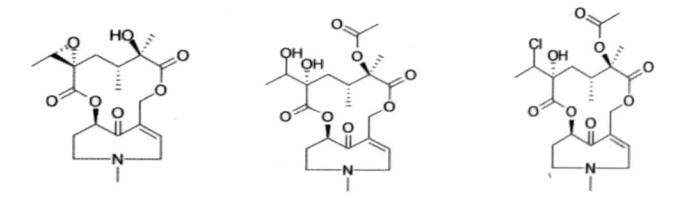

Doronine ($C_{21}H_{30}ClNO_8$)   Otosenine ($C_{19}H_{27}NO_7$)   Floridanine ($C_{21}H_{31}NO_9$)

Erythroxylum coca

Coca (Leaves)

Latin Binomial	Erythroxylum coca
Family	Erythroxylaceae
English Name	Coca
Urdu Name	Coca/Kuka

Medicinal Uses: The leaves of the flowering Erythroxylum coca plant are stimulant, antipyretic, anaesthetic and aphrodisiac in action. They are useful as cerebral and muscle stimulants during convalescence, relieving nausea, vomiting and stomach pains. The leaves are utilized as a general nerve tonic and also in treating asthma.

Traditional Uses: In South America, people chew Coca leaves to relieve hunger, altitude sickness, muscular and skeletal aches, as well as sadness, sexual impotence and to enhancement of physical performance. It is also used as an anaesthetic and analgesic to alleviate headaches, rheumatism, wounds, sores, etc.

Before more potent anaesthetics were available, the plant was also beneficial for broken bones, as an analgesic, in childbirth and skull operations (trepanning). The high calcium content in Coca leaves explains why people use it for bone fractures.

The traditional healers and herbalists also used the plant's leaves to treat ulcers, asthma, improve digestion, guard against bowel laxity as an aphrodisiac and also be credited with improving longevity. The Erythroxylum coca plant is not mentioned in classic Unani and Ayurvedic literature.

Biological Uses: The plant's extracts (methanol and ethanol) exhibited antioxidant, anti-cancer and anti-inflammatory effects. The leaf extract of Erythroxylum coca is antimicrobial in potential against microorganisms. The chloroform fraction of the plant shows anti-diabetic, antispasmodic and antiobesity properties. The plant leaf extracts show antihyperlipidemic activity.

Chemical Constituents: Cocaine is the principal tropane alkaloid found in the cultivated varieties of coca. The plant also contains other alkaloids (predominantly of either the pyrrolidine or the tropane types), flavonoids, tannins, terpenoids, glycosides, terpene, polyphenols, saponins etc.

Distribution: Erythroxylum coca is indigenous to Peru and Bolivia, is cultivated in Africa, North and South America, South Asia, Taiwan and Sri Lanka. It is one of the oldest cultivated plants in South America.

Note: Erythroxylum coca is known to have harmful effects during pregnancy. Pregnant women who use this plant or its alkaloid 'cocaine' have a high risk of placenta abruption. High doses of cocaine can also be associated with toxic reactions, including hyperthermia, rhabdomyolysis (degeneration of muscle tissue), shock and acute liver injury, which can be severe and even fatal.

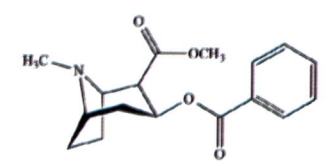

Cocaine ($C_{17}H_{21}NO_4$)

Fumaria officinalis

Shahtarah (Plant, Dried Plant and Flowers)

Latin Binomial	Fumaria officinalis/Fumaria indica
Family	Fumariaceae
English Name	Fumitory/Earth Smoke

Urdu Name   Shahtarah/Sahtaraj

Medicinal Uses: All above the ground parts of the flowering Fumaria officinalis herb can be used medicinally. The plant is alterative, diaphoretic, diuretic, stomachic in action and a blood purifier. This herb is helpful in all internal obstructions, particularly those of the liver and stomach, benefits scorbutic disorders and skin eruptions, including leprosy. It is the preferred herb used to purify blood in France and Germany and in some areas, it is smoked as tobacco.

According to the Wealth of India (encyclopedia of Indian herbs), Fumaria indica is useful in treating fever and influenza.

Traditional Uses: In Italy, the plant is used as a hypertensive, antispasmodic, respiratory stimulant and also anti-arteriosclerosis. It was said to aid in the removal of skin blemishes and freckles and ease dyspepsia and headaches. In Iranian folk medicine, the plant is used for skin diseases, in scabies, as an antiscorbutic and also for bronchitis.

Fumaria officinalis is effective in aches, pains, diarrhoea, fever, influenza and liver complaints in Unani and Ayurvedic medicinal systems. The herb, mixed with honey, is taken internally to prevent vomiting. A cold infusion of the plant helps treat children in wasting diseases, allowing cooling of the body during fever, treating of constipation and dyspepsia. Internally, it is useful as a blood purifier for skin diseases. A decoction of the Fumaria indica stem and leaves is a tonic, anthelmintic and aperient.

Externally, the plant's paste is used in chronic ailments like syphilis, scrofula, leprosy and fomentation for swollen joints. The dried plant (pulverized) with black pepper is also beneficial as an anthelmintic, diuretic, diaphoretic and for jaundice as well. The seeds help in the prevention of cutaneous eruptions such as eczema, psoriasis, scabies, syphilis, leprosy, tatters and itches.

The whole plant forms a constituent of many poly-herbal Unani blood purifier medicinal preparations like 'Itrifal-e-Shahtarah, Majun-e-Ushbah, Arq-e-Shahtarah,' etc.

Biological Uses: The plant's ethanolic extracts showed neural and analgesic effects, whereas methanolic fractions displayed antioxidant, antibacterial and anti-diabetic effects. The antiviral effect may be due to the presence of seco-phthalide isoquinoline alkaloids, e.g., narlumicine and oxysanguinarine.

Chemical Constituents: Fumaria officinalis plant contains isoquinoline alkaloids, with fumarine as the potent alkaloid and cryptopine. Other bioactive constituents isolated from the plant are flavonoids, glycosides, terpenoids, phytosterols, saponins, tannins, phenolic compounds, fixed oils and essential oils.

Distribution: The native range of the cultivation of Fumaria species is from Europe to Central Asia and North Africa. These countries include Turkey, the United Kingdom, Iran, Pakistan (mainly Baluchistan) and India, Mongolia and Afghanistan and two more species in the West of China.

Cryptopine ($C_{21}H_{23}NO_5$)

Galipea officinalis

Angostura (Plant, Barks and Leaves)

Latin Binomial	Galipea officinalis
Family	Rutaceae
English Name	Angostura

Urdu Name   Angusturaan

Medicinal Uses: The greyish-yellow, resinous, brittle bark of the evergreen shrub-like tree of Galipea officinalis is acrid, dysenteric, aromatic, digestive, febrifuge, and is a stimulant in action and is a tonic. It is considered an excellent treatment for intermittent fevers and is useful in treating yellow fever. In large doses, it is cathartic.

Traditional Uses: In folk medicine, traditional healers used this bark to cure fever and diarrhoea. The bark has exceptional soothing and anti-inflammatory properties that are useful in providing quick and safe recovery from numbness, palsy and involuntary muscle contraction (tremor). A decoction of the bark helps improve appetite, digestion, weight loss and it alleviates stomach pain. Excess water is removed from the body through perspiration and urination, which solves water retention (oedema). Galipea officinalis bark also helps in the efficient weight management of a person. The bark is still often used by Trinidadians in treating digestive problems.

The Galipea officinalis plant is not mentioned in classic Unani and Ayurvedic books and Pharmacopoeias; however, Galipea officinalis, now Galipea cusparia, is an official herb in the British Pharmacopoeia.

Biological Uses: The non-aqueous fractions of the Galipea plant exhibit anti-cancer, antimicrobial, antioxidant, anti-diarrheal, analgesic and wound healing effects on animals. The antioxidant and anti-inflammatory activities of the plant are also reported. The hydroalcoholic extracts of the plant have antibacterial and immunomodulatory properties.

Chemical Constituents: The plant contains quinoline alkaloids like cuspareine, cusparine, galipine and a newly isolated tetrahydroquinoline alkaloid angustureine, candicine and galipinine. The leaf is also rich in angustureine.

Distribution: Galipea officinalis plant is indigenous to South America (Venezuela).

Angustureine ($C_{14}H_{21}N$), Galipine ($C_{20}H_{21}NO_3$) Cuspareine ($C_{20}H_{25}NO2$) Galipinine ($C_{19}H_{21}NO_2$)

Holarrhena antidysenterica

Inderjo-Tulkh (Plant, Flower and Seeds)

Latin Binomial	Holarrhena antidysenterica
Family	Apocynaceae
English Name	Coral Swirl/Bitter Oleander
Urdu Name	Inderjo-Tulkh

Medicinal Uses: The seeds and bark of this flowering tree are useful for medicinal purposes. The plant is carminative, aphrodisiac, antidysenteric, astringent, diuretic in action and increases the formation of semen. Its stimulant and relaxant activities are mediated possibly through activation of histamine receptors and calcium channel blockers, respectively. Pulverized bark powder is given orally to cure stomach ache.

Traditional Uses: In Unani and Ayurvedic medicinal systems, dried bark powder is beneficial for children's diarrhoea. The bark extract is useful as an astringent, anthelmintic, febrifuge, diuretic, antiedemic, in piles, colic, dyspepsia and chest affections. It is also a remedy for diseases of the liver and skin. It has become a potent curative agent in acute or chronic dysentery and fever cases.

The seed of Holarrhena antidysenterica is antibilious and is used for promoting conception and toning up vaginal tissues after delivery. It is a valuable remedy in treating eczema, scabies, fungal infections and leprosy. The leaves pounded in water are taken to cure stomach ache. The juice from the fruit is helpful in controlling cough.

Many Ayurveda used this herb to treat renal stones, respiratory disorders, general weakness and burning sensation. They also considered this plant in treating rheumatoid arthritis, osteoarthritis and urinary tract infection. Holarrhena antidysenterica is known as 'white angel' in the Philippines and in Thailand, it is called 'Pudpitchaya.'

Biological Uses: The alcoholic extract of the fruit show anti-cancer effect against the nasopharynx's human epidermoid carcinoma (squamous cell carcinoma) in tissue culture. The aqueous fraction of fruit exhibits hypoglycaemic effects. Various non-aqueous extracts (methanol, ethanol and chloroform) of the seed and bark show significant antibacterial, anti-diabetic and antifungal activities against a wide range of human pathogens, including several antibiotic-resistant strains.

The bark extract also displayed antispasmodic properties. The aqueous extract of seeds shows a significant increase in urine output. The presence of steroidal alkaloid in the plant has anticholinesterase (a herb that inhibits cholinesterase activity) activities.

Chemical Constituents: Most of the stem bark contains alkaloids and the root bark has steroids from conanine or the closely related conamine, which also occur in other plant species. The primary steroidal alkaloid of the stem bark and root bark is conessine; other compounds are norconessine (kurchine), conessimine, kurchamine, kurchessine, kurcholessine, conimine, conamine and holarrhenine.

The plant also contains potent biologically active compounds such as flavonoids, triterpenoids, phenolic acids, tannins, resins, coumarins, saponins and ergosterol.

Distribution: Holarrhena antidysenterica flowering plant is native to tropical and southern Africa and South-East and Southeast Asia (Pakistan, India, Burma, Sri Lanka and Nepal).

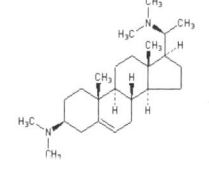

Kurchamine ($C_{22}H_{38}N_2$) Conessimine ($C_{23}H_{38}NO_2$) Kurchessine ($C_{25}H_{44}NO_2$)

Conessine ($C_{24}H_{40}N_2$)

Hyoscyamus niger

Ajwain Khurasani (Plant, Flowers and Leaf)

Latin Binomial	Hyoscyamus niger
Family	Solanaceae
English Name	Henbane
Urdu Name	Ajwain-e-Khurasani

Medicinal Uses: The leaves and flowering tops of Hyoscyamus niger plant are antispasmodic, hypnotic, a mild diuretic, sedative, mydriatic (herbs induce dilatation of the pupil) and anodyne in action. The herb has a milder narcotic effect than belladonna (Atropa belladonna) or stramonium (Datura stramonium) and is utilized in lessening muscle spasms and in reducing pain and nerve irritation. It is also helpful in cystitis, irritable bladder, hysteria, irritable cough, asthma, gastric ulcers and chronic gastric catarrh. Hyoscyamus tranquillizes people, affected by severe nervous irritability, when taken in small doses, repeated over time. The fresh leaves of the plant can be used as a poultice to relieve local pain from gout, neuralgia, cancerous ulcers, sores and swelling. The herb's solid extract helps produce suppositories, which helps relieve haemorrhoidal pain.

Traditional Uses: In Unani Medicine, the plant is called 'Ajwain-e-Khurasani.' It is used as a sedative, anti-phlegmatic and in treating productive cough. The leaves are beneficial in treating abdominal colic, pain due to worm infestation, toothache, pulmonary infections, pain due to tumours and pain associated with the urinary tract, especially kidney stones. It is a valuable plant in the Ayurvedic medicinal system in treating insomnia, psychiatric disorders, epilepsy, swelling, pain and breathlessness. The seed oil is used externally for neuralgic, dental and rheumatic pains.

Many Unani poly-herbal preparations contain 'Ajwain-e-Khurasani' as one of the active ingredients such as Bershasha, Hab-e-Jadwar, Majun Muqavi-wa-mumsik, etc.

Biological Uses: The seeds possess antimicrobial, antispasmodic, hypotensive, antipyretic, anticonvulsant, anticholinergic and anti-inflammatory effects. The plant methanolic extract also exhibits antiasthmatic and antiallergic, antibacterial and antifungal properties. The petroleum-ether, aqueous and methanolic fractions of the plant have shown anti-Parkinsonian and cytotoxic effects.

Chemical Constituents: The chief constituents of Henbane leaves are the tropane alkaloids, hyoscyamine, atropine and hyoscine. The plant also contains a glucocidal bitter compound called 'hyoscytricin,' volatile oils, terpenes, glycerides, saponins, flavonoids, coumarins and fixed oil. The seeds also contain fixed oil.

Distribution: Hyoscyamus niger plant is native to a broad region of Eurasia. The plant is distributed widely in East Asian countries, including China, Korea and Japan. It is cultivated as a medicinal plant in many other countries.

Note: Hyoscyamus is a poisonous plant and can only be used under medical advice.

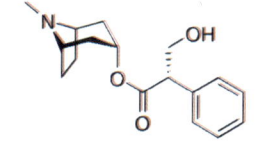

Hyoscyamine ($C_{17}H_{23}NO_3$) 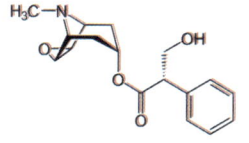   Hyoscine ($C_{17}H_{21}NO_4$)

Lobelia inflata

Tambaku Jangli (Leaves and Flowers)

Latin Binomial	Lobelia inflata/ Lobelia nicotianiefolia
Family	Campanulaceae/Lobeliaceae
English Name	Lobelia/Indian Tobacco

Urdu Name			Tambaku Jangli

Medicinal Uses: The herbaceous, flowering plant of Lobelia inflata is an expectorant, emetic, diaphoretic, antiasthmatic and a stimulant in action. The presence of alkaloids first acts as a stimulant and then as a depressive to the autonomic nervous system. In higher doses, the alkaloids paralyse muscular activity works in the same way as 'Curare' (Chondrodendron tomentosum of the **Menispermaceae family**).

Traditional Uses: This plant was passed to Europeans from Native American Indians and was used as an effective relaxant remedy for treating pain caused by muscle spasms. Thus, it is highly effective against asthma, bronchial complaints and lung problems. Lobelia inflata may help ease convulsive and inflammatory motor disorders such as epilepsy, tonsillitis, diphtheria and tetanus.

Externally, the herb is helpful in insect bites, ringworm and muscle spasms. It is an essential herbal remedy in modern usages. An infusion has been found beneficial in eye infections. The dried flowering herb and the seed are antiasthmatic, antispasmodic, diaphoretic, diuretic, emetic, an expectorant and nervine.

The use of Lobelia inflate, as an emetic, is debatable as to whether it would benefit the patient and its use be encouraged or discouraged by various herbalists. Lobelia inflata is a plant also used in traditional and homoeopathic medicine.

It is an aid to expel mucus from the respiratory tract; the plant is beneficial in treating respiratory problems. Besides, some individuals use lobelia to help those who wish to quit smoking, relieve muscle pain, and support alcoholism recovery. Excess doses may cause nausea, vomiting, drowsiness and respiratory failure.

Biological Uses: The essential oil of aerial parts of the plant possesses antioxidant, antifungal, antimicrobial activities. The non-aqueous fraction of the Lobelia inflata plant shows anti-cancer properties, delayed growth of the cutaneous tumour and reduced angiogenesis (a process of new blood vessel growth). The plant's water extract was recently shown to possess antitumor activity against lung, colon and liver cancers.

Chemical Constituents: The plant contains pyridine-piperidine alkaloids, lobeline, lobelanidine and nor-lobelanidine. The seeds have a much higher percentage of lobeline than the rest of the plant.

Distribution: Lobelia inflata is native to North America and is also grown in South Asia. The plant has been brought under cultivation in the hilly area of Pakistan.

Note: Excess doses may cause nausea, vomiting, drowsiness and respiratory failure. Overdose may cause many serious toxic effects, including sweating, very low blood pressure, collapse, coma convulsions, fast heartbeat, and possibly death.

Lobeline ($C_{22}H_{27}NO_2$)   Lobelanidine ($C_{22}H_{29}NO_2$)   Lobelanine ($C_{22}H_{25}NO_2$)

Mandragora officinarum

Mandrake (Plant, Roots and Flowers)

Latin Binomial	Mandragora officinarum
Family	Solanaceae
English Name	Mandrake
Urdu Name	Mardum Giyah

Medicinal Uses: The leaves and roots of the flowering, perennial, herbaceous Mandragora officinarum plant are emetic, purgative, cooling, anodyne and hypnotic in action. The fresh root is strongly emetic and purgative and the dried bark of the root also shares purgative qualities.

Traditional Uses: Ancient herbalists used the Mandragora plant to kill pain and to provide rest and sleep to patients and also for melancholy, convulsions, rheumatic pain and scrofulous tumours. Its most beneficial action is using small doses frequently given, as large ones cause violent evacuations and weakness. The leaves of the plant are harmless and have a cooling effect. The plant extracts help in making ointments and other external applications, for ulcers. The root extract is an ingredient in commercial cosmetic preparations as a skin conditioner and tonic.

People used Mandragora to trigger vomiting and increase interest in sexual activity. It is also helpful in motion sickness. The plant is seldom used in Unani and Ayurvedic systems of medicine.

Biological Uses: The methanolic extract of flowers possesses antioxidant properties. The ethanolic fraction of the root is antimicrobial and the fruit extract shows remarkable enzyme inhibitory activity.

Chemical Constituents: The plant contains tropane alkaloids like hyoscyamine, cuscohygrine, hyoscine, apoatropine, belladonnine and non-alkaloidal constituents such as sterols, essential oils, coumarins, carotenoids, flavonoids and terpenoids.

Distribution: Mandragora officinarum is native to regions around the Mediterranean Sea, within the borders of Tunisia, Algeria and Morocco in North Africa.

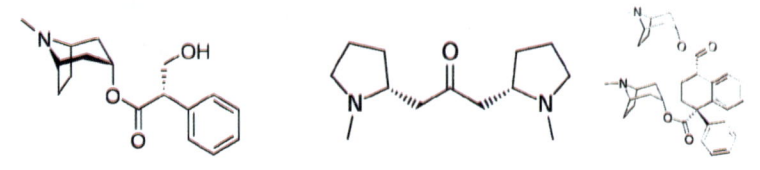

Hyoscyamine ($C_{17}H_{23}NO_3$)   Cuscohygrine ($C_{13}H_{24}N_2O$)   Belladonnine ($C_{34}H_{42}N_2O_4$)

Mitragyna speciosa

Kartom (Leaves and flowers)

Latin Binomial	Mitragyna speciosa
Family	Rubiaceae
English Name	Kratom
Urdu Name	Qartum

Medicinal Uses: The leaves of the evergreen, flowering Mitragyna speciosa are localized anaesthetic, aphrodisiac, stimulant, antidiarrhoeal, analgesic and antitussives in action. The leaves extract is used to heal wounds and intestinal infections.

Mitragyna speciosa leaves have common side effects like loss of appetite, erectile dysfunction (impotence), hair loss and constipation. Mitragyna speciosa, taken in large, sedating doses of dried leaves, may initially produce sweating, dizziness, nausea and dysphoria. Still, these effects are in a short while, superseded by calmness, euphoria and a dreamlike state that last for up to six hours. The tree/leaves are currently illegal in some countries but are legal and widely available in the United States, in a green powdered supplement.

Traditional Uses: Traditionally, in some South Asian areas, the chopped, fresh and dried leaves of the tree are chewed or made into tea by local manual labourers to combat fatigue and improve work productivity. Its leaves are traditionally chewed by Thai and Malaysian farmers and manual labourers as it causes a numbing and stimulating effect. Also, leaf preparations have been used for centuries during social-religious ceremonies and for the treatment of various medical conditions. Mitragyna speciosa leaves are used widely by women in villages, as a household remedy for common ailments such as fever, cough, hypertension, diabetes, pain and anxiety.

The leaves can cause hallucinations and euphoria. These are also applied as a wound poultice and are believed to be a deworming agent and appetite suppressor. It is also used in traditional medicine as an opium substitute.

Biological Uses: The aqueous and non-aqueous extracts (methanol and ethanol) possess antioxidant, antifungal and antimicrobial activities.

Chemical Constituents: The plant contains indole alkaloids, mitragynine and ajmalicine (same as in Rauwolfia serpentina) and paynantheine. These alkaloids have morphine-like effects. The plant also has some valuable bioactive constituents like flavonoids, phenolic compounds, steroids, terpenoids, tannins and resins.

Distribution: Mitragyna speciosa is native to South Asia. It is also indigenous to Thailand, Malaysia and Myanmar.

Note: A regular use of Kratom may produce dependence on it. Human withdrawal symptoms are relatively mild and typically diminish within a week. Craving, weakness and lethargy, anxiety, restlessness, rhinorrhea, nausea, sweating, muscle pain, jerky movements of the limbs, tremor, sleep disturbances and hallucination may occur.

Mitragynine (C$_{23}$H$_{30}$N$_2$O$_4$)   Ajmalicine (C$_{21}$H$_{24}$N$_2$O$_3$)

Nicotiana tabacum

Tambaku (Plant and Leaves)

Latin Binomial	Nicotiana tabacum
Family	Solanaceae
English Name	Tobacco
Urdu Name	Tambaku

Medicinal Uses: The leaves of the herbaceous Nicotiana tabacum plant are sedative, antispasmodic, expectorant, emetic and antiseptic in action. Medically, tobacco leaves are useful internally for hernia, constipation, tetanus and hysterical convulsions. It is best utilized externally as a plaster or poultice to ease cutaneous diseases, haemorrhoids and facial neuralgia.

Traditional Uses: The use of Tobacco has a long history by traditional healers as a relaxant, antispasmodic, diuretic, emetic, expectorant and sedative. They used it externally to treat rheumatic swelling, for skin diseases and scorpion stings. A leaf rolled into a suppository, has been beneficial in strangulated hernia, for obstinate constipation, due to spasms of the bowels and urine retention. Wet tobacco leaves can be applied to stings to relieve pain and cure piles. The plant should be used with great caution when taken internally. It is an addictive narcotic. The active ingredients can also be absorbed through the skin. A homoeopathic remedy is made from dried leaves to treat nausea and travel sickness.

The herb's excessive use produces dyspepsia, chronic inflammation of bronchial mucous membrane, diseases of the liver and sleeplessness. In Nepal, the leaf juice is quite effective externally, in treating scabies. In Haiti, a decoction of the dried leaves is taken orally for bronchitis and pneumonia. In Brazil, dried leaves are also used as an insecticide, for ulcerated abscesses, fistulas, sores and in many other ailments. It is seldom used in Unani medicines. In Ayurveda texts, Nicotiana tabacum is a drug of choice in urinary tract disorders and diseases related to the urinary bladder.

Biological Uses: The non-aqueous extracts (ethyl acetate and butanol) possess antibacterial, anti-Alzheimer and anthelmintic activities. The ethanolic fractions show antifungal, anticonvulsant, anthelmintic and antispasmodic properties. The methanol leaf extract of Nicotiana tabacum has antinociceptive (any substance that inhibits nociception) actions.

Chemical Constituents: The plant contains pyridine and piperidine alkaloids, nicotine, anabasine, anatabine and myosmine. Other biologically active constituents are sterols, triterpenoids, essential oils, flavonoids, phenolic compounds, resinous substances, minerals and vitamins.

Distribution: Nicotiana tabacum is indigenous to South America and is cultivated or grown in almost all the countries of the world. Pakistan produces one of the finest tobacco products and most of the agricultural cultivation is based in Charsadda, Mardan, Nowshera and Swabi districts of Khyber Pakhtunkhwa.

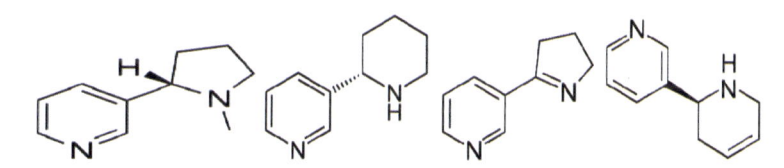

Nicotine ($C_{10}H_{14}N_2$)   Anabasine ($C_{10}H_{14}N_2$)   Myosmine ($C_9H_{10}N_2$)   Anatabine ($C_{10}H_{12}N_2$)

Papaver somniferum

Afiyum (Flower, Poppy (capules) and Seeds)

Latin Binomial	Papaver somniferum
Family	Papaveraceae
English Name	Opium
Urdu Name	Afiyun

Medicinal Uses: The seeds, fruits and dried juice (latex) of the flowering Papaver somniferum plant are analgesics, sedative, anodyne, hypnotic, antispasmodic and narcotic in action.

Poppy seeds are demulcent and nutritive and also mildly astringent. At first, the plant or its extract stimulates the brain, heart, and respiration, but this affect is soon followed by general depression. It relieves pain after abortion and delivery and is also an aphrodisiac tonic.

Traditional Uses: According to Unani and Ayurveda literature, Opium possesses the most significant therapeutic values. As a mild astringent, it is given with sugar and cardamoms (burnt) and is useful in diarrhoea and dysentery. Poppy seeds are used in syrup form against cough and asthma, as they are destitute of the narcotic constitutes and are used in confectionery and also against insomnia.

The seeds pounded in milk and made into a paste are effective against dandruff. The purification of opium has been described vividly in both Unani and Ayurvedic classic books. In Unani medicines, seeds (Khas-Khas in Urdu) are a valuable ingredient in many mono and poly-herbal formulations like Khamira-Khas-Khas, Majun-e-Muqavi Mumsik, Sharbat-e-Sadar etc.

Traditional healers (Hakims and Ayurveda) of the Indo-Pak subcontinent used Opium to treat moderate to severe pain of pleurisy, sciatica, chronic cold, cough due to nerve irritation, chronic dysentery and inflammation of the eye. It is also helpful for premature ejaculation, bilious meningitis, melancholia and schizophrenia. Externally, warm seeds made into a paste and applied over gouty parts render sound effects and alleviate rheumatic pains.

The capsule and seeds contain a large percentage of fixed oil, pale-golden in colour, with an agreeable odour, which dries quickly and the oil is used as food or oil for lamps. A liquid alcoholic extract named 'Elixir Paregorico' is extensively used for diarrhoeal diseases, in Brazil.

Biological Uses: The oil of Poppyseed possesses antioxidant properties and is beneficial for skin and hair health. The hydroalcoholic extract of the root produces better antibacterial activity than the ethanolic fraction. The aqueous and ethanolic extracts of these seeds have shown anti-acne properties.

Chemical Constituents: Opium produces some of the most widely used medicinal alkaloids like morphine, codeine, thebaine and porphyroxine, which are the essential component of this plant. The plant contains some valuable nutrients like vitamins A, C, E, K and minerals such as calcium, magnesium, iron, phosphorus, zinc, manganese and selenium. Its oil does not contain opiate alkaloids and has no narcotic properties. The Poppy seeds are very rich in Vitamin E (alpha tocopherols).

Distribution: Papaver somniferum plant is native to Turkey. Burma is the world's largest producer of opium poppies, followed by Iran and then Afghanistan. The region in Southwest Asia that stretches from Iran through South Afghanistan into Pakistan is known as the Golden Crescent. It produces about 820 tons (2009) compared to 700 tons of South East Asia, known as the Golden Triangle.

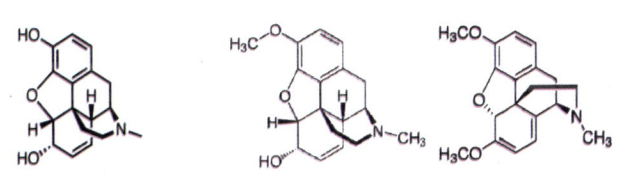

Morphine ($C_{17}H_{19}NO_3$) Codeine ($C_{18}H_{21}NO_3$) Thebaine ($C_{19}H_{21}NO_3$)

Peganum harmala

Harmal (Plant Parts, Flower and Seeds)

Latin Binomial	Peganum harmala
Family	Zygophyllaceae/Nitrariaceae
English Name	Syrian Rue

Urdu name   Harmal/Aspand

Medicinal Uses: The seeds of the herbaceous, flowering Peganum harmala plant are asthmatic, aphrodisiac, sedative, alterative, stimulant and antispasmodic in action.

Traditional Uses: Traditional healers (Hakims and Ayurveda) of the Indo-Pak subcontinent used seeds mostly in aphrodisiac preparations, for fevers, asthma and cold. Powdered seeds are beneficial as an anthelmintic in treating intermittent and remittent fevers. The leaves are considered a practical application externally and systemically in rheumatism. The whole plant can cure many diseases, like stomach complaints, urinary and sexual disorders, epilepsy and menstrual problems. The seeds and the entire plant of Peganum are beneficial in traditional medicines in Iran, Turkey, China and Egypt in relieving pain in hypertension, diabetes, asthma, coughs and also as an antiseptic agent.

In Unani and Ayurvedic medicinal systems, these seeds help treat asthma, insomnia and mental disorders. Peganum is effective in relieving fevers and chronic malaria. A decoction and infusion of seeds helps reduce challenging and painful menstruation and regulate menstrual periods. Traditionally, Peganum harmala plant is beneficial in treating diabetes, in some parts of the world.

The seeds of Peganum harmala plant form a constituent of the famous Unani poly-herbal aphrodisiac preparations like Majun-e-Aspand and Majun-e-Raig-Mahi.

Biological Uses: The plant aqueous and non-aqueous (methanol, ethanol, petro-ether, chloroform and ethyl acetate) extracts have antibacterial, antifungal properties, antioxidant, antitumor and also show cytotoxic activities.

Chemical Constituents: The plant contains harmaline and harmine; both are fluorescent indole alkaloids. It also has some essential biologically active constituents such as relatively new alkaloids 'dipegine,' flavonoids, saponins, volatile oils, glycosides, terpenoids, other alkaloids and tannins.

The seeds and roots contain the highest alkaloids and are absent in leaves and flowers. Harmine is also present in the plant's roots. It pharmacologically resembles 'harmaline' in its action, but is less toxic.

Distribution: Peganum harmala is native to arid and semi-arid regions of Northern African and Asian deserts (Pakistan, India, Afghanistan, Iran and Turkey) that have spread to parts of the South-Western United States and Northern Mexico.

Note: A high dose of Peganum shows severe side effects. Use only under medical supervision.

Harmaline ($C_{13}H_{14}N_2O$) Harmine or Banisterine ($C_{13}H_{12}N_2O$)

Pilocarpus jaborandi

Jhalar (Plant Parts and Leaves)

Latin Binomial	Pilocarpus jaborandi/Pernambuco jaborandi
Family	Rutaceae
English Name	Jaborandi
Urdu Name	Jhalar

Medicinal Uses: The dried leaves of flowering Pilocarpus jaborandi shrub or a small tree are aromatic, stimulant, diaphoretic and expectorant in action. Jaborandi is useful against psoriasis, deafness, baldness, chronic catarrh, tonsillitis, dropsy and catarrhal jaundice **(infectious hepatitis)**. It is also helpful in removing fat from the heart, heart disease, pleurlsy, chronic renal diseases and reduces thirst in patients with fever.

The extracted alkaloid has an antagonistic effect on atropine and causes the contraction of the eyes. It is a fast and highly effective diaphoretic drug, increasing gland secretions and breast milk flow. The plant may irritate the stomach, causing vomiting even when given as an injection, so care should be advised when prescribing this herb. The leaves are considered anti-inflammatory, diaphoretic, diuretic, febrifuge, galactagogue and sialagogue in action.

The presence of the alkaloid 'pilocarpine' in the plant is now widely used to treat glaucoma (Kala-motiya) and is useful in some eye surgeries and procedures.

Traditional Uses: Pilocarpus, in traditional medicine in South America is useful, where native people have employed the plant as a natural remedy for epilepsy, convulsions, gonorrhoea, fever, influenza, pneumonia, psoriasis, neurosis and as an agent to promote sweating. Despite serious safety concerns, Jaborandi is used to treat diarrhoea, gastrointestinal inflammations, kidney disease and to bring about sweating. In large doses, Pilocarpus jaborandi leaves are emetic. The leaves are suitable as a hair tonic. They may open pores and clean hair follicles and prevent hair loss.

Biological Uses. The plant extracts (aqueous, methanol, ethanol and ethyl acetate) possess anti-inflammatory, photosensitizing, antibacterial, antifungal and sleep-enhancing properties. The essential oil of Pilocarpus jaborandi plant exhibited bactericidal activity against Bacillus subtilis, Salmonella typhimurium, Escherichia coli and Pseudomonas aeruginosa. One of the plant's ingredients, 'pilocarpine,' has been utilized to treat dry mouth caused by radio or chemotherapy for throat cancer.

Chemical Constituents: The plant contains imidazole alkaloids, among which pilocarpine, a parasympathomimetic alkaloid (isolated in 1875), is the most important. Other alkaloids are isopilocarpine, pilocarpidine, jaborine, pilosine, pseudo-pilocarpine and isopilosine. The plant also contains valuable phytochemicals like flavonoids, steroids, coumarins, terpenoids and essential oils. The leaves are a good source of essential oil (volatile jabonine), giving off an aromatic balsam smell when they are crushed.

Distribution: Pilocarpus jaborandi is indigenous to South America and is specially grown in Brazil. It is also found in Venezuela, the Caribbean Islands and Central America.

Note: Jaborandi contains chemicals that might cause congenital disabilities or a miscarriage. Avoid taking by mouth or using it in the eyes if pregnant.

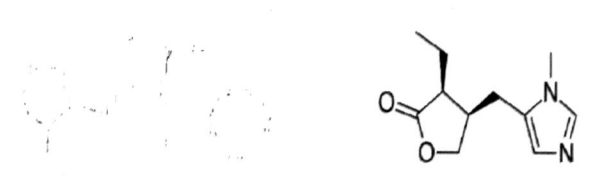

Pilosine ($C_{16}H_{18}N_2O_3$)   Pilocarpine ($C_{11}H_{16}N_2O_2$)

Piper longum

Filfil Daraz (Plant, Leaves and Fruits)

Latin Binomial	Piper longum
Family	Piperaceae
English Name	Long Pepper
Urdu name	Filfil Daraz/Piplamul

Medicinal Uses: The fruit of the perennial, climber, flowering Piper longum plant is digestive, an appetizer, astringent and carminative in action. It is also helpful in lung problems, including asthma, bronchitis and cough. Piper longum is a good remedy for treating gonorrhoea, menstrual pain, sleeping problems, chronic gut-related pain and arthritic conditions.

Traditional Uses: In Unani and Ayurvedic medicinal systems and traditional healers (Hakims and Ayurveda) of the Indo-Pak subcontinent, the fruit of the plant is a valuable stomachic, liver tonic, aphrodisiac, laxative, antidysenteric, helpful in urinary discharges, jaundice and hiccups. The roots are beneficial in the management of heart diseases. An infusion of the root is used for parturition, to provide assistance in the placenta's expulsion. Piper longum is a valuable remedy in various herbal compositions. It forms a useful liniment in case of paralysis. The roasted fruits are mixed with honey to treat rheumatism. A decoction of dried young fruit and root effectively treats acute and chronic bronchitis.

In the Ayurvedic medicinal system, the root is also valuable in beriberi (deficiency of vitamin B_1), throat infections, enlargement of the spleen, an immune booster and a hair tonic. The most extensively beneficial species in Ayurvedic medicine are reportedly used in at least 320 classical medicinal formulations. Mature but unripe spikes are useful in medicines.

Piper longum is an essential ingredient in many poly-herbal Unani preparations such as 'Jawarish -e-Jalinus, Hab-e-Azraqi and Majun-e-Falasfa.'

Biological Uses: Non-aqueous extracts (ethanol and petro-ether) of the fruit possess antifungal, antitumor, antioxidant and antimicrobial activities, whereas aqueous fractions have anti-diabetic, hepatoprotective and anti-inflammatory properties. The chloroform extract shows antitubercular action. Its oil is an antiseptic, antibacterial and an antioxidant. An alcohol (95 per cent) extract of the fruit exhibited hyperlipidemic properties.

Chemical Constituents: The plant contains piperine alkaloids, piperine, piperlongumine, pipermonaline, piperlingumin, pipermonaline, piperundecalidine, etc. Piper longum also has volatile oils, sterols, resins, a waxy-alkaloid, sesamine, saponins, terpenoids, phenols and carbohydrates. The essential oils of the fruit of Piper longum are a complex mixture of terpenes.

Distribution: Piper longum is a native to the Indo-Malayan region. It is also widely cultivated in tropical areas. This plant is also considered a native of South Asia.

Piperine ($C_{17}H_{19}NO_3$)

Piperlonguminine ($C_{16}H_{19}NO_3$)

Sesamin ($C_{20}H_{18}O_6$)

Piperundecalidine ($C_{23}H_{29}O_3$)

Piper nigrum

Kali Mirch (Plant, Fresh and Dried Fruits)

Latin Binomial	Piper nigrum
Family	Piperaceae
English Name	Black Pepper
Urdu Name	Kali Mirch

Medicinal Uses: The fruit of the flowering Piper nigrum is stomachic, carminative, alterative, aromatic and stimulant in action.

Traditional Uses: The herb is useful in treating constipation, gonorrhoea, prolapsed rectum, paralysis of the tongue and acts on the urinary organs. Pepper work's as stimulant properties on the gastrointestinal system to aid in digestion, ease flatulence and nausea. Piper nigrum is also beneficial in diarrhoea, cholera, scarlet fever, vertigo, paralytic and arthritic disorders. Ground pepper with acetic acid (sirka) is applied externally over the spleen region to resolve inflammation.

A decoction or cold water infusion of the leaves helps treat body aches and fevers. The macerated leaves and stems are helpful as antivenom against snake bites. Externally, the leaves are warmed and used as a poultice around joints to relieve arthritic pains and topically around the affected area to treat aches, pains and strains.

Black pepper is a commonly used herb in Unani, poly-herbal preparations like Jawarish-e-Kmuni, Barshahsha, Hab-e-Kabid and a popular carminative tablet 'Carmina'.

Biological Uses: The pepper oil has antispasmodic properties and relieves spasms, muscle pulls, cramps, convulsions and possesses antioxidant properties. The plant also exhibits antimicrobial, anticholinesterase, antitumor, anti-inflammatory and antioxidant activities. The leaf extract of the plant is antifungal. A petroleum ether fraction of the fruit shows a stimulant effect on the respiratory tract. In the presence of piperidine alkaloid piperine, the ethanolic fraction possesses potent antidepressant properties.

Chemical Constituents: Black pepper contains piperine alkaloids, chavicine, piperidine peronaline, iperonaline, piperettine, asarinine, pellitorine and piperetine (isolated from Piper arboretum). The presence of a colourless volatile oil gives an aromatic odour to pepper.

Distribution: Black pepper is considered 'The King of Spice' throughout the World. Piper nigrum is native to the Malabar Coast of India. Vietnam is the largest exporter of pepper, followed by Brazil, Indonesia and India.

Chavicine ($C_{17}H_{19}NO_3$)   Piperetine ($C_{19}H_{21}NO_3$)

Rauwolfia serpentina

Asroal (Plant, Flowers, Root and Seeds)

Latin Binomial   Rauwolfia serpentina

Family   Apocynaceae

English Name		Rauwolfia
Urdu Name		Asroal/Choti Candan/Sarpagandha

Medicinal Uses: The root of an erect, perennial flowering; evergreen Rauwolfia serpentina shrub is antihypertensive, sedative, psychotropic, stimulant, hypnotic in action and helps increase uterine contractions.

Traditional Uses: In Unani and Ayurvedic medicinal systems, the root of the shrub, Rauwolfia serpentina, is an antihypertensive, sedative, stimulant and antipsychotic in action. The powdered root is beneficial in the relief of insanity, hysteria, high blood pressure, epilepsy and insomnia. The decoction of the root has also been valuable in increasing uterine contractions; therefore, it is not suitable for pregnant women. The roots of the plant also serve as a remedy for the central nervous systems, in dysentery and in insomnia. It also acts as a febrifuge and in oedema.

The legendary Hakim Ajmal Khan (my great-grandfather) of Delhi, was a renowned Unani physician, a respected politician and a great philanthropist. He founded the Tibbiya College in Delhi to promote advanced learning and research, in Unani medicine.

As a part of bringing Unani Medicine and other indigenous traditional healing systems of India into the modern world, Hakim Ajmal Khan recognized the vital importance of laboratory research and clinical trials in proving traditional Unani's therapeutic efficacy of Ayurvedic medicinal herbs. Perhaps, the best-known example is his collaboration with the chemist, Dr Salimuzzaman Siddiqui[4], to chemically isolate and analyze the indigenous Unani and Ayurvedic herb's active constituents Rauwolfia, whose Latin binomial is Rauwolfia serpentina, of the Apocynaceae family. The work of the great chemist led to discovering the modern drug Ajmaline. Salimuzzaman Siddiqui named the antiarrhythmic agent 'ajmaline' in honour of his mentor Ajmal Khan. He named some other Rauwolfia alkaloids after Hakim Ajmal Khan, namely, ajmalicine, isoajmaline and neoajmaline. Other very important indole alkaloids are reserpine and yohimbine.

In addition to Unani and Ayurvedic, the root of the plant is also helpful in Siddha medicine in curing hypertension-associated headaches, dizziness, hysteria,

---

[4] Born at October 19, 1897 in Subeha, district Bara Banki, UP, India. Dr Salimuzzaman Siddiqui can be called the last Renaissance man, as he was a polymath of social and natural sciences. He was a chemist, philosopher, artist, critic of literature and a visionary of science.

amenorrhea, insomnia, oligomenorrhoea, dysmenorrhea abnormalities and in the treatment of psychiatric diseases.

The famous Unani, poly-herbal medicinal preparation for hypertension known as Ajmaline-54, contains Rauwolfia as an active ingredient.

Biological Uses: The leaves' non-aqueous (methanol) extract possesses antidiarrhoeal property. Its ethanolic extract has anti-inflammatory, antipyretic, anti-diabetic and anti-cancer effects. Various non-aqueous (methanol, petroleum ether, benzene and chloroform) fractions of leaf, stem and root have shown antibacterial and antifungal activities.

Chemical Constituents: Rauwolfia, in addition to valuable alkaloids, also contains useful secondary metabolites like flavonoids, saponins, tannins, steroids, cardiac glycosides, phenols and triterpenoids.

Distribution: Rauwolfia serpentina is native to the Indo-Pak subcontinent and East Asia from India to Indonesia.

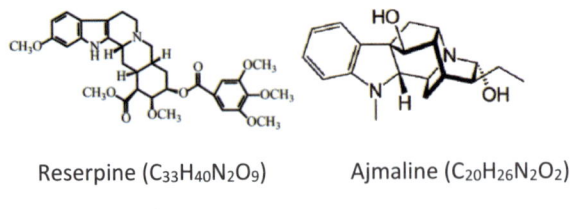

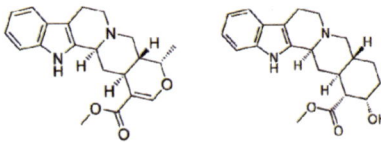

Reserpine ($C_{33}H_{40}N_2O_9$) Ajmaline ($C_{20}H_{26}N_2O_2$)

Ajmalicine ($C_{21}H_{24}N_2O_3$) Yohimbine ($C_{21}H_{26}N_2O_3$)

Scopolia carniolica

Scopolia (Plant, Flowers and Rhizome)

Latin Binomial	Scopolia carniolica/Hyocymus scoplia
Family	Solanaceae
English Name	Scopolia/Henbane bell
Urdu Name	Skubulia Karnywlyka

Medicinal Uses: The rhizome of the poisonous, flowering Scopolia carniolica plant is hypnotic, antidiarrhoeal, narcotic in nature and also causes dilation of the pupil. This plant's therapeutic activity resembles belladonna (Atropa belladonna of the Solanaceae family), but it is more narcotic in nature. The plant is rich in alkaloids as compared to Belladonna and Henbane (Hyoscyamus niger of the Solanaceae family). The German Commission E-Monographs, a therapeutic guide to herbal medicine, approves Scopolia carniolica for liver and gallbladder disorders.

Traditional Uses: The dried root is hypnotic, mydriatic and narcotic in nature. It induces sleep that resembles normal sleep. It helps treat chronic diarrhoea, dysentery, stomachache and manic-depressive states. The herb is very useful in alleviating sexual stimulation. The root extract is also beneficial in fluid retention (oedema) and the digestive tract's spasms. The powdered rhizome is applied externally as a patch to prevent nausea and vomiting or recovery from anaesthesia after surgery. Scopolia carniolica plant is seldom used in Unani and Ayurvedic systems of medicine.

Biological Uses: The aqueous-alcohol extracts exhibit antipyretic, antibacterial, antimicrobial, antihyperglycaemic and antioxidant properties. The methanol fraction of the stem is very beneficial in colon cancer.

Chemical Constituents: Hyoscine is in the anti-muscarinic family of medications and works by blocking some of the acetylcholine's effects within the nervous system. It contains tropane alkaloid scopolamine, also known as hyoscine and atropine. The concentration of atropine is the highest in the roots. The plant also has useful bioactive constituents such as flavonoids, coumarins, chlorogenic acid and phenolic compounds.

The United States Pharmacopoeia officially permitted the use of Scopolia Carniolica roots that need not enclose lower than 0.5 per cent alkaloid content for producing an extract and a fluid extract.

Distribution: It is native to Europe, Austria, Hungary and Russia. The plant is also occasionally cultivated in the gardens for decorative purposes.

Note: The Scopolia carniolica is a potent poison used only under medical direction. Common side effects include drowsiness, blurred vision, dilated pupils and dry mouth. It is unclear if its use during pregnancy is safe or not, but its use appears safe during breastfeeding.

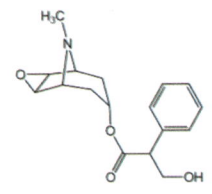

Scopolamine ($C_{17}H_{21}NO_4$)

Sida cordifolia

Beej-Band/Loofa (Flower, Seeds and Leaves)

Latin Binomial	Sida cordifolia/Malva tomentosa
Family	Malvaceae
English Name	Country Mallow
Urdu name	Beej-Band/Loofa

Medicinal Uses: The seeds, roots, leaves and oil of the perennial, flowering Sida cordifolia plant are useful for medicinal purposes. Its seeds are vicious, demulcent, anti-inflammatory and aphrodisiac. The roots are also anti-inflammatory and tonic, while the leaves are demulcent and anti-haemorrhage in action. Its oil is a nervine tonic. The plant contains ephedrine and pseudoephedrine. These compounds are responsible for their cardiovascular and central nervous system stimulant effect.

Traditional Uses: In Unani and Ayurvedic medicinal systems, it is considered the best nervine tonic and is rejuvenating for all kinds of respiratory and blood circulatory disorders. The entire herb contains stimulant alkaloids, which plays an essential role in shedding extra fats and thus, is suitable for weight loss. A decoction of its root is highly beneficial against tuberculosis, especially when taken with honey. A decoction is also a treatment for fevers.

The leaves are crushed in water and the juice is valuable in treating spermatorrhea and gonorrhoea. The stems are demulcent, emollient, febrifuge and diuretic. The roots are considered to be astringent, cooling, stomachic and tonic. An infusion is beneficial in treating nervous problems, urinary diseases, blood, bile disorders, in asthma and heart problems. Externally, the root juice is an effective remedy for healing wounds.

The seeds contain much larger alkaloid quantities than the leaves and roots. The seeds are helpful as an aphrodisiac. They are also used to treat gonorrhoea, cystitis, colds and cramping rectal pain.

Sida cordifolia is also considered beneficial in Chinese and Brazillian traditional medicinal systems as an antirheumatic, antipyretic, antiasthmatic, laxative, diuretic and hypoglycemic agent. The oil is valuable topically in massaging sore muscles, joint pain and also in rheumatism. The plant has a depressant rather than a stimulant effect on the central nervous system.

Biological Uses: The plant's aqueous fraction is reported to have hepatoprotective properties. The leaf's methanol extract shows an antibacterial effect and the root extract is an antioxidant. Research studies have shown that it possesses a significant blood-sugar-lowering activity and may reduce fat storage in fat cells. Sida cordifolia is used as a weight-loss product through its hypoglycaemic (blood sugar lowering) activity.

Chemical Constituents: The herb's chemical composition comprises alkaloids β-phenethylamines, carboxylated tryptamines, quinazoline alkaloids, ephedrine, vasicine, vasicinone etc. The plant also contains essential biologically active constituents such as flavonoids, essential oils, saponins, steroids, other alkaloids and reducing sugars.

Distribution: Sida cordifolia is native to the Indo-Pak subcontinent. It has been naturalized throughout the world and is considered an invasive weed in Africa, Australia, the southern United States, Hawaiian Islands, New Guinea and French Polynesia.

Note: The plant-specific name, Cordifolia, refers to the heart-shaped leaf.

Vasicine ($C_{11}H_{12}N_2O$) Vasicinone ($C_{11}H_{10}N_2O_2$) 2-Phenylethylamine ($C_8H_{11}N$)

Strychnos nuxvomica

Kuchla (Plant, Seeds and Fruit)

Latin Binomial	Strychnos nux vomica
Family	Loganiaceae
English Name	Nux Vomica
Urdu name	Kuchla/Azraqi

Medicinal Uses: The seeds of the evergreen Strychnos Nux vomica tree are stimulant, aphrodisiac, emetic, emollient, laxative and a tonic for the digestive system and the bladder. Nux vomica is utilized as a general tonic, mainly when combined with other herbal remedies, to treat neuralgia, dyspepsia, chronic constipation and general debility. The seeds can also be beneficial in cardiac failure, surgical shock, or poisoning by chloroform and in raising blood pressure and in increasing pulse rate, but they can cause violent convulsions.

Traditional Uses: This plant is a common remedy in Unani and Ayurvedic medicinal systems for facial paralysis, gout, general paralysis, backache, digestive debility and impotence. Seeds (after detoxification) combined with dried ginger powder effectively elevate blood pressure. In the Ayurvedic medicinal system, seeds are also helpful in dyspepsia and rheumatism.

Traditional healers of the Indo-Pak subcontinent, use the root of this herb as anthelmintic, in cholera, intermittent fever and wound infection. Externally, the paste of seeds is effective in treating facial paralysis. A poultice of leaves is beneficial for chronic ulcers and wounds for quick healing, while a decoction of the leaves is very effective in paralytic complaints.

Biological Uses: The hydroalcoholic extract of the seed possesses much better anti-diabetic activity than a methanolic fraction.

Chemical Constituents: The seeds contain Indole alkaloids, strychnine (isolated by French chemist P. J. Pelletier in 1820), brucine and strychnicine. The plant also has some biologically useful active compounds like glucosides, flavonoids, other alkaloids, steroids, triterpenoids, fixed oil and tannins. The indole alkaloid occurs in the seed, root, wood, bark, fruit pulp and its hard fruit shell.

Distribution: Strychnos nuxvomica is native to the Indo-Pak subcontinent and now is also grown in Burma, China, Australia and Indonesia.

Note: Nux vomica should only be used in limited circumstances and under strict control. Strychnine is very poisonous.

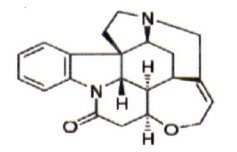

Strychnine ($C_{21}H_{22}N_2O_2$)   Brucine ($C_{23}H_{26}N_2O_4$)

Tinospora cordifolia

Gilu (Plant's Stems, Fresh and Dried)

Latin Binomial	Tinospora cordifolia
Family	Menispermaceae
English Name	Tinospora/Gurjo

Urdu Name　　　　　　Gilu/Sat-e-Gilu/Sat-e-Rumi

Medicinal Uses: The bark of the herbaceous Tinospora cordifolia plant is antipyretic, antispasmodic and anti-inflammatory in action and is also a blood purifier. The plant is known for its potent aphrodisiac nature and its rejuvenating nature. A decoction of the leaves is known to treat gout and ulcers and its root is emetic. An extract of the stem of Tinospora is beneficial against fever, skin diseases and is also an antidote for snake bites.

Tinospora cordifolia is useful in modern medicine for the prevention of cold and flu and skin disorders, liver disorders, immune support, gout, arthritis and lately is being used to overcome adverse chemotherapy effects.

Traditional Uses: The plant is one of the most commonly used herbs of Unani and Ayurvedic medicinal systems. The traditional healers (Hakims and Ayurveda) of the Indo-Pak subcontinent have used this herb to treat various diseases. For example, the aqueous plant extract is beneficial as a febrifuge and can influence bile liquids secretion and enrich blood constituents.

The fruit (powder) is helpful in treating jaundice and rheumatism. An infusion and aqueous extract (decoction) prepared from dry stem and root is a valuable tonic in debilitating conditions, intermittent fevers and dyspepsia. The decoction of the root is also used for gout treatment.

Tinospora cordifolia is one of the chief ingredients of the Unani products 'Safuf-e-Ziabetis' and 'Arq-Maul-Laham-Mako–Kasni-Wala' and is helpful in managing diabetes.

Biological Uses: The non-aqueous extract (ethanol) possesses antiulcer and antioxidant properties. Aqueous fraction has anti-inflammatory, antitumor, hepatoprotective and hypoglycaemic effects. The powdered leaf shows higher retention of antioxidant activity than the stem extract.

Chemical Uses: The plant mainly contains alkaloids, glycosides (cardiac glycosides), steroids, sesquiterpenoids, diterpenes, essential oils, a mixture of fatty acids and flavonoids. The alkaloids include berberine, palmatine, choline, tinosporin, glucosides and non-glycosides gelonin and gilosterol.

Distribution: Tinospora cordifolia is a deciduous climbing shrub native to East Asia, Myanmar, Sri Lanka, Thailand, Philippines, Indonesia, Malaysia, Vietnam, Bangladesh and South Africa.

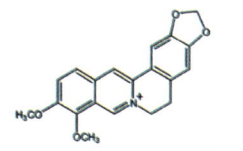

Berberine ($C_{20}H_{18}NO_4^+$) 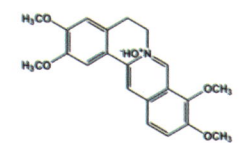 Palmatine ($C_{21}H_{24}NO_4^+$) 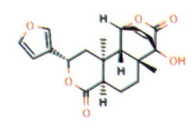 Tinosporin ($C_{21}H_{26}O_8$)

Tylophora indica

Anantmul (Plant, Stems and Flowers)

Latin Binomial	Tylophora indica
Family	Asclepiadaceae
English Name	Tylophore/Indian ipecac
Urdu Name	Anantmul/Antmool

Medicinal Uses: The root and leaves of the flowering Tylophora indica plant are stimulant, emetic, cathartic, expectorant and diaphoretic in action. They are useful in treating asthma, bronchitis, dysentery and diarrhoea. The plant is known to cure cold, psoriasis, anaphylaxis (severe allergic condition), respiratory infections and leucopenia (reduced white cells) diarrhoea. It is an inhibitor of the Schultz-Dale reaction (a reaction of anaphylaxis carried out *in vitro* with isolated tissues).

In modern herbal medicine, it has an antispasmodic and antiprotozoal action.

Traditional Uses: The emetic and asthmatic properties of the leaf and root of Tylophore indica are well established in both Unani and Ayurvedic medicinal systems. The leaves are expectorant and are used to treat respiratory infections, bronchitis and whooping cough. Fresh leaves of Tylophora indica chewed and swallowed daily with water, in the early morning, on an empty stomach, for a week gives moderate or complete relief from asthma symptoms. Its root or leaf powder helps in diarrhoea, dysentery and intermittent malarial fever.

The leaves are beneficial in the treatment of fever and allergies. Tylophora indica root also has analgesic properties, giving relief in earache, cystitis and lumbago. The root acts in similar ways to Ipecac (Carapichea ipecacuanha of the Rubiaceae family). It helps treat bronchitis, asthma, rhinitis, hay fever and allergy of the respiratory tract.

Biological Uses: The non-aqueous extracts (methanol and ethyl acetate) of leaves and stem of Tylophora indica showed high antioxidant and anti-inflammatory activities. Tylophora indica leaf extracts (aqueous and ethanol) possess a protective effect against ethanol-induced hepatotoxicity in rats. Its antitumor, immunomodulatory, antiulcer, antiasthmatic, antihistaminic, antiallergic, hypotensive, analgesic, anticonvulsant and antirheumatic activities are also scientifically proven. The non-aqueous (acetone, ethyl acetate and ethanol) fraction of the crude plant shows significant antibacterial activity against the tested pathogens. Bacillus subtilis (a gram-positive bacterium) is most susceptible to the extracts.

Chemical Constituents: Tylophora indica contains several medically active constituents, including isoquinoline alkaloids (tylophorine, tylophorinine also known as pergularinine and tylophorinidine), tannins, glycosides, flavonols (kaempferol, quercetin), saponins, sterols, resin and glucose. The plant also contains minerals such as zinc, copper, manganese, iron, silica, calcium, potassium and phosphorus.

Distribution: It is a native to tropical and subtropical Pakistan, India, Sri Lanka, Thailand, Malaysia and Borneo, Africa and Australia.

Tylophorine ($C_{24}H_{27}NO_4$)   Tylophorinidine ($C_{22}H_{23}NO_4$)

Pergularinine ($C_{23}H_{25}NO_4$)

Wrightia tinctoria

Inderjo Shirin (Plant, Pods, Leaves and Dried Bark)

Latin Binomial	Wrightia tinctoria/Wrightia rothii
Family	Apocynaceae
English Name	Inderjo Sweet
Urdu Name	Inderjo Shirin

Medicinal Uses: The bark, leaves and seeds of the deciduous, flowering Wrightia tinctoria shrub or tree are useful for medicinal purposes. It is a uterine sedative, aphrodisiac, astringent, antidiarrhoeal in action and a tonic for the stomach.

Traditional Uses: In Unani and Ayurvedic medicinal systems, the bark of the plant is effective as a galactagogue. It is also beneficial in abdominal pain, skin diseases, antipyretic, antidysenteric, antidiarrhoeal and an antidote for snake poison. The powdered bark is helpful in treating kidney stones. Wrightia tinctoria plant is also valuable for treating local pain, rheumatism, chronic cough and bronchitis. The leaves are suitable as a poultice for mumps and herpes and relieve toothache. The seeds are useful as a tonic, carminative, anthelmintic, astringent and aphrodisiac. A decoction of the leaves and bark Is valuable as a stomachic.

In folk medicine, the dried and powdered roots of Wrightia and other herbs are mixed with milk and orally administered to women for improving fertility. The bark and seeds are effective against psoriasis and non-specific dermatitis. It has anti-inflammatory and anti-dandruff properties and is valuable in hair oil preparations. The juice of fresh leaves is useful in jaundice treatment. The plant is traditionally beneficial in curing breast cancer. The oil obtained from the leaves mixed with coconut oil, helps treat psoriasis. The plant (bark, leaves and seeds) also has an aphrodisiac effect. In South Indian states, the tree's name is 'curative jaundice tree.'

Biological Uses: An ethanol extract of the bark shows significant anti-diabetic activity. The leaf extracts (petro-ether, chloroform, acetone and ethyl-acetate) exhibit anthelmintic and anti-inflammatory properties. The ethanolic fractions of the plant have antiulcer, antioxidant, cytotoxic, anti-HIV and antimicrobial activities.

Wrightia tinctoria plant extract considerably increases urine volume, acting as a strong kaliuretic (a process of excreting potassium in the urine). Non-aqueous extracts (ethyl-acetate, methanol and acetone) of Wrightia root showed antinociceptive and immunomodulatory properties.

Chemical Constituents: The plant's phytochemical studies have shown pyrrolizidine alkaloids, triterpenoids (cycloaretane and wrightial), flavonoids, saponins, tannins, steroids (cycloartenone and cycloeucalenol) and alpha and beta amyrin. Its flowers are fragrant and contain essential oils. The root contains cardiac glycosides. The stem bark of Wrightia tinctoria also contains alkaloids, lupeol, beta-sitosterol, stigmasterol, flavonoids and steroids. Wrightia tinctoria fruit peel and cellulose extracts are rich in phytochemical activity.

Distribution: Wrightia tinctoria plant is native to the Indo-Pak subcontinent, Burma, Australia and is found throughout the world.

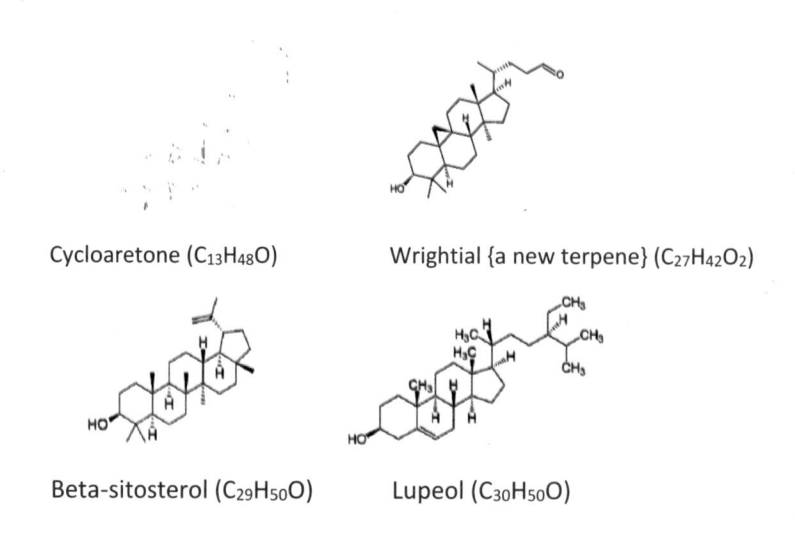

Cycloaretone ($C_{13}H_{48}O$)

Wrightial {a new terpene} ($C_{27}H_{42}O_2$)

Beta-sitosterol ($C_{29}H_{50}O$)

Lupeol ($C_{30}H_{50}O$)

Medicinal Plants
Plants containing Carbohydrates

Carbohydrates

Carbohydrates contain carbon, hydrogen and oxygen. The last two elements, hydrogen and oxygen, are usually present in the same proportions as in water, 2:1, respectively. They are among the most abundant constituents of both plants and animals. Simple carbohydrates such as sugars are generally water-soluble and have a sweet taste, while those which are more complex and have high molecular weights, are insoluble and tasteless.

Monosaccharide (simple sugars) consists of one sugar unit that cannot be further broken down into simpler sugars. Examples of monosaccharides in foods are glucose, fructose and galactose. These sugars contain three to nine carbon atoms, but those with five and six carbon atoms (pentoses, $C_5H_{10}O_5$ and hexoses, $C_6H_{12}O_6$) are present in plants; in the greatest quantity.

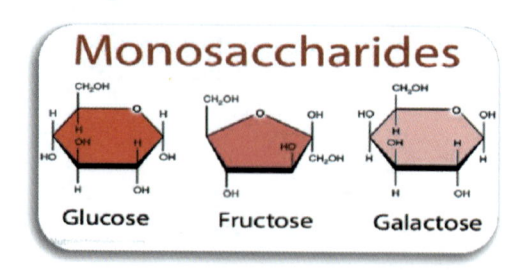

Configuration of monosaccharide: Like many chiral molecules, the two stereoisomers of glyceraldehydes will gradually rotate the polarization direction of linearly polarized light as it passes through it, even in solution. The two stereoisomers are identified with the prefixes D- and L-, according to the sense of rotation: D-glyceraldehydes are dextrorotatory (rotate the polarization axis clockwise). At the same time, L-glyceraldehydes are levorotary (rotate it counterclockwise).

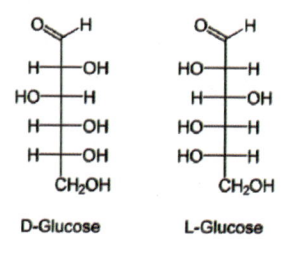

Carbohydrates (Functions)

- Glucose provides energy for the brain and ½ of the energy for muscles and tissues.
- Glycogen is stored in glucose.
- Glucose is immediate energy.
- Glycogen is reserved energy.

Carbohydrates also play a vital role in the metabolism and oxidation of protein.

Di, Tri and Tetrasaccharides: These sugars may also be called bioses, trioses and tetroses. They are theoretically derived from two, three and four monosaccharide molecules, respectively, with eliminating one, two and three water molecules.

Disaccharides: Examples of disaccharides are sucrose, maltose and lactose.

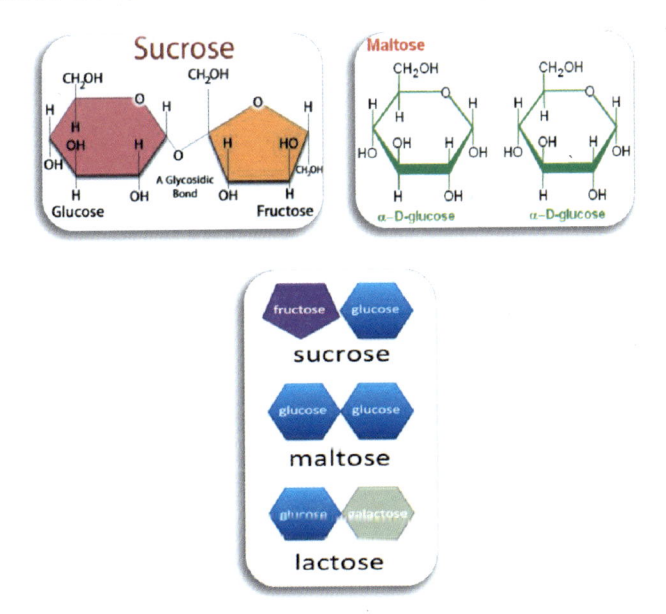

Polysaccharides: These are polymeric carbohydrate molecules composed of long chains of monosaccharide units bound together by glycosidic linkages (bond). Hydrolysis gives the constituent monosaccharides or oligosaccharides (containing a small number of monosaccharides). They range in structure from linear to highly branched compounds. Examples include storage polysaccharides such as starch and glycogen and structural polysaccharides such as cellulose and chitin.

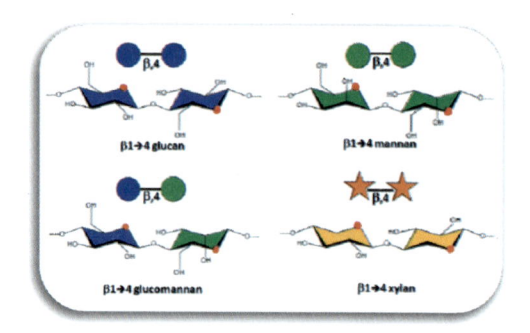

Tests for Carbohydrates Theory

Carbohydrates are polyhydroxy aldehydes and ketones or substances that hydrolyse to yield polyhydroxy aldehydes and ketones. Aldehydes (–CHO) and ketones (--C=O) constitute the carbohydrates' major groups.

Molisch's Test: In a test tube, add 2 ml of the test carbohydrate solution and two drops of α-naphthol solution. Carefully incline the tube and pour concentrated H_2SO_4, dropwise, using a dropper, along the sides of the tube. Observe the violet colour at the junction of the two liquids. (This is due to the formation of an unstable condensation product of beta-naphthol with furfural produced by the dehydration of carbohydrates).

Fehling's Test: In a test tube, add 2 ml of the carbohydrate test solution and add equal volumes of Fehling A & Fehling B and place it in a boiling water bath for a few minutes. When the contents of the test tube come to boil, mix them and observe any change in colour or precipitate formation. The production of a yellow or brownish-red precipitate of cuprous oxide indicates reducing sugars in the given sample.

Benedict's test: In the test tube with 2 ml of Benedict's reagent, add 5 - 6 drops of the carbohydrate test solution and mix well. Place the test tube in a boiling water bath for 5 minutes and observe any change in colour or precipitate formation. Cool the solution. Observe the colour change from blue to green, yellow, orange, or red, depending upon reducing sugar present in the test sample. If the saccharide is a reducing sugar, it will minimise copper (Cu (II) ions to Cu (I) oxide or Cu^{2+} to Cu_2O.

Barfoed's Test: To 2 ml of the test solution, add about 2-3ml of Barfoed' reagent Mix it well, boil it for one minute in a water bath and stand it for a few minutes. The formation of a red precipitate of cuprous oxide at the bottom and along the test tube's sides confirms monosaccharides' presence. Since Barfoed's reagent is slightly acidic, this test is specific for monosaccharides. If the saccharide is a reducing sugar, it will reduce copper (II) ions (Cu^{2+}) to copper (I) oxide Cu_2O.

Seliwanoff's Test: To 2ml of Seliwanoff's reagent, add two drops of the test solution. The mixture is heated to near boiling temperature. A cherry red condensation product will be observed, indicating ketoses in the test sample. There will be no significant change in colour produced for aldose sugar. When in reaction with the Seliwanoff reagent, ketoses reacts within 2 minutes, forming a cherry red condensation product. (Aldopentoses react slowly, creating the coloured condensation product).

Bial's Test: To 5ml of Bial's reagent, add 2 – 3 ml of the test solution and warm gently in a hot water bath for 2 minutes. The formation of a bluish-green product is indicative of pentoses. Hexoses generally react to form muddy brown products. The furfurals formed produce condensation products with a specific colour.

Iodine Test: Add two drops of iodine solution to about 2 ml of the carbohydrate-containing test solution. A blue-black colour is observed, which is indicative of the presence of polysaccharides. Iodine forms coloured adsorption complexes with polysaccharides.

Osazone Test: To 0.5 g of phenylhydrazine hydrochloride, add 0.1 gram of sodium acetate and ten drops of glacial acetic acid. Add 5 ml of the test solution to this mixture and heat under a boiling water bath for about half an hour. Cool the solution slowly and examine the crystals under a microscope. Needle-shaped yellow osazone crystals will be observed for glucose and fructose, whereas lactosazone shows mushroom-shaped and maltose produces flower-shaped crystals. They are reducing sugars forms osazone in treating with phenylhydrazine.

Colour Tests

Molisch's	Fehling's	Barfoed's	Bial's	Iodine	Osazone

Avena sativa

Oat (Plant Parts, Seeds Fresh and Dried)

Latin Binomial	Avena sativa
Family	Poaceae
English Name	Oat
Urdu Name	Jau

Medicinal Uses: The seeds of flowering Avena sativa are stimulant, antispasmodic, nutritional, demulcent, emollient in action and a tonic for the heart and brain. Oats form a nutritious and easily digestible food for convalescent patients who are exhausted after fevers. Oat extract or tincture is helpful as a nerve and uterine tonic. The plant's colloidal preparation effectively treats inflammation of the skin, itching, acne and eczema. The American Botanical Council reported in an article that 'liquid paraffin' with colloidal Oatmeal reduced itching and is used as antihistamine in acute burn patients compared to liquid paraffin alone. Oat straw tea can be highly beneficial when fighting addictions, especially smoking and nicotine withdrawal.

Oat grain is an ingredient in a wide range of food products including breakfast cereals, porridge, cookies, bread, muffins, crackers and snacks, beverages, meat extenders and baby foods.

Traditional Uses: In Europe, there is a tradition of using Oat straw in baths to treat rheumatism and painful muscles and kidney problems. Oat grain is valuable in restoring vigour and strength during recovery from weakness. Oats ease blood sugar in the Unani and Ayurvedic medicinal systems when used in a daily diet. It also reduces high cholesterol, reduces the risk of heart diseases and is beneficial in ulcerative colitis symptoms. Avena sativa seeds are helpful as an antidepressant and externally, as an emollient.

Biological Uses: The Oat extracts possess antioxidant, anti-inflammatory, wound healing, anti-diabetic and antihypercholesterolemic (herb reduces cholesterol levels) properties.

Chemical Constituents: Oat is a rich source of protein. Avena sativa contains minerals like magnesium, phosphorus, manganese, potassium (traces), zinc and polysaccharide. The plant also has biologically active constituents such as an indole alkaloid (avenanthramides), flavonoids, flavonol, lignans, triterpenoid, saponins, lipids, sterols and carbohydrates.

Distribution: Avena sativa is native to **Eurasia and Africa.** Russia is the largest Oat producer, followed by Canada, Poland and Finland.

Avenanthramide A ($C_{16}H_{13}NO_5$)

Beta vulgaris

Chuqandar (Plant and Fruits)

Latin Binomial	Beta vulgaris
Family	Amaranthaceae/Chenopodiaceae

English Name	Beetroot
Urdu Name	Chuqandar

Medicinal Uses: The root of herbaceous, biennial (infrequently perennial) Beta vulgaris plant contains pure fruit sugar, which is readily taken up by the body. The Beetroot juice is said to have a cleaning, digestive quality to 'open up obstructions of the liver and spleen' and ease headaches. The Beetroot may also provide a wide range of possible health benefits, such as reducing blood pressure, improving digestion and lowering the risk of diabetes. It is also beneficial in anaemia, inflammation and liver and spleen diseases.

Traditional Uses: In Unani and Ayurvedic medicinal systems, the roots are helpful primarily as haemagglutination (clumping together of red blood cells), antifertility, antifungal, as a diuretic and in some respiratory disorders. The roots are carminative, emmenagogue, haemostatic, stomachic and a tonic for women. A decoction prepared from the seed is beneficial in intestinal tumours. The roots also help in relieving constipation, decreased libido, gout, joint pain and in controlling dandruff.

The Beetroot and its leaves are valued as a vegetable. Most often, people use Beetroot for athletic performance. It is also helpful for liver diseases, reducing muscle soreness after exercise, high blood pressure and other conditions.

Biological Uses: Extracts (ethanol) of the plant possess antiseptic, antioxidant, antibacterial and anti-cancer activities. The aqueous extract of fresh leaves is beneficial in acne. In Iraq, the plant is ranked among the ten most potent vegetables concerning antioxidant capacity, anti-inflammatory, antiulcer, hepatoprotective, and antitumour properties.

Chemical Constituents: Beta vulgaris contains sugar, tannins, flavonoids, alkaloids, carotenoids and phenolic compounds. The root is a good source of vitamins like B_3 (niacin), B_5 (pantothenic acid), B_6 (pyridoxine), B_9 (folic acid), C (ascorbic acid) and minerals such as potassium, sodium, phosphorous, calcium, magnesium, copper, iron and zinc. The chemical adipic acid rarely occurs in nature but happens to occur naturally in Beetroot.

Distribution: The Beetroot plant is a native to Southern Europe. Russia is the largest producer of Beetroot, followed by France, the United States, Germany and Turkey. Beta vulgaris is commercially grown in Pakistan in Khyber Pakhtunkhwa and Punjab; it is also produced as a vegetable in Sindh and Baluchistan.

Adipic acid (C$_6$H$_{10}$O$_4$)

Citrus x aurantifolia

Nibu (Tree and Fruits)

Latin Binomial	Citrus x aurantifolia
Family	Rutaceae
English Name	Lemon/Key Lime
Urdu Name	Nibu

Medicinal Uses: The fruit of the evergreen Citrus x aurantifolia tree is aromatic, stimulant, refrigerant, carminative and anti-scorbutic (counteracting scurvy) in action. It is beneficial in acute rheumatism and in counteracting narcotic poisons such as opium. It may be freely used as such or in syrup; it is a popular remedy in coughs and colds. It is also a popular drink for its weight loss benefits.

In addition to a low-fat diet, Lemon water prevents fat and cholesterol deposition in the body. The presence of vitamin C inhibits low-density lipoprotein (LDL) oxidation and controls the clogging of the arteries. The presence of pectin (heteropolysaccharide) in Lemon, also reduces high cholesterol.

Traditional Uses: In Unani and Ayurvedic medicinal systems, the fruit's infusion is valuable in dyspepsia and flatulence. The plant immature is beneficial as a fortifier, cardiotonic, laxative and antihelminthic. The seeds are for heart patients. The essential oils are acrid, astringent, alexiteric (preservative against infectious diseases) and suitable for stomach disorders. Lemon oil is a strong external rubefacient and also has stomachic and carminative properties. The flowers of the plant are helpful as an antidote to poisons and the leaves are useful in preventing vomiting, hiccupping and dysentery. A decoction of the flowers is beneficial in fevers. The fruit is valuable as a tonic for treating the swelling of the spleen.

In India and Pakistan, some traditional healers (Hakims and Ayurveda) use various Lemon species as appetisers, cardio-stimulants and antiemetics. Squeezing Lemon in lukewarm water and drinking on an empty stomach cleanses the system, purifies impurities in the blood and energizes the body.

In traditional Chinese medicine, the ripe or unripe fruit's dry pericarp is useful mainly as an expectorant and stomachic. With other herbs, it is beneficial in treating hernia. The dried fruit is among anti-shock herbs used in traditional Chinese medicine, known as 'Tai-fu,' which generally treats shock, symptomatically.

Biological Uses: The fruit has antiseptic, antibacterial and anti-inflammatory properties. The lemon extract reduces the risk of many types of cancer, including breast cancer. It may probably be due to flavanone glycoside, hesperidin and *d*-limonene. The lemon oil possesses antiseptic, antioxidant and antibacterial activities.

Chemical Constituents: The plant contains glycosides, volatile oils, tannins, sugar, flavonoids and vitamin C. The lemon is also rich in minerals like sodium, potassium, calcium, copper, zinc and phosphorus. Pectin, a heteropolysaccharide, is produced commercially as a white to light brown powder, mainly extracted from Citrus fruit.

Distribution: The genus Citrus is native to South Asia, East Asia, Melanesia and Australia. The United States is the largest producer of different lemon species, followed by Brazil, China, India, Mexico and Iran. Citrus x aurantifolia is cultivated in the four provinces of Pakistan: Punjab, Sind, Baluchistan and Khyber-Pakhtunkhwa. Among all four provinces, Punjab is considered the hub of Citrus production.

Hesperidin ($C_{28}H_{34}O_{15}$)

Ficus carica

Anjeer (Tree, Fresh and Dried Food)

Latin Binomial	Ficus carica/Ficus racemosa
Family	Moraceae
English Name	Fig
Urdu Names	Anjeer

Medicinal Uses The fruit of the evergreen, flowering Ficus carica tree is nutritive, tonic, emollient, demulcent, laxative in action and resolvent of inflammations. It is generally helpful in laxative confections and syrups with senna (Cassia angustifolia) and carminatives. Demulcent decoction prepared from Fig is effective in treating catarrhal afflictions of the nose and throat. The three preparations of the Fig of the British Pharmacopoeia are 'Syrup of Fig' a mild laxative suitable for administering to children; 'Aromatic syrup,' an excellent laxative for children and delicate persons and a 'Compound herbal preparation' containing senna (Cassia senna) and rhubarb (Rheum emodi).

Traditional Uses: The therapeutic utilities of Ficus carica are indicated in traditional medicinal systems such as Unani, Ayurvedic and herbal. For example, Fig (fresh and dried) is useful as a diuretic, mild laxative and expectorant. The plant is helpful in treating disorders of the endocrine system (diabetes), respiratory system (asthma and cough), gastrointestinal tract (ulcer and vomiting), reproductive system (menstrual pain) and infectious diseases (skin disease, scabies and gonorrhoea). The milky juice of the freshly-broken stalk of a Fig has helped remove warts on the body. Ficus carica juice of the stems and leaves is very acrid and is used in some countries for blisters. The leaves are expectorant, diuretic, anthelmintic and beneficial in anaemia. The root is a useful tonic in treating leucoderma and ringworm infections. The leaves have shown an irritant property.

Fig leaves are valuable in treating tuberculosis in Malaysia and in the Mediterranean countries. The Fig, is a nutritious diet. In Pakistan, the fruit is used as antiplatelet, anti-inflammatory and gut motility. The bark, leaves and latex are used in anorexia. Figs have long been employed for their nutrient value, both in their fresh and dried state and they form a large part of food of the natives of both Western Asia and Southern Europe.

One of the famous Unani, poly-herbal expectorant medicinal preparations known as 'Sherbet-e-Zufa' containing Fig as one of the active ingredients.

Biological Uses: The plant extracts (methanol and ethanol) possess antioxidant, hypoglycemic, anti-cancer, hypolipidemic (lipid-lowering herbs) and antimicrobial properties.

Chemical Constituents: The plant's leaves and fruits contain phenolic compounds, flavonoids, vitamin C, glucosides, alkaloids, saponins, coumarins, tannins, organic acids and essential oils. Dried Figs are rich in fibre and in minerals like calcium, copper, manganese, potassium, magnesium and vitamin K. Figs contain more calcium on a weight basis than apples, bananas, dates, grapes, prunes and raisins.

Distribution: Ficus carica **is native to the Mediterranean and Western Asia.** Most of the global production of Figs is harvested in Turkey, followed by Egypt, Algeria, Iran, Afghanistan and Morocco.

Ipomoea paniculata

Bidari-kand/Shaqar Qand   (Flower, Leaves and Rhizomes)

Latin Binomials	Ipomoea paniculata/Batatas paniculata
Family	Convolvulaceae
English Name	Sweet Potato
Urdu Names	Bidari-kand/Shaqar Qand

Medicinal Uses: The rhizome of Ipomoea paniculata plant is edible, appetitive, aphrodisiac, lactagogue, demulcent, restorative and anti-inflammatory in action.

Traditional Uses: In Unani and Ayurvedic medicinal systems, the plant rhizome helps treat liver and spleen enlargement. The plant (root and rhizome) is valuable as an aphrodisiac, is a tonic and helps increase breast milk. Raw rhizomes' flour is beneficial for treating hepatosplenomegaly (spleen and liver disorders). The powder of the root is useful in spermatorrhoea. Ayurveda has also recommended its use in uterine pain, infertility, gastric ulcer and ulcerative colitis.

In the Philippines, Papua New Guinea, Malaysia, Indo-China and India, the seed of Ipomoea pes-caprae (one of the species of Ipomoea) is useful as a remedy for stomach ache and cramps. In Malaysia, a poultice of the rhizome is useful against headache.

In China, the seeds are regarded as diuretic, anthelmintic and de-obstruent and are also prescribed for dropsy and constipation to promote menstruation. In the West Indies, a decoction of the leaf is a remedy for asthma and rheumatism. It is also drunk daily in the last month of pregnancy to promote easy delivery. A strong decoction of Ipomoea paniculata root is abortifacient. In Nigeria, the dried leaves are a remedy for burns and finely crushed leaves are smeared on stiff joints and burns. The stem is bound to provide relief from pain.

Biological Uses: The plant's extracts (aqueous, methanol and ethanol) showed anti-inflammatory, anti-diabetic, antioxidant and galactagogue activities. Some Ipomoea species exhibit antimicrobial, analgesic, spasmolytic, spasmogenic, hypotensive and anti-cancer properties. The rhizome's crude fraction is more potent than that of the purified compound, probably due to the combination of anthocyanins and other phenolic constituents.

Chemical Constituents: Ipomoea paniculata plant contains carbohydrates, polyhydroxylated indolizidine alkaloids, resin glycosides, phenolic compounds, coumarins (scopoletin), flavonoids, steroids (ecdysteroid), triterpenoids octadecyl (E)-p-coumarate ($C_{27}H_{44}O_3$) and taraxerol ($C_{30}H_{50}O$). The plant is also rich in vitamins (A, B_1, B_2, B_6, C and D,) and minerals (sodium, potassium, calcium, iron and magnesium). The rhizome of sweet potatoes is a good vitamin D source, vital for calcium deposition and for storage in the body. Sweet Potatoes are among the top ten natural foods with a high nutrient value other than maize, white and brown rice, wheat, cassava, soybean, etc.

Distribution: Ipomoea paniculata is native to West Africa. The chief countries producing Ipomoea are China, Uganda, Indonesia, Vietnam and Nigeria.

Musa acuminata

Kela (Tree and Fruit before and after processing)

Latin Binomial	Musa acuminata
Family	Musaceae
English Name	Banana
Urdu Name	Kela

Medicinal Uses: The fruit of a herbaceous, evergreen Musa acuminata plant is anti-diabetic, antihypertensive, antiulcer, anti-inflammatory, antiemetic, antidiarrhoeal and antiurolithiasis in action.

The Food and drug administration (FDA) has also confirmed the importance of Banana fruit in reducing blood pressure and stroke risk due to its high potassium and low salt content. A decoction of the banana tree stems helps control blood sugar levels. The Banana plant (leaves, fruit and flowers) is documented in treating various diseases such as fever, cough, bronchitis, dysentery, allergic infections, sexually transmitted infections and non-communicable diseases.

Traditional Uses: In Unani and Ayurvedic medicinal systems, almost all parts of the Musa acuminata plant are useful in treating various diseases. The fruit is rich in iron; it helps in anaemia, constipation, heartburn, stress and ulcer. The plant's flower helps treat ulcers, dysentery, bronchitis and cooked buds are suitable for people with diabetes.

The astringent ashes of the unripe Banana peel and leaves are valuable for treating dysentery, diarrhoea and treating malignant ulcers. The root is powerfully astringent and has been used to arrest the coughing up of blood and in treating convulsions.

A paste made from the fruit gives immediate relief from pain if spread over a burn or wound. The stem is beneficial for treating the armpits, groin swellings and haemorrhoids. An infusion of the stem pulp is a remedy for treating dysentery.

Biological Uses: The non-aqueous extracts (ethanol) of the Banana plant possess anti-ulcer, antilipemic (herbs beneficial in lowering blood cholesterol), antiviral, antifungal and antioxidant properties. The Banana flower extract has anti-glycemic action. The methanolic fraction of dried, unripe banana shows protective effects against aspirin-induced erosion.

Chemical Constituents: The plant contains carbohydrates, glycosides, tannins, saponins, steroids, alkaloids, flavonoids, dietary fibres, minerals (potassium and magnesium) and vitamins (A, B_6, B_{12} and C). Musa acuminate (fruit) is an excellent source of potassium. Potassium can be found in various fruits, vegetables and even meats. However, a single banana provides 23 per cent of the potassium that one needs daily. Potassium benefits the muscles as it helps maintain their proper working and prevents muscle spasms.

In general, the flour of unpeeled Banana exhibits better nutrition values with higher minerals, dietary fibre and total phenolics. Therefore, the flour fortified with peel shows relatively higher antioxidant activity.

Distribution: Generally, bananas are said to have originated in Southeast Asia and the South Pacific. India is the largest Banana producer, followed by China and the Philippines.

Banana is grown commercially in Sindh and KPK provinces, Pakistan. In Pakistan, Sindh is most suitable for cultivating Musa acuminata (Hari chhal 'Basrai' banana variety). It is mainly produced in Hyderabad, Mirpur Khas, Badin, Thatta, Nawabshah, Sanghar, Noushero Feroze and Khairpur districts of Sindh. It is also grown in small areas in some parts of Khyber-Pakhtunkhwa and Punjab.

Note: Banana's vivid colour is caused by the artificial ripening process with ethylene (C_2H_4) gas. Traditionally, banana leaves are used to serve food in South India, Thailand, Malaysia and Indonesia.

Oryza sativa

Chawal (Plant and Fruits)

Latin Binomial	Oryza sativa
Family	Poaceae
English Name	Rice
Urdu Name	Chawal

Medicinal Uses: The seeds of the Oryza sativa plant are nourishing, soothing and a tonic. The plant is a diuretic, reduces lactation, improves digestion and controls sweating. The seeds are taken internally in the treatment of urinary dysfunction. The seeds or the germinated seeds are also beneficial in managing excessive lactation. The rhizome is taken internally in treating night sweats, especially in tuberculosis and in chronic pneumonia cases.

In European herbal books, rice is nutritive, demulcent and refrigerant in action. Boiled rice is good in treating upset digestion, bowel problems and diarrhoea. Finely pulverized rice flour is useful for burns, scalds and erysipelas (common bacterial infection).

Traditional Uses: In Unani and Ayurvedic medicinal systems, rice is considered acrid, oleaginous, a tonic, an aphrodisiac, a diuretic and useful in biliousness (a type of liver disorder). Oryza sativa, in the Ayurvedic medicinal system, is considered a 'healthy food' for the treatment of rheumatoid arthritis, paralysis, neurodegenerative diseases and in rejuvenation therapy.

Pharmacopoeia of India prescribes rice water as an ointment to counteract an inflamed surface. This plant is also mentioned in the Medicinal books of Malaysia, the Philippines, Cambodia and China.

In China and Cambodia, mature rice plants' hulls (husk) are considered useful in treating dysentery and that it promotes diuresis. The Chinese believe that rice strengthens the spleen and stomach, increases the appetite and cures indigestion. They use red rice yeast for various ailments. In Malaysia, boiled rice is a remedy for eye inflammation and skin diseases. In Cambodia, mature plants' hulls are considered beneficial for treating dysentery. In the Philippines, rice polish (bran, tiki-tiki) is extracted and used as an excellent vitamin B source to prevent and cure Beriberi.

Biological Uses: Orizaterpenol and the known momilactone B (an allelopathic agent) are found to have cytotoxic effects against murine leukaemia cells. The ethanolic fraction of the plant has anti-inflammatory and antioxidant properties. The presence of flavonoids, and phenolic compounds appear to have antioxidant and antiviral effects.

Chemical Constituents: The plant contains carbohydrates, fibres, cellulose, phytosterols, flavonoids, minerals (potassium, phosphorus, copper, magnesium and zinc) and vitamins (E, B_1 and B_3). Four new compounds, namely, (a) orizaterpenols, (b) orizaterpenoids, (c) orizaterpenyl benzoate and (d) orizanor-diterpenyl benzoate, along with nine known compounds were also isolated and identified from the rice hulls of Oryza sativa. Rice bran contains an important flavonoid type compound known as 'tricin.'

Distribution: Oryza sativa is native to South East Asia. China is the largest rice producer, followed by India, Indonesia and Bangladesh.

Rice is grown in many areas of Pakistan. In Punjab, it is cultivated in the district of Gujranwala, Gujrat, Sargodha, Faisalabad and Kasur. In Sindh, Jacobabad, Larkana, Badin, Thatta, Shikarpur and Dadu districts are well-known for rice cultivation. In Pakistan, rice is an important cash crop of the country and is important for the overall national economy.

Tricin ($C_{17}H_{14}O_7$)

Phoenix sylvestris

Khajur/Khurma (Tree and Fruits)

Latin Binomials	Phoenix sylvestris /Phoenix dactylifera
Family	Palmae/Arecaceae
English Name	Date
Urdu Names	Khajur/Khurma

Medicinal Uses: The fruit of Phoenix sylvestris tree is edible, aphrodisiac, diuretic, digestive in action and a tonic for the nerves and the heart. The juice of the fruit is cooling and is a laxative.

Traditional Uses: In Unani and Ayurvedic medicinal systems, Dates are useful in liver problems, respiratory disorders, fever, constipation and are also a tonic. The fruit is beneficial in heart complaints, abdominal complaints, fevers, vomiting and loss of consciousness. The seeds are a remedy in stopping bleeding. A paste made from the seeds helps bring down the temperature (antipyretic).

Traditional healers (Hakims and Ayurveda) of the Indo-Pak subcontinent have prescribed this fruit with boiled milk as a refreshing tonic and an aphrodisiac. A gum from the slit tree trunk helps cure diarrhoea, acting as a diuretic and a remedy for genitourinary diseases. A decoction of the roots can cure toothache. The fruit intake helps in getting relief from constipation. The central tender part of the plant is beneficial in treating gonorrhoea.

Biological Uses: An extract of Phoenix sylvestris fruit shows antioxidant, antimutagenic (herb capable of reducing the frequency of mutation), cytotoxic, anti-inflammatory, gastroprotective, hepatoprotective, nephroprotective, anti-cancer, antibacterial and immune-stimulant activities. Ethanolic fraction of the root has anthelmintic quality.

Chemical Constituents: The aqueous and non-aqueous (methanol, ethanol and acetone) extracts of the Date fruit show the presence of carbohydrates, fibres, fat, phenols, flavonoids, tannins, alkaloids and terpenoids. The plant also contains micronutrients such as vitamins A, B_1, B_2, B_3, B_6 and C and minerals like sodium, potassium, calcium, manganese, phosphorus, copper, zinc and iron.

Distribution: Phoenix sylvestris is native to an area starting from the Canary Islands in the West, across Northern and Central Africa, to the extreme Southeast of Europe (Crete) and continuing throughout Southern Asia and from eastern Turkey to southern China and Malaysia. Egypt is the leading country in growing dates, followed by Iran, Saudi Arabia and Iraq. Pakistan is the fifth largest producer of dates in the world.

Note: The leaves of Phoenix sylvestris are useful in making bags and mats. The stems help make local houses.

Saccharum officinarum

Ganna (Field, Fruits and Refined Sugar)

Latin Binomials	Saccharum officinarum/Saccharum bengalense
Family	Poaceae
English Name	Sugar cane
Urdu Name	Ganna

Medicinal Uses: The whole herb and the root of Saccharum officinarum plant are demulcent, laxative, diuretic in action and a high energy source.

Traditional Uses: According to Unani and Ayurvedic medicinal systems, the roots are astringent, emollient, diuretic, lithotriptic (a herb that affects renal calculus dissolution) and purgative. It is valuable for the treatment of dyspepsia and respiratory troubles. It is also beneficial in liver disorder and is recommended for jaundice patients. Patients should take in a large amount of juice for immediate relief. One of the vital health benefits of sugarcane juice is that it is diuretic in action; it helps treat urinary tract infections, kidney stones and ensures proper kidney function.

Traditional healers (Hakims and Ayurveda) in the Indo-Pak subcontinent also believed that the root is a cardiac tonic, a blood thinner, antiulcer, laxative and expectorant. A decoction of roots is useful in whooping cough and the juice is valuable in catarrh. It is a folk remedy for arthritis, bedsores, boils, colds, cough, eyes, fever, hiccups, inflammation, skin disorders, sores, sore throat, spleen disorders and wounds.

Biological Uses: These traditional medicinal systems' assumptions have been supported by modern pharmacological studies, which have indicated that sugar cane has various bioactivities like anti-inflammatory, analgesic, antihyperglycemic and hepatoprotective effects. The ethanolic extract (95 per cent) of fresh leaves and shoots are analgesic in property. The aqueous fractions of the stem and dried root are anti-hepatoprotective and diuretic in action. Other non-aqueous (methanol, ethanol, chloroform and ethyl acetate) fractions of the plant have antithrombotic, antihypercholesterolemic and anti-inflammatory activities.

An *in vivo* study of animals to molasses of Saccharum officinarum produced an immunosuppressive effect. The refined sugar from Saccharum officinarum consumption has also been linked with reproductive dysfunction in males. The consumption of sugar-sweetened snacks and drinks is related to low spermatozoa concentration.

Chemical Constituents: Sugar cane, in addition to plentiful carbohydrates, also contains an abundance of micronutrients that include: potassium, calcium, magnesium, iron, manganese, zinc and vitamins like thiamin (Vitamin B_1), riboflavin (Vitamin B_6) and several amino acids. Antioxidants such as flavonoids and poly-phenolic compounds boost overall health and oxidative stress. The plant also contains glycosides such as orientin, vitexin and schaftoside.

Distribution: Sugar cane is native to South East Asia. Brazil is the top country in sugar cane production globally, followed by India, China, Thailand and Pakistan. Pakistan is the 5th largest producer of sugarcane in the world.

Orientin (C$_{21}$H$_{20}$O$_{11}$)   Vitexin (C$_{21}$H$_{20}$O$_{10}$)

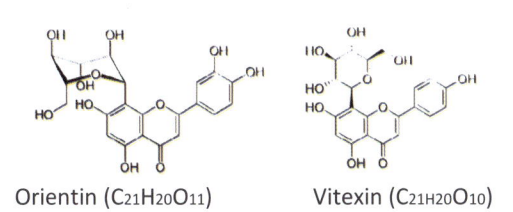

Solanum tuberosum

Aalu (Leaves, Flowers and Fruits)

Latin Binomial	Solanum tuberosum
Family	Solanaceae
English Name	Potato
Urdu Name	Aalu

Medicinal Uses: The tubes of the flowering Solanum tuberosum plant are alternative, diuretic, emetic and lactagogue (herb that promotes the secretion of milk) in action.

Traditional Uses: In Unani and Ayurvedic medicinal systems, potatoes are useful in the treatment of burns, corns, cough and cystitis. The peels of the tubes are said to be a folk remedy for tumours. Moderate consumption of the juice from the tubes helps treat peptic ulcers and a relief from burning pain and acidity. Potato skins are used in many parts of Asia to treat gum and heal burns. Due to the catecholase enzyme, it is an excellent tonic for the skin (brightening the skin and getting rid of dark spots).

A poultice has been made from boiling potatoes in water and is applied, as hot as can be borne, to rheumatic joints, swellings, skin rashes and haemorrhoids, etc.

Biological Uses: Extracts (aqueous, methanol and ethanol) of the whole plant (peel, tubers, leaves, flowers, etc.) showed antioxidant, anti-diabetic, anti-inflammatory, anti-platelet and anti-cancer activities. Ethanol extracts of the leaves have antifungal properties. An extract of leaves, seeds and tubers showed antimicrobial activity against gram-positive and gram-negative bacteria. The leaves are also antispasmodic.

Chemical Constituents: Potatoes are full of phytonutrients, organic components of plants thought to promote health. A Potato contains polyphenols, carotenoids (tetraterpenoids), flavonoids (anthocyanin, gives colour to potato), caffeic acid, vitamins (B_3, B_6 and C) and minerals (potassium, manganese and phosphorus). Solanine is a glycol-alkaloid poison found in the nightshade family species within the genus Solanum, such as the potato (Solanum tuberosum) and tomato (Solanum lycopersicum). One property of these alkaloids is reducing digestive secretions, including acids produced in the stomach.

Distribution: China is the largest producer of Potato, followed by India, Russia, Ukraine and the United States. The Potato is widely cultivated for its edible tubers in Pakistan.

Tamarindus indica

Imli/Tamar-Hindi (Flowers,Fruits and Seeds)

Latin Binomial	Tamarindus indica
Family	Caesalpiniaceae/Fabaceae
English Name	Tamarind
Urdu Name	Imli/ Tamir Hindium/Tamir Hindi

Medicinal Uses: The pulp of the ripe fruit of the evergreen, flowering Tamarindus indica tree is antibilious, febrifuge, digestive, refrigerant, carminative and anti-scorbutic in action. The fruit is aperient and a laxative. Fresh fruit is useful for curing fevers and controlling gastric acid. The fruit pulp may be beneficial as a massage in treating rheumatism as an acid refrigerant, a mild laxative and also in treating scurvy. Seeds (in powder form) are a remedy for dysentery and diarrhoea.

Traditional Uses: In Unani and Ayurvedic medicinal systems, almost all parts of the plant are valuable for medicinal purposes. When used internally, the bark is an astringent and a tonic and its ash aids digestion. The ash of the bark combined with common salt, helps treat intestinal obstructions, colic and indigestion. Tamarind leaves are also useful in loss of appetite and disinclination for food. The bark's lotions or poultices may help relieve sores, ulcers, boils and rashes. Young leaves may be beneficial in fomenting rheumatism and are applied to sores and wounds or administered as a poultice for joint inflammation, to reduce swelling and relieve pain.

The leaves sweetened decoction is good against throat infection, cough, fever and even intestinal worms. The seeds are helpful in curing infertility in men and also increasing sperm quality. The syrup, made from the ripe fruit, is drunk to keep the digestive organs in good condition and is also a remedy for coughs and colds. The fruit increases intestinal liquid volume and acts as an aperient. Local application of the flowers' poultices helps cure conjunctivitis. The juice of the flower is used to help cure bleeding piles. A decoction of the root was prescribed for alleviating sprue syndrome, piles and alcoholism. The paste of root bark is topically applied on freckles to clean them.

In the Indo-Pak subcontinent, the most famous and popular preparations of Tamarind are 'Imli-Ke Golyea', which acts as a carminative and another mouth-watering food product is called 'Imli- ke-Chatni.'

Biological Uses: Methanolic extract of Tamarind seeds shows significant analgesic and anti-inflammatory effects. Ethanolic extract of the leaves and the bark possess anthelmintic activity. The leaf extract (methanol and butanol) exhibits a significant antiemetic impact. Aqueous and non-aqueous extracts (methanol) of different parts of the plant have antimicrobial, hepatoprotective, hypolipidemic, anti-diabetic and immunomodulatory effects. The non-aqueous fraction of the leaf exhibits antioxidant activity.

Chemical Constituents: A single cup of Tamarind contains 68 grams of carbohydrates in the form of sugar, which is equivalent to 17 teaspoons of sugar. The Tamarind plant also has essential bioactive constituents like polysaccharides, volatile oils, sesquiterpene, tannins, flavonoid C-glycosides (vitexin, iso-vitexin, orientin and iso-orientin), alkaloids, gum and pectin. The pulp contains free organic acids (citric, tartaric and malic) and their salts. The plant is also a good source of minerals such as magnesium, potassium, calcium, iron, phosphorus, copper, zinc and vitamins like B_1, B_2 and B_3.

Distribution: Tamarindus indica, a long-lived and beautiful fruiting tree, is native to tropical Africa. However, it has been cultivated in the Indo-Pak subcontinent for so long that it is sometimes indigenous. Tamarindus indica, as the name indicates, is grown in India as a wild plant. It is also grown in Sudan, Nigeria, Kenya and Tanzania etc. The plant may be indigenous to tropical Africa. In Pakistan, the plant is cultivated in Punjab and Sind.

Triticum aestivum

Gandum (Plant, Fresh and Dried Fruits)

Latin Binomial	Triticum aestivum
Family	Poaceae
English Name	Wheat
Urdu Name	Gundum

Medicinal Uses: Wheat is one of the most versatile grains in nutritional value and health. It improves body metabolism and prevents Type 2 diabetes. Triticum aestivum plant was known to reduce symptoms in patients with rheumatoid arthritis and to reduce the severity of rectal bleeding in patients with ulcerative colitis. Wheatgrass is beneficial as it has the property of optimizing blood sugar levels. Nowadays, its use as an anti-diabetic agent is being popularized.

Traditional Uses: In the Unani system of medicine, Wheatgrass powder can facilitate a smooth digestion process, boost immunity, maintain healthy cholesterol levels and increase body weight. Triticum aestivum is mentioned in the Ayurvedic medicinal system books, as an immune-modulator, as antioxidant and astringent, as a laxative, diuretic and is used in acidity, colitis and kidney malfunction.

In China, the seed is said to contain sex hormones and promote female fertility. They are also useful in treating malaise, sore throat, thirst, abdominal coldness, spasmodic pains, constipation and cough. The plant is also revealed to be of great importance in menstrual disorders.

Biological Uses: The extract (ethanol) of the Triticum aestivum plant possesses anti-diabetic, hypolipidemic and antioxidant activities. The Wheat germ oil houses massive quantities of omega-3 fatty acids. The plant also has anti-cancer activity. The concentrated extract of methanol of the plant exhibits anti-obesity property.

Chemical Constituents: Phytochemical analysis of the whole plant in aqueous and ethanol extracts showed the presence of alkaloids, steroids, carbohydrates, phenols, tannins, flavonoids, saponins, triterpenoids and coumarins. Wheat germ oil is exceptionally high in octacosanol (a straight-chain aliphatic 28-carbon primary fatty alcohol). Solanine is a glycoalkaloid poison. The plant is an excellent source of many different vitamins, e.g., B_1, B_3, B_6, E and minerals such as iron, selenium, manganese, phosphorus and copper.

Distribution: China is the largest Wheat producer, followed by India, Russia, the USA and Australia. Pakistan is the seventh-largest producer of wheat in the world.

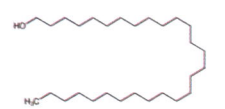

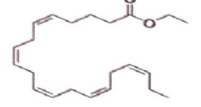

Octacosanol ($C_{28}H_{58}O$)   Omega 3 acid ethyl esters

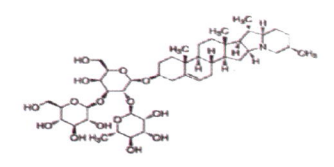

Solanine ($C_{45}H_{73}O_{15}$)

Vitis vinifera

Angoor/Kishmish (Fruits-Kishmisc-Munnaqqa)

Latin Binomial	Vitis vinifera
Family	Vitaceae
English Name	Grapes
Urdu Names	Angoor/Kishmish

Medicinal Uses: The Vitis vinifera fruit is nutritious, stimulant, laxative, diuretic, antihypertensive, fattening in action and an excellent tonic for the heart. Grape juice was formerly helpful in Europe for epilepsy. It is also useful for thrush in children and invaluable in severe colds and fevers. The juice of sour grapes is beneficial for bruises and sprain. Researchers at Georgetown University (Washinton DC) have shown that grape juice, similar to red wine, lowers the risk of developing blood clots that may lead to heart attacks. Further, grape juice is a good alternative for people who do not drink alcohol or want to limit their consumption.

Traditional Uses: In Unani and Ayurvedic medicinal systems, the fruit helps treat diseases like bilious dyspepsia, nausea, cholera, fever, etc. The fruit is astringent and useful in diarrhoea, whereas the ripe fruit acts as a laxative.

Traditional healers (Hakims and Ayurveda) of the Indo-Pak subcontinent also prescribed aqueous cold and hot extracts of the fruit for iron deficiency (anaemia), cough, constipation, cystitis, etc. The leaves and seeds of the plant help herbal formulations as dietary supplements. The flowers are useful in chronic bronchitis and dysmenorrhoea. They also use ashes of the plant's stem for joint pains, swelling of the testicles and piles.

In the formulation of the famous Unani, poly-herbal, semisolid preparations known as 'Majun-e-Falasfa and 'Majun-e-Zabeeb, Vitis vinifera (Maweez munaqqa) is an essential ingredient.

Biological Uses: Pharmacological studies show that the plant possesses antioxidant, antimicrobial, hepatoprotective, anti-inflammatory and analgesic properties. The ethanolic fraction of the seeds has antifungal activity against Candida albicans. The stem of the white grape plant has potent antibacterial activity against Staphylococcus aureus and Enterococcus faecalis.

There is no evidence of resveratrol (a type of natural phenol) on human cancer.

Chemical Constituents: The plant contains carbohydrates, tannins, organic acid (malic acid), flavonoids, terpenoids, resin, vitamins (B_1, B_2, B_6, C, K) and minerals (potassium, manganese, copper and phosphorus). Grape seeds are a valuable source of phenolic compounds, including resveratrol (stilbenoid). The amount of total dietary fibre in Vitis vinifera is quantitatively more significant than carbohydrates, proteins and lipids. This indicates that the fruit could be included in the daily diet as a food supplement.

Distribution: Vitis vinifera is thought to be native to the Caspian Sea area in South-Western Asia. It is one of the most produced fruits in the world. China is the largest producer of grapes, followed by Italy, the United States, Spain, France and Turkey.

Pakistan's grapes are cultivated in a 15,000-hectare area, while annual productivity is 64,500 tonnes. Baluchistan grows most of this fruit. Over 70 per cent of the grapes are grown in Balochistan, while there is some acreage in Khyber Pakhtunkhwa that also grows grapes.

Resveratrol ($C_{14}H_{12}O_3$)

Malic Acid ($C_4H_6O_5$)

Zoological Origin (Z/O)

Apis mellifera

Shahed (Bee, Honey and Honey Comb)

Latin Binomials	Apis mellifera/Apis dorsta
Family	Apidae of Order Hymenoptera (Z/O)

English Name		Honey
Urdu Name		Shahed/Easal/Asal

Medicinal Uses: Honey produced by Apis mellifera, or Apis dorsta bee of the Apidae family, is nutritive, demulcent, laxative, antiseptic and styptic (stop the flow of blood) in action.

Traditional Uses: In Unani, Ayurvedic and other traditional medicinal systems, honey is used for internal and external applications. It is useful in treating eye diseases, cough, thirst, phlegm, hiccups, haematemesis (blood in vomit), leprosy, diabetes, obesity, worm infestation, vomiting, asthma, diarrhoea and in healing wounds. It is helpful as a natural preservative and as a sweetener in many Unani and Ayurvedic medicines. It is also useful as a vehicle in some medications to improve the efficacy or to mitigate the side effects.

The traditional healers (Hakims and Ayurveda) of the Indo-Pak subcontinent say honey is valuable in keeping the teeth and gums healthy. Fresh Honey helps treat eye diseases, throat infections, bronchial asthma, fatigue, worm infestation, constipation and is nutritious. It promotes semen quality, mental health and is suitable for cosmetic purposes. It has been used for centuries to treat insomnia because it has hypnotic action. Additionally, honey is also recommended for skin disorders (such as wounds and burns), cardiac pain, palpitation, all imbalances of the lungs and in anaemia.

Honey is very useful in cosmetic treatment; it helps prepare facial washes, skin moisturizers, hair conditioners and creams for pimples.

Biological Uses: The phytonutrients in Honey are responsible for their antioxidant properties, and have antibacterial and antifungal power. Raw Honey has shown immune-boosting and anti-cancer benefits. It is antiseptic and supportive. It may be locally applied; it may act as a styptic (stop blood flow).

Chemical Constituents: Honey contains carbohydrates (glucose, fructose, sucrose, etc.), fat, protein, vitamins such as B_2, B_3, B_5, B_6, B_9, C and minerals like calcium, magnesium, phosphorus, potassium, manganese and zinc.

Distribution: China is the world's leading country in producing Honey, followed by New Zealand, Argentina, Germany, Ukraine and India. Honeybee flora is present in vast areas in all the provinces of Pakistan.

Medicinal Plants
Plants containing Fixed Oils

Fixed Oils

Definition: Fixed oil is a non-volatile oil of vegetable and animal origin. A mixture of esters of fatty acids is usually triglyceride. Fixed oils are esters of fatty acid with glycerol.

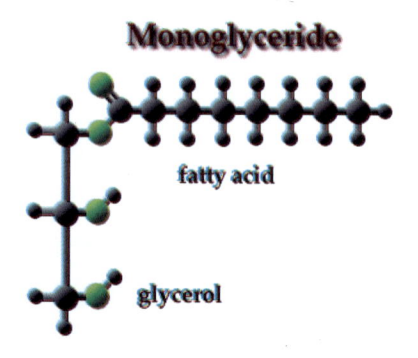

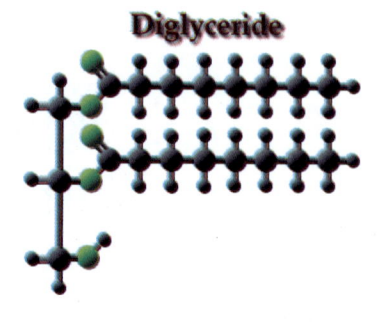

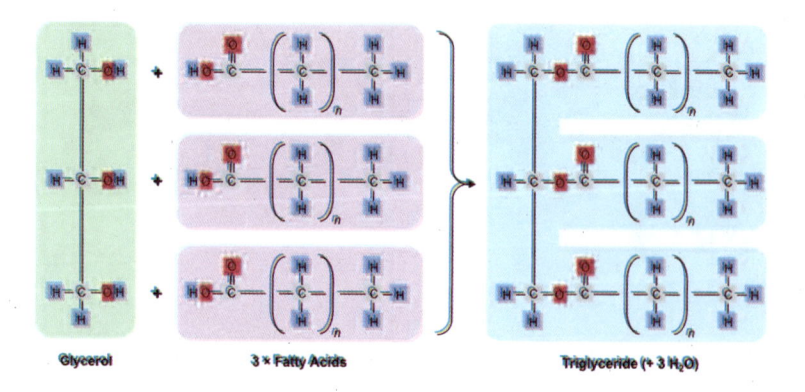

Classification:
Based on their ability to absorb oxygen from the air, fixed oils are classified as:

a) Drying oil
When exposed to air, it undergoes oxidation and forms a tough and hard film. These are usually used in paints and varnishes, for example, Linseed oil.

b) Non-Drying oil
These oils neither undergo oxidation nor form a tough and hard film, such as Olive oil.

c) Semi-Drying oil
When exposed to air, it undergoes a little bit of oxidation and forms a tough and thin film, for example, Cottonseed oil.

METHODS OF OBTAINING FIXED OILS

1. Direct extraction/expression
2. Solvent extraction
3. Steam treatment + extraction

Difference between Volatile Oil and Fixed Oil

Volatile oil	Fixed Oil
Also called essential oil.	Also called non-volatile natural oil.
Volatile oil can evaporate when placed at room temperature.	Fixed oils do not evaporate at room temperature.
They can be extracted easily by the distillation process.	They require some specific techniques for extraction.
There is no spot (no permanent stain) left after evaporation.	Some spot (permanent stain) left after evaporation.
They are unable to undergo saponification.	Fixed oils can be easily saponified.
Mixtures of cleoptenes & stearoptenes are termed volatile oils.	Esters of higher fatty acids & glycerin are called fixed oils.
The oil possesses a high refractive index.	The oil possesses a low refractive index.

These are optically active.	These are optically inactive.
Their primary source is leaves, roots, petals and bark.	Their primary source is the seeds of the plant.

Analytical Parameters of Fats and Oils

The following are the parameters used to analyze the fats and oils.

1) **Iodine value: (IV)** The iodine value is the mass of iodine in grams consumed by 100 g of fats or oils. An iodine solution is violet in colour and any chemical group in the substance that reacts with iodine, will make the colour disappear at a precise concentration. The amount of iodine solution required to keep the solution violet is measured by the iodine's sensitive, reactive groups. It is a measure of the extent of un-saturation and the higher the iodine value, the more chances of rancidity.

2) **Saponification value (SV)**: The saponification value is the number of milligrams of potassium hydroxide required to saponify 1 g of fat under the specified conditions. It measures the average molecular weight of all the fatty acids present.

3) **Hydroxyl value (HV)**: The hydroxyl value is the number of mg of potassium hydroxide (KOH) required in neutralizing acetic acid combined with hydroxyl groups when 1 g of a sample is acetylated.

4) **Ester value (EV)**: The ester value is the number of mg of potassium hydroxide (KOH) required in saponifying the ester contained in 1 g of a sample.

5) **Unsaponifiable Value (USV)**: The principle is fat or oil saponification by boiling under reflux with an ethanolic potassium hydroxide solution. The unsaponifiable matter is then extracted from the soap solution by diethyl ether. The solvent is evaporated and then the residue is dried and weighed.

6) **Acid value (AV)**: It is defined as the weight of potassium hydroxide in mg needed to neutralize the organic acids present in one gram of fat and it is measured of the free fatty acids (FFA) present in the fat or oil.

As the glycerides in fat slowly decompose, the acid value increases.

7) **Peroxide value (PV)**: One of the most widely used oxidative rancidity tests, the peroxide value measures the concentration of peroxides and hydro-peroxides formed in the initial stages of lipid oxidation. Milli-equivalents of peroxide per kg of

fat are measured by titration with iodide ion. Peroxide values are not static and care is taken in handling and testing samples. It is difficult to provide a specific guideline relating to the peroxide value to rancidity. High peroxide values indicate rancid fat, but moderate values may deplete peroxides after reaching high concentrations.

Arachis hypogaea

Mong-Phali (Plant Parts, Fruits, Oil, Leave and Flowers)

Latin Binomial	Arachis hypogaea
Family	Fabaceae
English Name	Peanut
Urdu Name	Mong-Phali

Medicinal Uses: The fruit and oil of the annual, herbaceous, flowering Arachis hypogaea plant are stimulant, anti-diabetic, emollient, anti-hypercholesterolemic, anxiolytic (herb reduces anxiety), aphrodisiac, antihypertensive in action and is a useful tonic for skin, heart and brain.

The oil of Peanut enhances immunity and stimulates the entire body. It eliminates free radicals that are the cause of chronic ailments such as Alzheimer's disease and cancer. Arachis hypogaea oil increases good cholesterol and lowers harmful cholesterol levels. It prevents the chances of cardiac disorders such as heart attacks, coronary artery diseases, strokes and atherosclerosis. Externally, the mono-saturated fats and vitamins make peanut oil beneficial for the skin and hair.

Traditional Uses: In Unani and Ayurvedic books, the fruit of Arachis hypogaea is mentioned as a general tonic and is useful in arthritis and skin diseases. Maceration of peeled seeds is drunk to treat gonorrhoea.

In China, Peanuts are a valuable demulcent, pectoral and useful in peptic ulcers. The oil helps relieve constipation and as an emollient. They are taken internally with milk to treat gonorrhoea and externally in treating rheumatism.

In Zimbabwe, the Peanut is beneficial in folk remedies for plantar warts, haemostatic and vasoconstrictor. In some African countries, pod extracts are taken as a galactagogue and used as eye drops to treat conjunctivitis (also known as pink eye). The plant is also helpful in relieving cough. In South America, peanuts are fermented into alcoholic drinks. In the United States and Argentina, most of the crop is valuable as food, but the peanut's primary use is in the oil market in most other countries.

Biological Uses: Pharmacological studies show that peanuts exert antioxidant, hypolipidemic, anti-inflammatory and sympathomimetic effects. The presence of stilbene (a diarylethene) and other similar biologically active compounds in Arachis, possess potent fungal growth inhibition (antifungal) properties.

Chemical Constituents: Arachis hypogaea plant consists of 47 - 50 per cent oil content, which has a more significant percentage of unsaturated fatty acids, making it an edible oil, of choice, for human nutrition and good health. A powerful antioxidant, vitamin E, is often found in high amounts in fatty foods. The Peanut is also a good source of minerals, e.g., manganese, magnesium, phosphorus, zinc, calcium and iron.

Distribution: Arachis hypogaea plant is one of nature's most nutritious seeds and one of the world's most popular and universal crops, cultivated in nearly 100 countries on all six continents. The USA is the world's fourth-largest producer of peanuts after China, India and Nigeria.

Chakwal, Attock, Jhelum and Rawalpindi in Punjab, Karak and Swabi in Khyber Pakhtunkhwa and Sanghar in Sindh, are the major growing areas of Peanut in Pakistan.

Note: The monograph of Peanut oil is present in almost all Pharmacopoeias of the world, e.g., USP, BP, EP, NP and IP.

Cocos nucifera

Nariyal (Tree, Fruits and Oil)

Latin Binomials	Cocos nucifera/Lodoicea maldivicia
Family	Palmae/Arecaceae
English Name	Coconut
Urdu Names	Nariyal/Khopra

Medicinal Uses: The fruit and root of Cocos nucifera tree are alexipharmic (an antidote against poison or infection), preservative, aphrodisiac in action and a tonic for the skin. It contains high polyphenol content. It can maintain the expected levels of cholesterol and other lipid parameters and helps prevent the development of atherosclerosis (heart problems) and is suitable in Alzheimer's disease. The unripe Coconut fruit's water is fine-flavoured, a cooling refrigerant drink, useful for thirst, fever and effective in urinary disorders.

Traditional Uses: The Coconut has been traditionally beneficial in Unani and Ayurvedic medicinal systems, in alopecia (baldness), hair loss, premature greying of hair, bronchitis, fever and a general debility. The fruit pulp is beneficial as an appetizer, is diuretic, astringent and laxative, whereas its oil is valuable as a hair tonic, as an appetizer, is digestive, disinfectant and is an insecticide. The root is useful in treating stomachache and blood in the urine. The oil is rubbed onto stiff joints. It is also helpful in treating rheumatism and back pains or as an ointment to maintain smooth and soft skin. Coconut milk is a diuretic. It is also beneficial in conditions such as pain, dehydration and bleeding disorders in the Ayurvedic medicinal system. Four spoons of ginger in Coconut water is an emmenagogue.

Famous Unani, poly-herbal, semi-solid preparations such as Majun-e-Filasfa and Majun Ruh-al-Mominin contain Coconut as one of the ingredients.

Biological Uses: The methanol extract has antioxidant, antibacterial, antifungal, antiviral and possesses antimicrobial properties. The liquid bark fraction has anticonvulsant, antiblennorrhagic (preventive of mucous discharge) and antimalarial effects.

Chemical Constituents: The Coconut water contains alanine, arginine, aspartic acid, cystine, histidine, sugar, etc. Phytochemical studies of coconut fibre (mesocarp) and ethanol extract reveal tannins, phenols, flavonoids, triterpenoids, steroids and alkaloids. The Coconut is high in minerals such as calcium, magnesium, phosphorus, sodium, selenium, copper, iron, zinc and vitamins like B_1, B_2, B_3, B_6, B_9, C, E, A and K.

Distribution: The plant is cultivated in South Asia, Pakistan (Karachi), the Philippines, Thailand, Malaysia, Indonesia, Sri Lanka and the Maldives.

Elaeis guineensis

Palm (Fruits and Oil)

Latin Binomial	Elaeis guineensis
Family	Arecaceae
English Name	Palm
Urdu Name	Tarr

Medicinal Uses: The Palm oil extracted from the fruit mesocarp of the Elaeis guineensis tree is traditionally helpful in treating headaches, pains, rheumatism, cardiovascular diseases and arterial thrombosis (blood clot in an artery) and atherosclerosis (hardening of the walls of the artery).

Traditional Uses: As hair oil, it reduces hair loss. The leaves are used to treat cardiovascular diseases, kidney diseases and in wound healing. The roots are analgesic. Used topically, Palm Oil restores hydration to dry skin, preventing further dryness by sealing in moisture. The leaf sap is valuable in preparations in treating skin infections.

The roots are analgesic. Preparations made from the palm heart are beneficial in treating gonorrhoea, menorrhagia and abdominal pain. It is laxative, antiemetic and diuretic. In folk medicine, the oil is helpful as a liniment for indolent tumours. Different parts of the plant are valuable as a laxative, diuretic and a cure for gonorrhoea in traditional African medicine.

Biological Uses: The methanol extract of the plant shows anti-candidal activity. Palm oil, obtained from the fruit, is used in making soaps, cosmetics and candles.

Chemical Constituents: Palm oil is the largest natural source of tocotrienol (vitamin E family). The antioxidant properties of palm oil boost immunity and delay the onset of wrinkles. The oil is composed of fatty acids, esterified with glycerol, palmitic acid, alpha-linolenic acid, stearic acid, etc. The methanol extract of fruit also has saponins, phenols and tannin.

Distribution: Indonesia is the world's largest Palm oil producer, followed by Malaysia, Nigeria and Thailand. Pakistan imports more than two million tonnes of oil and fats annually, of which Palm oil is the chief import.

Alpha-Linolenic acid ($C_{18}H_{30}O_2$)   Alpha-Tocotrienol ($C_{29}H_{44}O_2$)

Eruca sativa

Jarjir/Tara-Mira/ Banafsha Shab-boo (Leaves and Seeds)

Latin Binomials   Eruca sativa/Eruca vesicaria

Family	Cruciferae/Brassicaceae
English Name	Rocket
Urdu Names	Jarjir/Tara-Mira/Banafsha Shab-boo

Medicinal Uses: The leaves of the edible, annual flowering Eruca sativa plant are digestive, carminative, stimulant, anti-scorbutic and stomachic in action. The taste is best of the fresh, well-grown plant with a distinctly spicy flavour. The seeds are stimulant and rubefacient.

Traditional Uses: In Unani and Ayurvedic medicinal systems, the plant is useful as a tonic, laxative, emollient and stimulant. It also increases sexual desire. Eruca sativa plant is beneficial as a carminative; it alleviates abdominal discomfort and improves digestion. The seed oil with sugar is helpful in treating dysentery. It is said that massaging your hair with seed oil twice a week, will remove dandruff, lice and stress. It eliminates the factors that irritate the scalp and hair follicles and also prevents hair fall. The oil also protects the skin from UV rays. The seeds and tender leaves are known in Arabian countries to increase sexual desire and be considered an aphrodisiac.

Biological Uses: Non-aqueous extract (ethanol) of seeds possesses potent antioxidant, renal protective and has diuretic activities. The oil is beneficial in killing cancer cells of the melanoma of the liver. The powdered seed (extract of methanol) possesses antibacterial activity. The ethanolic extract of Eruca sativa plant has androgenic properties. It stimulates testicular steroid production, enhancing the preputial gland and increasing spermatogenesis in the testis of the male mice.

Chemical Constituents: Eruca sativa seeds are known to have high oil, protein and glucosinolate content. The oil is known as 'Tara-Mira,' which is produced from the seeds and erucic acid is the principal constituent of the oil. Eruca sativa contains vitamin B complex and other vitamins, e.g., C, A, E and K, which work together to enhance the cell's metabolism and health. The plant also has some valuable bioactive compounds like flavonoids, glycosides, saponins, glucosinolates, flavonols, phenolic compounds and minerals (calcium, copper, phosphorus, selenium, manganese and zinc).

Distribution: Eruca sativa is native to the Mediterranean and cultivated in North and North-East Africa, the Balkans and East and Central Asia. It is also produced in the Indo-Pak subcontinent, America and also in South-East Asia.

Glucosinolate Structure ($C_8H_{15}NO_9S_2$)

Gossypium herbaceum

Binola/Panbah Dana (Plant, Oil and Seeds)

Latin Binomial	Gossypium herbaceum
Family	Malvaceae/**Brassicaceae**
English Name	Cotton seeds
Urdu Names	Binola/Panbah Dana/Kapas

Medicinal Uses: The seeds and oil of the flowering Gossypium herbaceum plant are aphrodisiacs, emollient for the chest, fattening, expectorant and lactagogue (herb promotes the flow of milk) in action. The root bark is useful in inducing abortion or miscarriage as it causes the contraction of the uterus. It helps treat abnormal uterine bleeding, mainly when linked to fibroids and in case of difficult or obstructed menstruation. The preparation helps induce labour (at full time) to aid safe delivery. It is said to be used in sexual lassitude (sexual disorders).

Traditional Uses: In the Unani medicinal system, the plant's leaves are beneficial in childhood diarrhoea and its seeds are helpful in inadequate lactation. Internally, the seeds are valuable in treating dysentery, intermittent fever and fibroids. Externally, the seeds help treat herpes, scabies, wounds and inflammation of the testicles. The leaves are taken internally in the treatment of gastroenteritis.

Externally, the leaves are helpful in treating thrush, scalds, bruises and sores. The leaves with rose oil are valuable in gout. It is an alternative to ergot (Claviceps purpurea of the Clavicipiitaceae family) for inducing uterine contractions.

The oil is suitable for skin cleansing products, eye makeup, skin and hair care products. The bark and the seed oil contain a substance known as gossypol. This compound has the effect of lowering sperm production and possibly causing infertility in males.

The dried flower is a constituent of the famous Unani poly-herbal anti-metrorrhagia medicinal preparation known as Akseer-e-Niswan.

Biological Uses: The extracts (aqueous, methanol, ethanol and ethyl acetate) of leaves and seeds of the plant possess antibacterial, antiviral, antiulcer, anticonvulsant, anti-diabetic, antimalarial, antioxidant and antitumor activities. The ethyl acetate-ethanol extract of leaves has a diuretic action. The methanol fraction of the root demonstrates anti-fertility properties.

Chemical Constituents: The plant's seed extracts contain glycosides, resins, tannins, steroids, saponins, phenolic compounds and valuable minerals like phosphorus, iron, calcium, magnesium, manganese and sulphur. The leaves are rich in condensed tannins and the major constituents of the plant are flavonoids, tannins, carbohydrates, saponins, terpenoids and glycosides. More flavonoids are present in leaves than seeds.

Distribution: Gossypium herbaceum is native to North Africa, Asia Minor and Indo-Pak subcontinent. The five major cotton-producing countries are China, India, the USA, Pakistan and Brazil.

Pakistan is the fourth-largest producer of Cotton (1.40mn tonnes) globally. Cotton is grown mainly in the provinces of Punjab and Sindh, with the former accounting for 79 per cent and the latter for 20 per cent of the nation's cotton-growing land. It is also grown in Khyber Pakhtoon Khwah (KPK) and Baluchistan provinces.

Gossypol ($C_{30}H_{30}O_8$)

Helianthus annuus

Suraj-Mukhi (Field and Flower)

Latin Binomial	Helianthus annuus
Family	Asteraceae
English Name	Sunflower
Urdu Name	Suraj-Mukhi

Medicinal Uses: The seed of the large phorb, flowering Helianthus annuus plant itself is edible and its oil is used throughout the world for frying and cooking. The Sunflower seeds have a compound named 'phytosterol', which helps counter cholesterol absorption in the bloodstream. The Sunflower oil has cleansing properties: both as a diuretic and as an expectorant. The seeds are very rich in protein and essential fatty acids. These nutrients are vital for the excellent health of the nerves, brain, eyes and general health. It is useful in ethnomedicine for treating several disease conditions, including heart disease, bronchial, laryngeal, pulmonary infections, coughs, colds and whooping cough.

This notable medicinal, nutritional and culinary benefit has resulted in the historically growing popularity of the Sunflower, worldwide. The oil is rich in vitamin E and is considered by many to be important in improving skin health and regenerating cells. The oil is also a good source of vitamin A, C and D, making it good in the treatment of acne.

Traditional Uses: In Unani, Ayurvedic and modern herbal, seeds, oil, shoots and herb tincture have been valuable for anti-inflammatory, antipyretic, astringent, cathartic, diuretic, emollient, expectorant, vermifuge and vulnerary properties. More than half a Sunflower seed contains valuable and highly nutritious Sunflower oil.

Biological Uses: The Sunflower seed and sprouts contain essential antioxidant, antimicrobial, anti-inflammatory, antihypertensive, wound-healing compounds. The *n*-Butanol-soluble fraction of a methanol extract of the ligulate of Sunflower petals possesses marked anti-inflammatory activity.

Chemical Constituents: The phenolic compounds and flavonoids, polyunsaturated fatty acids and vitamins provide cardiovascular benefits. The seeds of the Sunflower supply a multitude of nutritious components, including protein, unsaturated fats, fiber, vitamins (especially E), minerals like selenium, copper, zinc, folate, iron, and more. The Sunflower seed contains 35–42 per cent oil and is naturally rich in linoleic acid and oleic acid (classified as a monosaturated omega-9 fatty acid).

Distribution: Helianthus annuus plant is native to the United States, Canada and Northern Mexico. The flower Helianthus annuus is the national flower of Ukraine and Ukraine is the world's largest producer.

It is cultivated all over the world. In Pakistan, it is produced on 2.6 million hectares (mostly in Sind) with an annual production of 3.3 million tonnes.

Linum usitatissimum

Alsi/Katan (Field, Seeds and Flowers)

Latin Binomial	Linum usitatissimum/Linum humile
Family	Linaceae
English Name	Linseed/Flaxseeds
Urdu name	Alsi/Katan

Medicinal Uses: The flowering Linum usitatissimum plant's seeds are emollient, demulcent, pectoral and expectorant in action. A poultice of Linseed meal, either alone or with mustard, effectively relieves pain and irritation from boils, ulcers, inflamed areas, or abscesses. Flax is generally utilised as an addition to cough medicines, while linseed oil is sometimes given as a laxative or to remove gravel and stones from the kidneys. When mixed with lime water, the oil is excellent for burns and for use in salads.

In the modern scientific view, Flaxseeds are useful in diabetes, high blood pressure, irritable bowel and in lowering the total cholesterol and low-density lipoprotein (LDL) in cholesterol levels in the blood. Flaxseed may help manage prostate cancer due to the presence of lignans (polyphenols). It inhibits the growth and proliferation of prostate cancer cells. Daily consumption can help improve glycemic control.

Traditional Uses: In Unani and Ayurvedic medicinal systems, a decoction of seeds is useful against dyspnoea, asthma, bad cough and bronchitis. A teaspoon full of seeds helps relieve constipation. Flaxseed oil fibres and flax lignans have potential health benefits, such as reducing cardiovascular disease, atherosclerosis, diabetes, cancer, arthritis, osteoporosis, autoimmune and neurological disorders.

Flax protein helps in the prevention and treatment of heart disease and in supporting the immune system. As a domestic remedy for colds, coughs and irritation of the urinary organs, Linseed tea is most valuable.

In Ayurveda, Flaxseeds regulate cholesterol and fat metabolism in the body. They can boost HDL or good cholesterol and reduce LDL or bad cholesterol and triglycerides. Externally, the use of Linseed oil on the skin might help manage skin allergies, skin inflammation and speed up wound healing due to its antioxidant property.

Biological uses: The crude extracts isolated fractions of Linum usitatissimum exhibited significant anti-inflammatory, anti-obesity, anti-diabetic, anti-diarrheal, antimalarial, hepatoprotective, renoprotective, immunosuppressive, anti-cancer, antiarrhythmic and cognitive effects. Flax is also beneficial for hair as it promotes hair growth and controls dandruff due to its antioxidant and antibacterial activities. Flaxseed might be considered a functional additive in cosmetics as it is beneficial for the skin. The methanolic extract of the plant, also has antifungal, antiviral and antibacterial properties.

Chemical Constituents: Linseed contains mucilage, fixed oil, iridoid glycoside (aucubin), protein, a mono-terpenoid and cyan-genetic glycoside 'linamarin.' Flax seeds are rich sources of vitamins like B_1, B_2, B_3, B_5, B_6, B_9 and C and minerals such as calcium, iron, magnesium, phosphorus, potassium and zinc.

Distribution: Linum usitatissimum is not a new crop and is native to West Asia and the Mediterranean coastal lands, Asia Minor, Egypt, Algeria, Tunis, Spain, Italy and

Greece. In all these areas, only fibre flax is cultivated. It is grown as a wild plant in Punjab and KPK, Pakistan.

Aucubin ($C_{15}H_{22}O_9$)   Linamarin ($C_{10}H_{17}NO_6$)

Olea europaea

Zaitoon (Oil and fruits)

Latin Binomial	Olea europaea
Family	Oleaceae
English Name	Olive
Urdu Name	Zaitoon

Medicinal Uses: The fruit of the evergreen, flowering Olea europaea tree is demulcent, laxative, emollient, nutritive, nervine stimulant and resolvent in action and significantly reduces the risk of heart diseases. Olive oil may fight Alzheimer's complaints.

Traditional Uses: In traditional (Unani and Ayurvedic, etc.) medicinal systems, Olives are useful as diuretic, hypotensive, emollient, laxative and as a skin cleanser. The oleuropein contained in the leaves and resulting oleacein of the drying process are responsible for blood pressure-lowering properties.

The decoction of leaves or bark is beneficial as a remedy for malaria. The leaves are taken orally for stomach and intestinal diseases and are suitable as a mouth cleanser.

The fruit is also used externally as a skin cleanser. The dried leaves of this plant are ideal as tea substitutes.

Biological Uses: The various extracts of this oil have anti-inflammatory qualities and are antioxidant in nature. The oil also has anti-cancer properties. The plant's isolated fractions exhibit antimicrobial, antihyperglycemic, immunomodulatory, antiviral antihypertensive, antiulcer and antinociceptive activities. The antihyperglycemic and antioxidative properties of the plant may be due to oleuropein, a glycosylated seco-iridoid.

The plant aqueous and non-aqueous extracts have shown a broad spectrum of *in vitro* and *in vivo* pharmacological activities, like analgesic, antiseptic, anticancer, anti-diabetic, anticonvulsant, antioxidant, anti-inflammatory, immunomodulatory and antimicrobial activities. The leaves are also antifungal and antiviral. Extra virgin Olive oil has shown remarkable anti-inflammatory activity due to oleocanthal, a phenylethanoid.

The leaves (ethanolic extract) of Olea europaea is a good source of glycosylated seco-iridoid known as 'oleuropein and secologanoside' oleuropein type of phenolic bitter organic compounds. The oleuropein has been proposed as a proteasome (a highly sophisticated protease complex) activater.

Chemical Constituents: In addition to fixed oil, the plant also contains essential biologically active constituents such as iridoid glycosides, secoiridoid, flavonoids, flavon glycosides, resin, oleo-resin, triterpenes, biophenols, tannins and poly-unsaturated fatty acids. The phenolic compounds (ligstroside), flavonoids, secoiridoids and secoiridoid glycosides are present in almost all parts of the plant.

Distribution: Spain is the largest Olive producer, followed by Italy, Turkey, Greece and Morocco.

In Pakistan 'Pothwar' region in the north-eastern part of the country is being developed into an 'Olive Vally' after being recognized as an area appropriate for olive cultivation because of its topography and local weather.

Note: One persistent rumour is that Olive oil will lose its health benefits when heated. This rumour is false. Olive oil is primarily monounsaturated fat. Cooking with oil will not change its fat composition.

Oleuropein ($C_{25}H_{32}O_{13}$)   Oleacein ($C_{17}H_{20}O_6$)   Secologanoside ($C_{17}H_{24}O_{11}$)

Prunus amygdalus

Badam (Tree, Fruits, Oil and Flowers)

Latin Binomial	Prunus amygdalus
Family	Rosaceae
English Name	Almond/Sweet Almond
Urdu Name	Badam

Medicinal Uses: The fruit (seed) of the evergreen, flowering Prunus amygdalus tree is laxative, demulcent, emollient in action and a nerve tonic. The oil produced is emollient, demulcent, nourishing and slightly laxative, mainly used in cosmetics and taken internally as a medicine. Sweet Almond is made into emulsions with barley water or gum Arabia to treat gravel, stone, kidney disorders, bladder and bile duct problems.

Externally, sweet Almond oil, with its wound-healing and anti-inflammatory properties, can also treat cutaneous stress, dermatitis, burns, crevasses or sunburns.

Research suggests that eating raw almonds daily for four to nine weeks might lower total cholesterol and 'bad low-density lipoprotein (LDL) in high cholesterol people. However, eating almonds does not appear to improve 'good high-density lipoprotein (HDL) cholesterol or blood fats called triglycerides.

Traditional Uses: Almond oil is useful against constipation. The burnt shell of the almond fruit is regarded as a traditionally acclaimed tooth powder. Almonds are a popular household remedy and are believed to increase brain power, rejuvenate the nervous system and are trusted for their beneficial effects on deteriorating eye-sight. Almond oil with hot water is used to relieve sore throat. Almond powder with Cochlospermum gossypium (Gond Katira) of the Cochlospermaceae family is effective in dry cough. According to the famous Persian polymath Abu Ali Ibn-e-Sina (d. 1037 AD), Almond oil is the best remedy for renal pain, dysuria, renal and bladder stone and hysteria.

Fruit of the Almond is rich in magnesium and nutrients, which promote hair growth. Almonds are a great solution for puffy eyes, dark circles and eye wrinkles. According to Unani classical books, the fruit is useful alone (oil of Almond) or with other herbs as compound formulation like Laouq-e-Badam, a brain tonic memory enhancer and demulcent.

Biological Uses: The fruit also possesses various pharmacological properties like antidepressant, antioxidant, hypoglycaemic, hepatoprotective, anti-ageing., immune-stimulant, hyperlipidemic and is also a memory enhancer.

Chemical Constituents: In addition to fixed oil, the plant is also a rich source of minerals like potassium, calcium, iron, phosphorus, copper, magnesium, iodine and zinc.

Distribution: Prunus amygdalus is native to Iran. The United States is the world's largest producer of Almond, followed by Spain, Iran and Morocco. The Almond tree, in ancient days, symbolized the hastening of events.

Pakistan ranks 17th among the top Almond producing countries of the world. In Pakistan, Balochistan is the major producer of almonds; production in other provinces is negligible. Pakistan produced about 26,487 tonnes of almonds during 2008-2009 from an area of 11,002 hectares.

Note: Sweet and Bitter Almond: Sweet almond is more famous for obvious reasons. Like the olive, the almond provides food and oil and both are produced with little effort from the former. A compound called 'Amygdalin' (is a cyanogenic glucoside) differentiates the bitter Almond from the sweet Almond.

In the presence of water (hydrolysis), amygdalin yields glucose and the chemicals benzaldehyde and hydrocyanic acid (HCN). HCN, the salt of which is known as cyanide, is poisonous. The bitter almond is slightly broader and shorter than the sweet almond and it contains about 50 per cent of the fixed oil that occurs in sweet almonds. Bitter almonds yield 4 - 9 mg of hydrogen cyanide per almond. Aamara has always been bitter. If the almond oil is extracted from bitter almonds, make sure that the label says that it's free of cyanide as this is toxic/poisonous for internal use.

Ricinus communis

Arand (Plant Parts, Oil and Seeds)

Latin Binomial	Ricinus communis
Family	Euphorbiaceae
English Name	Castor
Urdu Name	Arand

Medicinal Uses: The oil of the perennial, flowering Ricinus communis plant is purgative, cathartic, laxative, vermifuge and galactagogue (herb promotes secretion of milk) in action. The seeds are useful as an expectorant. Castor oil is one of the best laxative and purgative preparations available. It is particularly beneficial for children and pregnant women due to the mild action in easing constipation, colic and diarrhoea due to slow digestion.

When applied externally, the oil reduces cutaneous complaints such as ringworm, itch and leprosy. It is also valuable as carrier oil for the solution of pure alkaloids, e.g., atropine or cocaine from Atropa belladonna, which can be used in eye surgery.

Traditional Uses: The Castor oil has been widely beneficial in traditional medicinal systems (Unani, Ayurvedic and Homeopathic), such as abdominal disorders, arthritis, backache, muscle aches, snail fever, chronic sciatica, chronic constipation, period pains and insomnia. The oil acts as an osmotic laxative in mild to moderate constipation. An infusion of the leaves helps tooth ache and is a lotion for relief to the eye.

Castor oil has also been used in cosmetic products, including creams and moisturisers. This gel helps treat non-inflammatory skin diseases and is an excellent protection in occupational eczema and dermatitis cases. The oil helps to speed up hair growth.

Biological Uses: The seeds' extracts showed antibacterial, antifungal, antioxidant and anti-inflammatory activities. The aqueous-ethanol extract possesses antifertility properties. As revealed by several studies, the anti-cancer activity of the plant suggests that Ricinus communis may be a good source of anti-cancer therapeutic compounds. The aqueous extract of the plant exhibits better anti-anthelmintic activity than an ethanolic fraction.

Chemical Constituents: The plant contains alkaloids, isoprenoids, flavonoids, steroids, benzoic acid derivatives, coumarins, saponins, tocopherols and fatty acids.

Distribution: The plant is native to Africa. The Asia Pacific region controls the market; it has a high concentration of Castor oil consumers in the World. In Pakistan, Castor is cultivated in Punjab, Sind and Balochistan.

Sesamum indicum

Kunjad (Plant Parts, Leaves and Seeds)

Latin Binomials	Sesamum indicum/Sesamum orientale
Family	Pedaliaceae
English Name	Sesame
Urdu Names	Til/Kunjad

Medicinal Uses: The flowering Sesamum indicum plant seeds are aphrodisiac, laxative and fattening in action. Sesame oil is helpful in rheumatoid arthritis, depression and hypertension. The leaves and seeds are astringent.

Traditional Uses: The oil is beneficial in Unani and Ayurvedic medicinal systems because of its antibacterial and anti-inflammatory properties. The seed is diuretic, emollient, laxative, galactagogue and a tonic for the liver and kidney. It is commonly used in beauty treatments for the skin because it is an excellent moisturizer, promotes healthy skin regeneration and has anti-ageing properties. It is also used extensively as a massaging oil because of its warming property and its ability to seep deep into the skin.

Biological Uses: Sesame oil contains sesamol and sesaminol, two antioxidants that may positively affect health.

Chemical Constituents: It is well-known that a diet rich in unsaturated fats is good for heart health (beneficial for our heart). Sesame oil comprises 82 per cent of unsaturated fatty acids. Oleic and linoleic are the principal unsaturated fatty acids, while palmitic and stearic are the primary saturated fatty acids present in the oil. The phytochemical analysis of Sesamum indicum reveals alkaloids, flavonoids, tannins, phenols. The leaves of the plant are rich in alkaloids and flavonoids. The plant also contains minerals, e.g., sodium, phosphorus, calcium, potassium and magnesium.

Distribution: Tanzania is the largest producer of sesame seed globally, followed by Myanmar, India, China and Sudan. In Pakistan, the Sesamum is cultivated in all four provinces.

Theobroma cacao

Chocolate (Tree, Leaves and Fruit)

Latin Binomial	Theobroma cacao
Family	Malvaceae
English Name	Chocolate Tree
Urdu Names	Chocolate Tree/Koka Darakht/Thiubruma Alkakaw

Medicinal Uses: Theobroma cacao is a small evergreen tree called 'coca tree.' Although the Theobroma cacao tree's oil is primarily valuable as food, Cacao also has some therapeutic value. The seed contains a range of medically active constituents, including xanthenes, a fixed oil and endorphin (chemicals produced by the body to relieve stress and pain). It is a bitter, stimulant diuretic herb that stimulates the nervous system, lowers blood pressure and dilates the coronary arteries.

Cacao powder and butter are edible; the latter also soothes and softens damaged skin. It is principally helpful for its diuretic effect due to renal epithelium's stimulation. The plant is especially beneficial in fluid retention.

The leaf contains gentisic acid (a is dihydroxybenzoic acid) and it is antirheumatic and analgesic. An infusion of the dry pods is helpful in decreasing leprosy. Internally, Cacao powder is beneficial in treating angina and high blood pressure.

Theobroma cacao is an ingredient in cosmetic ointments and pharmacy for coating pills and preparing suppositories. It has excellent emollient properties and is used to soften and protect chapped hands and lips.

Traditional Uses: In folk remedy Cacao is useful for alopecia, burns, cough, dry lips, eyes and fever. The seed is valuable in Central America and in the Caribbean as a heart and kidney tonic. An infusion of the baked seed membranes is drunk to remedy anaemia. The rural people in the Amazonas State, Brazil, rub Cocoa butter on bruises. The use of this oil is not mentioned in Unani and Ayurvedic pharmacopoeias and classic literature.

Biological Uses: The presence of theobromine in the plant shows the antioxidant property. Other beneficial compounds exhibit antibiotic, antitumour, antiviral, anti-inflammatory, immunomodulatory, enzyme inhibiting, cardiovascular, analgesic, anti-and diabetic effects. The non-aqueous (methanol) stem bark extract has antibacterial activities against Escherichia coli and Pseudomonas aeruginosa bacteria.

The presence of polyphenols in Theobroma cacao also increases high-density lipoprotein (HDL), or good cholesterol protection against cardiovascular disease. These compounds also are mild inhibitors of platelet activity, thinning blood in action, similar to aspirin.

Chemical Constituents: The plant contains a wide range of chemical compounds like theobromine, theophylline, oleic acid, stigmasterol, flavonoids, terpenoids, alkaloids, tannins, saponins and glycosides.

Distribution: The Theobroma cacao tree is native to North America. Nearly 70 per cent of the world crop today is grown in West Africa (Ivory Coast, Ghana, Cameroon and Nigeria). Ghana is the world's second-largest cocoa producer, it earned just around $2bn.

Note: Due to the small amount of caffeine it contains, along with related compound, theobromine, chocolate can be stimulating, making it hard for people to fall asleep after a late-night snack.

Gentisic acid ($C_7H_6O_4$)   Xanthenes ($C_{13}H_{10}O$)

Zea mays

Makai (Plant Parts, Oil and Fruits)

Latin Binomial	Zea mays
Family	Poaceae
English Name	Corn
Urdu Name	Makai

Medicinal Uses: The Zea mays plant's Corn silks is cholagogue (a herb that promotes the increased flow of bile), demulcent, diuretic, mildly stimulant and vasodilator in action. It also acts to reduce blood sugar levels and is used in treating diabetes mellitus, cystitis, gonorrhoea and gout. The decoction of the leaves and roots helps treat strangury (painful spasmodic discharge of urine drop by drop) and dysuria.

The cob's decoction helps treat nose bleeds and menorrhagia. The seeds are diuretic, emollient and a mild stimulant; they are widely helpful in treating cancer, tumours and warts. The seeds contain the cell-proliferation and wound healing substance 'allantoin,' which is generally beneficial in herbal, homoeopathic and Ayurvedic medicines. The plant is said to have anti-cancer properties and is experimentally hypoglycemic and hypotensive.

Traditional Uses: Traditional healers (Hakims and Ayurveda) of the Indo-Pak subcontinent used different parts of the Zea mays plant to treat kidney stones, constipation and excessive menstrual bleeding. A decoction of the leaves, cob and roots is used in the treatment of strangury, dysuria, nose bleeding, menorrhagia and gravel. The Corn seed is diuretic and mild stimulant. In Ayurvedic plant is also used for general disability, anorexia and haemorrhoids.

Biological Uses: The non-aqueous (methanol) extract of Corn stem has antioxidant and neuroprotective properties. Various non-aqueous (ethyl acetate, chloroform, ethanol, methanol and petroleum ether) fractions of Cornsilk exhibit antibacterial, antiviral, anti-inflammatory, cardioprotective, hepatoprotective, antimicrobial and anti-diabetic properties. They also possess antiproliferative, antimutagenic, antifungal, antilithiatic (prevents the formation of or relieves the symptoms of kidney stones) and antihyperlipidemic activities.

The aqueous-alcoholic extract of the Cornsilk exhibited anti-fatigue, hepatoprotective and renal protective activity, and inhibit lipid peroxidation. The presence of flavonoids have been reported to reduce oxidative stress and show anti-fatigue activity in mice. Phytosterols have many health benefits. Dietary consumption of phytosterol is negatively related to cholesterol absorption, serum total and LDL cholesterol

Chemical Constituents: Various parts of the plant such as silk, seeds, stem, leaves and roots are a good source of bioactive compounds like fixed oil, tannins, saponins, bitter alkaloids, steroids, phenols, flavons and resin. Zea mays also has vitamins C and K and minerals like zinc, manganese, phosphorus, magnesium and copper. The presence of zeaxanthin (carotenoid alcohols) in the Corn plant, is one of the most common plants that contain carotenoids (also called tetra-terpenoids). In humans, it improves eye health. Zea mays hair also has various bioactive constituents comprising protein, vitamins, minerals, salts, steroids and flavonoids.

Distribution: Maize ranks as the third most grown crop in the world. The United States of America is the largest Corn producer globally, followed by China, Brazil, Argentina and Mexico. Corn is the second-largest grown crop in the world.

In Pakistan, Maize is the fourth largest grown crop after wheat, cotton and rice. KhyberPakhtoon Khawah (KPK) is the leading producer of Corn, followed by Punjab, Sind and Balochistan.

Note: Corn is a good source of fibre, 100 grams of popcorn contains 15 grams of fibre, which is 40 and 60 per cent Daily Value {DV} for women and men, respectively).

Allantoin ($C_4H_6N_4O_3$)

Zeaxanthin ($C_{40}H_{56}O_2$)

Zeaxanthin ($C_{40}H_{56}O_2$)

Medicinal Plants
Plants containing Glycosides

Polygonum viviparum

Cichorium intybus

Aloe vera

Moras alba

Glycoside

Definition: Glycoside is a molecule in which sugar is bound to another functional group via a glycosidic bond. Thus, the glycoside comprises of two parts: the sugar (glycone) and the non-sugar (aglycone).

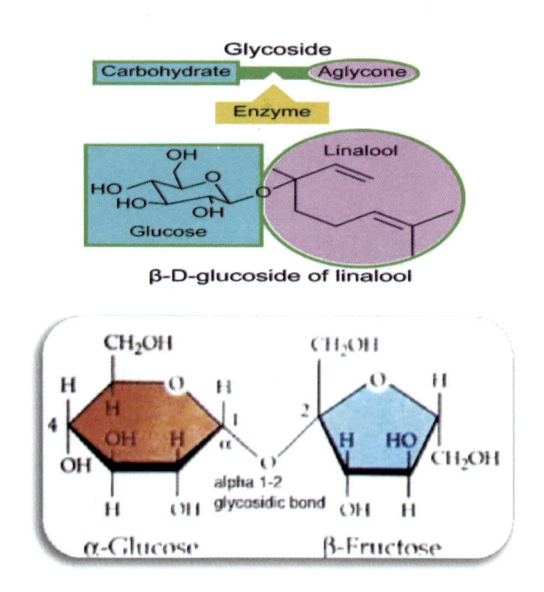

Physicochemical Properties of Glycosides:-

1. They are soluble in water and insoluble in non-aqueous solvents (Glycone: Water-soluble, Aglycone: soluble in non-aqueous solvents).

2. They are optically active.

3. They are bitter to taste.

4. They are readily hydrolyzed by acids and enzymes.

5. They play essential roles in living organisms.

6. They are amorphous and non-volatile.

7. Some have beautiful colours for the pollination process (flavonoids and anthraquinone).

The functions of Glycosides in plants:-

▶ Converting toxic materials to non-or less harmful materials.

▶ Transfer water-insoluble substances by using monosaccharides.

▶ Source of energy (sugar reservoir).

▶ Storing harmful products, such as phenol.

▶ Regulation for specific functions (growth).

▶ Some glycosides have antibacterial activity, protecting the plants from bacteria and diseases.

Isolation of glycoside

The method by which glycoside is isolated is called the stas-otto method. The drug-containing glycoside is finely powdered and subjected to successive extractions in a Soxhlet apparatus in alcohol or a suitable solvent. After extraction, collect the extract and treat it with lead acetate to precipitate tannins and filter it. The filtrate passes through H_2S gas (the lead acetate will precipitate as lead sulphide) and filters it. The filtrate is subjected to fractional crystallization. Distillation or chromatography gives pure components. The extract molecular structure is determined by the spectrophotometer, ultraviolet assays, infrared, NMR, mass spectroscopy etc.

Classifications

Classification of glycosides on the bases of linkage (Glycosidic Bond between glycone and aglycone:-

O-Glycosides: The sugar part is attached to the aglycone's oxygen atom in these glycosides. They are common in higher plants, for example, Senna, Rhubarb. They are hydrolyzed by treating an acid or an alkali into the glycon and aglycon portions.

S- Glycosides: In these glycosides, the sugar is linked with the aglycone sulfur atom. This glycoside is restricted to isothiocyanate glycoside like sinigrin in black mustard is formed by the condensation of sulphydryl group aglycon to OH group of glycon.

N-Glycodes: The sugar is linked with the aglycone's amino group's nitrogen atom in these glycosides. The most typical representation of this is a nucleoside, where the amino group reacts with the OH group of ribose or deoxyribose, resulting in N-glycoside.

C-Glycosides: In these glycosides, the condensed sugar is linked with the aglycone's carbon atom. Some of the anthraquinone glycosides like cascaroside in cascara and aloin in aloes shows the particular linkage.

C-glycosides are called aloin type glycosides, present in aloes. They do not hydrolyse by heating with dilute acid or alkalis but by oxidative hydrolysis with $FeCl_3$. Cochical contains c-glycoside in the form of a colouring matter called carminoic acid.

Classification of glycosides based on glycone (Sugar) part:-

(I) Glucose-Sennoside (II) Rhamnose-Frangullin (III) Digitoxose-Digoxinb
(IV) Glucose-Rhamnose-Glucorhamnoside-Glucofrangulin (V) Rhamnose-Glucose-Rhamnoglucoside-Rutin

Classification of Glycosides based on the therapeutic nature of Glycoside:-

Cardiac glycosides, e. g. Digitalis

Laxative glycosides, e.g., Senna

Anti-ulcer glycosides, e.g., Liquorice

Bitter glycosides, e.g., Quassia wood

Classification of glycosides based on the chemical nature of aglycone:-

(a)- Aldehyde glycosides, e.g., Vanilla folia (Vanilla), Cinnamomum zeylanicum (Darchini) and Cinnamomum tamala (Tezpat).

(b)- Anthraquinone glycosides, e.g., Cassia senna or Cassia angustifolia (Senna Maki), Aloe barbadensis (Ailwa), Rheum emod (Rewand Chini), Rhamnus purshianus or Croton tiglium (Jamal Gotta) and Cassia fistula (Amaltaas or Khayar Shanber).

(c)- Cardiac glycosides, e.g., Digitalis purpurea (Dijtalis or Zehar-al-Kashatabeen), Urginea indica or Urginea maritima (Jangli Piyaz), Strophanthus hispidus (Kombe), Cheiranthus and cheiri (Todri Surkh).

(d)- Flavonoid glycosides, e.g., Ruta graveolens (Sadab), Polygonum bistorta or Polygonum viviparum (Anjbar), Morus alba (Shahtut), Smilax glabra (Chob Chini), Borosma butulina (Buchu), Echinops echinatus (Barham Dandi), Adiantum capillus veneris (Pershiaoashan), Symplocos racemosa (Lodh Pathani), Ginkgo biloba (Ginkgo)and Curcuma longa (Haldi).

(e)- Cyno-genetic glycosides, e.g., Brassica nigra (Rai), Prunus amygdalus amara (Badam -Talkh), Zanthoxylum armatum (Kabab-e-Khandan) and Polygala senegra (Maar- Beekh/Saanp-ke-Jarr).

(f)- Coumarin glycosides, e. g. Psoralea corylifolia (Babchi), Cichorium intybus (Kasni) and Melilotus officinalis (Aklil-Ul- Mulik).

(g)- Alcoholic Glycosides, e. g. Salix purpurea (Bed–Mushk).

(h)- Saponin glycosides. See chapter 'Plants containing Saponins'.

(i)- Miscellaneous glycosides, e.g., Caesalpinia bonduc or Guilandinia bonduc (Karanjwa), Swertia chirata (Chiraitah), Picrorhiza kurrooa (Kuthi) and Citrullus colocynthis (Indrain Talkh or Hanzal).

Aldehyde Glycosides If the aglycone part of a glycoside contains an aldehyde group, it is called an Aldehyde Glycoside.

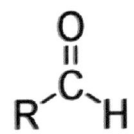

Aldehyde group

Anthraquinone glycosides (Anthracene Glycosides)
Definition: This type of glycoside contains the anthracene group or their derivatives as aglycone. On hydrolysis, they give aglycone part: Di-, Tri or Tetra hydroxyl-anthraquinones, also called anthracenedione.

Anthracene   Anthraquinone

Properties of Anthraquinone Glycosides
They are amorphous substances, soluble in water and insoluble in non-aqueous solvents. Anthraquinone glycosides are coloured substances, aromatic in nature and purgative in action.

Mechanism of Action: Anthraquinone glycosides are purgative in action because of their irritating action on the large intestine. They stimulate the muscular intestinal structure by increasing movement: which results in the evacuation of intestinal contents. Simultaneously, the mucus secretion is stimulated and water absorption is hindered and soft stool will be formed.

Cardiac glycosides:

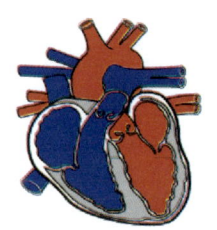

The Heart

Definition of Cardiac glycoside: Chemically, the aglycone part of cardiac glycosides is a steroidal moiety. They are either C_{23} or C_{24} steroids because of their 5 or 6 membered Lactones rings, respectively.

The five-membered lactone rings are called 'CARDENOLIDES' (One Bond), with six-membered rings called 'BUFADIENOLIDES' (Two Bonds).

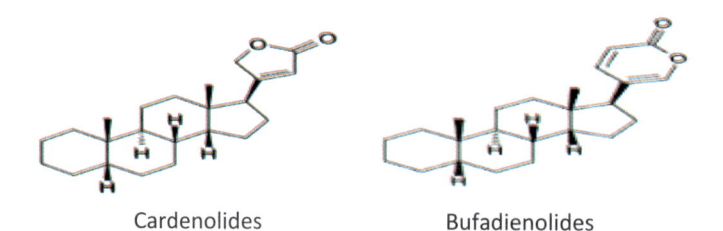

Cardenolides   Bufadienolides

Therapeutic uses of cardiac glycosides primarily involve the treatment of cardiac failure. Their utilities result from an increased cardiac output by increasing the contraction force. Cardiac glycosides occur in small quantities in the seeds, bark, roots, leaves and stems of plant families, Apocynaceae, Asclepiadaceae, Liliaceae, Ranunculaceae, Leguminosae, Scrophulariaceae and Euphorbiaceae etc. Bufadineolides are less widely distributed in nature than Cardenolides; therapeutically, they are less active and less toxic.

Flavone and Flavonoids Glycosides

Flavonoids (Flavus means yellow in Latin) are diverse phytonutrients (plant chemicals) found in almost all fruits and vegetables. They are responsible for the vivid colours in fruits and vegetables along with carotenoids.

Or

Flavonoids are polyphenolic compounds possessing 15 carbon atoms and two benzene rings joined by a linear three-carbon chain with the carbon skeleton C6-C3-C6. They are plant pigments and have a polar nature, soluble in methanol and water.

Flavonoids are a vast number of diverse compounds found throughout vascular plants. Vitamin P is the name once used to describe a group of plant-based substances we now know as flavonoids or bioflavonoids.

They fall into many classes depending on the degree of oxidation of the central pyran ring.

(a) Flavanones, e.g. Naringenin
(b) Flavones, e.g. Aurones, Chalcone
(c) Flavonols, e.g. Quercetin and (+)-Catechine
(d) Flavonoids, e.g., Leukoanthocyanidine
(e) Flavylium-salts, e.g., Cyanidine

(Flavonoids in Fruits and Vegetables)

Flavonoid

Flavonoids are classified according to their chemical structure

Flavones: These include luteolin and apigenin.

Flavanones: These include hesperetin, eriodictyol and naringenin.

Anthocyanidins: These include malvidin, pelargonidin, peonidin and cyanidin.

Flavonols: This widely distributed subgroup of flavonoids includes quercetin and kaempferol.

Isoflavones: This subgroup includes genistein, glycitein and daidzein. Isoflavonoids and Neoflavonoids can be regarded as abnormal flavonoids.

Benefits of Flavonoids: It has been reported that flavonoids are essential for human health because of their antioxidant, antibacterial, antiviral and anti-inflammatory properties.

Cyano-genetic glycosides

They are bioactive plant products derived from amino acids. Upon hydrolysis, these glycosides produce "Hydrocyanic Acid" (HCN). The active principle is "Prunasin," formed by a partial hydrolysis of "Amygdalin.

Plants contain many substances that can pose potential risks to users and one of these types of substances is cyano-genetic glycosides. There are approximately 25 known cyano-genic glycosides. These are generally found in the edible parts of the plant, which are fruits like apples, apricots, cherries and plums, particularly in the seeds. These chemicals are also found in almond, Zanthoxylum, Mustard Black, snakeroot, bamboo (shoots) and linseed/flaxseeds.

Coumarin Glycosides:
Coumarin is an aromatic organic chemical compound with the formula $C_9H_6O_2$. If an aglycone of glycosides contains coumarin or its derivative, it is known as Coumarin glycosides.
Coumarin is the *o*-coumaric acid lactone found mainly in plants' glycoside form.

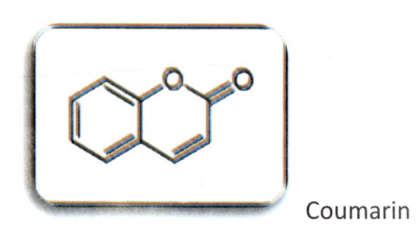

Coumarin

Alcoholic Glycosides

If an aglycone part of a glycoside is alcohol, it is called Alcoholic Glycosides.

Miscellaneous Glycosides

Several glycosides do not fall into the various classifications; therefore, they have been grouped under the head 'Miscellaneous Glycosides.'

Steroidal alkaloidal glycosides

(b) Thioglycosides
(c) Iridoid glycosides etc.

Steroidal Glycosides

Acalypha indica

Kuppa (Leaves, Flower and Root)

Latin Binomial	Acalypha indica
Family	Euphorbiaceae
English Name	Indian acalypha
Urdu Name	Kuppi

Medicinal Uses: The herbaceous, annual, flowering Acalypha indica plant is beneficial in bronchitis, asthma, pneumonia, scabies and other cutaneous diseases. The plant is listed in the Indian Pharmacopoeia as an expectorant in treating asthma and pneumonia. It was formerly listed in the British Pharmacopoeia.

Traditional Uses: The whole plant is useful in various countries' traditional medicines and has diuretic, purgative and antihelmintic properties. In Unani and Ayurvedic medicinal systems, the leaves have laxative properties and are useful as a substitute for 'senega' (Polygala senega of the Polygalaceae family). Mixed with garlic, they are effective as antihelmintic and as an ointment for scabies and other skin problems. The leaf's juice is a safe, specific and speedy emetic for children as an expectorant and helps chronic bronchitis, asthma and consumption. The juice is also beneficial in syphilitic ulcers and has a stimulating application in rheumatism.

The decoction is valuable in earache. The powder of dry leaves is helpful in bed sores. In congestive headache, a piece of cotton saturated with the plant juice or leaves, inserted into each nostril, is said to give relief by causing bleeding from the nose. **This plant is precious in traditional Siddha medicine as it is believed to rejuvenate the body.**

In Madagascar, the plant is used for skin parasites. In Mauritius, the sap of crushed leaves, mixed with salt or a decoction of the plant, is useful in scabies and other skin problems. In East Africa, the leaf sap is used for eye infections and the leaf powder is used for maggot (larva of a fly) infested wounds. In chronic cases of children's constipation, the plant leaves are ground into a paste and made into a ball and introduced into the rectum, which relaxes the sphincter and produces free motions. An infusion of the root or the root bruised in water, acts as a cathartic.

Biological Uses: The extracts of methanol showed analgesic and anti-inflammatory effects, whereas ethanolic extracts of the root possess antibacterial and antifungal activities. The petroleum ether and ethanol extracts have shown anti-implantation properties when given to female albino rats. This effect was reversible upon withdrawal of the treatment.

The aqueous extracts of the plant have shown negligible antimicrobial activity on tested pathogens, whereas the plant's methanol extract has shown maximum inhibition on Salmonella Typhimurium (gram-negative bacteria).

Chemical Constituents: The plant contains powerful bioactive constituents such as cyanogenic glycosides, flavonoid glycosides (Mauritanian, nicotiflorin and biorobin), steroids, saponins, other glycosides, alkaloids and tannins. Anthraquinones and triterpenoids were completely absent in all the aqueous and non-aqueous extracts.

Distribution: Acalypha indica plant occurs widely throughout the Old World tropics. In Africa, it grows in Nigeria, in West Africa and further widely throughout tropical Africa and the Indian Ocean islands. It also grows in Pakistan, India, South-East-Asia, Yemen and Australasia.

Mauritian ($C_{33}H_{40}O_{19}$)   Nicotiflorin ($C_{27}H_{30}O_{15}$)   Biorobin ($C_{27}H_{30}O_{15}$)

Adiantum capillus veneris

Pershiaoashan (Plants and Leaves)

Latin Binomial	Adiantum capillus veneris
Family...	Polypodiaceae/Pteridaceae
English Name	Maidenhair
Urdu Name	Pershlaoashan/Thandi Booti

Medicinal Uses: The leaves of the slow-spreading, semi-green Adiantum capillus veneris plant are expectorant, pectoral, demulcent and diuretic in action.

The plant is useful for chest complaints, coughs and throat problems. It is an ingredient of cough mixtures, its flavour masked by sugar and orange-flower water. Adiantum is good at easing pulmonary catarrh and is used in Europe as an emmenagogue.

Traditional Uses: In Unani and Ayurvedic medicinal systems, leaves are beneficial as antipyretic, expectorant, resolvent, diuretic, emmenagogue and siccative (herb produces dryness). The oral powders of the plant are extensively useful for gastrointestinal disorders such as diarrhoea, abnormal camps and jaundice. It is helpful as a headache-preventing agent. The plant also appears to be effective in dissolving the kidney calculi. The Adiantum plant is a potent anti-inflammatory agent; therefore, it is effective on a fistula in the form of an ointment.

In Iran's traditional medicine, the leaf infusion of Adiantum capillus-veneris helps in jaundice therapy. The leaves are beneficial as a detoxicant in alcoholism and in expelling worms from the body. Iranian traditional healers used this herb for female genital disorders such as amenorrhoea and jaundice. The decoction of the plant also helps in child-birth and in extracting the placenta. When used externally, the plant is a valuable hair tonic that treats alopecia, supports hair growth and stops dandruff.

The plant is frequently used in poly-herbal Unani medicines such as 'Laooq-e-Sapistan, Sherbat-e-Mudir and Sherbat-e-Faryad-Res.' Adiantum capillus veneris is mentioned in both Unani and Ayurvedic Pharmacopoeias of India.

Biological Uses: The plant extracts (methanol, ethanol and ethyl-acetate) have anti-inflammatory, antifungal, hypoglycaemic and antioxidant properties. Adiantum capillus- veneris contains flavonoid glycosides e.g. rutin, quercetin and adiantone.

The antibacterial property of this plant may be due to adiantone. A lectin from the plant leaves has a characteristic of glycoproteins, exhibiting agglutinating activity. The plant extracts also showed strong bioactivities, especially analgesic, antinociceptive, antiimplantation and antimicrobial activities. When applied topically, Adiantum capillus veneris shows less hair loss (better follicular density) than the testosterone group.

Chemical Constituents: The plant contains essential biologically active constituents such as terpenoids (mostly pentacyclic triterpenoids), terpenoids, flavonols, flavonoids (querciturone, isoquercitrin, nicotiflorin and naringin), essential oils, steroids, lipids, phenylpropanoids (coumarin derivatives), sterols (beta-sitosterol and stigmasterol), and saponin glycosides.

Distribution: Adiantum capillus-veneris is native to the Southern half of the United States, from California to the Atlantic coast, through Mexico and Central America, to South America. It is also native to Eurasia, Asia and Australasia.

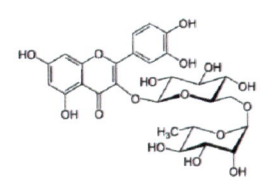

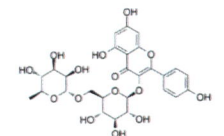

Rutin ($C_{27}H_{30}O_{16}$)   Nicotiflorin ($C_{27}H_{30}O_{15}$)   Adiantone ($C_{29}H_{48}O$)

Aloe vera

Ailwa (Field, Leaves and Gel)

Latin Binomials	Aloe vera/Aloe barbadensis
Family	Liliaceae/Asphodelaceae
English Name	Aloe
Urdu Name	Ailwa/Sibr

Medicinal Uses: The leaves and extract of the evergreen, perennial Aloe vera plant are emmenagogues, demulcent, stomachic, laxative, purgative and anthelmintic in action. Aloe is useful in constipation, dyspepsia, menstrual suppressions and piles. It is generally administered along with carminatives and anodyne drugs and acts on the lower bowel.

The antibacterial and antifungal properties of the Aloe vera plant increase blood flow to the affected area, thus helping the healing process. Aloe juice resolves a range of digestive diseases. It supports the digestive system's detoxification, improves the digestion and the function of the kidneys, the liver and the gallbladder.

In Western society, this plant is one of the few herbal medicines in common usage and it has found widespread use in the cosmetic, pharmaceutical and food industries. The Aloe-gel is extensively helpful in cosmetology as a hydrating ingredient in liquid form or creams, sun lotions, shaving creams, lip balms and hair conditioners. As a tonic for the skin, the mucopolysaccharide (glycosaminoglycan) helps bind moisture into the skin.

Aloe vera might help in alleviating depression. It may be due to the presence of certain biochemical compounds such as flavonoids and amino acids

Traditional Uses: In Unani and Ayurvedic medicinal systems, Aloe leaf is beneficial in constipation, colic, skin diseases, worm infestation and infections. Aloe is a brain tonic, laxative, purgative (phlegm and bile), stomach tonic, blood purifier, liver tonic and emmenagogue in nature. The dried extract of the plant forms a constituent of many poly-herbal Unani preparations like 'Ayarij-e-Feqra, Basalaqoon-Kabir, Hab-e-Mudir and Halwa-i-Ghaikwar.'

In Chinese medicine, Aloe is often valuable in treating fungal diseases. Research backs up the ancient use of topical Aloe in skin disorders. The gel has been approved as a very effective local treatment for improving skin texture, acne and abrasions. Aloe tooth gel is effective as toothpaste in fighting cavities.

Biological Uses: The methanol extracts of the leaf skins and flowers of Aloe show remarkable antioxidant and anti-mycoplasmic activities. Petroleum ether extract has shown anti-implantation activity, whereas hydroalcoholic fraction is anti-inflammatory in property. The presence of 'aloin and emodin' in Aloe vera is analgesic, antibacterial and antiviral in action.

Chemical Constituents: It contains aloin, a crystalline anthraquinone glycoside and emodin. Anthraquinones' presence stimulates mucus secretion and increases the intestinal water content and intestinal peristalsis. The plant also contains some essential micronutrients such as vitamin B_1, B_2, B_6, A and E and minerals like iron, potassium, calcium, chromium, magnesium, zinc, vitamin C, essential fatty acids and amino acids. The presence of amino acids also softens hardened skin cells and zinc acts as an astringent in tightening the skin.

Distribution: Aloe vera is considered native only to the South-West Arabian (Arabian Peninsula) peninsula. Aloe vera cultivation is one of the most widespread among medicinal plants worldwide. Aloe is mainly cultivated in Pakistan, India, China, Bangladesh, Taiwan, and South Korea.

Note: Avoid Aloe vera during pregnancy as it may cause miscarriage by increasing uterine contractions.

Aloin ($C_{21}H_{22}O_9$)   Emodin ($C_{15}H_{10}O_5$)

Barosma betulina

Buchu (Flower, Fresh and Dried Leaves)

Latin Binomials	Barosma betulina/Agathosma betulina
Family	Rutaceae
English Name	Buchu
Urdu Name	Batshu/Buchu

Medicinal Uses: The leaves of the flowering Barosma betulina shrub are aromatic, diuretic, stimulant and diaphoretic in action. The plant directly affects the urinary organs, benefitting gravel remover, inflammation, catarrh of the bladder, cystitis and urethritis. Barosma betulina leaves are beneficial for an enlarged prostate. They contain flavonoids that induce urine production. Buchu leaves are also rich in the bioflavonoid known as rutin. This bioflavonoid has long been beneficial in improving blood circulation. It can strengthen and increase flexibility in blood vessels such as arteries and capillaries.

Traditional Uses: The plant is valued by the indigenous people of South Africa as a folk remedy for various disorders. Dutch settlers in early times used Barosma betulina, commonly called 'Buchu,' to make a brandy tincture. Buchu is still a suitable herb for medicinal tincture. Barosma betulina has made its way into the fragrance and flavour industries due to its sulphur-containing compounds and sensory properties. It helps enhance fruit flavours and fragrance and boosts the flavour of black currants (Ribes nigrum of the Grossulariaceae family).

Biological Uses: Buchu contains essential oils with antimicrobial, antioxidant and anti-inflammatory properties. The plant extracts (aqueous and ethanol) also demonstrate analgesic and antimicrobial activity against common urinary tract pathogens. The plant is classed as an official medicine in Great Britain.

Chemical Constituents: The Buchu leaves contain diosmin, a flavones glycoside and hesperidin, a flavanone glycoside. Its oil is rich in monoterpenes. The oil's primary ingredient is diosphenol, a potent diuretic and antiseptic. Other active ingredients in the essential oil are menthone, iso-menthone, limonene and pulegone.

Distribution: The plant is a small shrubby plant chiefly found in the South-West region of Cape Colony (South Africa).

Note: In some Pharmacognosy books, the plant is mentioned in the volatile oil chapter due to its strong aromatic nature.

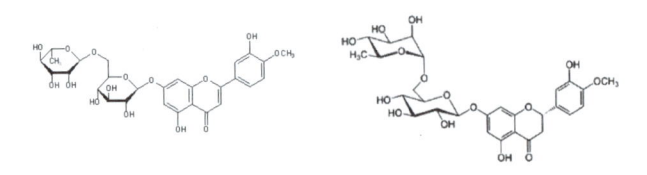

Diosmin ($C_{28}H_{32}O_{15}$)   Hesperidin ($C_{28}H_{34}O_{15}$)

Brassica nigra

Rai (Plant, Seeds and Flower)

Latin Binomials	Brassica nigra/Brassica juncea
Family	Cruciferae/Brassicaceae
English Name	Mustard Black
Urdu Name	Rai

Medicinal Uses: The seeds of the flowering Brassica nigra plant are irritant, stimulant, diuretic, emetic, digestive and rubefacient in action. In modern herbal medicine, it is mainly used as a poultice to relieve acute local pain. The herb draws blood to the skin surface, easing congestion of organs. The mustard oil is a powerful irritant and rubefacient when undiluted but is very useful when dissolved in spirit for chilblains, rheumatism and colic. A hot infusion of the seeds is a stimulating foot bath and aids the removal of common colds and headaches. Mustard flour, when taken internally, can act as an emetic.

Traditional Uses: In Unani and Ayurvedic medicinal systems, the seeds are useful in meningitis, paralysis, palsy, gout and rheumatism. They are also helpful in stomach pain. Black Mustard seeds help relieve water retention (oedema); this is done by increasing urine production. It also increases appetite. The seeds are suitable as a laxative, especially for older people.

The paste prepared by mixing Mustard seeds with water helps treat pneumonia, lower back pain, aching feet, arthritis and inflammation of the lungs' protective lining. A decoction of the seeds helps treat the liver and spleen's induration. It is also valuable in treating carcinoma, throat tumours and impostumes (swelling containing pus). Brassica nigra is an aperient ingredient of tea, useful in hiccups. In Traditional Chinese Medicine, brown mustard (Brassica juncea) seeds transform phlegm and stop cough. The oil of Mustard is said to stimulate hair growth and it is edible.

Biological Uses: The plant has antioxidant, antibacterial, antifungal, antiseptic and anti-inflammatory properties. The ethanol fraction of the leaf also possesses anti-inflammatory properties. The aqueous extract of seeds has antimicrobial activities. The plant's anti-cancer effect may be due to the presence of allyl isothiocyanate (an organo-sulfur compound).

Chemical Composition: The medicinal properties are allyl isothiocyanate, which is a local irritant and emetic. The chemical composition of Black Mustard seed contain a thioglycoside, e.g., alpha, beta glucopyranoside termed as 'sinigrin,' also known as malonate potassium allyl-glucosinolate, alkaloids, tannins, terpenoids, polyphenols, flavonoids, carotenoids and sterols. The plant also has some valuable minerals like selenium, magnesium, calcium, iron, manganese, phosphorus and zinc.

Distribution: Brassica nigra is native to Africa, Western and Central Asia and Europe. Brassica is a common crop in Pakistan. In one of the studies, it is reported that domestic oil production is only about 17 per cent of the total national demand. At the same time, the remaining is imported at the cost of substantial foreign exchange.

Sinigrin (C$_{10}$H$_{16}$KNO$_9$S$_2$)   Allyl isothiocyanate (C4H5NS)

Caesalpinia bonduc

Karanjwa (Plant Parts, Seeds and Pods)

Latin Binomials	Caesalpinia bonduc/Guilandinia bonduc
Family	Caesalpiniaceae
English Name	Bonduc Nut
Urdu Name	Karanjwa

Medicinal Uses: The flowering Caesalpinia bonduc plant is antipyretic, emmenagogue, antispasmodic, anti-flatulent in action and a blood purifier. The seeds have tonic and antipyretic properties and the bark and leaves have been helpful in lowering fevers. The oil extracted from the seeds helps treat discharges from the ear. The roasted pod is beneficial as a substitute for quinoline alkaloid 'quinine' (antipyretic). The root is suitable for relieving intestinal worms, fever, tumours, cough and amenorrhoea (not getting periods). The fruit is also effective in eliminating piles, wounds, leucorrhoea and urinary disorders. Boiled leaves of the Caesalpinia are helpful in fevers. In modern herbal medicine, the seeds are a help in febrile illness. A decoction of roasted seeds is an effective remedy for diabetes.

Traditional Uses: In the Unani system of medicine, the plant has been considered an essential remedy for treating several diseases. For example, the plant leaves pounded with Piper nigrum (Filfil-siyah) are useful in vitiated blood conditions. The seed-kernel, burnt in sesame oil, is applied to infected wounds and cutaneous affections. A prescription, Hab-e-Karanjwaa, is given in the Unani medicinal system as an anti-periodic in fever.

In the Ayurveda, the plant can treat various diseases, specifically, tumours cystic and cystic fibrosis. The leaves are beneficial as anthelmintic, emmenagogue and febrifuge and help in piles, intestinal worms, elephantiasis, amenorrhoea, pharyngodynia and fever. In folk medicine, the plant juice is given for two weeks after meals to cure intermittent fever. The seed-kernels, made into an ointment, are applied to hydrocele (a type of swelling in the scrotum). They are prescribed in haemorrhages and given as an anthelmintic mixed with honey or castor oil, as an infusion.

Biological Uses: The oil extracted from the seeds is used in cosmetic preparations to soften the skin. The aqueous fruit extract of Caesalpinia bonduc helps treat diabetes and coughs and exhibits antifungal, antiulcerogenic, anti-inflammatory and analgesic properties.

Chemical Constituents: The plant contains bitter-glycoside, caesalpinolide-A, an antibacterial and caesalpinianone, an antifungal agent. In addition, the plant also has valuable bioactive constituents such as flavonoids, tannins, phytosterols, saponins, coumarins, monoterpenoids (iridoids), triterpenoids, essential oils and alkaloids.

Distribution: Caesalpinia bonduc, a prickly shrub, is widely distributed worldwide, especially in the Indo-Pak subcontinent, Sri Lanka, China, Andaman and Nicobar islands.

Caesalpinolide-A ($C_{22}H_{32}O_6$)

Cassia fistula

Amaltass (Tree, Pods and Flowers)

Latin Binomial	Cassia fistula
Family	Caesalpiniaceae
English Name	Cassia Pod/Golden Shower
Urdu Name	Amaltaas/Khayar Shanber

Medicinal Uses: Most parts of the plant are used for medicinal purposes. The fruit of the handsome, flowering Cassia fistula tree is a laxative, purgative and emmenagogue. The plant is mentioned USP, BP, EP and in WHO monographs in 'Selected Medicinal Plants.'

Traditional Uses: The plant is effective in treating the common cold. Traditionally, the plant is used as an infusion, decoction or powder, either alone or in combination with other medicinal plants. The bark and fruit of the Cassia tree have excellent antioxidant properties and boost the body's immunity. Cassia pod leaves are laxative in nature and are used externally as an emollient; a poultice is useful for insect bites, swelling, rheumatism and facial paralysis. The juice of leaves helps dress for ringworms, relieving irritation and relief of dropsical swelling.

A decoction of the pulp is a remedy in curing kidney stones (nephrolithiasis). The root is a tonic, astringent, febrifuge and purgative. The flowers are antipyretic, abortifacient, demulcent and decrease inflammation. The seeds are emetic and are useful in constipation and have cathartic properties. The bark is used as a tonic and as an antidysenteric agent. The Heartwood (wood at the centre of the tree) traditionally helps as an anthelmintic.

Cassia fistula is one of the most commonly used plants in Unani and Ayurvedic medicines. The plant has been described as applicable against skin diseases, liver troubles, tuberculosis and its use in treating haematemesis, pruritus, leucoderma and diabetes. The anti-diabetic property appears to be in the Cassia pod's aqueous fraction. Externally, broken bones and tropical ulcers are bandaged with bark scrapings and leaf sap.

The Cassia pod forms a constituent of famous Unani poly-herbal, semi-solid, cold and catarrh medicinal preparation known as 'Laooq-e-Khayar Shambar and Majun-e-Kalkalang.

Biological Uses: The extract (ethanol-water 50:50) of the pods has shown anti-fertility activity in female albino rats. The plant's methanol fraction has documented analgesic, antioxidant and hepatoprotective activities. The aqueous extract of the pods has significantly decreased blood sugar and body temperature.

The seed fraction (methanol) of Cassia fistula exhibits antiepileptic properties. The aqueous and methanol extracts of the root bark exhibit anti-inflammatory activities. An alcohol fraction of the leaves has shown antibacterial activity *in vivo* against Staphylococcus aureus and Pseudomonas aeruginosa, plus accelerated wound healing. Antimutagenic and anticarcinogenic effects of Cassia fistula extracts were also studied.

Chemical Uses: Cassia contains anthraquinone glycosides, barbaloin (aloin), rhein (cassic acid), sennosides A-B, flavonols glycosides, tannins, proteins and carbohydrates. Anthraquinone derivatives and glycosides are responsible for the plant's laxative properties. The fruit pulp is rich in pectins and mucilage. The bark is a good source of tannins and is used for tanning and dying.

Distribution: Cassia fistula grows throughout Pakistan and other Asian countries such as India, China, Hong Kong, the Philippines, Sri Lanka, Malaysia, Indonesia and Thailand.

Note: Excessive use of Cassia fistula may cause nausea, vomiting, intestinal irritation, tenesmus, colic and possible abortion.

Barbaloin ($C_{21}H_{22}O_9$)   Rhein ($C_{15}H_8O_6$)

Cassia senna

Senna Makki (Plant, Leaves and Flower)

Latin Binomials	Cassia senna/Cassia angustifolia/Alexandrine senna
Family	Fabaceae/Caesalpiniaceae
English Name	Senna
Urdu Name	Senna Makki/Sennai Iskandaria

Medicinal Uses: The leaves of the flowering Cassia senna plant are laxative, purgative, anthelmintic and cathartic in action. It is deobstruent, a blood purifier and anthelmintic when combined with vinegar. The herb acts primarily on the lower bowel, acts locally upon the intestinal wall and increases the colon's peristaltic movements.

The taste of Senna is nauseating and prone to causing sickness and griping pains. The Senna pod has milder effects than the leaves and lack their griping effects. It is generally combined with aromatics, e.g., ginger or cinnamon and stimulants to modify Senna's effects. When the problems are overcome, Senna is a good medicine for children and elderly persons. Its also known as a 'Detox tea' based on its ability to eliminate toxins in the digestive system to improve nutrient absorption and metabolism. The American Herbal Products Association (AHPA) warns against Senna leaf's long-term use, but not Senna fruit. Senna is an FDA-approved, over-the-counter (OTC) laxative.

Traditional Uses: The Senna plant in Unani and Ayurvedic medicinal systems is widespread and popular. The leaves help treat constipation, loss of appetite, enlarged liver, indigestion, malaria, jaundice, anaemia and a brisk and are a safe purgative. A mixture of the powdered seeds of Senna and the fruit of Cassia fistula with curd, is a valuable ointment for the cure of ringworm.

A resin obtained from it is one of the ingredients of the famous Unani medicine known as 'Itrifal Ustukhudus,' a remedy for purging the brain and the stomach's viscid matter.

In the European market, Seena leaves are on sale as Senna tea. Roasted seeds as a substitute for coffee. In China, the leaves of Senna obtusifolia are helpful as a laxative and its decoction is useful in treating eye complaints. The Senna fruit seems to be gentler than the Senna leaf.

Biological Uses: Methanol extract of Cassia senna has antimicrobial activity. Aqueous and non-aqueous (methanol, ethanol, acetone and ethyl acetate) fractions of the leaves have anti-cancer, antinociceptive antibacterial, anti-inflammatory, antioxidant, antiulcer and antispasmodic properties.

Chemical Constituents: Senna contains glycosides Sennoside A and B, C and D, monomeric flavonol glycosides and anthraquinones. The plant also has valuable bioactive ingredients such as flavonoids, terpenoids, sterol glycosides, resin, mucilage, yellow flavanol (kaempferol), minerals, polysaccharides and traces of phlorotannins. The detailed studies on the water-soluble polysaccharides report the presence of several distinct hydrocolloids.

Distribution: Alexandrine senna is native to the upper and the middle Nile in Egypt and Sudan. Cassia angustifolia is indigenous to Arabia and is also cultivated in the Indo-Pak subcontinent. It is also grown elsewhere, notably in Africa (Somalia).

Note: More recently, in Pakistan, India and Britain (Asian citizens), the use of Senna became famous for the cure of COVID-19, the infectious disease caused by Coronavirus; however, there is no substantial scientific evidence that correlates the efficacy of Senna leaves in Covid.

Scientists are willing to concede the immunity boost it gives, but nothing more. The use of Senna in Covid-19 pandemic patients has been strongly discouraged due to its enormous side effects like; diarrhoea, water loss electrolyte imbalance and hypokalemia (low blood potassium).

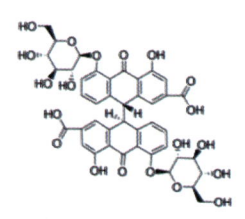

Sennoside A ($C_{42}H_{38}O_{20}$)

Cheiranthus cheiri

Todri (Plant, Seeds and Flower)

Latin Binomial	Cheiranthus cheiri
Family	Cruciferae/Brassicaceae
English Name	Wallflower
Urdu Name	Todri Surkh

Medicinal Uses: The seeds, oil, flowers and stem of the plant are suitable for medicinal purposes. The seeds of the herbaceous, perennial, flowering Cheiranthus cheiri plant are expectorant, a cardiac tonic, antimalarial and aphrodisiac in action. Cheiranthus cheiri (seeds) is cardiotonic and supports a failing heart like 'foxglove' (Digitalis purpura). A large dose is toxic.

The seeds are also valued as an aphrodisiac. The flowers possess cardiac stimulant and emmenagogue properties. The plant produces cardenolides, which are remarkable chemical compounds responsible for treating countless people with congestive heart failure.

Traditional Uses: In Unani and Ayurvedic medicinal systems, the plant is beneficial in congestive heart failure and the seeds are considered a tonic, diuretic, aphrodisiac and an expectorant. It is useful in tumours, jaundice and drug toxicity. The flowers and stems are antirheumatic, antiseptic, antispasmodic, nervine and purgative. They are also suitable for the treatment of impotence and paralysis. According to classical Unani literature, the leaves and oil may help in cancer treatment.

Cheiranthus cheiri plant is a constituent of many poly-herbal Unani formulations having kidney problems as their primary therapeutic indication, e.g. 'Jawarish-e-Todri, Laboob-e-Sagheer and Majun-e-Nuqra.'

Biological Uses: The juice of the seeds of the plant shows antibacterial activity against gram-positive and gram-negative bacteria. Cheirolin possesses goitrogenic (substances that disrupt thyroid hormones) properties. The aqueous and non-aqueous fractions of the plant have antioxidant, anti-inflammatory, analgesic and antifungal activities.

Chemical Constituents: The Cheiranthus plant contains cardio-active steroid glycosides, including cheirotoxin, erysimoside, glucoepysimoside and cheiroside-A. Cheirinine is an alkaloid isolated from its seeds that has quinine like action (antimalarial). Its fresh leaves contain 3-methyl thiopropyl isothiocyanate. The plant also contains beneficial bioactive ingredients such as alkaloids, glucosides, flavonoids and phenols.

Distribution: Cheiranthus cheiri plant is native to Europe. It is also widely cultivated as a garden plant.

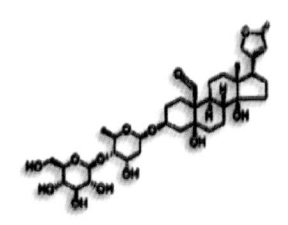

Erysimoside ($C_{35}H_{52}O_{14}$)

Cichorium intybus

Kasni (Flowers and Root)

Latin Binomial	Cichorium intybus/Cichorium endivia
Family	Compositae/Asteraceae
English Names	Endive/Chicory
Urdu Name	Kasni

Medicinal Uses: The root of the herbaceous, perennial, flowering Cichorium intybus plant is diuretic, laxative, demulcent, hepatoprotective, digestive in action and a blood purifier. A decoction of the root is beneficial in jaundice, gout, liver problems and rheumatic complaints. In modern herbal medicines, Chicory is well known as a coffee substitute but is also widely used medicinally to treat various ailments ranging from wounds to diabetes.

Traditional Uses: In Unani and Ayurvedic medicinal systems, the root is used for relief in pain, to promote appetite and digestion. It is also useful as a hepatoprotective and nephroprotective agent. The juice of the leaves and its tea are considered lithotriptic for eliminating internal mucus and for bile production. It is recommended as a treatment in jaundice, spleen enlargement, gastrointestinal problems such as digestive difficulties, lack of appetite, sinus problems, cuts and bruises.

In Italy, a decoction of the plant is helpful as a depurative. In South Africa, the weed, leaves, stems and roots are beneficial in making tea for jaundice patients. The syrup is commonly used as a tonic and purifying medicine for infants. In Turkey, an ointment is made from leaves for healing wounds.

According to the European monograph, the traditional use of Chicory roots includes the relief of symptoms related to mild digestive disorders such as abdominal fullness, flatulence, slow digestion and temporary loss of appetite.

Biological Uses: The plant extracts (water, ethanol, methanol and ethyl acetate) show antibacterial and antifungal activities.

Chemical Constituents: Cichorium intybus contains bitter glycoside chicoric acid and hydroxycinnamic acid. The plant also has useful phytoconstituents such as saponins, glycosides, flavonoids, alkaloids, volatile oils, phenolic compounds, steroids, carbohydrates and tannins.

Distribution: It lives as a wild plant on roadsides in its native Europe and is now common in North America, China, Pakistan, India and Australia, where it has become widely naturalized.

Chicoric acid ($C_{22}H_{18}O_{12}$)

Cinnamomum tamala

Tezpat (Fresh and Dried Leaves)

Latin Binomial	Cinnamomum tamala
Family	Lauraceae
English Name	Cinnamon leaves
Urdu Name	Tezpat/Tez-patta/Kari-patta

Medicinal Uses: The leaves of the evergreen Cinnamomum tamala tree are aromatic, carminative, antispasmodic and stimulant in action.

Traditional Uses: In Unani and Ayurvedic medicinal systems, the leaves are useful in treating colic and diarrhoea. The leaves of the tree have a clove-like taste and a faint pepper-like odour. Due to its aromatic nature, the leaves are kept in a cloth and chewed to eliminate mouth odour.

A decoction is helpful in headaches, in preventing recurrence of stones in the kidney and externally for scalp infection. The bark is beneficial as a stimulant, is carminative in rheumatism, colic, sexual weakness, gynaecological disorders, nausea and vomiting.

Its seeds are crushed and mixed with honey or sugar and administered to children for dysentery and cough. The oil of leaf is called 'Oil of Tezpat' and is medicinally used as a carminative, antiflatulent, diuretic and cardiac disorder.

Biological Uses: Cinnamon oil exhibits antioxidant, antidepressant, antiulcer and antimicrobial activities and a non-aqueous extract (methanol) of the bark possesses an antibacterial property. The methanolic extract of the leaves demonstrates a significant reduction in blood glucose. The plant is known to have antioxidant, antifungal, anti-inflammatory and antidiarrhoeal activities. The presence of tannin in the plant has the reducing power, which prevents liver injury by inhibiting the formation of lipid peroxides.

Chemical Constituents: The plant contains volatile oils (furanosesquiterpenoids) and aldehyde glycosides. Its dried leaves are used as a common ingredient in Indian cooking. The Cinnamon leaves contain a yellow oily liquid with a cinnamon odour and sweet taste 'cinnamaldehyde' and trans-cinnamaldehyde is a clear yellow liquid with an odour of cinnamon and a sweet taste.

Distribution: Cinnamomum tamala tree is native to India, Pakistan, Bangladesh, Nepal, Bhutan and China.

Cinnamomum zeylanicum

Darchini (Barks and Powder)

Latin Binomial	Cinnamomum zeylanicum
Family	Lauraceae
English Name	Cinnamon
Urdu Name	Darchini

Medicinal Uses The bark of an evergreen Cinnamomum zeylanicum tree is aromatic, carminative, antiseptic, astringent and stimulant in action. It is used as a local stimulant as a powder and as infusion and also generally combined with other herbs. Cinnamon stops vomiting and nausea, relieves flatulence, diarrhoea and can also be employed to control the haemorrhage of the womb.

Traditional Uses: In Unani and Ayurvedic medicinal systems, it is used as a spice and flavouring agent. Cinnamon is also added as a flavour in chewing gums due to its refreshing mouth effects on bad breath. The bark can also improve the colon's health, reduce colon cancer risk and acts as a coagulant that prevents bleeding and increases blood circulation in the uterus. Cinnamomum zeylanicum is used as a carminative, helps rheumatoid arthritis and reduces blood sugar levels. The bark is helpful and efficient in lowering cholesterol levels and strengthening the heart muscles.

Cinnamon has been traditionally used as tooth powder and in treating toothaches, dental problems, oral microbiota and for bad breath. The oil of Cinnamon is used for rheumatism, aching joint stiffness and sore gums. In Western medicine, cinnamon helps fight off bacteria, especially in the teeth. It is also an excellent antioxidant that can lower cholesterol. In traditional Chinese medicine, the uses of Cinnamon sticks include treating kidney disorders, lowering back pain, knee weakness, bladder infections and asthma. Cinnamon tea is gaining popularity in South Asian countries, mainly due to its beneficial compounds. These may offer various health benefits, including improving heart health, aiding weight loss, alleviating menstrual cramps, reducing inflammation and maintaining blood sugar levels. The Cinnamon barks are commonly added to rice and curry during the cooking process. Cinnamomum zeylanicum bark is one of the ingredients of 'Garam masala' (a mixture of spices).

Biological Uses: The extracts (ethanol, methanol and aqueous) of the bark possess antioxidant, antimicrobial, anti-inflammatory, anti-diabetic and anti-cancer activities. The oil from the bark and leaves has antibacterial and antifungal properties.

Chemical Constituents: The plant contains essential oils, aldehyde glycosides (cinnamaldehyde), steroids, flavonoids, saponins, triterpenoids and tannins.

Distribution: Cinnamomum zeylanicum tree is native to Sri Lanka and India's Malabar Coast. Indonesia is the leading producer of Cinnamon, followed by China, Vietnam and Sri Lanka.

Cinnamaldehyde (C_9H_8O)

Citrullus colocynthis

Indrain Talkh/Hanzal (Plant and Fruit)

Latin Binomial	Citrullus colocynthis
Family	Cucurbitaceae
English Name	Colocynth
Urdu Name	Indrain Talkh/Hanzal

Medicinal Uses: The fruit of the flowering Citrullus colocynthis desert plant is laxative, purgative, anthelmintic, diuretic, abortifacient and hydragogue in action. It is also used as a remedy for skin diseases.

Traditional Uses: In Unani and Ayurvedic medicinal systems, the fruit and seeds help treat diabetes and abdominal pain. The external use of the root and fruit extract helps cure pimples, acne and boils. Cotton, dipped in fruit juice, is also used for timely and easy delivery. A decoction of the root helps relieve constipation and boiled in milk, is helpful in amenorrhoea. The root is also beneficial in treating jaundice, urinary diseases, rheumatism, abdominal enlargements, cough and asthmatic attacks in children.

A poultice of the root paste is useful in addressing breast inflammation. The aqueous extract of the root shows a significant effect on reducing blood sugar levels. In Iran, it is used for constipation, oedema, cancer and diabetes.

A leading poly-herbal Unani medicine, 'Hab-e-Ayaraj' is valuable in treating headache, mood disorders and other brain-related medical issues as it contains Colocynth seeds as one of the ingredients.

Biological Uses: The bioactive constituents present in this herb influence insulin metabolism and show great positive activity in Type-2 diabetes. Extracts (aqueous and acetone) of the whole Colocynth plant possess anti-candidal (a type of fungus infection), antibacterial, anti-inflammatory and hypoglycaemic activities. The aqueous extract of the root, showed a significant reduction in blood sugar levels compared with chloroform and ethanol extracts.

The plant and its compound (cucurbitacin) might be a potential chemotherapeutic drug in treating breast and gastric adenocarcinoma cancers.

Chemical Constituents: The various important chemical constituents are elucidated from the entire plant (root, stem, leaves, fruit and seeds) and documented in literature, as imparting medicinal value to the genus are steroidal glycosides, alkaloids, flavonoids and terpenoids. Citrullus colocynthis proves to have several active chemical constituents like colocynthin, colocynthetin, cucurbitacins (tetra-cyclic-terpenoids), glycosides, flavonoids, flavone glycosides, etc. The seeds contain fixed oil. The fruit is the primary source of drugs. The seeds contain 30 – 34 per cent of pale yellow oil, which has an alkaloid, a glucoside and a saponin. The plant is also a rich source of ascorbic acid (Vit. C).

Distribution: Citrullus colocynthis is a viny desert plant native to the Mediterranean Basin and Asia, especially Pakistan, Afghanistan, Turkey and Izmir and North East Africa.

Colocynthin ($C_{38}H_{54}O_{13}$)   Cucurbitacins B ($C_{32}H_{46}O_6$)

Croton tiglium

Jamal-Gotta (Seeds, Plant Parts and Leaf)

Latin Binomial	Croton tiglium/Tiglium officinale
Family	Rhamnaceae/Euphorbiaceae
English name	Cascara Sagrada/Croton
Urdu Name	Jamal-Gotta

Medicinal Uses: The seeds of the flowering Croton tiglium plant and oil are irritant, rubefacient, cathartic and drastically purgative in action. It is a potent purgative herb that quickly evacuates the bowels in less than one hour. It causes vomiting and severe griping pains in large doses, which can be fatal. The herb is only suitable in cases of obstinate constipation where other herbs have failed. It is applied externally as a counter-irritant to relieve rheumatism, gout, neuralgia and bronchitis.

Traditional Uses: In Unani and Ayurvedic medicinal systems, the seeds are primarily beneficial for chronic constipation, dyspepsia, digestive complaints and in the treatment of piles. The bark is helpful as a remedy for cancerous sores and tumours, carbuncle, fever and paralysis. Croton oil is pale yellow to brown and it is transparent. It is useful in a minimal quantity for dropsy, intestinal obstruction, lead poisoning, cerebral affections like apoplexy convulsions and high blood pressure.

In Brazil, the leaves, stem and bark of the Croton species are used in traditional medicine to treat diabetes, high blood cholesterol and gastrointestinal disturbances. In the West Indies and North and South America, its bitter bark has been widely valued for treating digestive, hypotensive and stomachic issues. It is used to treat gastrointestinal disorders, intestinal inflammation and rheumatism in China. In Iran, the traditional name of the plant is 'Karchak' and it is used in gastrointestinal disorders. In Malaysia, one seed is eaten as a purgative and with coconut milk to stop the effect.

The seed oil may also be used to produce soap and candles. However, it can only be used outdoors for illumination as the smoke is toxic.

Biological Uses: The extract (aqueous-ethanol 50:50 per cent) shows an antioxidant property. The oil possesses antinociceptive (herb that reduces the sensation of pain), haemolytic and genotoxic activities. The ethanolic extracts of the stem and seed of Croton exhibit strong antidermatophytes (anti-fungus) activities.

Chemical Constituents: The oil comprises of fatty acids, oleic acid, linoleic acid, myristic acid, arachidic acid, palmitic, formic acid, etc. The plant also contains essential bioactive constituents such as biologically active glucoside (anti-cancer) called crotonoside (a purine nucleoside), resin, flavones, diterpenes and a protein called crotin. The root contains tannins, glycosides and toxic alkaloid 'ricinine' (is a pyridine alkaloid, a pyridone and a nitrile). The leaves yield two new compounds, badounoids A and B and nor-sesquiterpenoids. Two cyclopeptides, two tropane derivatives and two limonoids were also isolated from seeds of the Croton plant.

Distribution: Croton tiglium tree is found on the Malabar Coast of India, in Burma, Thailand, Cambodia, Vietnam, Malaysia and Indonesia.

Note: The use of the oil of the seeds should be monitored more carefully; it should only be administered in small doses. Excessive use of this plant can cause bloody diarrhoea, vomiting, the inability to urinate (acute urine retention) and loss of energy, depression and confusion.

The oil is a highly toxic and a violent irritant. The toxicity of Croton tiglium may be due to the presence of tetracyclic diterpenoids compound 'phorbol esters' (a member of the tigliana family of diterpenes) and crotonic acid along with other biologically active constituents.

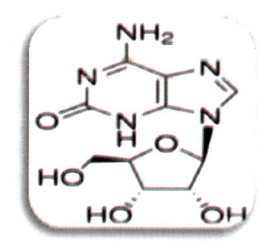

Crotonoside ($C_{10}H_{13}N_5O_5$) Ricinine ($C_8H_8N_2O_2$) Phorbol ($C_{20}H_{28}O_6$)

Digitalis purpurea

Zehar-al-Kashatabeen (Garden, Flowers and Leaves)

Latin Binomial	Digitalis purpurea
Family	Scrophulariaceae/Plantaginaceae
English Name	Foxglove
Urdu Name	Zehar-al-Kashatabeen

Medicinal Uses: The leaves of the herbaceous, biennial, flowering Digitalis purpurea plant are cardiac tonic, sedative, anti-asthmatic and diuretic in action. Administering digitalis increases all forms of muscle tissue activity, particularly the heart and arterioles. It causes a very high rise in blood pressure while the pulse slows and becomes regular.

Digitalis causes the heart to contract in size, allowing increased blood flow and nutrient delivery to the organ. It also acts on the kidneys and is a good remedy for dropsy, particularly when connected with cardiac problems. The herb provides benefit in treating internal haemorrhage, epilepsy, inflammatory diseases and delirium tremens.

The seeds are also described as cordial and diuretic. Digitalis purpura is an excellent antidote to aconite poisoning when given as a hypodermic injection.

Traditional Uses: Some traditional healers use Digitalis species to treat ulcers, boils, abscesses, headaches and paralysis. Externally, the plant is used for granulating poorly healing wounds and curing ulcers. Digitalis has a cumulative action whereby it is liable to accumulate in the body and have poisonous effects. It should only be used under medical advice.

The plant is seldom used in Unani and Ayurvedic medicines. A homoeopathic remedy made from the leaves is used to treat cardiac disorders.

Biological Uses: The plant possesses antioxidant, antibacterial, anti-diabetic, cytotoxic, hepatic, neuro and cardiac effects. The plant extracts also have cardiovascular immunological, hepatic, neuro and cardio-protective effects. The presence of saponin 'digitonin' is the Digitalis improves glucose tolerance and positivity affects serum lipids.

Chemical Constituents: Digitalis purpurea plant contains cardiac glycosides (digitoxin, digoxin, ouabain and oleandrin), essential oils, steroids and saponins.

Distribution: Digitalis purpurea is native to and widespread throughout most temperate Europe. It has also been naturalised in parts of North America and other temperate regions. The plant is a popular garden subject, with many cultivars available.

Note: Digitalis purpura is a poisonous plant. At low serum concentration, cardiac glycoside 'digitalis' is well tolerated. The most common adverse reactions are nausea, vomiting, anorexia, etc.

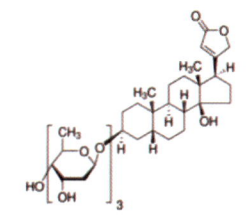

Digitoxin ($C_{41}H_{64}O_{13}$) 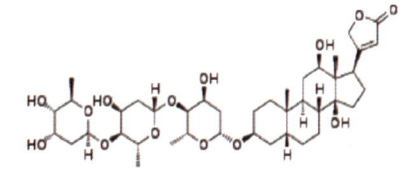   Digoxin ($C_{41}H_{64}O_{14}$)

Dioscorea sylvatica

Dioscori (Leaves, Plant Parts and Root-Tubes)

Latin Binomial	Dioscorea sylvatica/Dioscorea brevipes
Family	Dioscoreaceae

English Name	Wild Yam
Urdu Name	Ratalu/Waylad Yam

Medicinal Uses: The root tubes of the herbaceous Dioscorea sylvatica plant are antibilious (herb useful in liver disorders), antispasmodic, anti-inflammatory and diaphoretic in action. It is valuable in all forms of colic, abdominal, intestinal irritation, etc. It is also helpful in spasms, spasmodic asthma, vomiting and hepatic congestion.

Traditional Uses: Dioscorea sylvatica is useful in traditional medicine and the tubers contain pharmaceutical compounds such as steroidal saponins (tetracyclic triterpenoids) and other alkaloids. The plant is sold in Zimbabwe markets to treat skin diseases and physical disorders characterized by joint pain and swelling.

In Sudan, the root tuber is used against rheumatoid arthritis. In Cameroon and Madagascar, the pounded bulbs are applied to abscesses, boils and wound infections. When the freshly peeled rhizome is rubbed on the skin, a mild inflammation and itching soon appear. Dioscorea is generally considered safe in all trimesters of pregnancy and is traditionally indicated for nausea in pregnancy and the prevention of early miscarriage.

Biological Uses: The plant's non-aqueous extract (methanol) possesses antifungal, antibacterial and antioxidant activities. Aqueous and methanol fractions from the bulbils of Dioscorea bulbifera (variety Sativa) also have a potent antinociceptive effect. Other interesting biological applications include anti-inflammatory, anti-cancer (breast cancer), hypocholesterolemic and immune-stimulating remedies. The presence of diosgenin in the plant, has shown an anti-ageing effect due to the estrogenic receptors' stimulation in the skin.

Chemical Constituents: The plant contains steroidal saponins, often consisting of diosgenin glycosides (a spirostanyl glycoside). Dioscin is toxic and produces convulsions. The plant's bark also contains alkaloids, norditerpenoids, resins, sterols, phenolic compounds, batatasines, carbohydrates (starch) and mucilage. The plant is seldom used in Unani and Ayurvedic systems of medicine.

Distribution: The plant is native to tropical areas of America, Africa and Asia. Nigeria is the leading producer of Yam, followed by Ghana and the Ivory Coast. In Papua New Guinea, Wild Yam is called 'Kaukau.'

Note: Dioscorea sylvatica in larger doses or upon an intravenous injection of saponin glycosides causes hemolysis (destruction of red blood cells).

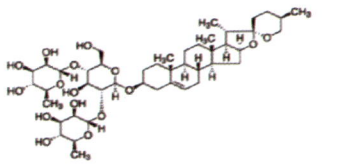

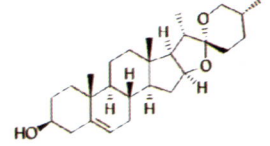

Dioscin ($C_{41}H_{64}O_{14}$) Diosgenin ($C_{27}H_{42}O_3$)

Echinops echinatus

Barham Dandi (Plant and Flowers)

Latin Binomial	Echinops echinatus
Family	Compositae/Asteraceae
English Name	Camel's Thistle
Urdu Name	Barham Dandi/Untkatara

Medicinal Uses: All above the ground parts of the plant have medicinal properties. The flowering Echinops echinatus plant is a nervine tonic, aphrodisiac, alternative and a blood purifier. The plant is also known as the purple coneflower. It has been valuable for centuries in traditional medicine systems and customarily as a treatment for the common cold, coughs, bronchitis, upper respiratory infections and some inflammatory conditions. The powdered form of all above the ground parts of this herb, is an effective tonic.

Traditional Uses: The roots, leaves, fruit and bark are extensively applicable in folk, Unani and Ayurvedic medicinal systems. The plant is alterative, analgesic, antifungal, anti-inflammatory, is a contraceptive, a diuretic, febrifuge, hepatic, nervine, ophthalmic and stomachic in nature. It is beneficial in treating hoarse coughs, hysteria, dyspepsia, scrofula and various eye problems. It also helps treat brain disease, chronic fever and pains in the joints and inflammation.

The root is abortifacient and aphrodisiac. The powdered root is applied to wounds to destroy maggots (larva of a fly) and a combined form, with the gum from Acacia (Gond Kikar) trees is applied to the hair to eliminate lice. The dried and powdered root bark is mixed with milk and used to treat diabetes. The gum is mixed with water to make a paste; the root-bark powder is applied to the male genitals one hour before intercourse to treat poor sexual vitality.

Unani and Ayurvedic, medicinal practices also consider the roots as an aphrodisiac. Ayurveda practitioners also consider the Echinops echinatus plant roots, as effective in facilitating childbirth.

The fumes obtained from burning the leaves and roots are inhaled in treating respiratory disorders, especially asthma, to get rapid and long-lasting relief. The seeds are sweet and aphrodisiac.

Biological Uses: The non-aqueous (methanol, ethanol and ethyl acetate) extracts of the plant have antioxidant, cytotoxic, analgesic, antipyretic, anti-inflammatory, antimicrobial, antibacterial and possess antifungal activities. The methanol and *n*-butanol fractions of the root have antioxidant and hepatoprotective properties. The plant extracts also show various biological activities such as antifungal, diuretic, antipyretic and hepatoprotective properties.

Chemical Constituents: The plant is known to contain biologically active compounds, including the flavanone, glycosides, polyphenol 'apigenin,' with anti-inflammatory activities, flavones sterols, triterpenoids, glucosides and essential oils

Distribution: It is native to Asia - Afghanistan, Pakistan, northern India, Myanmar and Sri Lanka. In Pakistan, Echinops echinatus is found in the Karakoram regions and Northern Areas.

Apigenin ($C_{15}H_{10}H_5$)

Gentiana lutea

Kiraat Root (Plant, Roots and Flowers)

Latin Binomial	Gentiana lutea
Family	Gentianaceae
English Name	Gentian
Urdu Name	Kiraat

Medicinal Uses: The flowering Gentiana lutea plant's root is stomachic, febrifuge, emmenagogue, anthelmintic and antiseptic in action and is a bitter tonic. The herb is probably the most effective bitter tonic remedy for exhaustion from chronic disease, general debility, weakness of the digestive organs and lack of appetite. The yellow Gentian is useful in many dyspeptic complaints, hysteria and jaundice. The roots are used in making an alcoholic beverage in Germany and Switzerland. Gentian is applied to the skin for treating wounds and cancer. Taking a Gentian root extract can reduce the number of calories eaten over the next 24 hours, but this does not reduce hunger or feeling of fullness.

Traditional Uses: Traditionally, the herb is used as a stimulant for gallbladder and liver, for them to function more efficiently. The plant is also a remedy for diarrhoea, for relaxation of mucous membranes, chronic malarial poisoning, dyspepsia, mental and physical depression, general debility and exhaustion.

In homoeopathy, a tincture of the root of Gentiana lutea is prescribed in anorexia, biliousness, dyspepsia, colic, diarrhoea, stomachache, fever and rawness of the throat and rheumatic pain. The extracts are useful in various foods, beautifiers and some anti-smoking products.

Externally, the plant helps heal wounds and internally to treat sore throat, arthritic inflammation and jaundice. The plant is seldom used in Unani and Ayurvedic medicines. However, its medicinal properties are mentioned in the Ayurvedic pharmacopoeia. In Iranian traditional medicine texts, the Gentian plant is valuable in treating urine retention, menstrual, liver, spleen dysfunctions and animal poison detoxification.

Biological Uses: The plant non-aqueous fraction possesses antioxidant, antifungal, antiulcer, anti-inflammatory, stomachic and immune-modulatory properties.

Chemical Constituents: The bitter ingredients of the Gentian root are secoiridoid glycosides 'amarogentin' and gentiopicrin. The former is one of the most bitter natural compounds known and is used as a scientific basis for measuring bitterness. The plant also has valuable phytochemicals such as alkaloids, triterpenoids, essential oils, pectin, tannins and flavones.

Distribution: Gentiana lutea herb is native to the calcareous alpine meadows, moist grasslands and open pastures of the Central and Southern European mountain ranges.

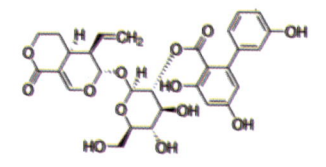

Amarogentin ($C_{29}H_{30}O_{13}$) 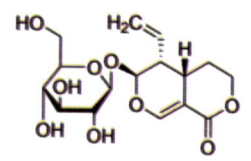   Gentiopicrin ($C_{16}H_{20}O_9$)

Ginkgo biloba

Ginkgo (Tree, Leaves and Fruits)

Latin Binomial	Ginkgo biloba
Family	Ginkgoaceae
English Name	Ginkgo
Urdu Name	Aljunaka/Ginkgo

Medicinal Uses: The leaves of the evergreen Ginkgo biloba tree are useful in treating altitude sickness, cerebral, vascular insufficiency, cognitive disorders, dementia, dizziness and sexual dysfunction. The leaf extract is used in memory loss, vertigo and vasodilator. The Ginkgo leaves and ginseng roots are beneficial in treating geriatric disorders. Studies show that Ginkgo improves arterial function. Several studies noted that these extracts improve walking distance in patients with the peripheral arterial occlusive disease, a condition in which arterial disease in the legs, leads to pain even with minimal exertion.

Traditional Uses: Traditional uses of these leaves include soothing a bladder infection and increasing sexual energy. Ginkgo has recently been introduced in the Unani herbal system into aphrodisiac products. Ginkgo nuts are eaten as a side dish in Japan ever since the Edo Period (1600 – 1867). In traditional Chinese medicine, the Ginkgo leaves are for brain disorders, circulatory disorders and respiratory diseases. Ginkgo nuts are traditionally helpful in getting rid of coughs, sputum, fever, stopping diarrhoea and toothaches, healing skin diseases, gonorrhoea and reducing micturition frequency.

Biological Uses: The non-aqueous fractions of the leaves (methanol, ethanol, ethyl acetate) have antioxidant, anti-inflammatory, hepatoprotective and antibacterial properties. Recently, the leaf extract of Ginkgo biloba has also shown beneficial effects in cancer.

Chemical Constituents: The leaf's extract contains flavonols, flavone glycosides, quercetin, kaempferol lactone derivatives, ginkgolides A, B, C, J, M, bilobalide and sterols.

Distribution: The tree species are native to Southeast Asia but was brought over to the USA in 1784. It has grown primarily in China, France and America.

Note: The male Ginko trees are highly allergenic.

Quercetin ($C_{15}H_{10}O_7$)   Bilobalide ($C_{15}H_{18}O_8$)   Kaempferol ($C_{15}H_{10}O_6$)

Melilotus officinalis

Aklil-ul-Mulik/Aspang (Plant, Seeds and Fruits)

Latin Binomial	Melilotus officinalis/Melilotus indicus
Family	Papilionaceae/Fabaceae
English name	Melilot/Crescent Lignum
Urdu Name	Aklil-Ul-Mulik

Medicinal Uses: The fruit of the flowering Melilotus officinalis plant is aromatic, carminative, demulcent and emollient in action. When applied as a plaster, ointment or poultice, the herb is good at relieving abdominal or rheumatic pain. Internally it is useful in easing flatulence. This plant was formerly used in cleaning the eyes, clearing headaches, healing wounds, ulcers and inflammation. It is also used to increase urine output and is widely used in treating venous issues such as – varicose veins and blood clots in the veins.

Traditional Uses: The Melilot's seeds help to warm up or tone up the various muscles and body organs in Unani and Ayurvedic medicinal systems, when massaged. It resolves the liver, spleen, stomach, uterus and inflammation of the testicles. The fruit is valuable as a demulcent. The plant is beneficial as an aromatic, emollient, demulcent, tonic, aphrodisiac, carminative in relieving flatulence and externally applied as a poultice for pains and aches. The tea of these flowers is useful for treating cold, respiratory disorders and gastrointestinal disorders. It also helps with idiopathic headaches, long-standing neuralgias, tenderness, menstrual colic, ovarian neuralgia and diarrhoea. An infusion is valuable in treating sleeplessness, nervous tension, palpitation and painful congestive menstruation. Externally, it helps treat eye inflammation, rheumatic pains and swollen joints.

An aromatic water (Arq) obtained from the flowering tops is an effective treatment for conjunctivitis (eye infection). The leaves are cooked as a vegetable. The seed forms a constituent of many poly-herbal Unani medicinal preparations like 'Hab-e-Jalinus, Majun Murraweh-Ul-Arwah, Jawarish-e-Zaruni-Ambri,' etc.

Biological Uses: A methanolic extract (plant) possesses an antimicrobial effect. The ethanolic extract shows antioxidant, hypotensive, hepatoprotective and anticoagulant properties. Methanol appears to be a better antitumor agent than ethanol fractions.

Chemical Constituents: The phytochemical analysis shows that Melilotus officinalis contains flavonoid, kaempferol-3-O-glucoside, steroidal glycosides, coumarins, melilotin glycoside, saponins, volatile oils, fats, triterpenes, anthraquinone glycosides, tannin and bis- hydroxycoumarin.

Distribution: Melilotus officinalis, a flowering plant, is native to Eurasia and was introduced in North America, Africa and Australia.

Kaempferol-3-O-glucoside (Dicoumarin)

Morus alba

Shahtut/Tut (Fruits and Leave)

Latin Binomial	Morus alba/Morus indica
Family	Moraceae
English Name	Mulberry
Urdu Name	Shahtut

Medicinal Use: The fruit, root and leaves of this tree are useful medicinally. The fruit of the medium-sized Morus alba tree is an expectorant, laxative, refrigerant in action and nutritive. The fruit juice is a beneficial drink for convalescent and cools the blood, after fevers. The root bark is antiasthmatic, antitussive and sedative.

Traditional Uses: In Unani and Ayurvedic medicinal systems, the fruit is an effective remedy against respiratory tract disorders, particularly as a repercussive. The plant of Morus alba is beneficial for treating dizziness, insomnia and premature ageing. The leaves also help in treating fever, sore throats, headaches and vertigo. An extract of the leaves is suitable when given by injection for elephantiasis (enlargement and hardening of the limbs). The root bark may help toothache, as a gargle, as a mouthwash and as a laxative. The twigs are efficacious in combating excess fluid retention and joint pain.

The tree bark has a purgative and a vermifuge effect on the body. The bark is also an expectorant, encouraging the loosening up of catarrh and is helpful in the treatment of cough. The syrup of the Mulberry (black) is esteemed for its beneficial effects on a sore throat, resolving pharynx and larynx inflammations. The fruit is also useful in preventing premature greying of the hair.

Mulberry has had all parts of it used in Traditional Chinese medicine for various purposes and recently, evidence of Morus alba, regarding its anti-diabetic properties has been recognised. In Brazil, the fruit is used for fever, lowering cholesterol, blood pressure and liver protection. A decoction of the leaves is also useful for sweating feet, dropsy and intestinal disorders.

The famous Unani medicine 'Sharbat-e-Toot-Siayah' contains Morus alba as an ingredient. It is a valuable remedy in chest congestion, effective for inflammation and pain in the throat. It also improves the voice pitch and acts as a febrifuge.

The Mulberry fruits and leaves are marketed as 'superfoods' on the European market because of their high antioxidant activity and vitamin and mineral content. The fruit is made into wine and jam.

Biological Uses: The plant contains many natural polyphenols and flavonoids, which have potential antioxidant, antimicrobial, anti-inflammatory, anti-cancer, antibacterial, anxiolytic and hepatoprotective properties. The aqueous-methanolic fraction of the root bark of the Mulberry plant is antidiabetic in nature due to the presence of a new glycoprotein (Moran 20K).

The non-aqueous fraction of Mulberry leaf or root barks exhibits free radical scavenging and antioxidant activities, thus benefiting depigmentation. The leaf extracts of the plant are useful in stopping atherosclerosis. The anti-cancer property of the plant may be due to the presence of 'albanol B' (a member of benzofurans).

Chemical Constituents: Compared to the stems and fruits, the leaves contain more phenolic compounds, flavonoids like kuwanons, sangennons-N, mulberroside mulberofurans, kuwanone G (is a tetrahydroxyflavone), moralbanone, glucosides and essential oils. The leaves are a good source of ascorbic acid, and they also contain vitamin B_1, B_9, D, carotene and leucovorin or folinic acid (5-formyl tetrahydrofolic acid).

Distribution: The Morus alba species is native to northern China, Pakistan, India and are widely cultivated and naturalized elsewhere in the United States, Mexico, Australia, Kyrgyzstan, Argentina, Turkey, Iran, etc.

Note: Its wood is valued for manufacturing sports goods due to its durability and elasticity. It is used mainly for tennis and badminton racquets and hockey sticks.

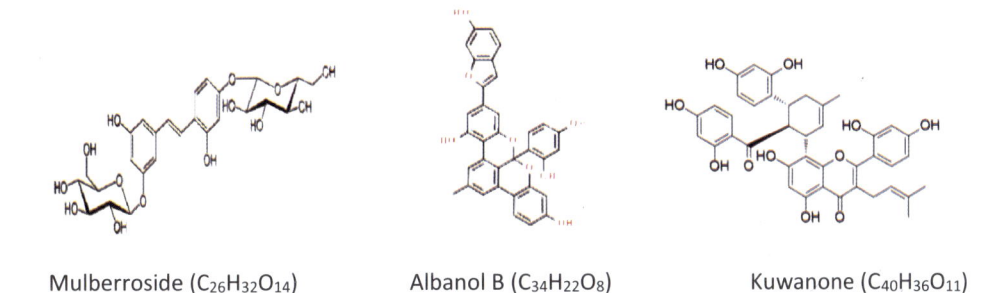

Mulberroside ($C_{26}H_{32}O_{14}$)   Albanol B ($C_{34}H_{22}O_8$)   Kuwanone ($C_{40}H_{36}O_{11}$)

Picrorhiza kurroa

Kuthi (Plant and Roots)

Latin Binomial   Picrorhiza kurrooa

Family	Scrophulariaceae
English Name	Picrorhiza
Urdu Name	Kuthi

Medicinal Uses: The root of Picrorhiza kurroa is antibilious (anti-nausea and vomiting), digestive, hepatoprotective, bitter and antispasmodic in action. In Modern herbal medicine, it is considered beneficial for immune-related diseases. The powdered root along or with 'neem' (Azadirachta indica of the Meliaceae family) bark proves as an effective antiperiodic. Picrorhiza kurroa is proved to be hepatoprotective, immunomodulatory and anti-inflammatory.

Traditional Uses: In Unani and Ayurvedic medicinal systems, the rhizome (root) is useful in skin disorders that cause white patches developing on the skin (vitiligo). The rhizome has hepatoprotective properties and thus supports the liver and spleen. The plant is beneficial in liver damage forms-cirrhosis and liver inflammation. It protects the liver against damage from the hepatitis C virus. The plant is also suitable for gastrointestinal problems such as acidity, diarrhoea and appetite stimulants.

In Nepal, Iran and Bhutan, the rhizome is considered an important medicinal plant for asthma, jaundice, malaria, snake bites and liver disorders. It helps other herbs in Chinese traditional medicine in treating dysentery and jaundice.

In Unani medicine, a preparation containing Picrorhiza known as 'Majun-e-Murraweh-Ul-Arwah' is suitable for treating tremors, tetanus, gout, strengthening nerves, and improving memory.

Biological Uses: The ethanol-water (95:5) leaf extract of the plant exhibits antioxidant property. The dichloromethane fraction of the plant shows efficient anticancer activity and may be recommended in exploring cancer therapy. The ethanolic extract of the plant's root reveals antiasthmatic activity.

Chemical Uses: The root contains 'bitter alkaloids' (kutkin), a mixture of two molecules, the iridoid glycosides known as picroside-I or kutkoside and picroside- II. Other bioactive ingredients present in the plant are apocynin, androsin and cucurbitacin glycosides.

Distribution: Picrorhiza kurrooa plant is native to Nepal and is also found in Pakistan, China, India, Nepal and Bhutan.

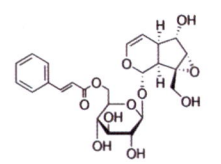

Picroside I ($C_{24}H_{28}O_{11}$) 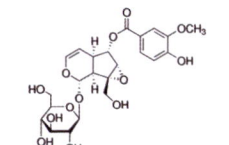   Picroside II ($C_{23}H_{28}O_{13}$)   Kutkin ($C_{23}H_{28}O_{12}$)

Polygonum bistorta

Anjbar (Plant Parts, Leaves and Rhizomes)

Latin Binomial	Polygonum bistorta/ Polygonum viviparum
Family	Polygonaceae
English Name	Bistorta
Urdu Name	Anjbar

Medicinal Uses: The rhizome of the flowering Polygonum bistorta plant is astringent, digestive, anti-haemorrhagic and antibilious in action and a tonic for the stomach and intestine. In modern herbal, it is mainly valuable for external bleeding and haemorrhage from the lungs or stomach. It can be beneficial in treating diarrhoea, dysentery, cholera and bowel complaints. The Bistorta is vital in alleviating diabetes and as a mouthwash or gargle to 'fasten loose teeth' and heal gum problems.

Traditional Uses: In Unani and Ayurvedic medicinal systems, the rhizome is suitable in stopping internal bleeding. A decoction of the rhizome is used in gleets and leucorrhoea; like in modern herbal, it is used as an excellent gargle to relax the sore throat, spongy gums and as an effective lotion for ulcers. The rhizome, with another herb gentian (Gentiana Verna), is useful in malaria and lithiasis (stone formation). As an antibilious, it is helpful in nausea and vomiting. Externally, it makes a good wash for minor burns and wounds and treats pharyngitis, stomatitis, vaginal discharge and anal fissure, etc. The seeds have diuretic action. It helps stop bleeding in traditional Iranian medicine, especially in the chest and lung. In China, it is beneficial in treating carbuncle, dysentery, haemorrhoids, snake bites and respiratory disorders. The Polygonum plant root forms a constituent of famous Unani poly-herbal medicinal anti-dysenteric preparation known as 'Sherbat-e-Anjbar.

Biological Uses: The ethanolic extract of Bistort has good antifungal activity against the tested fungal strains as compared to the methanolic extract. However, a methanol-aqueous extract of the root possesses anti-cancer properties.

Chemical Uses: The plant is a rich source of Tannins. Polygonum bistorta also contains important biologically active constituents such as flavonol glycosides, rutin, hyperfine, Isoquercitrin, luteolin, rientin, apigenin and Isovitexin. The rhizome contains essential oils.

Distribution: Bistorta species are native throughout much of the Northern Hemisphere, as far South as Mexico in North America and Thailand, in Pakistan, Iran, Iraq and India.

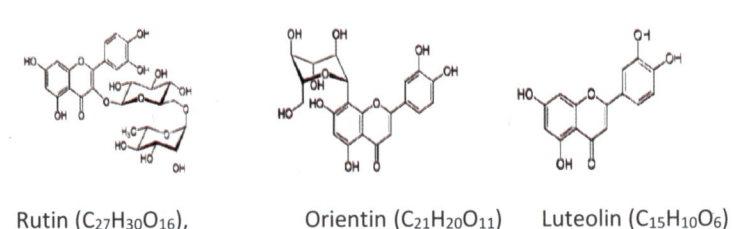

Rutin ($C_{27}H_{30}O_{16}$),   Orientin ($C_{21}H_{20}O_{11}$)   Luteolin ($C_{15}H_{10}O_6$)

Prunus amara

Badam Talkh (Garden and Seeds)

Latin Binomial	Prunus amara/Amygdalus communis
Family	Rosaceae
English Name	Bitter Almond
Urdu Name	Badam Talkh

Medicinal Uses: The fruit (seed) of Prunus amara tree is demulcent, mild laxative, stimulant in action and a nervine tonic. In addition to the fixed oil, Bitter almonds also yield on distillation, an essential oil containing 4 to 7 per cent of Prussic acid, 'hydrogen cyanide' (HCN). The bitter almond oil is helpful for a variety of health benefits. It helps muscle spasms, bacterial infections, fungal infections, pain, digestive issues and coughs.

Traditional Uses: The ancient Romans used bitter almond to get rid of intestinal parasites and intermittent fevers. In the middle Ages, people turned to bitter almond oil as a laxative and diuretic.

The fruit is a remedy for cough. In the traditional Mexican system, bitter almond is valuable as an alternative cancer treatment. In Chinese traditional medicine, it helps clear the phlegm and stops dyspnea (shortness of breath). It is also used as an expectorant.

In Germany, bitter almonds are sold in pharmacies and are an ingredient in Christmas fruitcake. In other parts of Europe, bitter almonds help make marzipan (confection). The Chinese consider it a symbol of enduring sadness and female beauty (not sure whether it is sweet or bitter almond).

Biological Uses: Almond aqueous and non-aqueous fractions have antioxidant, anti-inflammatory, antimicrobial, antiviral, hepatoprotective, antinociceptive activities and antimutagenic, inhibitory properties against several enzymes.

Chemical Constituents: The bitter almond contains a colourless, crystalline cyanogenetic glycoside, 'amygdalin,' fixed oil, flavonoids, tannins, terpenoids etc.

Distribution: Bitter almonds are native to Asia and the Middle East but can grow in the United States and the trees are used ornamentally in landscaping. In the U.S. A., only the nuts cannot be sold. It is mainly produced in the Hubei province in China.

Amygdalin ($C_{20}H_{27}NO_{11}$) classified as Cyanogenic Glycoside

Prunus armeniaca

Khubani (Flowers, Fruits and Seeds)

Latin Binomial	Prunus armeniaca
Family	Rosaceae
English Name	Apricot
Urdu Name	Khubani

Medicinal Uses: The fresh and dried fruit of Prunus armeniaca tree is demulcent, laxative, digestive and antibilious in action and is a nutrient. The fruit is nutritious, cleansing and mildly laxative. They are a valuable addition to the diet, working gently to improve overall health. The salted fruit is anti-inflammatory and antiseptic.

Traditional Uses: It is used medicinally in Vietnam to treat respiratory and digestive diseases. The decoction of the leaf is effective, in intestinal worms. The bark is astringent. The inner bark and/or the root are useful for treating poisoning caused by eating bitter almond and apricot seeds (hydrogen cyanide). One report says that a decoction of the outer bark helps neutralize hydrogen cyanide effects.

The decoction is also beneficial in soothing inflamed and irritated skin conditions. It helps treat asthma, coughs, acute or chronic bronchitis and constipation. Kernel paste is used to heal vaginal infections.

Biological Uses: The methanol extracts of powdered kernels possess higher antioxidant activity than methanol-aqueous extract. The latter extract, however, exhibits suitable antibacterial property. Cyanogenic glycosides (mainly amygdalin) in seeds are reported to be used as a medicament for cancer treatment.

Prunus armeniaca also show antitubercular, antimutagenic, cardioprotective, anti-inflammatory and antinociceptive activity.

Chemical Constituents: The plant contains cyanogenic glycoside amygdalin, norisoprenoids, terpenoids, phenols, essential oils, vitamins (A, C and E) and minerals (potassium, phosphorus, calcium, manganese and zinc).

Distribution: Prunus armeniaca tree is native to Asia. It is hugely popular in the Middle Eastern countries; Turkey and Iran are the world's largest fruit producers of apricots. In Pakistan, Apricot is being grown in Baluchistan province and Chitral, Swat, the KPK, Potohar and Murree Hills in the Punjab and Gilgit and in Chilas Baltistan.

Note: The oil contains olein and the glyceride of linoleic acid and it is substituted for the oil of almond in cosmetics because of its lower cost. It has a softening action on the skin. The flowers are tonic, promoting fecundity in women.

Prunus serotina

Cherry (Fruits, Leaf and Bark)

Latin Binomial	Prunus serotina/Prunus laurocerasus
Family	Rosaceae
English Name	Wild Cherry Bark
Urdu Name	Nibat Alkarz/Cherry

Medicinal Uses: The leaves and bark of Prunus serotina tree are useful for medicinal purposes. The tree of Prunus serotina is beneficial in coughs as an expectorant, is a sedative and a flavouring agent.

Traditional Uses: The leaves help produce distilled water, which is the principal herbal preparation made for this herb. It is good against coughs, dyspepsia, indigestion, whooping cough and asthma. The branches or the root's inner bark is dried and used in tea or extracted in syrup or tincture. The plant's cooling and anti-inflammatory actions help inflammatory conditions such as acute and chronic sinus inflammation and allergies.

As a bronchodilator, a decoction of the plant with other herbs helps relieve asthma. The cooling and anti-inflammatory action of the wild cherry is also recommended as an external wash for sores, ulcers, herpes and shingles. The Cherry Bark has properties that make the hair smooth and silky.

Biological Uses: The ethanol extract of this plant presents the most antioxidant activity as compared to methanol and acetone fractions. The methanol extract prepared from the bark of this tree exhibits anti-proliferative, anti-diabetic, antimicrobial activity. The plant has a potent anti-inflammatory and analgesic potential. The presence of essential oil in fruit, stems, leaves and the bark has antibacterial and antifungal properties.

Chemical Constituents: The active constituents in wild Cherry include cyanogenic-glycosides (prunasin and amygdalin), flavonoids, benzaldehyde, volatile oils, plant acids, tannins, calcium, potassium, magnesium, iron, vitamins (tocopherols and ascorbic acid) and carbohydrates.

Distribution: The species is widespread in North America and South America. In Pakistan, cherry cultivation is being done successfully in temperate zones, including Quetta, Pishin, Ziarat, Kalat, Zhob Mastung, Loralai, Swat and Murree.

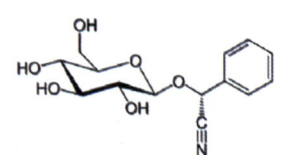

Prunasin ($C_{14}H_{17}NO_6$) 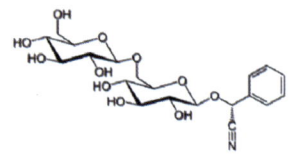   Amygdalin ($C_{20}H_{27}NO_{11}$)

Psoralea corylifolia

Babchi (Plant Flower and Seeds)

Latin Binomial	Psoralea corylifolia
Family	Leguminosae/Papilionaceae
English Name	Psoralea
Urdu Name	Babchi

Medicinal Uses: The seeds of flowering Psoralea corylifolia are laxative, anthelmintic, carminative and detersive in action and are a stomach tonic. These medicinal usages are reported in the Indian pharmaceutical codex, the British and the American pharmacopoeias.

Traditional Uses: Psoralea is a popular herb, which has long since been useful in traditional Ayurvedic, Unani and Chinese medicinal systems for its magical effects in curing various skin diseases. The most incredible aspect of this plant is that every part of it is valuable. The roots, stems, leaves, seeds and whatever blooms it has, are all used to treat various skin problems, such as leucoderma, skin rashes, infections, etc. The seed, root and leaves of Psoralea help treat skin conditions such as vitiligo, minor skin diseases, poisoning, conception, caries, deafness, filarial (a parasitic infection) and it is also wound rejuvenative. The seed oil is suitable in treating skin ailments like dermatitis, eczema, boils, scabies, leucoderma and ringworm. This plant has aphrodisiac properties that help alleviate reproductive problems in both men and women.

A famous poly-herbal Unani product known as 'Safuf-e-Bars' is an effective remedy for leucoderma, as it contains Psoralia as one of the ingredients. The seeds are a well-known blood purifier of Unani medicine.

Psoralea corylifolia is an ancient remedy for leucoderma. It has been used extensively not only by the practitioners (Hakims and Ayurveda) of the Indo-Pak subcontinent but by the Western system's followers as well. In Chinese traditional medicine, it helps in upgrading this plant's general vitality and that of its fruit, as a tonic for genital organs. The seeds of the plant are used as a famous traditional Chinese medicine, showing effects on kidney-related issues, impotence, warming the spleen and stopping diarrhoea and is included in the Pharmacopoeia of the People's Republic of China.

Biological Uses: The oil of Psoralea also has astringent, antibacterial, antimicrobial and antiseptic properties that treat weak gums, plaque and bad breath. This plant is also pharmacologically studied for its chemoprotective, antioxidant and anti-inflammatory properties.

Chemical Uses: The seeds contain coumarins glycosides (psoralidin, psoralen, isopsoralen and angelicin), flavonoids and triterpenoids, sesquiterpenoids, phenols and steroids. The seeds' chief active principal is an essential oil, fixed oil, and resin and it also occurs in large quantities, but these are not pharmacologically active substances.

Distribution: Psoralea corylifolia, a flowering plant, is native to the Indo-Pak subcontinent and Sri Lanka and is occasionally cultivated in Arabia for its medicinal properties.

Psoralidin ($C_{20}H_{16}O_5$)   Angelicin ($C_{11}H_6O_3$)

Rhamnus purshiana

Cascara-ke-Chaal (Plant, Leaves and Barks)

Latin Binomial	Rhamnus purshiana/Frangula purshiana
Family	Rhamnaceae
English name	Cascara/Chittem Bark
Urdu Name	Kasikarana/Post Cascara

Medicinal Uses: The bark of the large Rhamnus purshiana shrub primarily helps chronic constipation, dyspepsia, digestive complaints and treatment of piles. The bark also has tonic properties and is used as a laxative; it is taken internally to treat haemorrhoids, liver problems and jaundice.

Traditional Uses: The dried bark of Rhamnus purshiana was first used in conventional American medicine in 1877, after being introduced as a laxative by Mexican and Spanish priests in California. The Anglo-Saxons described it as a European counterpart (Rhamnus frangula) and the berries were mentioned in the 1650 London Pharmacopoeia.

Cascara is a non-prescription laxative. Since removing phenolphthalein from the US market in 1998, Cascara has replaced phenolphthalein in several laxative products.

Recently, in Europe, the Committee of Herbal Medicine adopted Herbal preparations equivalent to 10 - 30 mg hydroxyanthracene derivatives, calculated as cascaroside A, to be taken once, at night, to produce a comfortable soft-formed motion.

Products containing Cascara include concentrated 'milk of magnesia-Cascara,' 'Kondremul' (mineral oil preparation) and brown, rounded, film-coated Cascara natural laxative tablets.

Aloe-emodin, a constituent in Cascara, has been reported to have antiviral activity *in vitro*. Cascara may also be beneficial in the treatment of liver disorders. Studies by Chinese scientists found that glycoside emodin reduced fibrosis in rats' livers.

The German Commission of E-Monographs, a therapeutic guide to herbal medicine, approves Rhamnus purshiana for use in constipation. The Cascara bark is seldom used in Unani medicines.

Biological Uses: The Cascara bark extract has antibacterial, anti-inflammatory, analgesic, antioxidant, hepatoprotective and antimicrobial activities.

Chemical Constituents: Cascara contains about 6 to 10 per cent anthracene derivatives present both as normal O-glycosides and C-glycosides, free anthraquinones, e.g., cascarosides A, B, C and D, and two important aloins, barbaloin and chrysalion have also been identified. The plant also contains terpenoids, flavonoids, cardenolides, saponins, odorous volatile oil, malic and tannic acids. Steroids were also detected in the bark of the plant. The fresh Cascara bark contains anthranol derivatives, have griping and emetic properties. After storage for one year, anthranol derivatives are oxidized to anthraquinone derivatives and the bark loses its irritant properties.

Distribution: The plant is indigenous to the western part of North America and is also cultivated in Canada and Eastern Africa.

Note: Taking Cascara sagrada may lower blood potassium levels. Excessive use of this plant can cause bloody diarrhoea, vomiting, inability to urinate (acute urine retention), loss of energy, depression and confusion.

Aloin/Barbaloin ($C_{21}H_{22}O_9$)   Cascarosides-A ($C_{27}H_{32}O_{14}$)

Rheum emodi

Rewand Chini (Plant and Fresh/Dried Rhizomes)

Latin Binomial	Rheum emodi/Rheum officinale
Family	Polygonaceae
English Name	Rhubarb
Urdu Name	Rewand Chini

Medicinal Uses: The rhizome of the flowering Rheum emodi plant is stomachic, tonic, aperients, astringent and purgative in action. It has a mild purgative effect and is particularly useful for stomach trouble in infants and bowel looseness. A decoction of this plant's seeds helps ease stomach pain and increase appetite. The root of the Rhubarb is beneficial in removing freckles, nevus anemicus (a congenital disorder), moles and spots. The Rhubarb is also a great source of vitamin K_1, which is essential for blood clotting and bone health.

Traditional Uses: In Unani and Ayurvedic medicinal systems, Indian rhubarb is useful as a purgative and astringent tonic. Its primary action is mild purgation. However, it also has an astringent property, so it has a secondary effect in confining the bowels. Hence it is well fitted for use in simple diarrhoea, but not for constipation or any affection in which a continuous aperient action is necessary. It is a proper remedy for the ailments of children. Combined with ginger, it is valuable in tablet form when the bowels are sluggish.

The rhizome is regarded as a panacea in local home remedies and helps with stomach problems, cuts, wounds, muscular swelling, tonsillitis and mumps. Some people chew the rhizome, which is a good way of taking it.

The powdered rhizomes of this plant are used for cleaning teeth and are sprinkled over ulcers, for quick healing and brings about a significant decrease in menstrual pain (in single-blind, standard controlled trials).

Biological Uses: The extracts (aqueous and methanol) of the rhizome possess antibacterial, antifungal, antioxidant and anti-proliferative properties. The ethyl acetate extract of the rhizome has exhibited immune-enhancing activity.

Chemical Constituents: The rhizomes of Rhubarb have anthraquinone glycosides such as emodin, aloe-emodin, rhein and chrysophanol glycosides. The antioxidants in rhubarb include anthocyanins and are responsible for their red colour and also provide health benefits. Rhubarb is also high in proanthocyanidins and is also known as condensed tannins.

Distribution: Rhubarb is native to Central Asia and widely is distributed in China, Pakistan, India, Nepal, Myanmar and Bhutan.

Note: In large doses and long-term use of Rhubarb can cause side effects such as stomach and intestinal pain, watery diarrhoea, and uterine contractions.

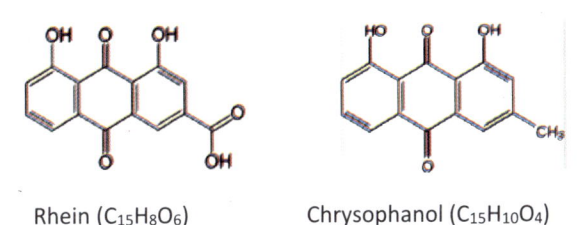

Rhein ($C_{15}H_8O_6$)

Chrysophanol ($C_{15}H_{10}O_4$)

Proanthocyanidins (Oligomeric flavonoids)

Rubia cordifolia

Majith (Stems and Roots)

Latin Binomial	Rubia cordifolia
Family	Rubiaceae
English Name	Madder
Urdu Name	Majith

Medicinal Uses: The root and stems are the active parts of the plant. The root of the flowering, evergreen Rubia cordifolia plant is anodyne, antitussive, astringent, diuretic, emmenagogue and styptic in action.

Traditional Uses: In Unani and Ayurvedic medicinal systems, Rubia cordifolia helps in treating joint pain, arthritis, dysmenorrhea, diabetes, discolouration of the skin and jaundice. The roots are beneficial internally, in treating abnormal uterine bleeding, internal and external haemorrhage, bronchitis, rheumatism, kidney stones and dysentery.

The plant is helpful in the treatment of blood disorders. Powdered dried roots and fruit are taken internally to treat the spleen and skin diseases.

Many traditional healers of the Indo-Pak subcontinent considered this plant valuable in tuberculosis, intestinal ulcers, liver diseases and jaundice. A decoction of the leaves and stems is beneficial as a vermifuge. The roots are used to lower blood pressure.

Rubia cordifolia is an essential ingredient of Unani poly-herbal medicinal preparation known as 'Majun-Dabidul-Ward. It is beneficial in hepatitis and liver diseases.

Apart from its medicinal value, this plant is also being valued as a natural food colourant and natural hair dye.

Biological Uses: Scientific studies show that the Rubiaceae family's anthraquinones exhibit some interesting *in vivo* biological activities, like antimicrobial, antifungal, analgesic, antimalarial, antioxidant and anti-leukemic. They also have an antibacterial action, inhibiting Staphylococcus aureus, S. Epidermidis and Pneumococci.

Chemical Constituents: Rubia cordifolia plant is known for its anthraquinones and naphtha-hydroquinones, phytochemical constituents. The significant phytoconstituents of Rubia cordifolia are rubiadin, rubicordone-A, rubiasins (new anthracene derivatives), iridoid glycosides and an essential ingredient quinine.

Distribution: The plant is native to Southern Europe, Africa and Asia (Pakistan, India, Afghanistan and China). In Pakistan, it is growing wild in northern hilly areas.

Rubiadin 'a dihydroxyanthraquinone' ($C_{15}H_{10}O_4$)

Ruta graveolens

Sadab (Plant, Flowers and Leaves)

Latin Binomial   Ruta graveolens

Family	Rutaceae
English Name	Rue
Urdu Name	Sadab

Medicinal Uses: The leaves of the strongly odoriferous, evergreen Ruta graveolens shrub are aromatic, stimulant, antispasmodic, emmenagogue, irritant and rubefacient in action. They are useful in treating coughs, croup (a type of respiratory infection), colic and flatulence. An infusion is also beneficial for nervous indigestion, heart palpitations and headache. In addition, the chemical 'rutin' in the plant strengthens weak blood vessels and aids in the treatment of varicose veins.

Traditional Uses: In Chinese medicine, Rue is valuable in insect and snake bites. When made into an ointment, it is effective in gouty and rheumatic pains, sprains, bruised tendons and chilblains. When a fresh leaf is chewed, it quickly flavours the mouth and relieves headache, giddiness, or hysterical spasm. Ruta graveolens is a potent herb and the dose administered should be kept low.

In Unani and Ayurvedic medicinal systems, a decoction of Rue, when used as an enema, relieves colitis, flatulence and flatulent colitis.

The leaves are analgesic and useful in chest pain caused by pneumonia and pleurisy. It is also helpful in dyspnoea, sciatica, gout, arthritis and flatulent colic. Externally, this herb and honey are a good treatment for paralysis, tremors, joint pain and nerve disorders.

The local application of the paste of Rue leaves, on the abdomen, is effective in dropsy. The herb is helpful in kidney and urinary bladder disorders and helps regulate these functions. It also relieves back and chest pain. The essential oil has a depressing effect on the central nervous system.

Biological Uses: The Rue leaves are not suitable in pregnancy as bioactive constituents in the plant may stimulate the uterus and vigorously promote menstrual bleeding. The Rue plant extract has antibacterial, analgesic, anti-inflammatory and anti-diabetic activities. The plant's essential oil, also known as 'Rue oil,' is antiseptic and antibacterial in nature.

Chemical Uses: The plant contains flavonol glycosides, rutin, quercetin, psoralen, methoxypsoralen (methoxsalen). The plant is rich in powerful biologically active ingredients such as acridone alkaloids (graveoline and graveolinine), coumarins, essential oils, terpenoids, flavonoids, tannins, etc., saponins. In addition, the leaves are a rich source of volatile oil.

Distribution: It is native to the Mediterranean region and is also grown worldwide. It is also cultivated as a medicinal herb, as a condiment and as an insect repellent, to a lesser extent.

Rutin ($C_{27}H_{30}O_{16}$)   Quercetin ($C_{15}H_{10}O_7$)   Graveoline ($C_{17}H_{13}NO_3$)   Methoxsalen ($C_{12}H_8O_4$)

Salix purpurea

Bed Mushk (Barks, Leaves and Flowers)

Latin Binomial	Salix purpurea/Salix aegyptiaca
Family	Salicaceae
English Name	Willow/Willow Barks
Urdu Name	Bed Mushk

Medicinal Uses: The bark of Salix purpurea is an analgesic due to 'salicin,' to an alcoholic glycoside beneficial for heart and brain tonics. In addition, it is astringent, diaphoretic, diuretic, hypnotic and a sedative. The leaves can be harvested throughout the growing season and used fresh or dried. The twigs help in the treatment of cancer, dysentery and ulcers.

Traditional Uses: In traditional medicine, it is useful as an aphrodisiac, sexual sedative, diuretic, astringent and as a general tonic. An extract of fresh leaves is effective against bloody diarrhoea. It also provides temporary pain relief. The leaves are suitable internally in treating minor feverish illnesses and colic, cancerous sores and chronic dysentery.

Biological Uses: The bark is anti-inflammatory, antioxidant and an antiseptic. The non-aqueous extracts of the plant have antibacterial properties. The antifungal activity is also evaluated against Candida guilliermondii, C. glabrata, C. parapsilosis and Fusarium oxysporum. Various non-aqueous fractions of the plant (petroleum ether, ether and chloroform) possess anti-cancer properties.

Chemical Constituents: The plant contains flavonol glycosides, e.g., epicatechin, rutin, quercetin, naringenin, chlorogenic, coumaric, volatile oils, flavonoids, terpenoids, rosmarinic and caffeic acid. It is a rich source of 'salicin,' of suitable for making aspirin.

Distribution: It is native to Europe and Northern Africa, east to temperate central Asia and Japan. One of the species of this plant, which is comparatively rich in tannins, is also mentioned in the chapter 'Plant containing Tannins.'

Note: The Willow bark is included in the Polish Pharmacopeia and the European monograph as a constituent of many herbal drugs, dietary supplements and weight loss enhancement remedies. The stems are very tough and flexible and are used in basket making.

Smilax glabra

Chob Chini (Plant, Roots and Leaves)

Latin Binomial	Smilax glabra/Smilax china
Family	Liliaceae/Smilacaceae
English Name	China Root
Urdu Name	Chob Chini

Medicinal Uses: The root of the climbing Smilax glabra plant is demulcent, diaphoretic, carminative in action and a tonic for vital organs. Its root is valued in cancer treatment, mercury poisoning, rheumatoid arthritis and syphilis. It is said to be 90 per cent effective in treating primary syphilis. The aerial tubers help in treating abscesses, boils, cystitis, diarrhoea etc.

Traditional Uses: in Unani and Ayurvedic medicinal systems, Smilax glabra is beneficial in treating old syphilitic cases. It helps certain skin diseases, including psoriasis, rheumatoid arthritis, gout, enteritis, urinary tract infections and skin ulcers. This plant is frequently useful as a blood purifier. The plant is also helpful as a cardiac tonic for digestive problems and liver disorders. The root is boiled in milk and administered orally to relieve rheumatism, gout and epilepsy. The root is also favourable as a diuretic; it improves urine frequency and volume. Externally, it is helpful in treating various skin-related disorders like psoriasis and eczema.

In Traditional Chinese Medicine, Smilax glabra roots belong to the Herbs that clear the heat and relieve toxicity. It is extensively suitable for clinical treatment of syphilis, acute bacillary dysentery, chronic nephritis and as an antitumor.

The root of Smilax glabra forms a constituent of Unani poly-herbal blood purifier medicinal preparations like 'Majun-e-Chobchini, Majun-e-Ushab and Arq-e-Chob-chini.'

Biological Uses: All extracts (methanol, ethanol and acetone) of the plant's leaf exhibited antioxidant, anti-inflammatory and antimicrobial activities. The plant also has antiproliferative, anti-hepatocarcinogenic and anti-cancer activities. Thirty biologically active constituents of the root of Smilax glabra were tested for their antimicrobial activity. The result showed that seventeen of these compounds have antimicrobial activity against gram-positive bacteria. Ten compounds displayed activity against the tested fungus, while eight compounds were antibacterial against gram-negative bacteria.

Chemical Constituents: It contains flavonoid glycosides, e.g., astilbin, neoastilbin, isoastibin and neoastibin (phenylpropanoid-glycoside), steroidal saponins, alkaloids, resin and gum. Phenolic compounds present in the plant are smiglabrone, smilachromanone, smiglastilbene, smiglactone, etc. The astringent property of this plant is due to the presence of tannins. A novel heteropolysaccharide with great immunomodulatory activity was isolated from the root of Smilax glabra by hot water extraction.

Distribution: Smilax china is native to China, the Himalayas and Indo-China.

Strophanthus hispidus

Kombe (Flower and Seeds)

Latin Binomial	Strophanthus hispidus
Family	Apocynaceae
English Name	Strophanthus
Urdu Name	Kombe

Medicinal Uses: The seeds of Strophanthus hispidus are a cardiac tonic. The plant influences the circulatory system. It is useful in chronic heart weakness, muscular debility of the heart and cardiac pains with difficult or laboured breathing. It acts in the same way as Digitalis (Digitalis purpurea of the Plantaginaceae family) but with increased digestive disturbance. Additionally, Strophanthus does not have a cumulative poisoning effect. The seeds have diuretic powers and are beneficial in dropsy, particularly heart problems. In urgent cases, the intravenous injection of strophanthus can increase circulation. The seed strength and power are highly variable and the seeds are so greatly poisonous that they can be taken as an arrow poison.

More recently, it has come to modern medicine's attention as a source of cardioactive glycosides, extracted from the seeds and used as a heart stimulant and for their influence on blood circulation, especially in cases of chronic heart weakness. A decoction of the bark or leaf sap is beneficial as an antidote against the effects of snakebites. The leaves are valuable internally in treating parasites, malaria, dysentery and gonorrhoea. A root decoction treats rheumatic afflictions. Externally, the root decoction is applied to treat skin diseases, leprosy and ulcers.

The British Pharmacopeia mentioned two preparations of this essential and valuable drug, a dry extract and a tincture.

Traditional Uses: Although poisonous, this plant has a long traditional history of medical use in Africa. The latex and seeds are arrow poisons. Decoctions of the root, stem and seeds are beneficial in treating leprosy, malaria, dysentery, ulcer, inflammation and other sexually transmitted diseases. The plant is seldom used in Unani and Ayurvedic systems of medicine. This plant is mentioned in the Homoeopathic Materia Medica.

Biological Uses: The extract (ethanol 90 per cent) exhibits antioxidant and anti-inflammatory properties. The antioxidant properties of this plant are due to the kombic acid. The root and leaf extracts are potent sources of anti-diabetic activity. The ethanol extract of the root possesses antinociceptive and antiulcerogenic activities. These properties justify using the extract in folklore medicine, in treating ulcers and rheumatic afflictions. The chloroform and ethanol extracts have hypoglycemic activities.

Chemical Constituents: The seeds have the highest concentration of cardiac glycoside (4.8 per cent), whereas the leaves, fruit and juice of the plants contain approximately 0.07, 0.0 and 0.036 per cent of glycoside respectively. Strophanthus contains a mixture of glycosides called K-strophanthin. The plant also contains flavonoids, alkaloids, saponins, resin, fixed oil, choline, trigonelline and kombic acid, an acid saponin.

Distribution: Strophanthus hispidus is native to west tropical Africa, and east, to Tanzania and South to Angola. It is naturalized in China.

Strophanthidin ($C_{23}H_{32}O_6$)   Trigonelline ($C_7H_7NO_2$)   Kombic Acid ($C_{27}H_{38}O_4$)

Swertia chirata

Chiraith (Leaves, Dried Plant and Flowers)

Latin Binomial	Swertia chirata
Family	Gentianaceae
English Name	Chirata
Urdu Name	Chiraita

Medicinal Uses: All above the ground parts of this plant are valuable for medicinal purposes. The flowering plant of Swertia chirata is bitter, antiseptic, febrifuge, diuretic, a blood purifier and aphrodisiac in action.

Traditional Uses: This plant is regarded by the traditional healers of the Indo-Pak subcontinent as a blood purifier and thus effective as an infusion in syphilis, gonorrhoea, itching, scabies, inflammation and ulcers. A decoction and a plant infusion are effective in chronic fevers with other suitable herbs. The herb's bitterness stimulates saliva and gastric juices, which helps stop nausea, bloating, indigestion and hiccups. It is also used for fever and in ridding the body of parasites.

The plant is a tonic for the heart and liver and can help relieve sciatica, cough, scanty urine and melancholia. The Chirata is helpful as a preventative measure for malaria during epidemics. It is suitable as a tonic for people convalescing from a long illness. The plant helps treat piles and provides relief from symptoms like itching, soreness and swelling around the anus.

Swertia chirata is commonly known as a bitter tonic in the traditional medicinal system (Unani and Ayurvedic) in treating fever, loss of appetite, digestive disorders, diabetes, skin and other diseases. The whole plant's decoction can cure malaria, liver disorders, dyspepsia, diarrhoea and intestinal worms. The plant paste is applied to treat skin diseases such as eczema and pimples.

The whole plant forms a constituent of many Unani poly-herbal medicinal preparations such as 'Arq-Murakkab-Musaffi-Khun, Majun-e-Juzam, Jawarish-e-Jalinus and Jawarish Zaruni Ambari.'

In traditional Iranian medicine, the plant is useful as a bitter tonic for stomach and skin disorders. In addition, its medicinal usage is well-documented in the Indian pharmaceutical codex, the British (PB) and the United States Pharmacopoeias (USP).

Biological Uses: The plant extracts (aqueous, ethanol, methanol and 70 per cent ethanol) have antibacterial, antifungus, antiviral, antiulcer, anti-cancer, antioxidant, antileishmanial *(*destroying protozoa) and anti-inflammatory activities. The ethanolic extract of the stem also has antibacterial properties. The aqueous extract of leaves is also an antioxidant.

Chemical Constituents: The most acerbic substance found is a secoiridoid bitter glycoside (swertiamarin, mangiferin and amarogentin). It doesn't taste delightful even at a dilution of 1:58,000,000 and can be procured from Swertia chirata.

The plant also contains important biologically active ingredients such as flavonoids, glycosides, steroids, alkaloids, iridoids, triterpenoids, saponins and volatile oils.

Distribution: Swertia chirata is indigenous to the temperate Himalayas, Nepal, Bhutan, Pakistan (Galyat region of Khyber Pakhtunkhwa) and India.

Swertiamarin ($C_{16}H_{22}O_{10}$)   Amarogentin ($C_{29}H_{30}O_{13}$)   Mangiferin ($C_{19}H_{18}O_{11}$)

Symplocos racemosa

Lodh Pathani (Barks)

Latin Binomial	Symplocos racemosa/Symplocos chinensis
Family	Symplocaceae/Styracaceae
English Name	Lodh Tree
Urdu Name	Lodh Pathani

Medicinal Uses: The bark of the flowering Symplocos racemosa tree is antipyretic, antidiarrhoeal, anti-inflammatory and astringent in action. Externally, it is helpful in ophthalmic diseases. A paste of the bark of this plant is applied around the eyes. It stimulates all of the secretory organs, relieves the mucous surfaces' irritation and checks excessive secretions. A decoction with milk is very effective for menstrual disorders. It cleanses toxins from the liver and purifies the blood.

Traditional Uses: According to Ayurveda, the bark reduces fever. The bark, finely powdered and added in some oil, is dropped into ears to stop abnormal discharge (associated with or without pain). The root is effective in healing female related health problems. It is a uterine tonic that relaxes the wall of the uterus and its tissues. It helps treat gynaecological issues such as heavy menstrual bleeding, frequent abortions, uterine bleeding and leucorrhoea.

The bark and other herbal decoctions and infusions treat ailments such as a fatty liver, liver cirrhosis, persistent dysentery and fevers. The bark, in large quantity, causes dizziness and gastrointestinal disorder.

In Unani and Ayurvedic medicinal systems, the bark is acrid, digestive and astringent to the bowels and it commonly helps treat diarrhoea. It reduces fever and cures spongy and bleeding gums. The plant's bark forms an ingredient of many Unani polyherbal medicinal preparations for leucorrhoea, such as 'Sufuf-Sailanur-Rehham and Sufuf Kalan.'

This bark of the plant is essential and beneficial in gynaecological disorders and leucorrhoea, in the traditional Chinese system.

Biological Uses: The plant extracts (methanol, *n*-butanol and ethyl acetate) possess antioxidant and anti-inflammatory activities and cytotoxic potential against the human hepatocellular carcinoma cells, without affecting the normal cells.

Chemical Constituents: The bark contains flavanol glycosides like symplocoside, symposide and alkaloids. Phytochemical studies indicate many bioactive ingredients such as flavonoid glycosides like symplocoside, pentacyclic-triterpenoids like betulinic acid, acetyl oleanolic acid, oleanolic acid and flavonoids, tannins, saponins, glycosides, resins and steroids.

Distribution: The evergreen Symplocos racemosa tree is found in tropical and subtropical regions of Asia, Australia, America and Malaysia. It is found in the North and East India and throughout the Himalayas.

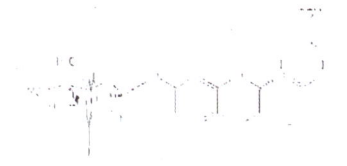

Symplocoside ($C_{22}H_{26}O_{11}$)

Urginea indica

PiyazJangli (Plant and Bulbs)

Latin Binomial	Urginea indica/Urginea maritima/ Drimia indica
Family	Liliaceae/Asparagaceae
English name	Squill/Indian Squill
Urdu name	Jangli Piyaz/Asqeel

Medicinal Uses: The bulbs of the flowering Urginea indica plant are diuretic, expectorant, cathartic, emetic in action and an excellent tonic for the heart.

Traditional Uses: In Unani and Ayurvedic medicinal systems, it is useful in arthritis, rheumatism, oedema, gout, male sterility, psoriasis, swellings, pulmonary troubles, cardiac stimulant and in subcutaneous parasitic infection. The bulbs are beneficial as an antidote for insect bites. The plant is also valuable as a laxative and expectorant. The bulbs, crushed or sliced, are applied to the soles of the feet to prevent a burning sensation. It is frequently employed in dropsy as a diuretic, whether due to the kidney's chronic diseases or renal congestion or chronic cardiac disorders. The traditional healers of the Indo-Pak subcontinent use the bulbs mainly in treating the heart and with its stimulating, expectorant and diuretic properties. Externally, they recommended the bulbs in the treatment of dandruff and seborrhoea.

Biological Uses: The plant extracts (methanol, acetone and chloroform) show antibacterial activities against gram-negative and gram-positive bacteria and fungi. The rhizome's dried powder extract (methanol) possesses high anti-inflammatory activity and effective anti-arthritic activities and moderately sound analgesic effects.

Chemical Constituents: The bulb consists of cardiac steroidal glycosides scilliroside, scillaren–A, proscillaridin, etc. They stimulate the heart and produce positive muscular contractions and negative chronotropic (change of heart rate) effects in heart insufficiency, angina pectoris, nephritic oedema (kidney disorders).

The aglycone of proscillaridin is called scillarenin ($C_{24}H_{32}O_4$). The plant also contains various flavonoids, including quercetin, kaempferol, poly-glycosides and minerals like iron, calcium, magnesium, sodium, potassium, copper, manganese and zinc.

Distribution: It is native to southern Europe, western Asia and northern Africa.

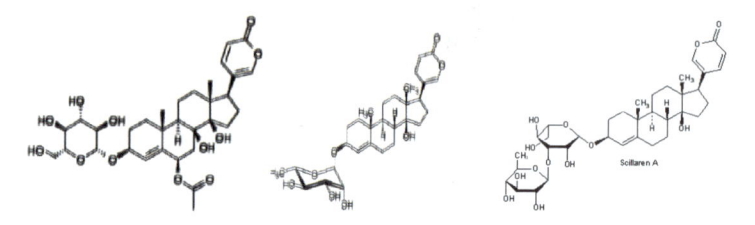

Scilliroside ($C_{32}H_{44}O_{12}$) Proscillaridin ($C_{30}H_{42}O_8$) and Scillaren -A ($C_{35}H_{52}O_{13}$)

Vanilla planifolia

Vanilla (Plant Parts, Flowers and Pods)

Latin Binomial   Vanilla planifolia

Family	Orchidaceae
English Name	Vanilla
Urdu Name	Fanilana/Vanilla

Medicinal Uses: Vanilla planifolia contains methyl or ethyl vanillin. The antibacterial properties of vanilla make it beneficial for the treatment of acne. Vanillin helps cleanse the skin through its antibacterial effects, reducing pimples and acne. Vanilla is rich in antioxidants, preventing and reversing skin damage caused by free radicals. In addition, the plant is helpful in the treatment of anxiety and depression.

Traditional Uses: It is seldom used in Unani and Ayurvedic medicine systems. Traditionally, the seed pods are valuable as an aphrodisiac, carminative, emmenagogue and stimulants. They are said to reduce or cure fevers, spasms and caries. According to pharmacopoeias, Vanilla extracts (especially tinctures) are used in pharmaceutical preparations such as syrups and flavouring agents.

Biological Uses: Vanillin's antimicrobial properties against yeast and other microorganisms have been evaluated. The plant also has aphrodisiac and antioxidant activities. The plant also possesses antimutagenic and anticarcinogenic properties.

Chemical Constituents: The plant contains aldehyde glycoside, vanillin, vanillic acid, essential oils, cyclic carboxylic esters 'lactones,' phenylpropanoid compounds, cellulose, sugar and valuable minerals magnesium, calcium, zinc, manganese, potassium and iron. The extract of Vanilla planifolia with vanillin contains several related phenylpropanoid (C_6–C_3) compounds. These compounds undergo a series of enzymatic reactions during curing, which brings about vanilla's characteristic aroma and flavour.

Distribution: Vanilla planifolia is native to Mexico, but it is now widely grown throughout the tropics. Indonesia and Madagascar are the world's largest producers.

Vanillin ($C_8H_8O_3$)   Vanillic acid ($C_8H_8O_4$)

Zanthoxylum armatum

Kabab-e-Khandan (Plant, Fruits and Seeds)

Latin Binomial	Zanthoxylum armatum
Family	Rutaceae
English Name	Zanthoxylum
Urdu Name	Kabab-e-Khandan

Medicinal Uses: The fruit of Zanthoxylum armatum plant is aromatic, stimulant, astringent, digestive, carminative in action and is a liver tonic. It is also valuable for the treatment of toothache. The Zanthoxylum is an important medicinal plant with various household, commercial and ethnomedicinal applications. The fruits, leaves, seeds and stem-bark help headaches, fever, toothache, tonsillitis, diarrhoea, dysentery and altitude sickness. The fruit contains an essential oil that possesses antiseptic, disinfectant properties, so it has a wide application in pharmaceuticals and flavouring industries. The seeds are aromatic.

Traditional Use: In Unani and Ayurvedic medicinal systems, a decoction prepared from Zanthoxylum armatum is beneficial as a stimulant for the digestive system and beneficial for treating fever and cholera. It is also suitable in overcoming general weakness. This herb's smoke helps treat asthma. As an astringent, it is recommended as an anti-diarrhoeal. This plant's juice helps with throat disorders, is used as a gargle and is also useful for dental problems.

The seeds of Zanthoxylum are stomachic and carminative. One of the essential ingredients in Unani poly-herbal formulation called 'Zuroor-e-Qula' is known to possess antimicrobial and anti-inflammatory properties and is also recommended in cases of stomatitis and gastric ulceration. The bark and seeds are a tonic for treating dyspepsia, fevers and cholera.

Many traditional healers suggest its use in common cold, cough and fever. It is believed to give warmth to the body. Young shoots of the plant are valuable as toothbrushes. Their aqueous extract is a remedy in expelling roundworms. Recently people have also started using pulverized fruit for cleaning teeth.

In Nepal, a decoction of the fruit and berries is made useful for rheumatism, abdominal pain, cholera and skin diseases. In China, scabies is treated by the plant, using a lotion applied to the skin and as a remedy for snake bites. In Japan, the seeds are for stomach problems and depression. It is also used for snakebites in Malaysia and Thailand. The natives of North America crush the bark and apply it to their gums for pain relief; hence it is known as a toothache tree.

Biological Uses: The plant's bioactive compounds are responsible for various biological activities like an antioxidant, antimicrobial, antifungal, antiviral and hepato-protective. The oil has antibacterial, antifungal and antiseptic properties. The crude extract of Zanthoxylum armatum shows spasmolytic effects. The methanol extract of the bark possesses anti-proliferative and anti-diabetic activities. The presence of linalool and linalyl acetate is known to achieve the anti-inflammatory activity.

The lipophilic extracts of the Zanthoxylum armatum fruit reduce inflammation (irritation and redness) in the mouth.

Chemical Constituents: The plant contains flavonoids, glycosides, coumarins, alkaloids, essential oils, sterol, steroids, terpenoids, phenolic compounds, benzoids and alkaloidal sterols. Monoterpenes like linalool and limonene are the major constituents of essential oils.

Distribution: Zanthoxylum armatum is a medicinal plant widely found in Pakistan, India, and from Kashmir to Bhutan at altitudes up to 2500 meters. In Pakistan, the plant is found in Dir, Swat, Hazara, Murree and Poonch hills and in Jhelum. It is also found in Taiwan, China, the Philippines, Srilanka, Nepal, Bangladesh, Indonesia, Malaysia and Japan.

Linalool (C$_{10}$H$_{18}$O)   Limonene (C$_{10}$H$_{16}$)   Linalyl acetate (C$_{12}$H$_{20}$O$_2$)

Fenchol (C$_{10}$H$_{18}$O)

Medicinal Plants
Plants containing Saponins

Saponins

'Sapo' is the Latin name for soap. Saponins are the plant glycosides possessing a distinct property of forming soapy lather in water. Therefore, they are primarily used as detergents. Saponins on hydrolysis give out sugars (glucose, galactose, or xylose, etc.) and aglycones 'sapogenin'.

Saponins consist of polycyclic aglycones attached to one or more sugar side chains. The aglycone part also called 'sapogenin,' is either steroid (C_{27}) or triterpene (C_{30}). The foaming ability of saponins is caused by the combination of a hydrophobic (fat-soluble) 'sapogenin' and a hydrophilic (water-soluble) sugar part. Saponins have a bitter taste. Some saponins are toxic, known as sapotoxin. Saponins have many beneficial effects on blood cholesterol levels, cancer, bone health and the immune system's stimulation.

Properties of Saponins

(a) Saponins are mostly amorphous in nature, soluble in alcohol and water, but insoluble in non-polar organic solvents like benzene, n-hexane, etc.
(b) In an aqueous solution, give froths, when shaken.

An aqueous solution absorbs and retains in solution a volume of gas (e.g., carbon dioxide) several times greater than that absorbed by an equal volume of water.

(c) An aqueous solution, shaken with oil and fats, produces emulsion, which is stable for a short time, varying from a few minutes to an hour or more. Emulsification is caused by the saponins lowering the surface tension between the oil and the water.

(d) An aqueous solution added to red blood corpuscles causes haemolysis, e.g., disintegration and solution of the corpuscles, to form a clear red liquid.

Classification of Saponins:

They are classified into two groups:

I. Tetracyclic triterpenoid saponins: (Steroidal Glycosides)

Cucurbitane (C$_{30}$H$_{54}$)   Steroidal Glycoside

(a) Dioscorea bark-Diosgenin

(b) Solanum Berries-Solasodine

(c) Asparagus roots-Sarsapogenin

II. Pentacyclic Triterpenoid Saponins

(a) Hemidesmus indicus

(b) Trigonella foneum-graeum

(c) Ginseng-Ginsenoside

(d) Licorice-Glycyrrhizin

Chemical tests for Saponin Glycosides:

1. Foam test: Shake the drug extract or dry powder vigorously in water. The persistent foam is observed.

2. Haemolytic test: Add the drug extract or dry powder to one drop of blood placed on a glass slide. A Haemolytic zone appears.

Note: Saponins are generally responsible for an expectorant action.

Solasodine (C$_{27}$H$_{43}$NO$_2$)   Sarsapogenin (C$_{27}$H$_{44}$O$_3$)   Diosgenin (C$_{27}$H$_{42}$O$_3$)

Achyranthes aspera

Charchita (Plant, Flowers and Leaves)

Latin Binominal	Achyranthes aspera
Family	Amaranthaceae
English Name	Chaff-Flower
Urdu Name	Charchitah

Medicinal Uses: All above the ground parts of the flowering Achyranthes aspera plant are useful for medicinal purposes. The plant is carminative, digestive, diuretic, expectorant, antiasthmatic and antiperiodic (herb stops reoccurring of symptoms) in action.

Traditional Uses: In Unani and Ayurvedic medicinal systems, Achyranthes aspera is beneficial in kidney diseases, as a diuretic and also in spleen enlargement. The dried leaf (powder) mixed in honey, is suitable for diarrhoea. The leaf juice is a valuable remedy for skin diseases like pruritus (itching) and scabies (a type of skin infection). The leaf paste is applied externally for toxic bites. The leaf is emetic. The juice of the whole plant helps treat boils, dysentery and haemorrhoids. The plant's coarse powder, boiled in water, helps in treating pneumonia.

A decoction of the root is effective against stomachache, flatulence, colic and ringworm. The whole plant ash is a good remedy for bleeding piles and abdominal problems. The ash mixed with mustard oil is believed to relieve pyorrhoea and toothache. The flowering spikes or seeds are ground and made into a paste with water and are beneficial as an external application for bites of poisonous snakes and reptiles. It is also used in night blindness and cutaneous diseases. The raw seeds of Achyranthes are useful in bleeding piles, as an expectorant and as a brain tonic. The seeds are a remedy for hydrophobia and skin diseases. Dried twigs can be used as a toothbrush.

Biological Uses: The alcoholic (ethanol) extract shows anti-inflammatory, antifertility, antidepressant, antiallergic and antioxidant properties, whereas methanol extract of the leaves has antiviral, antioxidant and anti-inflammatory activities. The presence of flavonoids in the plant, has been shown to prevent or slow cancer cell development.

Chemical Constituents: The plant contains triterpenoid saponin glycosides (saponins A, B, C, D and e) and other chemical constituents such as achyranthine, betaine, pentatriacontane, hexatriacontane, flavonoids, steroids, essential oils, oleanic acid, alkaloids, terpenoids, glycosides, tannins and a small amount of resin.

Distribution: Achyranthes aspera plant, probably is indigenous to South East Asia, Africa, Europe, Italy, Spain and America. The plant is commonly found in Baluchistan, Pakistan.

Pentatriacontane ($C_{35}H_{72}$) 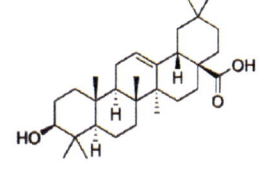   Oleanic acid ($C_{30}H_{48}O_3$)

Asparagus adscendens

Shaqaqul Misri/ Musli Safaid (Plant, Roots and Leaves)

Latin Binominal	Asparagus adscendens
Family	Liliaceae/Asparagaceae
English Name	Garden Asparagus

| Urdu Names | Shaqaqul Misri/Musli Safaid |

Medicinal Uses: The roots and leaves of the flowering Asparagus adscendens plant are demulcent, anti-diarrhoeal, antidysenteric, aphrodisiac and diuretic in action. The white Asparagus is very popular in Europe and Asia. It is generally beneficial in fluid retention, pain, anxiety, bronchitis, tuberculosis and dementia.

Traditional Uses: In Unani and Ayurvedic medicinal systems, it is generally used in genitourinary complaints, such as seminal weakness, impotence, spermatorrhoea and leucorrhoea. In Ayurvedic, it is considered a female tonic, beneficial in female infertility in increasing libido and curing inflammation of the sexual organs. The root, boiled in milk, helps relieve bilious dyspepsia and is useful in the treatment of nocturnal emission, gleet, chronic leucorrhoea and diabetes. The aqueous extract of the root significantly improves memory and reduces stress. Externally, it is used to treat stiffness in the joints.

Biological Uses: Asparagus possesses thrombolytic (dissolves blood clots), membrane stabilizing, antimicrobial and antioxidant activity. Asparagus alcoholic extract of the root has antihepatotoxic properties. The methanol extract of the root has antidepressant activity. Alcoholic and aqueous fractions of the root have antimicrobial and immunomodulatory properties against pathogenic bacteria, viruses and fungi.

Chemical Constituents: It contains steroidal saponins glycosides, e.g., sarsasapogenin, volatile oils, flavonoids (kaempferol, quercetin and rutin), sterols, polysaccharides, isoflavones, tannins, resin and minerals like zinc, magnesium, copper, manganese, potassium and selenium. The plant is also a good source of vitamins such as A, B_1, B_2, C and E.

Distribution: Asparagus adscendens grow in the Indo-Pak subcontinent, Afghanistan, Iran, China and Japan. In Pakistan, the plant is produced in Malakand, Kohat, Waziristan, Rawalpindi, Kashmir, etc.

Sarsasapogenin/Epismilagenin ($C_{27}H_{44}O_3$)

Asparagus racemosus

Satawar (Plans and Roots)

Latin Binominals...	Asparagus racemosus/Asparagus officinalis
Family	Liliaceae/Asparagaceae
English Name	Asparagus
Urdu Name	Satawar/Satawari

Medicinal Uses: The root of the flowering Asparagus racemosus plant is diuretic, demulcent, laxative, diarrhoeal, antidysenteric and aphrodisiac (increase viscosity of the semen) in action. The aphrodisiac property of the plant root may be due to steroidal saponins glycoside. The Asparagus root is recommended in the case of dropsy and it promotes healthy skin.

Traditional Uses: In Unani and Ayurvedic medicinal systems, Asparagus racemosus is generally beneficial in genitourinary complaints such as seminal weakness, impotence, spermatorrhoea and leucorrhoea. The root, when powdered is taken internally, is used to treat male infertility and loss of libido.

Traditional healers (Hakims and Ayurveda) of the Indo Pak subcontinent use the root of Asparagus for upset stomach (dyspepsia), constipation, stomach spasms and stomach ulcer. Some Ayurvedic practitioners use aqueous extract for nervous disorders, inflammation and specific infectious diseases. It is also suitable in fluid retention, pain, anxiety, cancer, diarrhoea, bronchitis, dementia and diabetes. Asparagus is packed with antioxidants and is also a helpful brain booster. Extracts from dried roots benefit various reproductive and hormonal issues in women.

Biological Uses: The ethanolic and aqueous extract of Asparagus racemosus possesses significant antidiarrhoeal activity due to the inhibitory effect, both on gastrointestinal propulsion and fluid secretion. Aqueous-non-aqueous (methanol and ethanol) fractions also show antibacterial, anti-inflammatory, antiulcer, antioxidant and antidepressant activities, which significantly affect lactating mothers, in increasing production. The presence of steroids 'shatavarin' show anti-cancer properties.

Chemical Constituents: Shatavari IV is a steroidal saponins glycoside of sarsasapogenin, present in the root. The plant contains volatile oils, alkaloid-aspargamine, flavonoids (kaempferol, quercetin and rutin), sterols, polysaccharides resin, minerals zinc, magnesium, and copper manganese, potassium and selenium. It is also a good source of vitamins such as A, B_1, B_2, C and E.

Distribution: Asparagus racemosus grows in the Indo-Pak subcontinent, Afghanistan, Iran, China and Japan. The plant is now grown on a commercial scale around Islamabad, Rawalpindi and Peshawar.

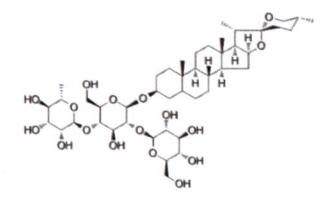

Shatavarin IV ($C_{45}H_{74}O_{17}$)

Glycyrrhiza glabra

Mulaithi (Plant Parts and Roots)

Latin Binominal	Glycyrrhiza glabra
Family	Papilionaceae/Fabaceae
English Name	Liquorice

Urdu Names   Mulaithi/Asalas-Soos

Medicinal Uses: The root of the herbaceous, perennial, flowering Glycyrrhiza glabra plant is an expectorant, demulcent, pectoral, emollient, diuretic, laxative and digestive in action. The plant is one of the World's oldest herbal remedies and is an excellent expectorant.

Traditional Uses: In the Unani system of medicine, the root is beneficial in asthma, irritation of the larynx and is mainly employed for relieving sore throat. It also helps in sexual debility, skin diseases, acidity, jaundice and hoarseness.

A decoction of the root or powder mixed in honey, is a remedy for anaemia. According to classical Unani text, Liquorices act as a demulcent, concoctive of phlegm and as an expectorant. It is widely helpful in cold (catarrh), cough, pharyngitis, hoarseness of voice etc.

The roots and rhizomes of Liquorice (Glycyrrhiza species) have long been used globally as a medicine and a natural sweetener. The root and rhizome parts of the plant are used in folk medicine, both in Europe and eastern countries. The plant's root forms a constituent of many Unani poly-herbal preparations like 'Laouq-e-Sapistan, Laouq-e-Khiyar-Shambar (Shambari), Joshanda, Sharbat-e-Sadder and Sharbat-e-Aijaz.'

Biological Uses: Glycyrrhiza glabra extracts possess many medicinal properties such as antitussive, anti-diabetic, antimicrobial, antioxidant, anti-inflammatory, antiulcer and anti-cancer, etc.

Chemical Constituents: Glycyrrhiza glabra (root) contains pentacyclic triterpenoids, saponins glycoside, flavonoids, coumarins, isoprenoids, flavones, essential oil, resins, sterols, tannins and various other substances. Liquorice is also rich in minerals such as calcium, phosphorus, magnesium, manganese, zinc and copper. Glycyrrhizic acid or glycyrrhizin is the diglucopyranosiduronic acid of glycyrrhetic.

Distribution: The plant is native to the Mediterranean and specific areas of Asia. Countries producing liquorice include Pakistan, India, Iran, Italy, Afghanistan, the People's Republic of China, Iraq, Azerbaijan, Uzbekistan, Turkmenistan and Turkey.

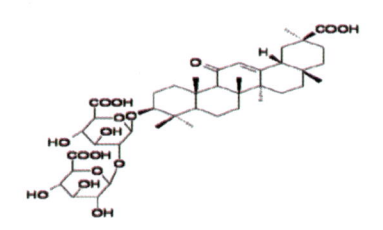

Glycyrrhizin (C$_{42}$H$_{62}$O$_{16}$)

Gynostemma pentaphyllum

Jiaogulan (Leaves and Roots)

Latin Binominal	Gynostemma pentaphyllum
Family	Cucurbitaceae
English Name	Jiaogulan
Urdu Name	Jayawjulan

Medicinal Uses: The herbaceous perennial plant (leaves and roots) of Gynostemma pentaphyllum is a tonic, improves blood circulation, stimulates liver function, strengthens the immune, nervous systems, reduces blood sugar and cholesterol levels. It also has sedative effects, relieving spasms and lowering blood pressure. Internally, it is beneficial in treating nervous tension, exhaustion, peptic ulcers, asthma, bronchitis and cancer.

Traditional Uses: In Traditional Chinese Medicine, the plant has anti-ageing benefits and aids in many common health conditions, including diabetes, high cholesterol and anxiety. It is an adaptogenic herb that helps the body acclimatize to stress, enhance memory, improve athletic performance and boosts the immune system. The plant, also known as 'Jiao-Gu-Lan' in Chinese, has been used as a folk remedy for many diseases, including metabolic syndrome, hepatitis, hypertension and neurodegenerative diseases in China and some East and Southeast Asia countries.

Gynostemma pentaphyllum is sometimes referred to as 'Southern Ginseng' because it grows in south-central China and is used similarly to ginseng. The Chinese have traditionally drunk tea made from this plant's leaves to give them the energy they need throughout a hard day of labour.

The plant was rated among the ten most essential tonic herbs at a conference on traditional medicines in Beijing. In Japan, it is designated as a diuretic, antipyretic and anti-inflammatory. The plant is also used in cosmetic products like vanishing cream, freckle cream, soap, shampoos and hair oil.

Biological Uses: Gynostemma pentaphyllum, namely gypenosides or gynosaponins, is believed to be the active compound responsible for various biological activities. The aqueous and methanolic extracts of the plant's root and leaves show antioxidant, hepatoprotective, anti-cancer and anti-diabetic activities. In contrast, the root's ethanolic extract exhibits poor antioxidant and anti-cancer properties. The seed oil is antiseptic and antioxidant.

Chemical Constituents: The plant contains tetracyclic triterpenoid saponin glycosides, flavonoids, alkaloids, resin, sterols, tannins, vitamins and minerals. The roots are very similar to ginseng and they are also rich in saponin glycosides, e.g., gynosaponin. One hundred and eighty saponins which are also known as 'gypenosides,' have been isolated. Polysaccharides are major components of the plant, where they are typically conjugated with proteins. Gynostemma also contains various trace elements like copper, zinc, iron, magnesium and manganese.

Distribution: This plant is usually grown in China, northern Vietnam, southern Korea and Japan.

Note: Gynostemma pentaphyllum may cause some side effects, such as severe nausea and increased bowel movements.

Gynosaponin {Saponin glycoside} ($C_{47}H_{80}O_{13}$)

Hemidesmus indicus

Ushbah (Roots, Leaves and Flowers)

Latin Binominal	Hemidesmus indicus
Family	Asclepiadaceae/Apocynaceae
English Name	Sarsaparilla
Urdu Names	Ushbah/Anantamul

Medicinal Uses: The rhizome of the flowering Hemidesmus indicus plant is alternative, diaphoretic, diuretic, stimulant and demulcent in action. The plant was introduced into Europe as a remedy for syphilis. It is used in other chronic diseases, particularly rheumatism and skin disorders. Sarsaparilla is still considered an excellent blood purifier. The cold aqueous extract of the rhizome is recommended for asthma.

Traditional Uses: In Unani and Ayurvedic medicinal systems, the rhizome is used in syphilitic and chronic rheumatic affections and is employed in chronic affections of the liver. The root is one of the best detoxifying herbs. It helps in purifying the blood and in improving skin texture. A paste of the plant's rhizome can be used externally to treat joint pain in osteoarthritis and gout. Apart from the above common pharmacological properties, traditional healers (Hakims and Ayurveda) of the Indo-Pak subcontinent also use rhizome of the plant to manage many gynaecological problems like leucorrhoea, dysmenorrhoeal (painful periods), etc.

Several Unani mono and poly-herbal formulations contain the root of Hemidesmus indicus as an ingredient, e.g. 'Majun-e-Ushbah, Sharbet Ushbah and Arq-e-Ushbah.' The syrup extracted from the rhizome, is utilized as a flavouring agent.

Biological Uses: The methanolic extracts of the rhizome show anti-inflammatory, antioxidant, immunomodulatory, antileprotic (a herb used to treat leprosy) antihyperglycemic properties, whereas ethanolic fraction possesses antibacterial activities. Hemidesmus indicus plant has remarkable anti-cancer potentials against breast cancer cell lines. The methanolic extract of the plant's rhizomes could be an excellent herb for treating breast cancer. The plant's chloroform extract shows promising activity against 'Helicobacter pylori' bacteria (a type of bacteria that may cause ulcers and stomach cancer). The ethanol (95 per cent) and chloroform fraction show antifungal activity.

Chemical Constituents: The rhizome contains saponins glycoside, lupeol, flavonoids, triterpenoids, volatile oils, resin, tannins and oleo-resin. The flowers are a rich source of flavonoid glycosides. The leaves contain cardiac glycosides, saponins and tannins. An acne and face whitening cream, known as 'Dasoni' containing 'lupeol' as an ingredient.

Distribution: The plant is found in Pakistan (Waziristan and Balochistan), India, Nepal, Iran, Bangladesh and Indonesia.

Lupeol 'a Pentacyclic triterpenoids' ($C_{30}H_{50}O$)

Panax ginseng

Ginseng (Plants and Roots)

Latin Binominals	Panax ginseng/Panax quinquefolium
Family	Araliaceae
English Name	Ginseng

Urdu Name   Jenseng

Medicinal Uses: The root of Panax ginseng plant is mildly stomachic, adaptogenic, stimulant, antiseptic, carminative and aphrodisiac in action. The root is also beneficial in dyspepsia, vomiting, nervous disorders, consumption (tuberculosis) and exhaustion.

Studies show that the American Ginseng reduces blood glucose levels in type 1 diabetics. Both species of Ginseng enhance immune function. In one study, a specific Asian Ginseng extract boosts the immune response to flu vaccine and reduces colds.

Traditional Uses: In the West, Ginseng helps treat loss of appetite, stomach problems, digestive problems, possibly from nervous and mental exhaustion. Ginseng is beneficial and works well against fatigue, old age infirmities (physical or psychological weakness) and helps convalescents recover their health. In healthy people, the drug increase vitality, cures pulmonary complaints, tumours and increases life expectancy.

Ginseng is the most valuable medicinal herb used in Korea, China and Japan. In Chinese traditional medicine, it is useful in anorexia, shortness of breath, palpitation, insomnia, impotence and diabetes. The root also improves memory and thinking skills and works against Alzheimer's disease and many other conditions.

Biological Uses: The ethanolic extract of the root of Panax ginseng showed increased cardiac output. Simultaneously, a decrease in heart rate was noticed when the aqueous fraction was used. In addition, laboratory research shows that extracts of both the whole root and isolated compounds act as antioxidants, affect the immune system function and combats inflammation. The presence of ginsenosides in the plant appears to be responsible for most Ginseng activities, including anticarcinogenic, anti-diabetic, anti-inflammatory, antiallergic, antihypertensive and anti-stress. The oil of Ginseng is antioxidant and has radical-scavenging properties.

Chemical Constituents: The major bioactive compounds in Ginseng are triterpenoid saponin glycosides (steroidal glycosides), which are also known as ginsenosides and are found in the root, leaves, stem and flowers. The plant also contains sterols, carbohydrates, terpenoids, saponins, ginseng oil, flavonoids, minerals (sodium, potassium, calcium, phosphorus and magnesium) and vitamins (B_1, B_2, B_{12} and C).

Distribution: The biggest Ginseng producer is China, followed by Korea, Canada, the United States and Japan.

Note: The species name 'ginseng' comes from the Chines word 'rensheng,' which means 'human' as ginseng root resembles the human body.

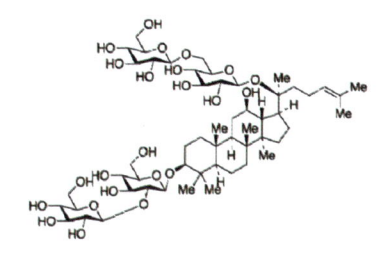

Ginsenosides

Pedalium murex

Bara Gokhru (Flowes, Fruits and Leaf)

Latin Binomial	Pedalium murex
Family	Pedaliaceae
English Name	Caltrops Large
Urdu Name	Gokhru Klaan

Medicinal Uses: The fruit of Pedalium murex plant is diuretic, demulcent and aphrodisiac in action. It is also helpful in nocturnal emission and spermatorrhoea. In modern herbal, the fruit of Pedalium is beneficial in treating puerperal diseases (infection of the uterus), stomach disorders, ulcers, fevers, wounds and general debility.

Traditional Uses: In Unani and Ayurvedic medicinal systems, this plant's fruit is recommended in spermatorrhoea, dysuria and impotence; it is also helpful in inflammatory conditions and uterine disorders. The viscid mucilage produced by soaking the plant, is used as a demulcent, diuretic, as a tonic in treating gonorrhoea and dysuria and it dissolves urethral stones. The traditional healers (Hakims and Ayurveda) of the Indo-Pak subcontinent use a decoction of the fruit for lower back pain, sciatica, inflammation of the pelvic, sacral region, kidney stones, dropsy and respiratory disorders. Many Unani poly-herbal preparations like 'Sherbet-e-Bazuri, Safuf Supari Pak and Sufuf Kalan' contain Pedalium murex's root as one of the ingredients.

Biological Uses: The non-aqueous extracts (ethanol, petro ether and methanol) of the root possess antiulcer, anti-inflammatory, anti-nephrolithiasis (kidney stone diseases), nephroprotective, antibacterial and antioxidant properties. The ethyl acetate fraction of the fruit exhibits the highest anti-inflammatory activity due to its high phenolic content.

Chemical Constituents: The leaves, fruits and roots contain triterpenoids saponin glycosides, alkaloids, flavonoids, essential oils, saponins, steroids, volatile oils and tannins. The flowers are rich in flavonoids.

Distribution: The Pedalium murex plant grows abundantly in the Indo-Pak subcontinent, Sri Lanka, Mexico and tropical Africa. In Pakistan, it is found in the Cholistan area.

Polygala senega

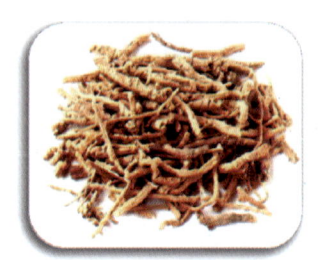

Maar Beekh (Plant, Flowers and Roots)

Latin Binomial	Polygala senega
Family	Polygalaceae
English Name	Senega/Snakeroot
Urdu Name	Maar Beekh

Medicinal Uses: The root of the flowering Polygala senega plant is diaphoretic, stimulant, diuretic, expectorant and emmenagogue (herb to stimulate menstrual flow) in action. The plant is highly effective in treating acute bronchial catarrh, chronic pneumonia and kidney-related dropsy.

The root has been used as an antitussive and has also demonstrated hypoglycemic, immunologic and anti-cancer effects. However, there are no clinical trials to support these uses. It is still used in modern herbals, where it is valued mainly as an expectorant, as a stimulant in treating bronchial asthma, chronic bronchitis and whooping cough.

Traditional Uses: Polygala senega is beneficial in croup (infection of the upper airway), whooping cough and rheumatism. In large doses, the root of Senega is emetic and cathartic. This plant's monograph is not mentioned in both Unani and Ayurvedic pharmacopoeias. However, the herb is officially listed in the Chines Pharmacopoeia. The rhizome of Polygala has been used in traditional Chinese medicine for the treatment of inflammation, learning and memory deficits, dementia, neurasthenia and cancer. Polygala root is also described in the 17th Edition of Japanese pharmacopoeia.

Biological Uses: The aqueous, ethanol and methanol extracts of the root possess anti-inflammatory, antirheumatic, antispasmodic and antibacterial activities. In contrast, a fraction of *n*-butanol has reduced blood glucose and triglyceride levels, in healthy mice.

Chemical Constituents: The root contains triterpenoid saponins glycoside (presenegenin glycosides and polygalic acid), flavonoids, coumarins, styryl-pyrones, fixed oil, gums, resins, sterols, starch and minerals. However, the root does not contain starch.

Distribution: Polygala senegra is native to North America and cultivated in India, Brazil and Japan. Canada is the largest exporter of the product, but the root is collected from the wild.

Note: Snakewood is a common name for several different plants. Do not mix Polygala senegra with Indian snakewood, Rauvolfia serpentina of the Apocynaceae family or African snake plant Sansevieria cylindrical of the Asparagaceae family.

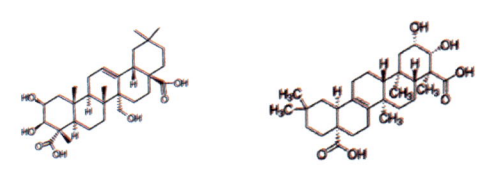

Presenegenin ($C_{30}H_{46}O_7$)   Polygalic acid ($C_{29}H_{44}O_6$)

Polypodium vulgare

Bisfaij (Plant and Roots)

Latin Binominal	Polypodium vulgare
Family	Polygonaceae/Polypodiaceae
English Name	Polypody
Urdu Name	Bisfaij

Medicinal Uses: The polypodium vulgare plant rhizome is a tonic, expectorant, aperients, pectoral (relating to the breast or chest) and analgesic in action. It is helpful as a laxative, tonic, dyspepsia and in appetite loss. The whole herb is also beneficial for skin diseases, cough, catarrh, hepatic complaints and parasitic worm. Polypodium rhizome with other herbs is valued in drying piles.

Traditional Uses: In Unani and Ayurvedic medicinal systems, the plant is beneficial as aperients, expectorant, deobstruent (herb removes obstructions) and alterative. Tea made from the roots is valuable for treating pleurisy, hives, sore throats, stomachache and is a mild laxative for children. It is beneficial for lung ailments and liver diseases. The poultice of the rhizome is applied to inflammations. Tea or syrup of the whole plant is anthelmintic. Traditional healers (Hakims and Ayurveda) of the Indo-Pak subcontinent also recommend this plant in digestive disorders as an expectorant, laxative, purgative, diuretic, antipyretic and as an antiepileptic agent. Many Unani poly-herbal preparations such as 'Majun-e-Najah, Majun-e-Ushbah, Itrifal Aftamoon and Sharbat-e-Ahmad Shahi' contain Polypodium vulgare as one of the ingredients.

The leaves can also be used as medicine but are less effective. The plant can be useful, either fresh or dried. The saponins in the new plant of Polypodium act as a cough suppressant.

The rhizome is useful in European, American and Chinese traditions. It is claimed to be efficacious in jaundice, dropsy, scurvy and when combined with mallow (Malva sylvestris of the Malvaceae family), it removes the spleen's hardness. In Europe, the rhizome of Polypodium vulgare is a useful cholagogue (an herb that increases bile discharge from the system) in congestion and bronchitis.

Biological Uses: The plant's rhizome has high antioxidant free radical scavenging activities. Essential oils, extracted from the aromatic plant, showed good antimicrobial properties. The extracts, both aqueous and non-aqueous of the whole plant and rhizome, show antiepileptic, analgesic, antiviral, antispasmodic and antihypertensive properties. The presence of 'polydin' in the dried Polypodium rhizome has been found to possess antibiotic activity and hence used in cough and cold.

Chemical Constituents: The rhizome contains steroid hormones 'ecdysteroids'. The plant contains a high-intensity sweetener, known as 'Osladin'; it is a saponin, sapogenin steroidal glycoside. It also contains flavonoids, triterpenoids, resin, glycosides, organic acids and essential oils. The rhizome is also a good source of tannins. In addition to saponin 'osladin,' another saponin isolated from the rhizome of the plant Polypodium vulgare is 'polypodosaponin.

Distribution: Polypodium vulgare is native to Europe (especially in France), Africa and Eastern Asia. The plant is almost found in every country of Europe.

Note: The plant is considered harmful for the kidneys and lungs. In large doses, it sometimes causes nausea and vomiting.

Osladin {Saponin Glycoside} ($C_{45}H_{74}O_{17}$)   Ecdysteroids ($C_{27}H_{44}O_6$)

Quillaja saponaria

Quillaia (Bark and Flower)

Latin Binominal	Quillaja saponaria/Quillaja brasiliensis
Family	Quillajaceae/Rosaceae
English Name	Quillaia bark
Urdu Name	Quillaia Ke Chaal

Medicinal Uses: The bark of the evergreen, flowering Quillaja saponaria tree is beneficial in common cold, bronchitis and high blood cholesterol. It is an emulsifying agent, particularly for tars and volatile oils. It is added in topical preparations for skin disorders and as a protective agent for cracks, bruises, frostbite and insect bites. The herb is highly irritating, causes nausea and is expected to consume internal consumption. It is a diuretic and a cutaneous stimulant. Recent research indicates that Quillaja saponaria extract can prevent Rotavirus infection in children and lessen its symptoms. Rotavirus causes severe diarrhoea in children and can lead to dehydration and death. The bark is suitable in preparing tooth powder, toothpaste, hair shampoos, hair tonics, tar solutions and metal polishes. Quillaja saponaria bark is mentioned in the British Pharmacopoeia (BP).

Traditional Uses: Quillaja has been used orally in traditional medicine to relieve cough, bronchitis, topically to alleviate scalp itchiness and dandruff. Reports show that Quillaja can depress cardiac and respiratory activity and induce localized irritation and sneezing. The bark extracts (alcohol), diluted with water, may be useful in washing the skin, especially the scalp, before treatment. Saponins are added to various liquids as a frothing agent but are not used as medicine. These are still used externally as a cutaneous stimulant in treating skin ulcers and eruptions.

Biological Uses: The plant extracts have antiviral, antifungal, antibacterial, antiparasitic, hepatoprotective and antitumor activities. The plant fraction mainly contains triterpene saponins controlled in vitro infections with P. Salmonis. It could be considered good candidates for a new, safe and sustainable method of controlling fish bacterial infectious diseases.

Chemical Constituents: The Quillaia bark contains triterpenoid saponins glycoside as a main bioactive compound and quillaic acid (an antioxidant agent), tannins, starch and minerals. Saponin glycoside on hydrolysis forms pentacyclic triterpenoid, quillaic acid, quillaia sapogenin, alkaloids, glucuronic acid and gypsogenin.

Distribution Quillaja saponaria plant is native to Chile and Brazil. It has been introduced as an ornamental plant in California. These have been acclimatized in Spain but are rarely cultivated there. A different species, 'Quillaja brasiliensis,' is native to Brazil.

Note: Since saponin is a powerful irritant and muscular poison, it can be fatal if used in too large doses and it is rarely used today. However, the bark has been used to produce a foam head on beverages and to wash clothes.

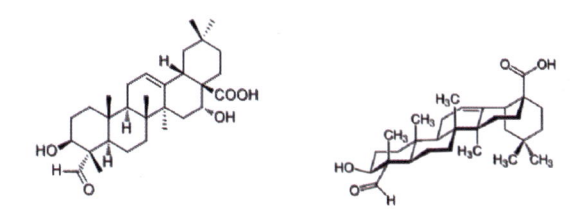

Quillaic acid ($C_{30}H_{46}O_5$)   Gypsogenin ($C_{30}H_{46}O_4$)

Saponaria officinalis

Gasol/Soap Plant (Plants Flower, and Roots)

Latin Binomial   Saponaria officinalis

Family	Caryophyllaceae
English Name	Soap Wort
Urdu Names	Gasol/Soap Plant/Saban Ka Pauda

Medicinal Uses: The root and leaves of Saponaria officinalis are alterative, detergent, tonic, diuretic and expectorant in action. This herb is helpful in scrofula (glandular swelling) and other skin complaints, jaundice and other visceral (internal organs of the body) obstructions. The root is also useful in chronic venereal diseases (syphilis) and rheumatism.

Traditional Uses: A decoction of the herb is applied externally to treat itchy skin. Traditionally, the plant is used as an expectorant. It is so irritating, that the gut's action stimulates the cough reflex and increases fluid mucus production within the respiratory passage. The whole plant, except the root, is alterative, is cholagogue (an herb that promotes bile discharge) and is purgative.

The plant in powdered form, if taken internally, is beneficial in jaundice and other visceral obstructions but is rarely used internally, in modern herbal medicines. This herb should be very carefully used due to the very poisonous nature of saponins. In large doses, Soap Wort is strongly purgative.

Like some other saponins containing herbs, it is also suitable in cleaning clothes, skin, hair and most herbal shampoos have them as ingredients.

Biological Uses: The flower's oil possesses antiseptic, antibacterial and anti-inflammatory properties.

Chemical Constituents: The plant contains flavones-saponarin, terpenoids, flavonoids, gums, tannins, resins, carbohydrates and mucilage. Flavonoids and vitamin C fight dark spots and free radicals that can cause ageing signs. The oil is rich in oxygenated sesquiterpenoids and nonterpenoids compounds.

In cosmetics, the root of the plant is used as a face cleanser, as a soap, hand cleaner and as a body wash.

Distribution: Saponaria officinalis tree can be found in Europe, including Great Britain, Scandinavia, Spain, Siberia and Asia.

Saponarin ($C_{27}H_{30}O_{15}$)

Tribulus terrestris

Gokhru (Flower and Fruits)

Latin Binomial	Tribulus terrestris
Family	Zygophyllaceae
English Name	Caltrops Small
Urdu Names	Gokhru/Khar-e-Khask

Medicinal Uses: The fruit of the flowering Tribulus terrestris herb is an antiseptic, demulcent, aphrodisiac and diuretic in action. It is useful in gonorrhoea, liver diseases like hepatitis and in rheumatism, headaches, kidney stones and in enhancing athletic performance. In the form of an infusion, it is helpful in gout, kidney and urinary tract diseases. The root and fruit have cardiotonic properties.

Traditional Uses: In Unani and Ayurvedic medicinal systems, the fruit of the plant is beneficial extensively in treating male infertility, painful urination, calculous affections, Bright's disease, immune disorders, eczema, psoriasis, kidney stones and improves blood circulation. The use of Tribulus for erectile dysfunction is common in alternative systems (Unani and Ayurveda) of medicine. Some early research shows that taking Tribulus for three months improves erection and sexual satisfaction in men, with or without a condition called partial androgen deficiency. However, Tribulus (Gokhru) affect on erectile dysfunction is still unclear.

Tribulus is one of the ingredients of many poly-herbal Unani medicines such as Sherbet-e-Bazuri, Sherbet-e-Mudir, Arq-e-Dasmol, Majun-Sang-i-Sar-i-Mahi, etc.

In traditional Chinese medicine, the fruit is valuable for treating eye trouble, oedema, abdominal distension, emission and sexual dysfunction. In Bulgaria, the plant is useful as a folk medicine for treating impotence. In Sudan, this plant's fruit is beneficial as a demulcent in nephritis and in the treatment of inflammatory disorders.

Biological Uses: Ethanolic extracts of the fruit show antiurolithic, anti-diabetic, anti-inflammatory, antispasmodic and anti-cancer properties, whereas methanolic fraction is found to be anthelmintic. The aqueous fraction of the fruit of Tribulis has shown hypolipidemic property, whereas the methanolic extract is analgesic.

The ethanolic extract of the fruit of the plant also possesses significant anti-cariogenic activity against Streptococcus mutans (anaerobic, gram-positive coccus), the pathogen responsible for dental caries.

Chemical Constituents: The Tribulus fruit contains chemical compounds known as steroidal saponin glycosides, 'protodioscin.' Other plant parts have various biologically active ingredients such as flavonol glycosides, flavonoids, other steroidal saponins, alkaloids, resin and tannins.

Distribution: Tribulus terrestris is native to the Mediterranean region. It is found across warm temperatures and tropical areas of Asia (Pakistan, India and China) and in Europe, Africa, New Zealand and Austria. Tribulus terrestris is common throughout Pakistan in sandy soils of barren lands and cultivated fields as a weed.

Protodioscin ($C_{51}H_{84}O_{22}$)

Trigonella foenum-graeum

Methi (Plant Parts, Seeds and Leaves)

Latin Binomial	Trigonella foenum-graeum
Family	Papilionaceae/Fabaceae
English Name	Fenugreek
Urdu Name	Methi

Medicinal Uses: The seeds of Trigonella foenum-graeum plant are antipyretic, anti-diabetic, expectorant, carminative and laxative.

A preparation where seeds are soaked in water until they swell and form a paste, helps prevent fever, relieves the stomach and is used against diabetes. An alcoholic tincture helps prepare an emollient cream, ointments and plasters. Externally, the mucilage is suitable as a poultice for skin infections such as abscesses and scrofula. Fenugreek, with the usual dosage of conventional medicine, e.g., insulin, helps gout, diabetes, fatigue, headache and irritability associated chiefly with emotional disturbance (neurasthenia). It reduces cholesterol level. The seeds and leaves decrease blood pressure. The seeds also prevent constipation and possess the hypoglycemic effect. It is widely used as a flavouring for human food.

Traditional Uses: In Unani and Ayurvedic medicinal systems, seeds are beneficial against indigestion, dyspepsia and constipation. A soothing tea made with a combination of Fenugreek seeds, mint, cinnamon and honey reduces stress and alleviates anxiety. They are suitable for preventing anaemia and rundown conditions.

In the Indo-Pak subcontinent, traditional healers (Hakims and Ayurveda) use Fenugreek for diabetes mellitus. The aqueous extract of seeds helps against peptic ulcers by providing a coating of mucilaginous matter. Externally, the seeds are helpful in treating acne and help hair health. Fenugreek leaves and seeds help in blood formation.

In ancient Egypt, the seeds were beneficial in easing childbirth and increasing milk flow. The modern Egyptian women are still using them today, to relieve menstrual cramps and make 'Helba' tea for breast augmentation, hair growth, weight loss and to clean the skin. Arab women from Syria to Libya, eat fried Fenugreek seeds to give roundness to their breasts and hips, as round shapes are considered an ideal beauty in the East.

Biological Uses: The extracts (aqueous and non-aqueous) of seeds exhibited antitoxic, antioxidant, anti-inflammatory, anti-diabetic and immunomodulatory activities. *In vitro* studies of the ethanolic seed extract revealed its cytotoxic effect on several cancer cell lines, such as breast, prostate and pancreatic cancers. Fenugreek seeds help in the healing of wounds of several types of diabetes.

Chemical Constituents: The plant contains steroid sapogenin (fenugreekine, diosgenin), pyridine and piperidine alkaloids such as trigonelline, gentianine, carpaine. It also has essential biologically active compounds like flavonoids, tannins, terpenes, terpenoids and phenols (coumarin, scopoletin, chlorogenic acid and caffeic acid). The seeds of the Fenugreek are also a rich source of vitamins, namely, vitamin A, B_1, B_2, B_3, H, B_{12} and C and minerals like sulphur, phosphorus and calcium.

Distribution: Trigonella foenum-graeum plant is indigenous to Eastern Mediterranean countries and cultivated in Pakistan, India, South America, Africa and Europe.

Trigonelline ($C_7H_7NO_2$)   Carpaine ($C_{28}H_{50}N_2H_4$)   Gentianine ($C_{10}H_9NO_2$)

Diosgenin {Steroidal Saponin} ($C_{27}H_{42}O_3$)

Medicinal Plants
Plants containing Gum and Mucilage

Gums:

Gums are formed from the disintegration of internal plant tissues, mainly from the decomposition of cellulose in the process of gummosis (oozing of sap from the wound). They are polysaccharide complexes formed from sugar and uronic acid ($C_6H_{10}O_7$).

Galactomannan

Properties of Gums

Gums are amorphous translucent substances insoluble in alcohol and most organic solvents. They are soluble in water and give a viscous, sticky solution. Gums are swollen by absorbing water to form a jelly-like mass. Gums consist of calcium, magnesium and potassium salts of polyuronides. On hydrolysis, on prolonged boiling with dilute acids, they yield a mixture of sugar and uronic acid.

Occurrence

Gums are found in trees and shrubs in Leguminosae, Rosaceae, Cochlospermaceae, Mimosaceae and Rutaceae.

Formation:

Gums are abnormal products formed by injury to the plant under unfavourable conditions.

Constituents:

Gum consists of polysaccharides, glucose and rhamnose as the main monosaccharide components and also galacturonic acid, galactose, arabinose, and mannose.

Galacturonic acid ($C_6H_{10}O_7$) Galactose ($C_6H_{12}O_6$)   Arabinose ($C_5H_{10}O_5$)

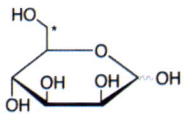

Mannose ($C_6H_{12}O_6$)

Differences between Gum and Mucilage

GUMS	MUCILAGES
Gums readily dissolve in water	Mucilages form slippery masses in water
Gums are pathological products	Mucilages are physiological products

Gums and mucilages have certain similarities

Both are plant hydrocolloids. They are also translucent amorphous substances and polymers of a monosaccharide or mixed monosaccharides and many of them are combined with uronic acids. Gums and mucilages have similar constituents and, on hydrolysis, yield a mixture of sugars and uronic acids. Gums and mucilages contain hydrophilic molecules, combined with water, to form viscous solutions or gels.

Uses

They are used as a tablet binder and disintegrating agents, emulsifiers, gelling agents, suspending agents, thickening agents, dental formulations and as bulk laxatives.

Acacia arabica

Gond Kiker/Aqaqia (Tree, Gum and Flower)

Latin Binomial   Acacia arabica/Acacia nilotica

Family	MimosaceaeFabaceae
English Name	Acacia
Urdu Name	Gond Kiker/Aqaqia

Medicinal Uses: The gum of the flowering Acacia Arabica tree is demulcent, astringent, emollient and antihaemorrhagic in action.

Traditional Uses: In Unani and Ayurvedic medicinal systems, this plant is beneficial in diarrhoea, dysentery, diabetes mellitus and sore throat. The extract of the gum is astringent and a tonic. It is useful in dry cough, amoebic dysentery, asthma and oral cavity lesions. It is also helpful as a demulcent for the respiratory, digestive and urinary tract inflammatory conditions. Externally, it is beneficial for burns. It acts as a cooling agent as an expectorant and is constipating and is a liver tonic. An infusion of the tender leaves is valuable as an astringent and a remedy for diarrhoea and dysentery.

Traditional healers (Hakims and Ayurveda) of the Indo-Pak subcontinent use Acacia gum in headaches, eczema, abscess, ophthalmic disorders, throat infection, urinary problems and gonorrhoea. Its tender leaves, crushed into a pulp, are valuable as a gargle in spongy gums and sore throat. Its flowers help reduce the body temperature, earaches, is antidiarrhoeal, antidysenteric and is a tonic. The bark is a powerful astringent; it is valuable in leucorrhoea, haemorrhages, wounds, ulcers, diarrhoea and vaginal secretions. The seed extract is astringent and is injected to ease irritation, in acute gonorrhoea and leucorrhoea. The seeds are eaten, roasted or raw, in times of acute scarcity. A decoction of the pods is valuable in urogenital diseases. This plant's tender twig is useful as a toothbrush in South-East Africa and the Indo-Pak subcontinent.

Biological Uses: The methanolic extract of the seed possesses antiviral and antifungal activities. Ethyl acetate fraction of the plant has the highest antispasmodic activity *in vitro* against Plasmodium falciparum. The hot aqueous extract of the root is antispasmodic. The bark extract (ethanol) is an antioxidant. The extracts of various parts of the plant have anti-cancer, antimutagenic, antispasmodic, antifungal, antibacterial and anti-inflammatory properties.

Chemical Constituents: The plant contains gums, e.g., galactose, l-rhamnose, l-arabinose, condensed tannins, phenolic compounds, saponins, apigenin (flavone glycoside) and flavonoids (quercetin). The bark is rich in tannins.

Distribution: The Acacia arabica tree is native to Africa (Egypt, Sudan, etc.), the Middle East and the Indo-Pak subcontinent, Burma and Australia. In Pakistan, it is found in Sind, Punjab, Balochistan and Khyber Pakhtunkhwa.

Anogeissus Latifolia

Ghatti Gum/Dhava (Leaf and Gum)

Latin Binomial	Anogeissus latifolia
Family	Combretaceae
English Name	Axle Wood tree
Urdu Name	Ghatti Gond/Dhava

Medicinal Uses: The gum of a small to medium-sized flowering Anogeissus latifolia tree is useful in treating cholera, toothache, diarrhoea, dysuria, urogenital tract infections, colds and cough.

Traditional Uses: The gum is beneficial in spleen enlargement and diabetes. The decoction of the plant is valuable in treating diabetes, jaundice, obesity and skin diseases. The powder is applied externally as a paste to treat wounds and for localised swelling and internally, it is used as an anti-diarrhoeal agent. The plant's gum is mixed with water and given if a patient is suffering from a scorpion or spider bite. The gum exudes from the trunk and is known as 'ghatti gum, has been used in sweetmeats as emulsifiers, in the food industry. It is also valuable in preparing powdered, stable oil-soluble vitamins.

Biological Uses: In an *in vivo* study, atherogenic animals treated with gum ghatti of Anogeissus, have significantly improved their lipid profile; this effect might be an additive in action, with other cholesterol-lowering regimes. The hydroalcoholic extract of the bark has antiulcer property. The methanol-aqueous extract (80 : 20) showed remarkable activity against gram-negative and gram-positive bacteria. The plant extracts, both aqueous and non-aqueous (ethyl acetate and methanol), also possess antiseptic, antifungal and antimicrobial properties.

Chemical Constituents: Gum Ghatti is a complex polysaccharide of a high molecular weight. It occurs in nature as mixed calcium, magnesium, potassium and sodium (salt). The gum tree also contains valuable biologically active phytochemicals such as flavonoids, tannins, flavanone (leucocyanidin), resinous matter, volatile oils, terpenoids, steroids and glycosides. In addition, the leaves and bark are a good source of tannins (gallotannins).

Distribution: Anogeissus latifolia tree is native to East Asia - India, Nepal, Sri Lanka and Myanmar.

Note: The gum of Anogeissus Latifolia tree is used as a substitute for Gum Arabica.

Bombax ceiba

Mochrus (Tree, Gum and Flowers)

Latin Binomial	Bombax ceiba/Salmalia malabarica
Family	Bombacaceae/Malvaceae
English name	Salmalia gum/Cotton Tree Gum
Urdu Name	Mochrus

Medicinal Uses: All parts of the tree are valuable for medicinal purposes. The gum of flowering, Asian tropical Bombax ceiba tree is useful in dysentery, diarrhoea, gonorrhoea, asthma, inflammation, and rheumatic pains.

Traditional Uses: Bombax gum is frequently used as a single or in compound formulations in Unani and Ayurvedic medicinal systems for dysentery, diarrhoea, abnormally heavy menstrual bleeding and as a tonic. The bark of the tree is astringent in action and the seeds are used for treating cystitis and gonorrhoea. The gum is valuable when combined with other herbs, in relieving seminal debility and premature ejaculation. A suppository moistened with the gum and kept in the vaginal passage helps to dry out vaginal discharges.

In addition to the gum, root, bark, flowers, fruit, the seeds are also beneficial in catarrhal affections, ulceration, inflamed surfaces and as tonics. As extensive use of the gum may exert contraceptive action. The leaves are applied topically to relieve inflammation. The flowers are bitter, acrid, cooling and have astringent in effect on the bowels, remove bile, purify the blood and are beneficial in spleen disorders. It is externally helpful in skin affections as a cooling agent and as an astringent. The seeds are helpful in chickenpox, smallpox, chronic cystitis and genitourinary diseases. A young plant is antipyretic in action.

The decoction of the bark is valuable as a demulcent styptic and is phlegmatic. An aqueous extract of the plant is useful in dysentery. The toothpowder containing gum, is beneficial for loosening teeth and bleeding gums. It improves skin complexion when used as a face mask. A well-known Unani poly-herbal preparation known as 'Majun-e-Moochrus' contains this gum; it is an effective remedy in strengthening the uterus and is helpful in leucorrhoea.

Biological Uses: Various aqueous and non-aqueous fractions of the plant confirm that the crude extracts or individual compounds from the plant show anti-diabetic, antimicrobial, anti-urolithiatic, anti-inflammatory activities, hepatoprotective properties as well as antihyperglycemic activity.

Chemical Constituents: The Salmalia gum from the bark contains katechuic acid, sugar, called 'semulrot' ash with $CaCO_3$, $MgCO_3$, tannic and gallic acids. The seed also contains volatile oils and tannins. The flowers are rich in flavonoids and saponins. The bark contains valuable bioactive constituents like beta-sitosterol, glycosides, flavonoids and terpenoids, whereas alkaloids and saponins are not present in the root.

Distribution: Bombax ceiba plant is widely cultivated throughout tropical and subtropical regions. It is native to south and eastern Asia and Northern Australia. It is also native to Southern, Eastern Asia and Northern Australia.

Cochlospermum gossypium

Gond Katira (Tree, Flowers and Gum)

Latin Binomial	Cochlospermum gossypium/Cochlospermum religiosum

Family	Cochlospermaceae/Buxaceae
English Name	Tragacanth
Urdu Name	Gond Katira/Katira

Medicinal Uses: The gum of the flowering Cochlospermum gossypium tree is demulcent, astringent, styptic and stomachic in action. Modern pharmaceutical uses this gum as a tablet binder, as an emulsifying agent in lotions, creams and pastes.

Traditional Uses: In Unani and Ayurvedic medicinal systems, it is useful in treating heatstroke. It is effective in increasing libido and also for treating sexual inadequacy or weakness in men. In addition to this, its long-term use can cure other sexual issues like erectile dysfunction, low semen count and premature ejaculation. It is also valuable as a laxative and for persistent cough and diarrhoea.

Tragacanth (gum) is an excellent anti-ageing supplement for the skin when used in a face mask. It reduces the appearance of wrinkles, fine lines and other signs of wrinkles and effectively manages wounds. Due to its cooling properties, it helps in lowering blood pressure in hypertension. It is effective in treating constipation due to its purgative properties. Traditional healers (Hakims and Ayurveda) of the Indo-Pak subcontinent use this herb to treat women with small breasts; it works as an effective breast enhancer.

The roots of this plant represent an ancient and well-known herb in Traditional Chinese Medicine for its usage as an antiperspirant, as a tonic, diuretic, immunomodulating and immune-stimulating agent. In Iranian traditional medicine, tragacanth is helpful as a demulcent for treating sore throat and hair loss due to seborrhoea. Several therapeutic effects, such as respiratory diseases, have been described in Iranian ancient medical books regarding this plant.

In South-Eastern Asian countries (Pakistan and India), Tragacanth's syrup (Sharbat-Gond-Katira) is a popular summer drink.

Biological Uses: Laboratory studies (*in vivo*) suggest using Tragacanth as an anti-cancer agent to slow down the cancer cell division rate. The methanol extract of leaves is effective against Staphylococcus aureus, while other bacteria were not affected. Moreover, the methanolic fraction of its fruit was most active against gram-positive and gram-negative bacteria. At the same time, moderate activity is observed in its petroleum ether and chloroform extracts.

The ethanol fraction displayed (a concentration-dependent) inhibition of Staphylococcus aureus and Escherichia coli.

Chemical Uses: The plant of Tragcanth contains gum, flavonoids (myricetin), tannins, steroids, phenolic compounds and alkaloids. The leaves also have glucosides (isorhamnetin-3-O-glucoside). The gum consists of a water-soluble fraction known as Tragacanthin and a water-insoluble fraction known as Bassorin.

Distribution: Cochlospermum gossypium is a flowering plant native to the Indo-Pak subcontinent, Thailand, Burma, in North and Western Iran's desert highlands, mainly the Zagros Mountain region.

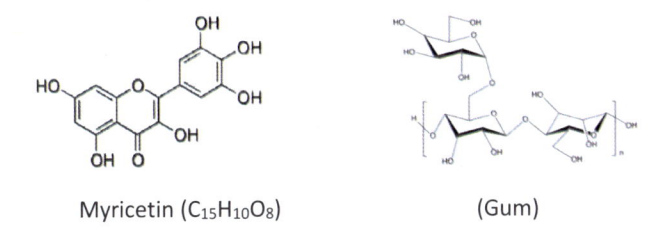

Myricetin ($C_{15}H_{10}O_8$)   (Gum)

Senegalia senegal

Kher (Gum, Leaves and Flowers)

Latin Binomial	Senegalia senegal/Acacia senegal
Family	Fabaceae
English Name	Sudan Gum
Urdu Name	Kher

Medicinal Uses: The gum of a small thorny Senegalia senegal tree is emollient, demulcent, astringent and styptic in action. The gum obtained from the trunk has soothing properties and forms a protective coating over inflamed tissue, reducing irritation and encouraging healing. It is taken internally, often in the form of pastilles, in treating sore throat, coughs and catarrh.

Traditional Uses: The Sudan gum has a naturally sticky texture. Materials with this property are often helpful in reducing irritation and inflammation. The gum is especially effective in easing stomach or throat discomfort. Senegalia senegal is also effective in lowering blood cholesterol. The Sudan gum is an excellent herbal treatment for nursing in low blood pressure. Externally, it is beneficial in treating sores, burns and leprosy. It is also favourable in providing relief in brain strokes like brain haemorrhage. The bark, leaves and gum contain tannins that are used as an astringent in treating colds, inflammation of the eye, diarrhoea and haemorrhages. The root is beneficial in treating dysentery, gonorrhoea and nodular leprosy.

The seeds contain fat (Pilu oil) which is useful in making medicine. A decoction of the bark and leaves is useful in traditional medicine in treating several conditions, including bleeding and diarrhoea. The powdered leaves or mixture of the pulverized stem bark with gum, is topically applied to treat any body injury and to cure wounds.

Biological Uses: The non-aqueous fraction of the plant's stem bark has antibacterial and anti-inflammatory properties. The non-aqueous extracts (ethanol, methanol, acetone, dichloromethane and ethyl acetate) of leaves, exhibit antiviral, antifungal, antibacterial, antimicrobial and anti-trichomonal (anti-protozoal) activities.

Chemical Uses: The gums from Acacia senegal are complex polysaccharides. They contain a small amount of nitrogenous material that cannot be removed easily.

Distribution: It is native to semi-desert regions, Sub-Saharan Africa (Angola, Botswana, Burundi and Cameroon), Oman, Pakistan (Cholistan area) and coastal India.

Sterculia urens

Karaya Gond (Gum and Flowers)

Latin Binomial	Sterculia urens
Family	Sterculiaceae/Malvaceae
English name	Sterculia Gum/Karaya Gum
Urdu Name	Ealakat Satirikyula

Medicinal Uses: The gum of Sterculia urens tree is used as a bulk-forming laxative to relieve constipation. It is used to increase sexual desire (an aphrodisiac) but swells up inside the gut to provide the bulk of material that gently stimulates peristalsis. The gum also helps treat infections. Gum Karaya is not digestible or absorbed systematically.

In manufacturing, Sterculia gum is suitable as a thickener in medications, cosmetics, in denture adhesives, as a binder and stabiliser in foods and beverages. The powdered gum is used in lozenges, pastes and denture fixative powder.

Traditional Uses: In the Ayurvedic medicinal system, it is useful as a laxative and due to its antibacterial and anti-inflammatory characteristics, it is an effective remedy for sore throat. It also maintains normal blood sugars.

Externally, it is beneficial in the treatment of wounds and sores. It increases granulation and improves healing, even in resistant or chronic bedsores. Some studies suggest that Gum Karaya decreases the plasma lipid levels and is beneficial for people suffering from high cholesterol and high triglyceride level. The root and bark are used in Chinese medicine in treating rheumatism, asthma, fractures and tumours. Sterculia urens gum forms a constituent of several Ayurvedic anti-diabetic preparations.

Biological Uses: The hydro-methanolic fraction of the root of Sterculia urens has antioxidant and antimicrobial activities. Other non-aqueous extracts of the whole plant have anti-cancer, antiulcer, anti-diabetic, antibacterial, antioxidant and anti-inflammatory properties.

Chemical Constituents: The Sterculia gum is a complex, partially acetylated polysaccharide obtained as a calcium and magnesium salt. The polysaccharide component of Sterculia has a high molecular weight and is composed of galacturonic acid, beta-D-galactose, glucuronic acid, L-rhamnose and other residues. Sterculia urens root is rich in bioactive compounds (flavonoids, alkaloids, saponins, glycosides, essential oils and phenolic compounds), which serve as a novel natural source for potential therapeutic applications.

Distribution: Sterculia urens is native to South Asia (Pakistan and India) and has been introduced into Burma, Australia, South Africa and Far East countries.

Note: Karaya gum is generally recognized as safe by the US Food and Drug Administration.

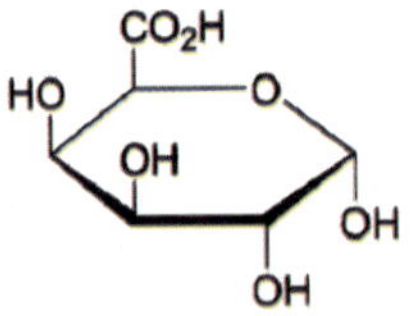

D-Galacturonic acid ($C_6H_{10}O_7$) 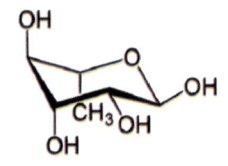 Alpha L-Rhamnose ($C_6H_{12}O_5$)

Mucilage

Mucilage is a gelatinous substance containing polysaccharides and protein, like gum, produced by plants and certain microbes. Chemically mucilage is a polar glycoprotein (contains oligosaccharide).

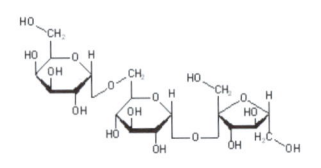

Raffinose ($C_{18}H_{32}O_{16}$)

Abelmoschus esculentus

Bhendi (Plant, Fruits {Pods} and Leaf)

Latin Binomial   Abelmoschus esculentus

Family   Malvaceae

English name	Okra/Lady Finger

Urdu Name	Bhendi

Medicinal Uses: All parts of the plant are functional, medicinally. The fruit (pod) of the flowering Abelmoschus esculentus plant is demulcent, anti-diabetic antispasmodic, diuretic, emollient and stimulant in action.

Okra mucilage has medicinal applications and is used as a plasma replacement or a blood volume expander. Okra's mucilage binds cholesterol and bile acid carrying toxins dumped into it by the liver.

Traditional Uses: The traditional healers (Hakims and Ayurveda) of the Indo-Pak subcontinent recommend the use of Okra water in diabetes and ulcers. Unripe pods (decoction) are beneficial as an emollient, demulcent and diuretic. The pods are known to exhibit antitumor activity. The root juice is suitable externally in treating cuts, wounds and boils. An infusion of the root is beneficial in the treatment of syphilis. The leaves furnish an emollient poultice and are valuable in treating catarrhal infections, dysuria and gonorrhoea. The seeds are antispasmodic, cordial and a stimulant. An infusion of the roasted seeds has sudorific (herb causes sweating). The fruit is crushed with young leaves and used to wash hair and treat dandruff. Flowers are beneficial in the treatment of bronchitis and pneumonia. The roots are very rich in mucilage, having a strongly demulcent action.

In Nepal, the root helps in treating boils and wounds. In Latin America, the leaves are used for action against tumours. In Turkey, the seeds are used for managing increased blood sugar concentration.

Biological Uses: The plant's methanolic fraction exhibits antioxidant, antibacterial and anti-diabetic effects. An ethanolic extract of the pods is effective against Gram-negative and Gram-positive bacteria. Okra contains a substance called 'myricetin,' which is known to improve and increase sugar absorption by the muscles and, thus, can lower the blood's high sugar level. Okra is also known for being high in antioxidants.

Chemical Constituents: The plant contains cellulose, pectin, polysaccharides (sugar, rhamnose, galactose and galacturonic acid), flavonoids, volatile oils, terpenoids and glycosides. This green vegetable (Bhendi) is filled with folic acid, vitamin B, vitamin C, vitamin A, vitamin K and minerals like calcium, potassium, magnesium, manganese and zinc. Okra seeds are a good source of white or pale yellow edible oil and protein.

Distribution: Its cultivation is spread throughout North Africa, Asia and the Middle East. The seed pods are eaten cooked and the seeds are toasted and ground and used as a coffee substitute. The plant is grown commercially in many countries such as Pakistan, India, Iran, Turkey, Afghanistan, Brazil, Malaysia, Thailand, etc. Pakistan is ranked third in terms of Okra production.

Myricetin ($C_{15}H_{10}O_8$)

Aegle marmelos

Bail-I-Giri (Leves and Fruits)

Latin Binomial	Aegle marmelos/Crataeva marmelos
Family	Rutaceae
English Name	Bael Fruit/Stone Apple
Urdu Name	Bail-I-Giri

Medicinal Uses: The fruit of the slow-growing, subtropical Aegle marmelos tree is demulcent, resolvent, expectorant, concoctive, diuretic in action and purgative for bile.

Traditional Uses: Aegle marmelos is a vital herb in the Unani and Ayurvedic medicinal systems, with multiple benefits. From its flowers to leaves, fruit, bark and roots, every part of the Bael tree has various pharmacological effects. The fruit is beneficial in digestive disorders like ulcerative colitis and lack of appetite. It is also successfully used against biliousness, fevers, amoebic dysentery, flatulent colic as a demulcent and febrifuge to people suffering from general debility. It also maintains healthy cholesterol and blood glucose levels in the body. The dried pulp is astringent. The leaves are beneficial in treating dyspepsia, gastritis, indigestion, colds and sinusitis. The root is antiemetic and relieves abdominal colic pain. The pith of the fruit also relieves colic pain and state of indigestion. The stem of the plant is valuable in the treatment of cold and coughs, in rheumatoid arthritis, improves digestive power and is carminative.

A decoction of the stem is beneficial for the heart. The flowers are useful in dysentery, diarrhoea and act as carminative. The Bail fruit is also extensively described in the Unani literature in treating various diseases like jaundice, chronic diarrhoea, dysentery, spermatorrhoea, eye disorders, ulcers, nausea and upper respiratory tract infections.

Biological Uses: The oil of the fruit is useful in pain and inflammation and improves skin complexion. The oil also possesses antiseptic, antifungal and antibacterial activities. The hydroalcoholic extract of Bael leaves shows radioprotective and anti-cancer (breast and colon) properties. The aqueous extract of the fruit exhibits hypoglycemic and chemopreventive effects.

Chemical Constituents: The plant contains a mucilaginous substance, alkaloids, coumarins, flavonoids, terpenoids, carbohydrates, tannins and volatile oils.

Distribution: The plant is native to the Indo-Pak subcontinent and presently grows in Sri Lanka, Thailand, Nepal and Bangladesh.

Althaea officinalis

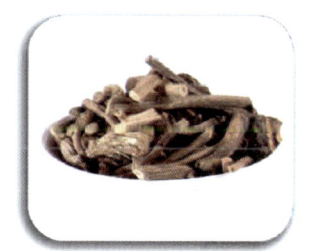

Khatmi (Plant, Flower and Roots)

Latin Binomial	Althaea officinalis
Family	Malvaceae

English Name	Marshmallow
Urdu Name	Khatmi

Medicinal Uses: The perennial, flowering Althaea officinalis plant is demulcent, emollient and expectorant in action. The plant is beneficial in inflammation and irritation of the alimentary canal and the urinary and respiratory organs. A decoction of the plant relieves diseases of the chest like coughs, bronchitis and eases the bowels after dysentery without any astringent effects. The root extract is effective against sprains, bruises, or muscle aches. It is frequently given as syrup to infants and children. The Marshmallow is traditionally used to relieve the mucous membranes, including a gargle for the mouth, throat, and gastric ulcers.

Traditional Uses: Althaea is an important herb in the Unani system of medicine, especially in cough syrups. It is recommended as an expectorant for cough and relieves pharynx and chest congestions. It works well for urinary problems; it eases the passage of kidney stones and is useful in combination with other diuretic herbs for kidney treatments, which help release gravel and stones. The roots are beneficial as a demulcent in bronchitis and the seeds help kidney and bladder disorders. The leaves and flowers are used on burns. This herb has been used for years as a wound healer and can be used externally as a poultice for skin eruptions and infections. It is also used externally for varicose veins, skin abscesses and dermatitis.

The flowers are an ingredient of many Unani poly-herbal medicinal preparations like 'Laooq-e-Sapistan, Joshanda, Joshina (Hamdard) and Laooq-e-Nazle.' The seeds are also used in Unani medicine known as 'Marham-e-Dakhyleyun (ointment).'

Perhaps of less importance than its medicinal powers is Japan's recent discovery that the Marshmallow may have a whitening effect on the skin. This action may interest the cosmetic industry, which has long incorporated the plant into moisturizing creams because of its softening and soothing properties.

In Russia, syrup of root is sold without a prescription by pharmacies to treat minor respiratory ailments. Herbalists in the West also use the root for countering excess stomach acid, peptic ulceration and gastritis. A hot infusion is given to treat cystitis and frequent urination. The seeds are not used in the Western herbal; but only the root, leaves and flowers are used.

Biological Uses: The non-aqueous extracts (methanol, aqueous and 80 per cent ethanol) of the plant possess antitussive, anti-inflammatory, anti-estrogenic, antimicrobial, antioxidant and cytotoxic activities. The extract of 1, 3, butanediol of Althaea officinalis root has an immunomodulatory effect.

Chemical Constituents: Althaea officinalis contains starch, mucilage, polysaccharides, carbohydrates, phenolic acids, flavonoids, glycosides and asparagine. The mucilage content is high in the root.

Distribution: Althaea officinalis is native to Eastern Europe, North Africa and Western Asia.

Bambusa arundinacea

Banslowchan/Tabasheer (Branch and Mucilage)

Latin Binomial	Bambusa arundinacea/Dendrocalamus strictus
Family	Gramineae/Poaceae
English Name	Bamboo Manna
Urdu name	Banslowchan/Tabasheer

Medicinal Uses: The giant, thorny, Bambusa arundinacea tree is astringent, digestive, antidysenteric and antiulcer in action. Bamboo Manna is used in chest complaints such as tuberculosis, bronchitis, cough and asthma.

Traditional Uses: In Unani and Ayurvedic medicinal systems, the leaves, stem and roots are beneficial as an astringent, laxative and diuretic. It helps relieve thirst and, due to its astringent and desiccative action, stops spermatorrhoea and bloody discharge from piles. It is also useful in some gynaecological disorders. The plant juice is rich in silica and is taken internally to strengthen the cartilage in conditions such as osteoarthritis and osteoporosis.

The root is astringent and cooling; it is valuable in the treatment of joint pain and general weakness. Some traditional healers in India use this plant as a tonic for the heart and lungs. It is a good diuretic as it helps balance urine flow, acts as an alkali, and prevents painful urination. An ointment from the root is a folk remedy for cirrhosis and hard tumour. The famous Unani poly-herbal antacid preparation known as 'Jawarish-e-Tabasheer' contains Bamboo Manna as an active ingredient.

In Chinese medicine, the Bamboo leaves are sweet, cold and somewhat bitter, so they are suitable for treating fevers, colds and congestion. They are especially beneficial for reducing heat in the chest, heart, lungs and overall health. The plant extract has been used in folk medicines to treat various inflammatory conditions.

The Bamboo extract is recommended in formulating cosmetic products with anti-irritant activity. It protects the skin and hair. In Japan, the plant is called 'Moso' and it is 'Mao-Zhu,' in China.

Biological Uses: Researchers reveal that using methanolic extract with a non-steroidal anti-inflammatory analgesic, offers a strong anti-inflammatory effect. As a result, it can help tackle chronic inflammatory conditions such as rheumatoid arthritis. The aqueous and non-aqueous fractions (hot aqueous, methanol and ethanol) show anti-inflammatory, anthelmintic, astringent, antiulcer, diuretic and antioxidant properties.

Chemical Constituents: The plant's various parts have a siliceous substance near the joint; inside is white camphor-like crystalline in appearance, slightly sticky to the tongue and sweet. Bamboo arundinacea leaves contain flavonoids, cyanogenetic glycosides, phenolic acids, tannins, lactones, triterpenes, flavonoids, polysaccharides and minerals. The Bamboo plant is a rich source of resins, arginine, silica, riboflavin, choline, thiamine, etc.

Distribution: Bambusa arundinacea, also known as 'Giant Thorny Bamboo,' is a species of tropical dense clumping bamboo native to Southeast Asia. It is also grown in Pakistan (Sargodha, Mandi Bhaudin, Lahore, Khusab and Kasur), India, Sri Lanka, America, Australia, especially in China, Malaysia, Maluku, Java and Japan.

Note: "A man can sit in a bamboo house under a bamboo roof, on a bamboo chair at a bamboo table, with a bamboo hat on his head and bamboo sandals on his feet. He can simultaneously hold a bamboo bowl at the same time. On the other hand, he can hold bamboo chopsticks and eat bamboo sprout." William Edgar Geil (1865-1925 AD).

Cordia latifolia

Sapistan (Tree Parts and Fresh and Dried Fruits)

Latin Binomial	Cordia latifolia/Cordia dichotoma
Family	Boraginaceae
English Name	Sebestan Plum
Urdu Name	Sapistan

Medicinal Uses: All parts of the plant are valuable for medicinal purpose. The fruit of the flowering Cordia latifolia tree is expectorant, demulcent, anthelmintic, diuretic and aperients in action. The bark and the unripe fruit are useful as a mild tonic. The leaves are useful in pulmonary diseases and stomach disorders.

Traditional Uses: The plant is beneficial In Unani and Ayurvedic medicinal systems for treating cold, cough, coryza, fever, dyspepsia, ulcers and skin diseases. The fruit of the tree is edible, slimy and heavy to digest. They are given in colic pain, blood disorders, seminal weakness and sexual disorders. Most genus Cordia species help treat wounds, boils, tumours, gout and ulcers. These species are also helpful as a blood purifier and febrifuge. A decoction of the leaves is used for treating flu, fever, cough, cold, asthma, snakebite and is a useful tonic. The bark is astringent in action and a hepatic stimulant.

A decoction of the root helps in curing tuberculosis, bronchitis and malaria. The seeds are anti-inflammatory. Externally, the leaf poultice is valuable in treating migraine, inflammation and wounds. The powdered seed is applied to skin eruptions and is a remedy for gonorrhoea. The fruit of the plants is very mucilaginous and beneficial as a demulcent, is a blood purifier, treats spleen diseases, kidney and lung diseases. It is useful as a cure for mouth ulcers, in powder form. The bark infusion is a remedy for mouth infection and the teeth are rubbed with the bark to strengthen them. The leaf tea is a tonic in asthma and tuberculosis.

In Unani medicines, Cordia is an important herb used in cough, catarrh preparations like Joshanda, Laooq-e-Sapistan, Dayaquza, Sharbet-e-Arzani, etc.

In Mali, the plant leaves are applied to wounds and ulcers. In Tanzania, the fruit pulp is useful in ringworm and the powdered bark is extensively used to treat skin diseases. In Iran, the fruit is popularly used to treat chest and urinary tract infections, lung diseases and spleen diseases. In Egypt, the dried fruit is still sold today in spice markets as 'sapistan' and is used as medicine. In Taiwan, the fruit is eaten pickled. In Latin America, the alcoholic bark extract is used in pain, myalgia, and sciatica. In Brazil, a decoction of leaves is valuable in washing wounds and taking care of inflammation.

Biological Uses: The primary pharmacological activities reported for extracts (methanol and ethanol) and isolated compounds include anti-inflammatory, antiulcer, antioxidant, hepatoprotective, antiparasitic, immunomodulatory, analgesic, cytotoxic, antimicrobial and antidiarrhoeal. The aqueous and hydroalcoholic extracts are the most effective against herpes simplex virus. In addition, the water extract of the leaves is reported to have a potent inhibitory action on HIV (anti-HIV).

Chemical Constituents: The principal secondary metabolites isolated from the genus include terpenoid, hydroquinone, diterpenoids, triterpenoids, prenylated hydroquinone, meroterpenoid, naphtha-quinone, polysaccharides, alkaloids, sesquiterpenes, flavonol, glycosides, steroids, gum, mucilage and saponins. Recently, four flavonoid glycosides (robinin, rutin, rutoside, datiscoside and hesperidin), a flavonoid aglycone (dihydrorobinetin) and two phenolic derivatives (chlorogenic acid and caffeic acid) were also isolated from the seeds.

The plant is a valuable source of micronutrients such as sodium, potassium, calcium, zinc and iron. The oil is obtained from the seeds and glue can be made from the mucilaginous fruit.

Distribution: Cordia latifolia is a flowering tree in the Borage family, native to Pakistan, India, China, Brazil, North Australia and West Melanesia (Fiji, New Caledonia and the Solomon Islands).

Cycas sphaerica

Kangi Palm (Tree and Fruit)

Latin Binomials	Cycas sphaerica/Cycas revoluta
Family	Cycadaceae
English Name	Cycas
Urdu Name	Kangi Palm/Sago Balm

Medicinal Uses: A gum of the evergreen, flowering Cycas sphaerica shrub resembling tragacanth (Cochlospermum gossypium) oozes from wounds in the plant.

The bark and the seeds are ground to a paste with vegetable oil and used as a poultice on sores, cuts, wounds and ulcers. The juice of tender leaves is helpful in the treatment of flatulence and vomiting. A decoction of the leaves is drunk to soothe cough. The plants contain alkaloids of carcinogens and amino acids that cause chronic nervous disorders. Both male and female flowers have narcotic, stimulant and aphrodisiac activity.

Traditional Uses: The plant yields gum, which is useful as a demulcent for the respiratory, digestive, snake bite, and urinary tract inflammatory conditions. Externally, the gum is beneficial for burns. The powdered root of Cycas circinalis is considered a refreshing and nourishing tonic for men.

The traditional healers in India use male cones of Cycas sphaerica for medicinal purposes. They collect male cones before pollen shedding for use in the Ayurveda system of medicine. In the Ayurveda system, people believe that the root can improve sperm count. The seeds are used as an aphrodisiac. Local herbalists in India also use male cones to cure rheumatoid arthritis and muscle pains.

The very young leaves are edible. The raw seed is poisonous, but after being cut into thin slices, dried, then steeped in water for a few minutes and dried again, they become edible. However, the leaves, stem and seeds do not have food or medicinal value. The whole plant is valuable in treating paralysis. The Cycas male cone is also called 'Rinbadam' in Malayalam.

Biological Uses: Hot aqueous extraction and non-aqueous (ethanol, ethyl acetate, methanol and chloroform) fractions of the powdered seeds have antimicrobial, antiulcer, antifungal and antibacterial activity.

Phenolic compounds have antioxidant, antidiarrheal and hypoglycemic properties. The presence of alkaloids shows its action on the nervous system and against debility. It also supports the therapeutic uses of Cycas sphaerica as an aphrodisiac, on neurological disorders and for paralysis. Also, the presence of flavonoids in the Cycas species exhibit antimicrobial and antiviral (*in-vivo*) activities.

The crude extracts of the plant exhibit biological activities such as antioxidant, cytotoxic, antileishmanial and anticancer.

Chemical Constituents: The phytochemical analysis of the plant revealed the presence of flavonoids, glycosides, alkaloids, fatty acids, benzenoids, terpenes, diterpenoids, triterpenoids, sterols, esters and steroids. The root is also a good source of flavonoids.

A plant containing saponins can form foam, which depends on the nature of the drug and the quantity of saponins present.

Distribution: The plant is native to south Japan and is widely cultivated in the Indo-Pak subcontinent and generally, it is found in tropical, moist deciduous forests and woodlands on hills.

Ocimum basilicum

Tulsi/Faranj-Mushk (Leaves and Seeds)

Latin Binomial   Ocimum basilicum/Ocimum sanctum

Family	Lamiaceae
English Name	Basil
Urdu name	Tulsi-Jangli/Faranj-Mushk/Niazbo

Medicinal Uses: The leaves of the flowering Ocimum basilicum plant are aromatic, demulcent, expectorant, carminative and refrigerant in action. These are exhilarant and febrifuge. The plant is useful in treating mild nervous disorders. Infusion of leaves is good for vomiting and nausea. It helps regulate bowel movement by drinking a hot decoction of the leaves.

Traditional Uses: In the Ayurvedic medicinal system, the flowers of the plant are stimulant, carminative, antispasmodic, diuretic and demulcent. The leaf juice is instilled in the nose for nose infection and nasal congestion. In sore throat, chewing leaves is helpful. The infusion is beneficial in treating gas, cramps, spasm, nausea and other digestive troubles. Since it has warming properties, it is also beneficial in cold, cough and respiratory illnesses.

An infusion of the mucilaginous seeds helps treat gonorrhoea, dysentery and chronic diarrhoea. The seeds are also valuable in the treatment of gonorrhoea and for hepatic and gastric disorders. Externally, the juice of the leaf cures acne and pimples. They are used as a flavouring agent and also in the preparation of salads.

Biological Uses: The essential oil obtained from the plant is antibacterial, antifungal and insecticidal. Ocimum basilicum seeds are rich in antioxidants and they help control diabetes and are also suitable for the skin. The seeds are rich in alpha-linolenic acid, which comes from high Omega-3 fatty acids present in the seeds. These acids help in boosting the fat burning metabolism of the body. It is also full of fibre, so it keeps the stomach satisfied for longer and prevents unwanted cravings (helps in weight loss). Basil seeds are high in fibre, particularly soluble fibre, fully loaded with protein, including pectin (heteropolysaccharide).

Tulsi seeds are antioxidants, meaning they protect our cells from damage from free radicals due to the presence of flavonoids. These plant compounds also have antiulcer, anti-inflammatory and anti-cancer properties. The plant non-aqueous extracts possess antihyperglycemic, hypolipidemic, antitoxic, anti-inflammatory, antibacterial and antifungal properties. These also exhibit antioxidant, antimicrobial and antihypertensive activities. The methanol and dichloromethane fractions show antiherpes potential.

Chemical Constituents: The plant contains essential oils, e.g., methyl chavicol, linalool, cineol, eugenol, heteropolysaccharide, methyl cinnamate, etc. It also contains vital biologically active compounds such as saponins, tannins and glycosides.

Distribution: Basil is native to central Africa's tropical regions and also to Southeast Asia.

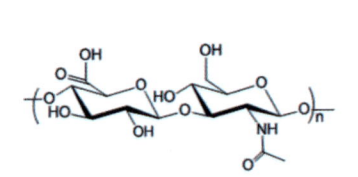

Heteropolysaccharide 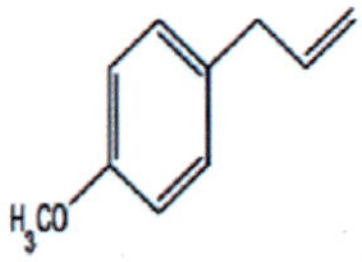   Methyl chavicol ($C_{10}H_{12}O$) 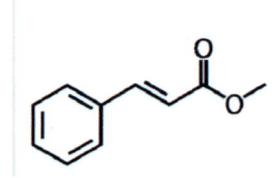   Methyl cinnamate ($C_{10}H_{10}O$)

Plantago ovata

Ispaghul (Plant and Seeds)

Latin Binomial	Plantago ovata/Plantago decumbens/Plantago ispaghula
Family	Plantaginaceae
English name	Spogel/Flea Seeds/Psyllium Husk
Urdu Name	Ispaghul

Medicinal Uses: The seeds of Plantago ovata plant are laxative, demulcent and emollient in action. Ispaghul seeds, when moistened, swell into a gelatinous mass, which lubricates the intestine at the same time, stimulating its normal activity. In general, the plant is also considered resolvent, as a local anaesthetic and anti-inflammatory.

The seeds are beneficial in preventing heart attacks by regulating serum cholesterol in modern therapeutics. It regulates blood glucose levels in insulin response, decreasing fat and glucose absorption. It detoxifies the gastrointestinal tract, resulting in the excretion of the toxins from the body. Plantago ovata prevents lethargy and gives a feeling of well being and strength.

The extracted mucilage powder of Plantago ovata exhibits faster drug dissolution and improved bioavailability and the powder can be effectively used as disintegrants and super disintegrants in tablet formulations.

Traditional Uses: In Unani and Ayurvedic medicinal systems, dried seeds and husk are beneficial as an emollient, demulcent and safe laxative. They are valuable in treating constipation, diarrhoea, haemorrhoids and high blood pressure. The seeds are considered cooling, diuretic and recommended for use in febrile conditions and in the affections of the kidney, bladder and urethra. A decoction of the seed is prescribed in cough and cold and a poultice of crushed seeds is useful for rheumatic and glandular swelling.

In Yemen, soaked seeds are used as a poultice for boils, ulcers and as a cosmetic for hair. A water extract of the dried seeds is used externally in Iran, for its inflammatory and emollient effects. Plantago ovate mixed with coconut juice is helpful as a diuretic. In Spain, the leaf is taken orally by infusion for cold, whereas in Thailand, the dried seeds husks' hot water extract is taken orally as a demulcent and also in diarrhoea. It was also helpful in treating skin irritations in the olden days, such as poison ivy reactions and insect bites and stings. Folk practitioners commonly use Psyllium husk pudding to reduce white discharge and leucorrhoea.

Biological Uses: The non-aqueous (ethanol and methanol) fractions exhibit antimicrobial and antioxidant properties at various concentrations. Plantago ovata helps treat hyperlipidemia and its anti-cancer effects and may be useful for glycemic control in patients with type-2 diabetes.

Chemical Uses: The phytochemical investigation of the Plantago species reveal their high potential in producing a wide array of secondary bioactive metabolites, such as iridoids, phenols, sterols, alkaloids, flavonoids, terpenoids, steroids, tannins and cumatines that have utilities as supplemented food and in treating human diseases. The oil in the seed embryo contains fatty acid (linoleic acid) and has been used to prevent atherosclerosis (hardening and narrowing of arteries).

Distribution: Plantago ovata is native to Mediterranean regions, including North Africa, Europe, Pakistan and India.

Pyrus cydonia

Behidana (Flower, Tree, Seeds and Fruit)

Latin Binomial	Pyrus cydonia/Cydonia vulgaris
Family	Rosaceae
English name	Quince Seeds/Quince Fruit
Urdu name	Behidana/Behi

Medicinal Uses: The fruit of the flowering Pyrus cydonia tree is nutritive, astringent, diuretic, diarrhoeal, demulcent in action and mucilaginous in nature. The fruit is edible and appetitive. It is suitable in preparing syrup, which helps relieve dysentery and diarrhoea. A decoction of the seeds is beneficial against gonorrhoea, thrush and irritable conditions of the mucous membranes. The liquid is also used as a skin lotion or cream and administered in eye diseases, as a soothing lotion.

Traditional Uses: In Unani and Ayurvedic medicinal systems, the fruit is edible and it has properties of being astringent, expectorant and a cardiac tonic. The unripe fruit is an effective remedy for diarrhoea. The juice can be taken as a gargle in treating mouth ulcers, for dysentery and other irritable mucous membrane conditions. The powdered seeds help remove dandruff and are useful as a skin tonic and also used in ulcers.

The leaves and bark are beneficial in Unani and Ayurvedic medicine as an antitussive, antipyretic, sedative and as anti-diarrheal. Some herbalists use the gel prepared from the seeds soaked in water for throat and vocal cord inflammation, in addition to skin rashes and allergies. Quince seeds are among the most common ingredients in the semi-solid compound preparations in the Unani system of medicine like 'Jawarish-Safar-Jali, Jawarish-e-Amla, Sharbet-e-Aijaz, Laooq-e-Sapistan, etc.

In Iran and Afghanistan, Quince seeds are collected and boiled and then ingested to combat pneumonia. Quince fruit dilution strengthens and improves the male organs and stomach functions in homoeopathic medicine. It may be helpful in cases of erectile dysfunction, premature ejaculation and prostate complaints. In Greece, a tea prepared by boiling the seeds of Pyrus cydonia in wáter is given in the inflammation of the bladder.

Biological Uses: The quince leaf and fruit have medicinal applications such as protective effect on spermatogenesis, hypercholesterolemia, antibacterial, antiulcer, antifungal, reno-protective, anti-atherogenic (herb prevents the fatty deposit in the arteries) and hepatoprotective potential. The leaves also have an anti-proliferative effect against colon cancer cells and have antioxidant property. The presence of polysaccharide mucilage, 'glucuronoxylan' of the plant, is used in dermal patches to heal wounds.

Chemical Constituents: The plant is rich in valuable bioactive secondary metabolites such as steroids, phenolic compounds, flavonoids, terpenoids, organic acids, tannins and glycosides. The plant is also rich in micronutrients such as minerals (potassium, phosphorous, sodium, magnesium and iron) and vitamins (B_1, B_2, B_3 and C).

Distribution: Pyrus cydonia is native to Iran and Turkey and is cultivated in Pakistan (North Waziristan, KPK), India, the Middle East, Europe and Africa.

Medicinal Plants
Plants containing Resins

"The value of these resins in the time of Christ is illustrated by the fact that the wise men brought them as gifts along with gold" (Gospel of Matthew 2. 11).

Definition:

The term 'Resin' is applied to the more or less amorphous product of a complex chemical nature. When heated, they soften (fuse) and melt.

Properties of Resins

1. Brittle, amorphous solids that fuse if heated.

2. Insoluble in water and are bad conductors of electricity.

3. Soluble in alcohol or other organic solvents.

4. On evaporation, these solutions deposit the resin as a varnish-like film.

5. Resins burn with a characteristic smoky flame.

6. Resins are usually hard, transparent and translucent. When heated, they become complex mixtures of resin acids, resin alcohols (resinol), resin phenol (resinotannol), resin ester and chemically inert compounds resenes.

7. Resins are used in varnishes but have primarily been replaced by better quality synthetic materials.

Resin

Classifications

Resins can be classified into three categories.

- Classification based on occurrence
- Classification according to chemical constituents
- Taxonomical classification (Biological classification)

Classification based on Occurrence

1. Gum resins: A mixture of gum and resin excreted from some plants or trees (Jalap, Ammoniacum and Gamboge).

2. Oleo-resins: A mixture of oil and resin excreted from some plants or trees (Mastic, Copaiba, Ginger and Turmeric).

3. Oleo-gum resins: A mixture of oil, gum and resin excreted from some plants or trees (Myrrh and Asafoetida).

4. Solidified resin: A mixture from which the volatile oil (terpene components) has been removed by distillation is known as Rosin.

Classification according to chemical constituents

1. Acid resins: Colophony (Abietic acid), Myrrh (Commiphoric acid) and Copaivic (Copaivic acid).

2. Ester resins: Benzoin (Benzoic acid + Benzoresinol + Cinnamic acid) and Storax (Cinnamyl Cinnamate).

3. Phenol resins: Tolu Balsum Toluresinotannol and Balsum of Peru Perruresinotannol.

4. Alcohol resins: Benzoin (Benzoresinol) and Storex (Storesinol).

5. Glyco-resins: Jalap Resin, i.e., Ipomea purge of the Convolvulaceae family and Podophyllum emodi of the Berberidaceae family.

6. Resene resins: Asafetida resins e.g. Ferula foetida of the Apiaceae family.

Taxonomical Classification: According to the botanical origin.

(1) Berberidaceae resins, e.g., Podophyllum.

(2) Coniferous resins, e.g., Colophony.

(3) Zygophyllaceae resins, e.g., Guaiacum.

Tests for Resins (Chemical):

(1) Dissolve about 0.1g of powdered resin in 10ml of acetic anhydride. Add one drop of sulphuric acid on a glass rod (care should be taken to see that the apparatus used

is dry; the concentrated sulphuric acid solution is cold when used). On adding the acid, the purple colour rapidly changes into violet.

(2) Mix a little powdered colophony with light petroleum. Give it a good shake and then filter it. Old resin samples are usually much less soluble in this solvent than the fresh ones. Shake the solution with twice its volume, of a dilute solution, of copper acetate. The petroleum layer becomes emerald-green due to Abietic acid's copper salt.

Constituents: Colophony contains resin acids (about 90 per cent) and neutral inert substances known as 'resenes' and esters of fatty acids. The extract composition varies with the biological source, preparation, age and storage method.

Alhagi maurorum

Turanjabin (Plant, Flowesr and Resin)

Latin Binomial	Alhagi maurorum
Family	Fabaceae
English name	Camel thorn/Caspian manna
Urdu Name	Taranjebin

Medicinal Uses: All parts of the plant, including roots, are useful for medicinal purposes. Alhagi maurorum plant is antirheumatic, laxative, anti-diarrhoeal, antiseptic, antidiuretic and expectorant in action and is a blood purifier. Today, resin-gum is also used in the pharmaceutical industries to produce laxative, diuretic and sweeteners.

Traditional Uses: In traditional and folk medicine, Alhagi maurorum is used in liver disorders, in treating constipation and parasite infection. Alhagi maurorum has been used locally in folk medicine to treat glandular tumours, nasal polyps and ailments related to the bile duct. It also soothes the chest, excretes burnt bile and phlegm and is also a tonic for the stomach, the intestines, as it decreases body heat and relieves internal inflammation.

A decoction made from the seeds is beneficial in curing kidney stones. Grandmothers have traditionally used it to treat neonatal jaundice. It is a laxative if taken in small amounts; however, it will act as a purgative in large quantities. The oil of the plant is useful in rheumatism. In south Asian countries, the plant is useful as a laxative and an expectorant. In Iran, a decoction of the plant is helpful in jaundice.

Taranjebin is a semi-solid or a liquid gummy substance that excludes the leaves and branches of the Alhagi species. It hardens into white granules, which gradually turn to yellow and brown. This gum resin is well documented in classic Unani literature to remedy general weakness and acts as a laxative and expectorant.

Biological Uses: The plant's aqueous extract shows antioxidant, anti-inflammatory, analgesic and antibacterial activities. The ethanolic extract of the roots completely suppressed histamine-induced (guinea pig ureter) contractions and increasing the dose of histamine did not reverse the inhibition. The whole plant extract (methanol) has hepatoprotective effects and the leaves and the flower fraction possesses cytotoxic properties. The oil is antiseptic and antibacterial.

Chemical Constituents: The plant contains many valuable biologically active compounds like flavonoids, alkaloids, sterols, steroids, tannins, resins, glycosides, essential oils and coumarins. The plant is also rich in minerals such as calcium, magnesium, iron, zinc, copper, potassium and chromium.

Distribution: The native range of cultivation of Alhagi maurorum is from Cyprus to Egypt, the East of Mongolia, West and South of India, Saudi Arabia and the Quetta-Pishin districts of Pakistan.

Alpine galangal

Khulanjan (Rhizomes, Flower and Leaves)

Latin Binomial	Alpine galangal/Alpine officinarum
Family	Zingiberaceae
English Name	Galangal
Urdu Name	Khulanjan

Medicinal Uses: The evergreen, flowering Alpine galangal plant's rhizome is aromatic, stimulant, carminative, sialagogue (herb promotes secretion of saliva) and antituberculosis in action.

Traditional Uses: The Galangal root is a spice closely related to ginger and turmeric and a popularly employed remedy in Unani, Ayurvedic and traditional Chinese medicinal systems. In the Unani medicine, Alpine galangal is called 'Khulanjan' and its actions and uses are mentioned in several Unani classical pieces of literature. It is beneficial as a single drug or as a compound medicine and it has actions such as expectorant, a nerve stimulant, as digestive, as an appetizer, carminative and a cardiac tonic. Galangal rhizome is also effective against phlegmatic, atrabilious affections and in treating skin diseases and spleen enlargement. A decoction prepared from the rhizomes is useful as a gargle in treating bleeding, swollen gums and other infections associated with gums.

The traditional healers (Hakims and Ayurveda) of the Indo-Pak subcontinent believe that a decoction or a fine powder of rhizome, also acts as a blood purifier. The seeds are beneficial for emaciation (extreme weight loss) and cleaning the mouth. The plant (flowers, leaves and rhizomes) has an active role in treating eczema, bronchitis and coryza. The famous Unani medicinal preparations like 'Jawarish-e-Jalinus, Jawarish Ood Shirin, Majun-e-Chobchini, Hab-e-Jadwar, etc., contain galangal rhizome as one of the ingredients.

In traditional Chinese medicine, Alpine galangal is helpful in treating indigestion, respiratory disorders, skin diseases, oedema and cancers. The oil of the rhizome is known as 'galangal.'

Biological Uses: The whole plant extracts (aqueous and methanol) possess many pharmacological properties such as anti-cancer, antioxidant, anti-inflammatory, antifungal and antibacterial. The rhizome shows weak antimalarial activity in mice. A petro-ether fraction of 95 per cent ethanol extract of the rhizome shows strong antioxidant activity. An ethanolic extract of the rhizome has shown to increase sperm count in rats.

Chemical Constituents: The plant contains essential oils, e.g., carotol, camphor, cineole, etc., resins, tannins, flavonol galangin, terpenoids, flavonoids, steroids and a small amount of glycosides.

Distribution: Alpine galangal is native to Southeast Asia and China. India is the world's largest Alpine galangal producer, followed by China, the United States and Spain.

Boswellia glabra

Loban (Plant and Gum-Resin)

Latin Binomial	Boswellia glabra
Family	Burseraceae
English name	Frankincense/Indian Olibanum
Urdu name	Loban/Kunder

Medicinal Uses: The gum resin of Boswellia glabra tree is anti-inflammatory, demulcent, stimulant, emollient, detersive and exhilarant in action. The extract of Styrax benzoin is a calcium absorption acceleration activator and can prevent and cure bone diseases due to calcium deficiency like osteoporosis. The gum, along with other ingredients, inhibits phagocytosis of melanosomes by keratinocytes (the primary cell) in the skin epidermis, thus inhibiting melanin's transport, produced by melanosomes, to the skin epidermis, giving the skin a brighter colour.

Some researches show that taking certain plant extracts can reduce pain by up to 65 per cent and can improve people's mobility with osteoarthritis in the joints. Other researchers indicate that taking a combination product containing resin (frankincense) and other herbal ingredients, can also reduce pain and improve people's mobility with osteoarthritis.

Traditional Uses: Boswellia serrata is one of the ancient and most valued herbs in Ayurveda. In Unani and Ayurvedic medicinal systems, different parts of the plant are useful in treating arthritis, asthma, ulcerative colitis (an inflammatory bowel disease), headache, blood purification and wound healing.

The aqueous extract of this plant appears to be very useful in diabetes. The gum resin, obtained from the plant is a vital tonic, especially in the urinary bladder. In the Middle Eastern countries, it is used as a stimulant for digestion, for strengthening teeth, as diuretic, as purgative, to enhance memory and for emotional and psychological problems.

Externally, Frankincense also helps in aromatherapy for asthma, bronchitis, coughs, laryngitis, inflammation, colds, flu, anxiety, nervous tension and painful menstruation. Boswellia is applied to the skin to tone the skin and decrease wrinkles.

Biological Uses: In Chinese traditional medicine, this oleo gum resin is quite popular owing to its wide range of beneficial biological properties like anti-inflammatory, antirheumatic, antimicrobial, analgesic and anti-cancer. It is also used to reduce skin damage caused during radiation treatments for cancer. Early research suggests that Boswellia might benefit people with brain tumours. Taking 4.2g of Boswellia daily seems to reduce the tumour size. The methanolic extract of the stem bark of the Boswellia plant has antinociceptive activities.

Chemical Constituents: One of the main constituents of Boswellia glabra is boswellic acid, a pentacyclic triterpenoid. The wild habitat of the plant contains a higher percentage of oxygenated monoterpenoids/benzenoids and sesquiterpenes, α-terpineol, terpinyl isobutyrate and eudesmol. The plant also contains essential biologically active compounds like alkaloids, flavonoids, cardiac glycosides, steroids, tannins and saponins.

Distribution: Frankincense trees are commonly grown in the gum belt in Africa and the Middle East (Ethiopia, Somalia, Oman and Sudan), Pakistan and India. China is the world's largest market for Frankincense and myrrh, where they are consumed mainly as medicinal products.

Boswellic acid ($C_{30}H_{48}O_3$)

Commiphora molmol

Murr (Tree and Resins)

Latin Binomial	Commiphora molmol/Commiphora myrrha
Family	Burseraceae
English Name	Myrrh
Urdu Name	Murr

Medicinal Uses: Myrrh is one of the oldest known medicinal plants used by the ancient Egyptians for medical purposes and mummification. Like any other resin, Myrrh is a local stimulant, antiseptic, anti-inflammatory, expectorant, astringent and anthelmintic in action. In naturopathic (herbal), this oleo-gum resin mixed with equal parts of honey and rose water, can be useful as a mouthwash for administration in inflammation of the mouth and lips and inflammation of the gums, for thrush and in diphtheria. The oleo gum resin of the Commiphora molmol tree is also used as perfumes.

Traditional Uses: In Unani and Ayurvedic medicinal systems, this plant is beneficial in leucorrhoea, chronic catarrh, ulcers and as a vermifuge. Resin is an essential ingredient in Unani, poly-herbal, semi-solid preparation known as 'Tiraqayat.

Myrrh is classified as a bitter and spicy resin in Chinese traditional medicine and is useful as a tonic for the heart, liver and spleen. It is also considered as blood moving powers to purge stagnant blood from the uterus. Commiphora molmol is, therefore, recommended for amenorrhoea, menopause and uterine tumour.

Biological Uses: The oil of Myrrh possesses antiseptic, antibacterial, anti-inflammatory and antioxidant activities. The resin has been developed as antihyperlipidemic and antischistosomal (a parasite trematode worm) agents.

Chemical Constituents: Myrrh contains essential oils. Other important resin components are alpha, beta and gamma camphoric acids and heeraboresene, commiferin, burseracin, elemol, cadinene, acadinene, furano-sesquiterpenes, resin, gum, sterol and tannins.

Distribution: Commiphora molmol is grown in the South Arabian Peninsula (Oman and Yemen) and Somalia. China is the biggest importer of Myrrh in the world.

Commiphora mukul

Muqil (Plant and Resin)

Latin Binomial	Commiphora mukul
Family	Burseraceae
English Name	Guggul
Urdu Name	Muqil/Gugal

Medicinal Uses: Commiphora mukul is a fragrant oleo gum resin secreted by the tree. The resin is used for arthritis, lowering high cholesterol, hardening the arteries (atherosclerosis), skin diseases and weight loss. It is a resolvent to inflammation. Evidence-based researchers have shown Commiphora mukul reduce the effects of thyroid suppressive drugs and its possible utility for hypothyroidism.

Traditional Uses: In Unani and Ayurvedic medicinal systems, extracts of the plant are valuable in inflammation, gout, obesity and lipid metabolism disorders. It is also beneficial in treating nervous diseases, hypertension, muscle spasms, skin and urinary infections. The fruit cures abdominal problems. Externally, it is applied as a paste in haemorrhoids, incipient abscesses and bad ulcers.

Commiphora mukul forms a constituent of many Unani, poly-herbal medicinal preparations like Majun, Hab, Itrifal and an ointment (Zimad in Urdu).

Biological Uses: The plant possesses antiseptic, antibacterial, anti-inflammatory and antioxidant properties. Ferulates (ferulic acid) is an important bioactive constituent identified from the guggul gum and it plays a significant role in *in vitro* cytotoxicity and is a cure for bleeding pile. Another possible effect is in treating some types of acne.

Commiphora seems to work as an antibiotic 'tetracycline' in treating nodulocystic (a severe form of acne) acne. Both treatments decrease the pain, the swelling and the redness (inflammation) and the number of acne outbreaks. *In Vivo* studies (mice) have shown the gum resin of Commiphora mukul tree may increase the uptake of iodine by the thyroid gland and enhance the activity of thyroid peroxidase enzymes.

An extract of the plant contains phytochemicals that lower cholesterol and triglycerides and one of these substances also decreases the redness and swelling that occurs in some acne types.

Chemical Constituents: The plant contains volatile oils, gum, resin, steroids, terpenoids, sugars, phyto-steroid (guggulsterone), flavonoids, tannins and glycosides.

Distribution: Commiphora mukul is mainly grown in Pakistan, India, Central Asian countries, Africa, Saudi Arabia and the UAE. In Pakistan, it is found in the Cholistan area.

Guggulsterone ($C_{21}H_{28}O_2$)

Ferulic acid ($C_{10}H_{10}O_4$)

Convolvulus scammonia

Saqmunia (Flower and Resins)

Latin Binomial   Convolvulus scammonia

Family	Convolvulaceae
English Name	Scammony
Urdu Name	Saqmunia

Medicinal Uses: The resin from the rhizome of the flowering Convoluvlus scammonia tree is a hydragogue, cathartic, anti-phlegmatic, antispasmodic, abortifacient (herb causing abortion) and anti-inflammatory in action. The plant is a prominent memory improving herb and reduces mental tension. It is an active stimulant in modern herbal medicine, which acts on the bowels and produces prompt watery stools. This resin is a drastic cathartic and hydragogue and should be used cautiously. The dried juice obtained from the root is called 'virgin scammony.'

Traditional Uses: In the Unani system of medicine, the resin is most beneficial in dropsy, anasarca (swelling of the whole body), cerebral affections, liver and intestinal catarrh with shiny intestinal mucous. It is also helpful as a diuretic, in painful joints, in skin disorders (boils on the skin, etc.), as anti-dandruff and in spider bites. A decoction of the plant is useful in cough, flu and treats painful joints and swelling. Aerial parts of the convolvulus plant help treat parasites and jaundice.

Convolvulus scammonia is also beneficial as a laxative, wound healer, antispasmodic and antihemorrhagic. In Unani medicines, the resin is functional after detoxification. It is one of the ingredients of poly-herbal preparations known as 'Itrifal-e-Zamani, Qurs-e-Mullayyan and Majun-e-Suranjan.'

Biological Uses: The extract (aqueous-ethanol) of aerial parts of the plant possesses antiseptic, antibacterial, antioxidant and hepatoprotective properties. A purified bindweed extract (80 per cent aqueous ethanol) is used to inhibit tumour growth and enhance immune function. Aqueous and alkaloid crude extracts of Convolvulus scammonia have an anti-cancer and cellular protective effect.

Chemical Constituents: The resin contains scammonium-I (also known as Jalapin, same as in Jalap of the Convolvulaceae family), volatile oils, rosin, tannins, flavonoids, sterol-triterpenes, alkaloids and sugar. Areal parts of the plant contain phenols, terpenes, flavonoids and tannins.

Convolvulus arvensis contains the tropane alkaloids, tropine, pseudotropine, tropinone and pyrrolidine alkaloid 'cuscohygrine ($C_{13}H_{24}N_2O$).'

Distribution: Convolvulus scammonia bindweed is native to the countries of the Eastern part of the Mediterranean basin; it grows in bushy waste places, from Syria in the South to the Crimea (Ukraine) in the North, and Africa.

Scammonium-1 {Glucoside}(C$_{50}$H$_{84}$O$_{21}$)   Tropine (C$_8$H$_{15}$NO)   Tropinone (C$_8$H$_{13}$NO)

Copaifera langsdorffii

Kapaiba (Tree Parts, Resin and Leaves)

Latin Binomial	Copaifera langsdorffii
Family	Leguminosae/Fabaceae
English Name	Copaiba
Urdu Name	Alkubiba

Medicinal Uses: The pale-yellow gum-resin of Copaifera lansdorfii tree is aromatic, antiseptic, diuretic and expectorant in action. It is useful in leucorrhoea and gonorrhoea. The resin is an aromatic stimulant herb with a bitter, burning taste. It is beneficial in treating sore throat and tonsillitis, as an antiseptic gargle. The resin is taken internally in treating a range of respiratory problems, such as tuberculosis, bronchitis, sinusitis and the urinary tract and reproductive system conditions such as cystitis, kidney, bladder infections, vaginal discharge and gonorrhoea. Externally, it helps cure a range of skin problems, including insect bites, eczema, chilblains, sores and psoriasis. It is also effective in treating wounds and bleeding.

Traditional Uses: In the Brazilian herbal system, the resin is used as a potent antiseptic, expectorant and is effective in urinary tract infection. Capsules of this resin are sold in stores and pharmacies in Brazil and are recommended for all types of internal inflammation, stomach ulcers and cancer.

The gum-resin is also used in Peruvian herbal medicine systems in reducing inflammation and in increasing urination. The oil of the plant improves digestion, has diuretic, expectorant effects and controls bacterial infections. The resin, as a whole, has demonstrated significant antimicrobial activity against gram-positive bacteria. However, in large quantities, the resin is purgative and can cause skin rashes and kidney damage. The plant and its resins are seldom used in the Unani system of medicine.

Biological Uses: The plant's bark and gum-resin are antibacterial, antimicrobial and cytostatic (herb causing inhibition and cell division). The anti-inflammatory affect is mainly due to the terpenoids, particularly caryophyllene (sesquiterpene), which has also demonstrated effective pain-relieving properties and antifungal properties. The resin shows significant antitumor activity.

Chemical Constituents: The gum resin contains volatile oils, resin, condensed tannins, whereas the whole plant has flavonoids, terpenoids, phenolic compounds and gallic acid. The essential oil contains alpha- and beta-caryophyllene, sesquiterpenes, resins and terpenic acids. The bark is a rich source of condensed tannins.

Distribution: Copaifera langsdorffii is a genus of large trees found in Brazil, mainly in the Amazon forest and the Atlantic forest and Brazilian highlands. It has also been found in other countries in South America. It is primarily found in the Congo, Cameroon, Guinea and Angola. The plant is also known as a 'diesel tree.'

Curcuma longa

Haldi (Flower and Rhizome)

Latin Binomial   Curcuma longa

Family	Zingiberaceae
English Name	Turmeric/Karukum
Urdu Name	Haldi

Medicinal Uses: The flowering Curcuma longa plant's rhizome is aromatic, carminative, antiseptic, deobstruent (removing obstructions) and stimulant in action.

Being rather a potent herb, Turmeric is helpful as a powder, an alcoholic extract or as a tincture in small doses, mixed with other herbs. It is mainly beneficial as a blood purifier that stimulates blood circulation and to bring on the female menstrual flow. Curcuma longa also cleanses the liver and improves the production and flow of the bile.

Traditional Uses: In Unani and Ayurvedic medicinal systems, a milk decoction of the rhizome is made as a tonic, to treat skin rashes, blemishes, rheumatism, muscular aches, pains and to speed up recovery from an athletic workout. Traditional healers (Hakims and Ayurveda) of the Indo-Pak subcontinent also recognize Turmeric's properties in scraping excess sugar, fats and cholesterol from the blood, in type two diabetes, high cholesterol and triglycerides

The rhizome is extensively used in Unani and Ayurvedic medicines, alone or in a combination of Turmeric rhizome with 'neem' (Azadirachta indica) to lower blood sugar.

The fine yellowish powder of 'Ubtan' is the oldest cosmetics form with many healing properties. Turmeric is used as an antirheumatic herb in Chinese medicine, and it is recognized chiefly for arthritic, rheumatic aches and pains of the shoulders, arms and upper extremities, either internally or topically.

Turmeric is probably the best known for its uses as a culinary herb, where it is the chief ingredient in curry powder, giving it the bulk of its flavour and aroma and its distinctive yellow colour. Because of all its valuable health benefits, those who eat curries and Turmeric in their diet, enjoy better health overall than people who do not. The chief advantages are blood purification, better blood circulation, better liver and intestinal health. Turmeric is valued as the main ingredient in curry powders because it has antioxidant and antimicrobial properties and helps the liver detoxify foods that may be toxic, impure, or less than perfectly fresh.

Biological Uses: The antioxidant, anti-inflammatory and antimicrobial properties of turmeric help heal wounds, fight eczema, reduce acne scarring and bring out a natural glow. The presence of curcumin in Turmeric causes the death of cancer cells without harming healthy cells. As piperine (as in Piper longum and Piper nigrum), it enhances curcumin absorption in the body by up to 2,000 per cent and combining the spices, magnifies their effects. Researchers around the world are showing tremendous interest in turmeric. In the United States alone, the National Institutes of Health is currently funding studies on turmeric and curcumin for various conditions, including colorectal cancer, pancreatic cancer, Alzheimer's disease, psoriasis, inflammatory bowel disease, irritable bowel syndrome and rheumatoid arthritis.

Chemical Constituents: The resin is oily and it is deep brown in colour. The oleoresin contains 35-40 per cent curcumin and 15 to 20 per cent curcumin oil. The primary active ingredients of Curcuma include three curcuminoids, curcumin, demethoxycurcumin and bisdemethoxycurcumin. The plant also contains valuable bioactive phytochemicals such as glycosides, steroids, flavonoids, alkaloids, tannins and saponins.

Distribution: Curcuma longa is native to the Indo-Pak subcontinent and is extensively cultivated in the tropical and subtropical regions of South and Southeast Asia, including China, Indonesia, Pakistan (Kasur and Bannu districts), India and some areas of Africa which have warm and wet tropical climate.

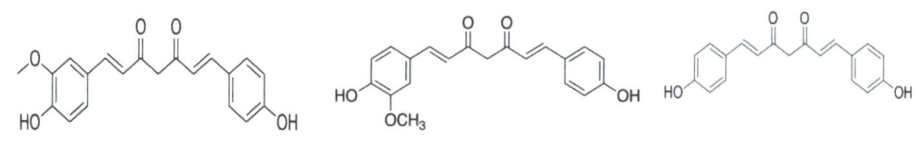

Curcumin ($C_{21}H_{20}O_6$)   Demethoxycurcumin ($C_{20}H_{18}O_5$)   Bisdemethoxycurcumin ($C_{19}H_{16}O_4$)

Daemonorops draco

Dammul Akhwain (Tree Parts, Extract/Resin)

Latin Binomial	Daemonorops draco/Calamus draco
Family	Arecaceae/Palmae

English Name	Dragon's Blood
Urdu Name	Damm-ul-Akhwain

Medicinal Uses: The resin of Daemonorops Draco tree is astringent, styptic and desiccative (dry out) in action. It is also helpful in menorrhagia (abnormally, heavy bleeding during menstruation) and bloody piles.

Traditional Uses: In Far East countries (Malaysia, Java and Sumatra), the plant resin is used as a tonic, as an antirheumatic and also in syphilis. Dragon's blood may offer some protection against or even kill pathogens like bacteria, fungi and viruses.

In Unani and Ayurvedic medicinal systems, it is mainly used in bloody piles and excessive blood loss during menstruation. Traditional healers (Hakims and Ayurveda) of the Indo-Pak subcontinent recommend this resin for strengthening the stomach and liver and as an astringent ingredient of collyriums (solution to clean eyes) and externally as a wash for further healing and to stopping bleeding. It has been used in dentifrices and as a mouth wash. The plant resin is a substance that is often used in traditional Chinese medicine (TCM) to treat chronic colitis and to improve blood circulation. It is also helpful with Frankincense (myrrh) for chronic ulcers. Dragon's blood is used to give the classic red colour to the herbal oils.

Biological Uses: The oleo resin possesses antiseptic, antibacterial, antioxidant and antifungal properties.

Chemical Constituents: The plant contains resin, gum, volatile oils, red-tannin derivatives, drocoresinotannol, cracoresen, flavonoids, phenols, alkaloids (traces), steroids and isoprenoids.

Distribution: Zambia and Gabon export high-quality Daemonorops draco globally.

Dorema ammoniacum

Ushaq (Plant Parts and Gum-Resin)

Latin Binomial	Dorema ammoniacum
Family	Umbelliferae/Apiaceae
English Name	Ammoniacum
Urdu Name	Ushaq

Medicinal Uses: The gum resin of the perennial Dorema ammoniacum herb is aromatic, anti-inflammatory, diuretic, emmenagogue and expectorant in action. The plant has been used in Western herbal medicine for thousands of years and is still an effective remedy for various chest complaints. This plant is listed in the British Pharmacopoeia as an expectorant and antispasmodic and is still of value in Western and Indian Medicine for chronic bronchitis and persistent coughs. It is also suitable for cosmetic industries.

Traditional Uses: In Unani and Ayurvedic medicinal systems, the resin is beneficial for anthelmintic and gastrointestinal disorders. It is often suitable, internally, in treating chronic bronchitis (especially in the elderly), asthma and catarrh. The resin has also been valuable traditionally, in the treatment of convulsions. Externally, it is helpful as a plaster for the swelling of the joints and for indolent tumours. The resin is dissolved in vinegar, and is applied as a liquid, to relieve pain and to heal wounds. It is also effective in dyspnoea.

Iranian traditional medicine suggests using this herb to reduce and manage inflammatory pain in joint diseases. In Uzbekistan, milky latex from the plant's roots is beneficial as a diuretic for headache and for respiratory organ disorders. A tincture from the green stem, is useful for heart diseases based on Azerbaijan's folk beliefs and also beliefs of the Armenian people. The Dorema species can treat many abnormalities, especially catarrh, bronchitis, diarrhoea and can also act as a diuretic.

Biological Uses: A wide range of pharmacological activities, including antimicrobial, anti inflammatory, antioxidant, cytotoxicity, anticonvulsant, anti-diabetic and hypolipidemic activities, have been reported in this genus in the modern medicine. These phytochemicals are derived from different parts of the Dorema species, such as the flower, fruit, leaf, stem and the root. The oil obtained from the plant has antibacterial and antioxidant properties.

Chemical Constituents: Numerous biologically active constituents, including terpenes (ammoresinol and ashamirone), coumarins and phenolic compounds, have been isolated from the Dorema species.

Medicinal Plants   Resins

Distribution: Dorema ammoniacum is a native to West Asia, Iran, Pakistan and Afghanistan.

Ammoresinol ($C_{24}H_{30}O_4$)

Dryopteris chrysocoma

Sarkhas (Plant, Spores and Leaves)

Latin Binomial	Dryopteris chrysocoma/Nephrodium filix-mas
Family	Pteridaceae/Dryopteridaceae
English Name	Filix-Mas/Male Fern
Urdu Name	Sarkhas

Medicinal Uses: The roots, leaves, oil and resin of this plant are used for medicinal purposes. Dryopteris chrysocoma is desiccant, abortifacient (herb causing abortion), anthelmintic, vermifuge, decongestant and irritating in action. It is probably the best herb known against tapeworm. It is usually given at night, after several hours of fasting. Then, followed by a purgative drug in the morning, e.g., castor oil, excellent results are obtained. It acts by paralyzing the worm's muscles, forcing it to relax its hold on the gut wall. The root is prescribed with a non-oily purgative. The Male Fern preparations are used externally for rheumatism, muscle pain, neuralgia and sciatica.

Traditional Uses: The traditional healers (Hakims and Ayurveda) of the Indo-Pak subcontinent use this herb as a contraceptive, when taken with honey and for oozing wounds and herpes. The root or its oleoresin is useful as a specific treatment for tapeworms. Externally, the root is beneficial as a poultice in treating abscesses, boils, carbuncles and sores. The plant is seldom used in Unani and Ayurvedic systems of medicine.

Biological Uses: The extract (aqueous and non-aqueous) of the root and resin possess antiseptic, antibacterial, anti-inflammatory, antiviral and anodyne properties. Anti-cancer, antifungal and antirheumatic activities are also reported. The crude extract (methanol) of the whole plant (leaves, stem and root) shows intense anti-inflammatory activity. The leaf's air-dried extracts (petro ether, acetone, methanol, and aqueous) are antibacterial in nature.

Chemical Uses: The active ingredient of the resin is filicin and filicic acid. The plant contains resin, volatile oils, flavonoids, gum, tannins and various salts. The root is a good source of tannins.

Distribution: Dryopteris chrysocoma grows throughout Europe, including Britain, Africa, America, Pakistan and Eastern Asia.

Note: The dose administered must be carefully assessed as the Male Fern is an irritant poison, in large quantity, causing muscle weakness, coma and possible damage to the eyesight.

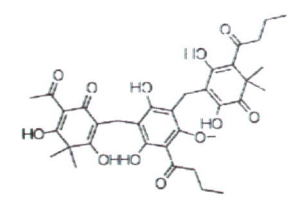

Filicin ($C_{36}H_{44}O_{12}$)

Ferula foetida

Hiltit (Plant, Flowers and Resin)

Latin Binomial	Ferula foetida/Ferula assafoetida

Family	Umbelliferae/Apiaceae
English Name	Asafoetida/Gum Foetida
Urdu Name	Hiltit/Hing

Medicinal Uses: The oleo gum resin of the flowering Ferula foetida plant is carminative, digestive, expectorant, stimulant, antispasmodic, antiflatulent and rubefacient in action. It is also helpful in modern herbal in treating hysteria, nervous conditions, asthma, whooping cough, as a laxative and as a sedative. The volatile oils present in the plant are eliminated through the lungs, making this an excellent treatment for asthma. Asafoetida has been esteemed among indigenous medicines, particularly in Asian countries from the earliest times.

In modern herbalism, Ferula foetida is helpful in the treatment of hysteria, some nervous conditions, bronchitis, asthma and whooping cough. It was at one time employed in the treatment of infantile pneumonia and flatulent colic.

Traditional Uses: It is widely used in the Indo-Pak subcontinent food and as a medicine in Unani and Ayurveda systems. Asafoetida has also been used as a sedative, diuretic, anti-diabetic, aphrodisiac and emmenagogue. It also thins the blood (antiplatelet) and lowers blood pressure. Ferula foetida forms a constituent of the famous Unani poly-herbal preparation known as Hab-e-Hiltit, a remedy for stomach disorders.

In Iranian traditional medicine, Asafoetida is considered to be a sedative, analgesic, carminative, antispasmodic and diuretic. In China, a decoction of the plant is taken orally as a vermifuge. In Egypt, the dried root's hot water extract is taken orally as an antispasmodic, diuretic and as a vermifuge. The gum is chewed for amenorrhoea (absence of menstruation) in Malaysia and is an anti-epileptic agent, in Morocco. In Afghanistan, the dried gum's hot water extract is taken orally for hysteria, whooping cough and ulcers.

Biological Uses: Ferula foetida possesses antibacterial, antiseptic, antiviral, antioxidant, anti-inflammatory and antimutagenic activities. This oleo-gum-resin has been known to possess antifungal and anti-diabetic activities. The extract of ethanol (95 per cent) of the dried plant has anti-cancer, hypotensive and molluscicidal (a phylum of invertebrate animals) properties. The plant's hot water extract, administered to female rats, was inactive on the estrogen of the uterus. The methanol fractions from several Ferula species have exhibited cytotoxicity and anticonvulsant activities.

Recent studies have shown several promising actions, particularly neuroprotective, memory-enhancing, digestive enzyme, antioxidant, antispasmodic, hypotensive, antiobesity, anthelmintic and hepatoprotective.

Chemical Constituents: The plant contains volatile oils, resin, gum, flavonoids, tannins and sugar. The oil's disagreeable odour is mainly due to the disulfide.

Distribution: It is grown primarily in Iran and Afghanistan, from where it is exported to the rest of the world.

Ferula galbaniflua

Jawashir/Ganda Behroza (Plant Parts and Gum-Resin)

Latin Binomial	Ferula galbaniflua/Ferula jaeschkeana
Family	Umbelliferae/Apiaceae
English name	Galbanum
Urdu name	Jawashir/Ganda Behroza

Medicinal Uses: The gum resin of the flowering Ferula galbaniflua plant is aromatic, stimulant, expectorant, demulcent, anti-phlegmatic, carminative in action and a tonic for the nerves. The oil increases circulation in the body, helping with arthritis, rheumatism and circulation-related issues. It also relieves chest congestion due to bronchitis and other upper-respiratory problems.

Traditional Uses: Ferula galbaniflua is useful as an antispasmodic and an intermediate between ammoniac and asafoetida for relieving the lungs' air passages. Externally the gum resin is used as a plaster for inflammatory swellings. The oil and resin were traditionally incorporated into pastes for boils, wrinkles and other skin diseases. Ferula galbaniflua has historically been used as anti-hysteria and for the treatment of dysentery.

The rhizomes of this plant which are known as Al-Kalakh in Arabic, are used in Saudi Arabia as a traditional remedy for the treatment of skin infections, while the roasted flower buds are used against fever and dysentery

In the Unani medicinal system, the resin is mainly valuable in ointments known as 'Zimadad and Marhamain.'

Biological Uses: In recent studies, the antimicrobial, anti-inflammatory, antiepileptic and spasmolytic properties have been confirmed. The oil of the plant is antiseptic and antibacterial. Extracts of the Ferula species have shown a broad spectrum of *in vitro* and *in vivo* pharmacological properties, including antidiabetic, antiproliferative and cytotoxic activities.

Chemical Constituents: Ferula galbaniflua contains gum resin (galbanum), mineral constituents, volatile oil, umbelliferine, sesquiterpene coumarins, galbaresino-tannol (resin alcohol) and tannins. The primary constituent of the fruit is a crystalline mixture of the 5-(O)-angeloyl and isovaleroyl (an ester of 1-oxojaeskeanadiol).

Distribution: Turkey and Iran are the two major producers of Ferula galbaniflua (galbanum).

Ferula persica

Kundal/Sak (Plant and Resin)

Latin Binomial	Ferula persica/Ferula szovitsiana
Family	Umbelliferae/Apiaceae
English name	Sagapenum gum Kundal/Sak
Urdu name	Kundal/Sak

Medicinal uses: The oleo gum resin of the flowering Ferula persica plant is a stimulant, anthelmintic, diuretic, emmenagogue and attenuant (a herb that dilutes the fluids) in action.

Traditional Uses: In Iran, it is traditionally used as a laxative, carminative, antihysteric and for the treatment of diabetes. Externally, it is useful for backache and rheumatism. The plant extract also shows some sedative properties. It is seldom used in Unani medicines.

Biological Uses: The extracts of this plant show a broad spectrum of pharmacological properties including, antiseptic, antibacterial, antifungal and anti-cancer. The resin is antiseptic, antibacterial, anti-inflammatory and the plant extract possesses antioxidant properties. A decoction of leaves and flowers exhibit antibacterial and antiviral activities. In a study, the galbanic acid extracted from Ferula persica inhibited angiogenesis and the proliferation of the tumour cells in lung cancer cell lines. The essential oil of the fruit exhibits antiepileptic activity.

Chemical Constituents: The plant contains resin, gum, volatile oils, sesquiterpene coumarins, sulphur-containing compounds, glycosides and a small amount of tannins.

Distribution: Ferula persica is a native to central Asia, particularly Eastern Iran and Afghanistan. Ferula persica is a well-known species of the genus Ferula in Iran and has two varieties: 'persica and latisecta.'

Fraxinus ornus

Turanjbin (Tree, Plant secretion and Leaves)

Latin Binomial	Fraxinus ornus
Family	Oleaceae
English Name	Manna Ash/Flowering-Ash
Urdu Name	Turanjbin/Gond Jawasa

Medicinal Uses: The bark, flowers, leaves and gum resin of the plant are useful for medicinal purposes. The gum resin of Fraxinus ornus tree is laxative, purgative, antipyretic, aphrodisiac, emetic, antirheumatic in action and a blood purifier. In the British Pharmacopoeia Codex (BPC, first published in 1907), syrup of gum resin of the Fraxinus ornus is prescribed as a mild laxative for children, in the proportion of one part of the resin and ten parts of water.

Traditional Uses: The honey-like secretion of the thorny bush called Alhagi maurorum is called 'Turanjbin' by the Unani physicians. In Unani and Ayurvedic medicinal systems, it helps treat nausea, fever, excessive thirst, cough and chest pain. It is valuable in asthma and piles. It is bitter and acrid with a distinct flavour; it is antipyretic, laxative, diuretic, digestible, refrigerant, aperient and attenuated. It removes excess fat, cures leprosy, skin diseases, brain affections, bronchitis, is good for piles, for the opacities of the cornea and a persistent unilateral headache. It is useful in a bleeding nose, allays thirst and improves appetite. The flowers are useful in piles.

In the northern areas of Pakistan, the root, bark and leaves of the plant have been traditionally suitable for the cure of malaria and pneumonia. The oil from the leaves is helpful in treating rheumatism.

The bark is a gentle laxative and a tonic. It is precious for children and pregnant women. Its action usually is very mild, though it does sometimes cause flatulence and pain. A decoction of twigs is beneficial in the treatment of cough in children. The seeds are antihypertensive and antihyper-triglyceridemic in action.

Biological Uses: The incredible range of pharmacological properties of Fraxinus ornus have been well documented, including its anti-cancer, anti-inflammatory, antioxidant, anti-ageing, antimicrobial and neuroprotective properties. The bark extract (ethanol) exhibits a pronounced antioxidative activity and possesses intense wound healing properties.

Oleuropein (a glycosylated seco-iridoid) isolated from Fraxinus can be used as a neuroprotective agent against colchicine induced neurodegenerative diseases, as it significantly recovers memory and helps learning retention.

Chemical constituents: Fraxinus ornus plant possesses various secoiridoids, gum, resin, glucosides, phenylethanoids, flavonoids, resins, tannins, essential oils and coumarins. The Fraxinus plant is rich in hydroxycoumarins.

Distribution: Fraxinus ornus is a native to Southern Europe and South-Western Asia, China, the Northern area of Pakistan, India and Afghanistan.

Garcinia morella

Usarah-e-Rewand (Plant Parts, Fruits and Resins)

Latin Binomial	Garcinia morella/Garcinia cambogia
Family	Clusiaceae/Guttiferae
English Name	Gamboge
Urdu Name	Usarah-e-Rewand/Farfeeran

Medicinal Uses: The gum resin of the evergreen Garcinia morella tree is a powerful hydragogue, carminative, anthelmintic, antispasmodic and a mild diuretic in action. It is helpful in getting rid of toxins. The root bark is antirheumatic.

Traditional Uses: In Unani and Ayurvedic medicinal systems, the fruit is beneficial in treating dysentery, gastritis and it is said to have anti-inflammatory properties. In Ayurvedic medicine, the plant is also useful in treating cough, cold and fever; however, it is seldom used alone. The yellow fruit is esteemed as a dessert fruit.

Biological Uses: The yellow coloured gum resin possesses antifungal, hepatoprotective, antiviral, antibacterial, antioxidant and cytotoxic properties. The methanol extracts of the fruit show better anti-cancer activity than the gum resin. The ethyl acetate fraction of the bark possesses wound healing properties The chloroform extract contains garcinol (a polyisoprenylated benzophenone), which may possess anti-cancer activities.

Chemical Constituents: The plant contains resin, gum, terpenoids, phenolic compounds, flavonoids, tannins and volatile oils. The gum resin is rich in myristic acid, palmitic acid, palmitoleic acid, oleic acid, linoleic acid, etc.

Distribution: Gamboge fruit is native to Southeast Asia, specifically the tropical countries bordering the Bay of Bengal, including Southern India, Malaysia, Thailand, Myanmar and Cambodia.

Ipomoea hederacea

Kaladana/Hab-ul-Neel (Flowers and Seeds)

Latin Binomial	Ipomoea hederacea
Family	Convolvulaceae
English Name	Pharbitis Seeds
Urdu Name	Kaladana/Habul-ul-Neel

Medicinal Uses: The seeds of the flowering Ipomoea hederacea plant are cathartic, carminative, diuretic emmenagogue in action and are a blood purifier. The seeds are also useful as anthelmintic, anticholinergic, antifungal, antispasmodic, antitumor, diuretic and are laxative. They contain small quantities of the hallucinogen lysergic acid diethylamide, LSD. This has been used medicinally in the treatment of various mental disorders.

Traditional Uses: In Unani and Ayurvedic medicinal systems, the seeds are useful in treating oedema, oliguria, ascariasis and constipation. A decoction of the root is an emmenagogue. The plant is also beneficial in treating abdominal diseases, fevers, headache and bronchitis. The grounded plant is valuable as a hair wash to rid it of lice. The juice of the leaves is suitable in treating eye inflammations. Externally, the dried, powdered seed paste or ointment is applied over the leucodermal, vitiliginous patches and the skin's irritative parts. The seeds are rubbed on the male genitals to treat erectile dysfunction, female genitals for lubrication purposes and enhancing sexual desire. It is also used as a contraceptive in Korea.

In China, it is used as a diuretic, antihelmintic and deobstruent. In the Philippines, Papua New Guinea, Malaysia, Indo-China and India, the seeds help reduce stomach ache and cramps. In Nigeria, the plant is valuable as a love charm.

Biological Uses: Studies have shown that the plant's oil and non-aqueous extracts (methanol) possess antioxidant, nematicidal, hepatoprotective and antibacterial properties. Some of these species of Ipomoea also show antimicrobial, spasmolytic, spasmogenic, hypoglycemic, hypotensive, antiviral, anticoagulant, anti-inflammatory, psychotomimetic and anti-cancer activities.

Chemical Constituents: The active principle in the Ipomoea hederacea is resin (about 12 to 15 per cent) and is called 'Pharbitism.' It is considered comparable to the resin of 'Jalap' or the 'convolvulin' from Ipomoea purge of the Convolvulaceae family. This medicinal herb contains some valuable phytochemicals such as ergoline alkaloids (chanoclavine, penniclavine, etc.), terpenoids, saponins, flavonoids, fixed oil, essential oils and tannins.

Distribution: The Ipomoea species are native to the Americas and have recently been introduced into North America.

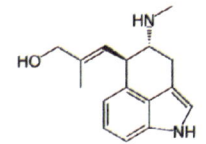

Chanoclavine ($C_{16}H_{20}N_2O$) 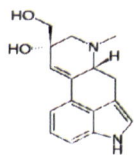   Penniclavine ($C_{16}H_{18}N_2O_2$)

Ipomoea purge

Jalapah (Flower and Roots)

Latin Binomial	Ipomoea purge/ Exogonium purge
Family	Convolvulaceae
English Name	Jalap/John's Root
Urdu Name	Jalapah

Medicinal Uses: The root of flowering Ipomoea purge is purgative, anti-phlegmatic, antispasmodic, antirheumatic, emetic and antibilious in action. It is generally utilized in all pulmonary ailments, bladder problems and urine suppression.

Traditional Uses: In the Unani system of medicine, Jalap root is emetic and causes loose motions, acting as a violent purgative. Jalapa is regarded as a safe drug in eliminating 'mal-humours' that cause disorders like dropsy, chronic and habitual constipation, facial paralysis, general paralysis and rheumatism, sciatica, as well as general catarrhal affections. Jalap is either taken alone or powdered, in chicken soup or lukewarm water. It can also be combined with other suitable laxatives. A decoction of the root is an emmenagogue. The pounded plant is used as a hair wash.

Biological Uses: Extracts (aqueous and non-aqueous) of flowers, leaves and fruit of Ipomoea showed analgesic, spasmolytic (to relieve spasms), hypotensive, spasmogenic (induce spasms), antibacterial and anti-cancer properties. A methanolic extract from the seeds presents biological activity against Herpes. Analgesic properties have been attributed to indolizidine alkaloid, e.g., ipalbidine. The leaf fraction shows no antimicrobial activity.

Chemical Constituents: The plant contains resin, gum, ergoline, indolizidine and nortropane alkaloids, isoprenoids, terpenoids and coumarins. The root also contains tannins, phenolic compounds, glycosides, flavonoids, steroids and saponins.

Distribution: Ipomoea purge is native to Mexico and naturalized to other parts of the neotropics (South and Central America and the Caribbean).

Operculina turpethum

Tarbud (Flower, Plant and Rhizomes)

Latin Binomial	Operculina turpethum/ Ipomoea turpethum
Family	Convolvulaceae
English Name	Turpeth/Indian Jalap
Urdu Name	Tarbud/Tubut

Medicinal Uses: The roots or rhizomes of the flowering Operculina turpethum plant are aromatic, hydragogue cathartic, hepatic stimulant, anti-phlegmatic, antiepileptic and antiarthritic. The glycol-resin and other phytochemicals present in the plant possess antiseptic, antibacterial, anti-inflammatory and ulcer protective properties.

Traditional Uses: The plant has been incorporated into 'ten purgative herbs' in the Ayurvedic medicinal system. Turpeth, combined with other herbs, is particularly beneficial in rheumatic, paralytic (causing paralysis) and epileptic conditions in the Unani medicinal system. In both Unani and Ayurvedic medicinal systems, this herb's purgative action helps various stomach disorders like flatulence, indigestion and unsatisfactory bowel movements. The root is also useful in treating fever, oedema, anorexia, hepatosplenomegaly (enlargement of the liver and spleen) and intoxication. A concentrated aqueous decoction of the root is used externally in oozing and scaling skin diseases. The root is also helpful in gout, bilious disturbances in general, jaundice and intestinal worms. A decoction of the leaves is a tonic after childbirth.

Unani poly-herbal medicinal preparations, e.g., Itrifal, Majun, Jawarish and Qurs, contain Turpeth as one of the ingredients.

Biological Uses: The chloroform fraction of the plant shows antibacterial activity. The etheric, alcoholic and aqueous extracts have anti-inflammatory, antioxidant and antimicrobial properties. Oral administration of the hydro-alcoholic and methanolic stem bark extracts of Operculina turpethum exhibit potential, anti-ulcer activity. The ethanolic extract possesses a hepatoprotective effect. A study of the ethanolic fraction of the stem of the plant has antioxidant activity and may play a protective role against 2, 4-Dimethoxybenzaldehyde (DMBA) induced breast cancer.

Chemical Constituents: The chemical constituents of Operculina turpethum plant are resins, a mixture of alfa and beta turpethein, glycosides, coumarins, scopolamine (hyoscine), saponins, flavonoids, steroids and carbohydrates.

Distribution: Operculina turpethum is a convolvulaceous plant found throughout India, Pakistan, China, Sri Lanka, Africa and Australia. It is occasionally cultivated in botanical gardens as an ornamental plant.

Turpethein ($C_{10}H_{16}$)   Copolamine ($C_{17}H_{21}NO_4$)

Pinus roxburghii

Behroza (Tree and Resin)

Latin Binomial	Pinus roxburghii/Pinus longifolia
Family	Pinaceae
English Name	Chir Pine/Long leaf Indian Pine
Urdu Name	Behroza/Sat-e-Behroza

Medicinal Uses: The oleo resin of the evergreen Pinus roxburghii tree is anti-inflammatory, calorific (relating to heat production), carminative, laxative and stimulant in action.

The gum resin has a good effect on the vagina and uterus diseases. An ointment prepared from the resin, applied to affected parts, regularly before bedtime, will soften scar tissue and heal boils and cracks. The resin is also valuable in treating ulcers, snakebites, and skin diseases. The Pine wood is diaphoretic and also a stimulant. The needles can be suitable as a diuretic. The bark, roots and stems of Pinus roxburghii are also beneficial in anti-diabetic in ethnopharmacology. The resin removes joint inflammation caused by rheumatism, which helps restore movement and alleviate pain.

Traditional Uses: In China, the resin from a particular Pine tree is useful in treating abscesses. Various parts of the plant are prescribed for coughs, colds, influenza, tuberculosis, bronchitis as antiseptic, diaphoretic, diuretic, rubefacient, stimulant and febrifuge. These are also useful in treating inflammations, piles, diseases of the liver and spleen, urinary discharges, lumbago, tuberculosis, scabies and epilepsy. The gum has shown good response in diseases of the vagina and uterus. In the Unani system of medicine, Pinus roxburghii is mainly valuable in Zamadat and Marh (ointments).

Biological Uses: The Pine oil possesses antiseptic, antibacterial, antioxidant and antifungal properties. The dried hydro-alcoholic extract of the plant also has antioxidant and anti-inflammatory activities. The needle oil shows maximum activity against Staphylococcus aureus and Bacillus subtilis, while no activity was observed against Escherichia coli. The isolated compound (sesquiterpene) of the plant, has an anti-mosquito property.

Chemical Constituents: The plant contains resin, gum, volatile oils, tannins, quercetin, sterols and resin, whereas the oil is rich in caryophyllene, alpha-humulene and terpineol.

Distribution: Pinus roxburghii or its species grow in almost all counties of the world.

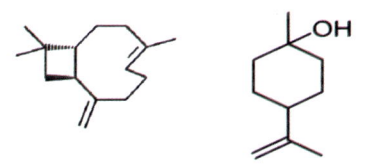

Caryophyllene ($C_{15}H_{24}$)   Terpineol ($C_{10}H_{18}O$)

Pistacia lentiscus

Mastaghi (Plant and Resins)

Latin Binomial	Pistacia lentiscus
Family	Anacardiaceae
English Name	Mastic
Urdu Name	Mastaghi

Medicinal Uses: The aromatic resin of the dioecious, evergreen Pistacia lentiscus tree is diuretic, restorative, emmenagogue (increases menstrual flow), is a tonic and is absorbent in action. Pistacia Lentiscus is a powerful aphrodisiac herb that is potent in increasing libido. It is an excellent herbal remedy for healing wounds and cuts. It supports liver functions and strengthens them in preventing liver diseases. It protects the digestive tract from ailments that cause peptic ulcers. Mastic in alcoholic solutions, introduced into a carious tooth cavity, helps relieve toothache and provides temporary filling.

Traditional Uses: In Unani and Ayurvedic medicinal systems, Mastic resin is widely used in ulcer healing, is antispasmodic and aphrodisiac. Pistacia lentiscus resin helps treat heartburn, gastritis, ulcer and indigestion.

Mastic is one of the essential ingredients of many Unani polyherbal, semisolid preparations known as 'Jawarish Mastagi, Qurs Tabasheer, Majun-e-Jiryan, Arq Maul-Laham,' etc.

Biological Uses: Fractions of various plant parts exhibit antioxidant, antibacterial, anti-inflammatory, antiprotozoal and wound healing properties. The methanol fraction the fruit oil is antimicrobial, anti-cancer, whereas aqueous extracts have antihyperlipidemic, hypoglycaemic and anticholinesterase activities.

Chemical Constituents: The plant contains resin, abietic acid, essential oils, tannins, flavonoids, diterpene rosin acids and sugar. Oils from the plant's leaves mainly consist of volatile hydrocarbon oils, e.g. myrcene, limonene, germacrene, etc.

Distribution: Pistacia lentiscus is a native of the Mediterranean region, and from Morocco and the Iberian Peninsula (Portugal, France, Andorra and Gibraltar) and from Turkey to Iraq and Iran.

Preparation of Rosin

The crude resin is mixed in a heated stainless steel vessel with 20 per cent (w/w) turpentine after filtration, it is allowed to stand to separate water and other impurities. The dilute oleo resin is then distilled over.

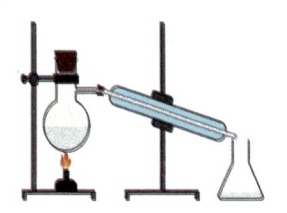

Distillation and Distillation Units

Balsam: This **is** an aromatic, resinous substance, such as balm, exuded by various trees and shrubs and it is used as a base for certain fragrances and medical preparations. Balsam is a resinous mixture with large proportions of benzoic acid and cinnamic acid or both.

Benzoic acid ($C_7H_6O_2$)   Cinnamic acid ($C_9H_8O_2$)

Differences between Balsams vs Resins

According to Elena Vosnaki (is a historian, archaeologist and fragrance author):

"The distinction between resin and balsam is one form, on a fundamental level. Simply put and generalizing, Resinous materials come in the form of solidified, gum-like 'tears' seeping from the elixir vita (a substance Alchemists attempted to make to restore youth, prolong life and turn metals into gold) circulating into the bark of big trees, such as the Boswellia glabara (which produces frankincense). On the other hand, Balsams are sticky materials, not necessarily tree secretions, often coming from flower pods or bushy twigs (such as Vanilla orchids or the Mediterranean rockrose)."

Commiphora stocksiana

Balsam (Tree, Parts and Resin)

Latin Binomial	Commiphora stocksiana
Family	Burseraceae
English Name	Balsam
Urdu Name	Balsan

Medicinal Uses: The wood, fruit and resin of the flowering Commiphora stocksiana tree are expectorant, anti-inflammatory, styptic and anti-haemorrhoidal in action. Balsam is useful in all chronic mucous afflictions, catarrh, leucorrhoea, diarrhoea and dysentery.

Traditional Uses: In Unani and Ayurvedic medicinal systems, it is beneficial for curing inflammations, rheumatism, indolent ulcers, bronchitis, laryngitis, tonsillitis, leucorrhoea and chronic endometritis (inflammation of the inner lining of the uterus). Balsam is a stimulant, expectorant and parasiticide in action. It is also helpful in scabies, irritant skin diseases and acute eczema. It helps in treating discharges from the genitourinary organs. Commiphora stocksiana is applied locally as a paste in haemorrhoids, incipient abscesses and bad ulcers. Externally, the gum is suitable in cleansing and healing wounds, bad ulcers, sores, etc. The oil may be applied to sore nipples and discharges from the ears to effect healing. The fruit is carminative, expectorant and stimulant.

Biological Uses: The oil of Commiphora stocksiana possesses antiseptic, antiviral, anti-inflammatory and antibacterial properties.

Chemical Constituents: The plant contains resin, oils, gum, flavonoids, sugar and tannins.

Distribution: Pakistan and India are the primary producers of Commiphora stocksiana. In Pakistan, the Commiphora tree is common on dry river beds of Sind and Balochistan coastal regions.

Liquidambar orientalis

Maya Amber Dasi (Tree, Leaf and Balsam)

Latin Binomial	Liquidambar orientalis
Family	Altingiaceae/Hamamelidaceae
English Name	Storax/Sweet gum

Urdu Name	Maya Ambar Desi/Silaras

Medicinal uses: The balsam of the deciduous, slow-growing Liquidambar orientalis tree is aromatic, stimulant, expectorant and diuretic in action. Like most balsams, it acts beneficially upon the mucous membranes and has been used internally for asthma, bronchitis, catarrh and pulmonary affections; externally in gleets and leucorrhoea. The ointment of the balsam is a practical application for several cutaneous disorders such as scabies, ringworms, etc.

Traditional Uses: In Unani and Ayurvedic medicinal systems, a decoction of the Liquidambar orientalis plant, made into a syrup's consistency, effectively reduces the throat's roughness and cough. It is taken internally to treat strokes, infantile convulsion, common heart diseases and pruritis. It is also beneficial in the treatment of cancer. Externally, it is mixed with oil and used in treating scabies, wounds, ulcers, etc. The leaves, fruit and roots are used in similar ways to the resin and are also considered an antidote, parasiticide and vulnerary.

Biological Uses: The Balsam shows remarkable antiseptic, antibacterial, anti-inflammatory and antiparasitic activities. It has the same action as the balsam of Tolu and balsam of Peru.

Chemical Constituents: Balsam contains cinnamic acid, cinnamyl alcohol, resin alcohol and volatile oils. An extract of its leaves contains terpenoids.

Distribution: Liquidambar orientalis tree is native to Turkey, Rhodes Island (Greece) and the United States

Myroxylon balsamum

Tolu Ka Gond (Leaves, Tree and Balsam)

Latin Binomial	Myroxylon balsamum
Family	Leguminosae/Fabaceae

English Name	Tolu Balsam
Urdu Name	Tolu Ka Gond

Medicinal Uses: Tolu Balsam is considered a pathological product produced in the new wood, formed due to inflicted injury. Tolu's Balsam was first documented in the German Pharmacopeia in the 17th century. Peru Balsam, a resinous substance derived from Myroxylon balsamum plant, has been a beneficial topical ointment for various skin conditions such as scabies, poorly healing wounds, eczema and haemorrhoids.

Traditional Uses: The essential oil extracted from the Myroxylon balsamum plant is valuable as an ingredient in commercial cosmetic preparations, for perfumes. It is used extensively as an expectorant in cough mixture and is an antiseptic. Besides, it is a cough suppressant and respiratory aid used in cough lozenges, syrups, sore throats and a vapour inhalant for respiratory ailments. The balsam is applied directly to the skin to treat bedsores, cracked nipples, cracked lips and minor skin cuts. It has also been useful in suppositories for the symptomatic treatment of pain, pruritus and feelings of congestion associated with the acute attack of piles and other anal disorders.

The tree or its balsam is not mentioned anywhere in the Unani and Ayurvedic books and Pharmacopoeias.

Biological Uses: The alcoholic extract of the plant has been reported to inhibit Mycobacterium tuberculosis, as well as the common ulcer-causing bacteria, Helicobacter Pylori, in *in vitro* studies. The non-aqueous extract (ethanol) has antibacterial, anti-inflammatory, antioxidant and hepatoprotective properties. The oil also exhibits antibacterial and antiviral activities.

Chemical Constituents: The yellowish-brown or brown semisolid resinous mass of the plant that contains resin esters, essential oils, benzoic acid, cinnamic acids, cinnamein, small amounts of terpenes, as well as traces of eugenol and vanillin. Toluene is a volatile solvent that acts as a central nervous system depressant. It occurs naturally in the tolu tree (Myroxylon toluiferum) and its crude oil.

Distribution: Myroxylon balsamum is found in Central America and northern and western South America (Peru, Chile, Brazil, Colombia, etc.).

Cinnamein (C$_{16}$H$_{14}$O$_2$)   Toluene (C$_7$H$_8$)

Myroxylon pereirae

Peru Ka Gond (Tree Parts and Balsam)

Latin Binomial	Myroxylon pereirae/Myroxylon balsamum
Family	Leguminosae
English Name	Peru Balsam
Urdu Name	Peru Ka Gond/Byru Bilisam

Medicinal Uses: The Balsam of Peru of the emergent Myroxylon pereirae tree is aromatic, stimulant and parasiticide in action. Peru Balsam is used as a miticide to heal indolent wounds, as scabicide and parasiticide. It is also beneficial in diarrhoea, ulcer therapy and as a local protectant rubefacient. It is an antiseptic and vulnerary and a stimulating expectorant. In dentistry, Peru balsam is incorporated in products used to treat 'dry socket,' a painful condition that sometimes follows tooth removal.

Peru balsam has been described in many national pharmacopoeias of Argentina, Austria, Belgium, Brazil, Chile, France, Germany, Italy, Japan, Mexico, Netherlands and Spain. It has been in the U.S., Pharmacopeia since 1820, with documented uses for bronchitis, laryngitis, dysmenorrhoea, diarrhoea, dysentery and leucorrhoea.

Traditional Uses: It is valuable for use in scabies, in irritant skin diseases and in acute eczema. The balsam is good in all chronic mucous afflictions, catarrh, leucorrhoea, diarrhoea and dysentery. It stimulates the heart and raises blood pressure. The oil or liquid may be used for sore nipples and discharges from the ear. The fruit is primarily useful in treating itching, for which it is claimed to be the best remedy.

Myroxylon pereirae is also employed in perfumery and some chocolate flavourings, also in the making of odours.

Biological Uses: Peru balsam possesses antibacterial, antifungal, antiseptic, parasiticide and rubefacient activities. Like Tolu of Balsam, it is also suitable in suppositories for the symptomatic treatment of pain, pruritus and feelings of congestion associated with an acute attack of piles and other anal disorders. People take Myroxylon pereirae for cancer and parasitic intestinal infections despite serious safety concerns when by mouth and when applied to the skin.

Chemical Constituents: The Peru balsam contains a mixture of resin, benzyl benzoate, benzyl cinnamate, cinnamyl cinnamate, peruviol, vanillin and cinnamic acid. The plant also contains an acyclic sesquiterpene alcohol, 'farnesol.' This colourless liquid is used as a deodorant in cosmetic products. Farnesol is also present in Polianthes tuberose of the Asparagacesia family, Cymbopogon martini of the Poaceae family, Cyclamen persicum of the Primulaceae family and Citrus aurantium of the Rutaceae family.

Distribution: Myroxylon pereirae is found in Central America and Northern and Western South America (Peru, Chile, Brazil, Colombia, etc.).

Note: Systemic toxicity following the application of Peru balsam to the nipples of breastfeeding mothers has been reported.

Myroxylon pereirae (balsam of Peru) is one of the ingredients in the famous cream for haemorrhoids 'Anusol' the American multinational 'Johnson and Johnson.'

Farnesol ($C_{15}H_{26}O$)

Medicinal Plants
Plants containing Tannins

Tannins

Definition: Tannins are naturally occurring complex organic compounds possessing nitrogen-free poly-phenols of high molecular weight. They form a colloidal solution with water giving acid reactions. They also precipitate proteins and alkaloids.

Properties of Tannins

Tannins are dark brown or reddish-brown in colour. Their solutions are acidic and have an astringent taste.

They are non-crystalline (amorphous).

Tannins are soluble in water, alcohol, dilute alkalis, glycerol and acetone.

In solution, they show an acidic reaction due to the presence of phenols.

Tannins are insoluble in non-aqueous solvents except acetone.

The solution of tannin precipitates protein and alkaloids.

Tannins are precipitated by salts of copper, tin and lead.

They are precipitated by a strong potassium dichromate solution of chromic acid.

Tests for Tannins

Gelatin test:

An aqueous gelatin and sodium chloride solution is added to a tannin solution. A white buff coloured precipitate is formed.

Goldbeater's skin test:

A small piece of Goldbeater skin (membrane prepared from the intestine of an ox) is soaked in 20 per cent hydrochloric acid, ringed with distilled water and placed in a solution of tannin for 5 minutes. The skin piece is washed with distilled water and kept in a ferrous sulphate solution; brown or black colour is produced on the skin due to tannins' presence.

Phenazone test:

A mixture of aqueous extract of a drug and sodium acid phosphate is heated, then cooled and filtered. A solution of phenazone is added to the filtrate. A bulky, coloured precipitate, is formed.

Match stick test (Catechin test):

A match stick is dipped in an aqueous plant (drug) extract, dried near the burner and moistened with concentrated hydrochloric acid (HCl). The matchstick wood turns pink or red due to phloroglucinol formation on warming, near the flame.

The chlorogenic acid test:

An extract of the chlorogenic acid-containing drug is treated with aqueous ammonia. The green colour is formed on exposure to air.

The vanillin-hydrochloric acid test:

To a sample solution of tannins, add vanillin-hydrochloric acid reagent (Vanillin 1 gm, alcohol 10 ml, concentrated hydrochloric acid 10 ml). A pink or red colour is formed due to the formation of phloroglucinol.

Classification of tannins

1. True Tannins: They are high in molecular weight, polyhydroxy phenolic compounds and give a positive Goldbeater's skin test.
2. Pseudo-Tannins: Are phenolic compounds of lower molecular weight and do not show the Goldbeater's skin test.

Goldbeater's	Match Stick's	Chlorogenic's	Phenazone's	Vanillin's
(Black)	(Red)	(Green)	(White)	(Pink)

Chemical Classification of tannins:

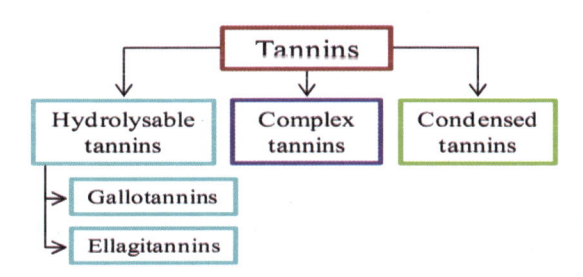

```
                    Tannins
          ┌────────────┼────────────┐
          ↓            ↓            ↓
    Hydrolysable    Complex     Condensed
      tannins       tannins      tannins
          ↓
    Gallotannins
          ↓
    Ellagitannins
```

1. Hydrolysable tannins: These tannins are hydrolyzed by acids or enzymes and produce gallic acid and ellagic acid. The tannins derived from gallic acids are known as gallitannins and ellagic acid as ellagitannins. Gallictannins occur in rhubarb, chestnut, rose petals, cloves and Turkish gallons. The ellagitannins sources are pomegranate bark, myrobalans (Terminalia chebula), oak and eucalyptus leaves, etc.

Gallic Acid ($C_7H_6O_5$)   Ellagic Acid ($C_{14}H_6O_8$).

Condensed tannins: These tannins are resistant to hydrolysis and they are derived from flavonols, catechins and flavan-3, 4-diols. On treatment with acids or enzymes, they are decomposed into phlobaphenes. On dry distillation, condensed tannin produces catechol. Condensed tannins are found in the bark of cinnamon, cinchona, wild cherry, willow, acacia, etc. They are also present in roots and rhizomes of krameria and the male fern and in the seeds of cacao, areca and guarana. Condensed tannins are also present in the extracts of catechu, acacia and gum butea.

Catechin ($C_{15}H_{14}O_6$)

3. **Complex Tannins** Complex tannins are defined as tannins in which a catechin unit is bound glycosidically to either a gallotannin or an ellagitannin unit. As the name implies, this compound structure can be very complex.

Acutissimin–A ($C_{56}H_{38}O_{31}$)

Classification of Tannins Based on the plant part where tannins are obtained, they are classified into the following four groups:

Wood: Quercus baloot wood of the Fagacae family, Acacia catechu of the Mimosaceae family and Quebracho colorado of the Anacardiaceae family.

Bark: Acacia arabica of the Mimosaceae family, Cassia absus and Cassia fistula of the Caesalpiniaceae family.

Fruit: Fruit of Caesalpinia bonduc of the Fabaceae/Caesalpinia family, Zizyphus jujube of the Rhamnaceae family, Terminalia chebula and Tamarindus indica of the Combretaceae family.

Leaf: Leaf of Emblica officinalis of the Myrsinaceae family and Carissa carandas or Schinopsis lorentzii of the Apocynaceae family.

Acacia catechu

Katha (Branch, Extract and Barks)

Latin Binomials	Acacia catechu/Mimosa catechu
Family	Fabaceae
English Name	Catechu
Urdu Name	Katha

Medicinal Uses: The wood and foliage of the deciduous, thorny, Acacia catechu tree, on boiling, produces a dark brown sticky substance known as 'catechu' (Katha in Urdu). This substance crystallises upon cooling and has been a vital trade article in medicinal herbs. The bark and wood of Acacia catechu are a powerful astringent due to the presence of tannins. The Catechu plant is antifungal, antiseptic, antibacterial and is antigingivitis. This therapeutically active plant helps in clotting blood in excessive bleeding (blood coagulation).

Traditional Uses: In Unani and Ayurvedic medicinal systems, the extract of the bark is useful in asthma, cough, bronchitis, diarrhoea, dysentery, sore throat, skin afflictions and gonorrhoea. The decoction of the plant helps wash sore or cracked nipples. The plant helps fight all kinds of skin irritation and itching. An ointment containing Catechu is useful in bedsores and in the swelling of the liver and spleen. Externally, it is also used as a wash to treat nose bleeds, haemorrhoids, skin eruptions, mouth ulcers, sore throats, dental infections, etc.

It is one of the principal ingredients used in preparing Asian Chewgum, known as 'Paan' from betel leaves for chewing purposes and when combined with lime, it gives the characteristic red colouration. People of different ages use it to heal sore throat because of its astringent and soothing effect. Tannins present in Acacia catechu are responsible for this property.

Biological Uses: Catechu possesses antiseptic (in very dilute aqueous solution), antioxidant, anti-inflammatory, hypoglycaemic, antimycotic and antipyretic properties. Acacia catechu's bark contains alkaloids and many other potent active compounds that show antimicrobial activity.

Chemical Constituents: The aqueous bark extract contains tannins (gallic acid derivatives), alkaloids, glucosides, sterols and flavonoids. The bark is also a rich source of tannins (30 to 60 per cent) and flavonoids (20 to 30 per cent).

Distribution: These trees grow in a dry, open forest in the West of Thailand. They also grow in the arid plains of South Asia.

Bauhinia variegata

Kachnar (Flowers and Fruits)

Latin Binomial	Bauhinia variegata
Family	Fabaceae
English Names	Camel's Foot Tree/Orchid Tree

Urdu Name   Kachnar

Medicinal Uses: The tree of the flowering Bauhinia variegata is astringent and haemostatic (herb helpful in stopping bleeding) in action. The bark is astringent and is a tonic.

Traditional Uses: Bauhinia variegata has been widely used as a medicinal plant in the Unani and Ayurvedic medicinal systems. The leaves are beneficial in treating skin diseases and inflammation of the mouth and lips. The plant roots are valuable in snake poisoning, dyspepsia, flatulence and are carminative. The dried buds are useful in treating piles, diarrhoea and worms. The juice of the bark is helpful in curing amoebic dysentery and the juice of the flowers is also beneficial in treating diarrhoea and other stomach disorders. The fruit is known to be valued as an antitumour and also helps in obesity.

Biological Uses: The plant is believed to possess antimicrobial, anti-inflammatory, antioxidant, anti-goitrogenic (decreases the bioavailability of iodine), hepatoprotective and clearing of haemagglutination (clumping together of red blood cells) properties. The ethanolic and hydro-alcoholic concentrated extracts of the leaves and stem bark reduce the blood sugar level. The chloroform extract of the bark has anthelmintic action. The methanol and chloroform fractions have wound healing properties.

Chemical Constituents: Bauhinia variegata bark produces tannin. It also contains cardiac glycosides, steroids, flavonoids, terpenoids and gum. The oil of this plant is rich in volatile hydrocarbon oils.

Distribution: Bauhinia variegata is a tropical dry mixed deciduous and moist forest tree. The plant is native to the Indo-Pak subcontinent, East Asia, China, Nepal, Bhutan, Vietnam and Thailand.

Butea monosperma

Butea (Leaves, Gum and Flowers)

Latin Binomial	Butea monosperma/Butea frondosa
Family	Fabaceae/Papilionaceae
English Name	Butea tree/Flame-of-the-Forest
Urdu Names	Palas/Tesu

Medicinal Uses: The bark of a medium-sized, slow-growing, deciduous, flowering Butea monosperma tree yields a red juice known as 'Butea gum.' Its pharmacological properties include anthelmintic, anti-conceptive, anticonvulsive, anti-diabetic, hypoglycaemic and wound healing properties.

Traditional Uses: In Unani and Ayurvedic medicinal systems, the stem bark helps treat dyspepsia, diarrhoea, dysentery, diabetes, ulcers, sore throat and snake bites. The flowers and leaves are aphrodisiac, astringent and diuretic. The flowers are also useful in the treatment of liver disorders.

The seeds contain oil, called 'Moodoga oil,' which is an effective treatment for hookworms. The seeds, ground into a paste with honey, are used for their anthelmintic, antifungal and antibacterial properties. The seed paste, mixed with lemon juice, is used as a rubefacient. The flowers (Gul-e-Tesu in Urdu) are used as astringent, diuretic, depurative and aphrodisiac. In folk medicine, the leaves are helpful in urine retention. The seeds act as an anthelmintic.

Biological Uses: An ethanol extract of the flowers exhibits significant blood glucose reductions, serum cholesterol reduction and improve glucose tolerance. The crude aqueous fractions of the bark showed significant hypoglycaemic and antihyperglycemic effects in normal and alloxan-induced diabetic albino rats, respectively. A potential antiasthmatic agent has been reported from the use of the bark.

Chemical Constituents: The gum contains condensed tannins (proanthocyanidins). The flowers contain triterpenes (butrin, isobutrin, coreopsin, sulphurein, isocoreopsin and monospermoside), glycosides and saponins. The presence of compounds butrin, isobutrin have been shown to have antihepatotoxic principles. The gum of Butea contains mucilaginous material, volatile oils and tannins. The flowers of the Butea monosperma tree are rich in glucosides.

Distribution: Butea monosperma tree is native to tropical and subtropical parts of the Indian subcontinent and Southeast Asia, India, Pakistan, Bangladesh, Nepal, Sri

Lanka, Myanmar, Thailand, Cambodia, Malaysia, Vietnam and western Indonesia. It is found in the plains of the Jhelum valley and Sialkot districts in Pakistan.

Carissa carandas

Kakronda (Tree, Leaf and Fruits)

Latin Binomial	Carissa carandas
Family	Apocynaceae
English Name	Karanda
Urdu Name	Kakronda

Medicinal Uses: The leaves and barks of the evergreen, deciduous, flowering Carissa carandas shrub are astringent, antiscorbutic (prevents scurvy), stomachic in action and very effective against piles and conjunctivitis.

Traditional Uses: In Unani and Ayurvedic medicinal systems, the fruit of the plant is useful in treating acidity, indigestion, skin and urinary disorders. It is beneficial in treating malaria, epilepsy, pain relief, dog bite, itch, leprosy, female libido, intestinal worms and liver dysfunction.

The traditional healers (Hakims and Ayurveda) of the Indo-Pak subcontinent use this plant to treat scabies, intestinal worms, as an astringent, in rheumatism, anthelmintic, mouth ulcer and in sore throat. A decoction of leaves is helpful against fever, diarrhoea and earache. The roots serve as a stomachic, vermifuge and a remedy for itches. The stem part of the plant is valuable in strengthening tendons (soft tissue by which muscle attaches to bone).

Biological Uses: The extract (methanol and petroleum ether) of the plant shows antimicrobial, antifungal, analgesic, antioxidant, anti-inflammatory and antiscorbutic activities.

Chemical Constituents: The leaves of Carissa are a rich source of tannins. The plant also contains biologically active compounds such as alkaloids, glycosides, saponins, flavonoids, steroids, triterpenoids, tannins and Vitamin C.

Its fruit has been utilized in processed products such as jam, jelly, squash, syrup, chutney and are in great demand in the international market.

Distribution: The Carissa carandas plant is native to Africa, Australia and south-east Asia. It grows naturally in the Indo-Pak subcontinent, Nepal, Sri Lanka, Afghanistan and Bangladesh.

Note: The extracts of the plant were assessed for *in-vivo* toxicity and found safe up to 2grams/kg body weight in mice.

Emblica officinalis

Amla (Plant, Fruits and Leaves)

Latin Binomials	Emblica officinalis/Phyllanthus emblica
Family	Euphorbiaceae/Phyllanthaceae
English Name	Indian Gooseberry
Urdu Name	Amla

Medicinal Uses: The fruit of the deciduous, flowering Emblica officinalis tree is carminative, refrigerant, diuretic and laxative in action.

Traditional Uses: All parts of the plant are useful in various traditional herbal, Unani, Ayurvedic and Homeopathic preparations, including the fruit, seed, leaves, root, bark and flowers. It is widely applicable in Ayurvedic medicines and is believed to increase defence/immune power against diseases. The fruit is beneficial in digestive system disorders, dyspepsia, gastritis, hyperacidity, constipation, colic, colitis and haemorrhoids. It is also suitable for metabolic disorders, anaemia, diabetes, gout and lung diseases (cough and asthma). Emblica enhances the production of red blood cells and strengthens teeth, hair, nails and regulates blood sugar. The juice of the bark used with honey and turmeric, is beneficial in gonorrhoea, hepatitis, osteoporosis, liver and spleen problems.

The plant is used both as single and in compound formulations as it is the main ingredient in Jawarish-e-Amla, Jawarish-e-Shahi, Anushdaru and Itrifalat.

Biological Uses: The fruit extract (methanol and ethanol) of the plant possesses antioxidant, antimicrobial, anti-cancer and anti-diabetic properties. The aqueous extract has antidepressant effect. Ethanol and acetone fractions of fruit show moderate antifungal activities, whereas no effects have been seen in the plant's ethanol extract.

Chemical Constituents: The plant contains tannins (gallic acid, ellagic acid and phyllembelin), vitamin C, alkaloids (phyllantine, phyllantidine), essential oils, flavonoids, terpenoids, fixed oil and minerals like phosphorus, iron and calcium. The bark of Emblica also contains leukodelphinidin, a hypoglycemic agent.

Distribution: Emblica officinalis is a medium-sized deciduous tree. The plant species are native to the Indo-Pak subcontinent, also growing in Sri Lanka, Uzbekistan, South East Asia and China. It is planted in the plains and in gardens on both sides of the Indus in Pakistan.

Leukodelphinidin ($C_{15}H_{14}O_8$)

Hamamelis virginiana

Witch Hazel (Tree Parts, Flower-Stem)

Latin Binomial	Hamamelis virginiana
Family	Hamamelidaceae
English Name	Witch-hazel
Urdu Name	Alssahiruh Hazil

Medicinal Uses: The bark and leaves of the deciduous Hamamelis virginiana are aromatic, astringent, tonic and sedative in action. They also relieve swelling, skin irritation, anxiety and burning caused by haemorrhoids.

Researchers used a Witch hazel ointment on 230 children with diaper rash, skin inflammation and minor skin injuries and a pharmaceutical ointment on 78 children with similar conditions. The dose and duration of treatment were left to the primary care physicians discretion, for each child and symptoms were rated for 7 to 10 days. Both the Witch hazel and the pharmaceutical ointment improved skin appearance and symptoms over the treatment period.

Traditional Uses: Hamamelis virginiana plant is most valuable in checking internal and external haemorrhages and bleeding piles. An ointment made from the bark is useful for local application. A decoction helps against tuberculosis, gonorrhoea and menorrhagia (abnormal menstrual periods). Hamamelis virginiana contains tannin, the most important healing constituent in the plant, giving the shrub its astringent efficacy. Tannins allow the plant to be used effectively against bruises and skin conditions like atopic eczema (dermatitis) and inflammation. It is widely used as an external application for sore muscles, varicose veins, sore nipples, inflammations, etc. The leaf tea is ingested for colds, sore throat, dysentery, cough and asthma. The bark tea is astringent and can be suitable for piles and eye ailments. Tannins in the bark are responsible for their astringent and haemostatic properties.

In cosmetics and personal care products, Hamamelis Virginiana (Witch Hazel) water and its leaf water are useful in the formulation of bath products, cleansing products, deodorants, hair conditioners, shampoos, skincare products, eye makeup and aftershave lotions.

This plant is not mentioned anywhere in Unani and Ayurvedic literature. However, the plant's characteristics are given in the Homoeopathic 'Materia Medica.' A homoeopathic remedy made from fresh bark is used to treat nosebleeds, piles and varicose veins.

Biological Uses: The plants hydrochloric extracts show antiviral and antiphlogistic activities. Other non-aqueous (methanol, ethanol and ethyl acetate) fractions have anti-inflammatory, antibacterial, antigenotoxic, antioxidant and cytotoxic properties.

Chemical Constituents: The plant contains essential oils, flavonoids such as kaempferol, quercetin and quercitrin, saponins and polyphenols. The plant is also a rich source of both hydrolysable and condensed tannins.

Distribution: Hamamelis virginiana tree is native to woodlands, forest margins and stream banks in Eastern North America, from West Nova Scotia to Minnesota and South to Central Florida and Eastern Texas.

Lawsonia inermis

Mehndi (Plant, Leaves and Powder)

Latin Binomials	Lawsonia inermis/Lawsonia alba
Family	Lythraceae
English Name	Henna
Urdu Name	Mehndhi/Henna

Medicinal Uses: The small-sized evergreen, flowering plant of Lawsonia inermis is aromatic, detergent, diuretic, astringent in action and a blood purifier. The plant has analgesic, hypoglycaemic, hepatoprotective, antioxidant and anti-cancer properties.

Traditional Uses: In Unani and Ayurvedic medicinal systems, Henna is beneficial for arthritis, liver, skin disorders and as a blood purifier. An infusion of the flowers is a valuable application in bruises, whereas a decoction of the flowers is helpful as an emmenagogue. A decoction of the bark is applied to burns and scalds. It is also given internally, in various affections, such as jaundice, enlargement of the spleen, calculus, as an alternative in leprosy and for obstinate skin affections.

The root is considered a potent medicine for gonorrhoea and herpes infections. The root is also an astringent that may be pulped and used for sore eyes. The pulped root may also be applied to children's heads for boils. The root is supposed to help treat hysteria and nervous disorders. The seeds are used in deodorants. An ointment prepared from the leaves is effective for curing wounds and ulcers. Henna is useful in cosmetic preparations as a colouring and cosmetic ingredient in many ways. It is valuable for years as a hair colour, nail colour, decoration of feet, palms and hands.

Biological Uses: The extracts (methanol, ethanol, acetone and chloroform) of different parts of the plant possess antioxidant, antibacterial, antiulcer, hepatoprotective, anti-inflammatory, antifungal, immunomodulatory and anticarcinogenic activities. The chloroform, ethanol and water extracts of the Lawsonia plant leaves also show antiparasitic effects.

The butanol and chloroform fractions show more potent anti-inflammatory, analgesic and antipyretic effects as compared to the crude extracts, of the butanol. The acetone soluble fraction of the petroleum ether extract of Lawsonia inermis leaves, exhibited a prominent nootropic (**a substance that enhances cognition and memory and facilitates learning**) activity.

Chemical Constituents: The leaves contain hennotannic acid (Lawsonia), also known as lawsone, gallic acid and amino acid. Lawsone dissolves in an alkaline solution to give an intense orange-red colour. Henna leaves and flowers also contain flavonoids, essential oils, steroids (beta-sitosterol), resin, tannins, saponins, coumarins (coumarin), alkaloids, terpenoids, phenolic compounds and xanthones.

Distribution: Lawsonia inermis is native to Asia. Linguistics and biogeography evidence supports an origin in Baluchistan (Iran/Pakistan) to Western India (Rajasthan), where it can still be found growing in the wild and is exported worldwide.

Lawsone or Hennotannic acid ($C_{10}H_6O_3$)

Myrica nagi

Kaiphal (Leaves, Barks and Fruits)

Latin Binomials	Myrica nagi/Myrica esculenta
Family	Myricaceae
English Names	Box Myrtle/Bay Berry
Urdu Name	Kaiphal

Medicinal Uses: The dioecious, evergreen tree or large shrub of Myrica nagi is aromatic, astringent, carminative, anti-catarrhal and antiseptic in action.

Traditional Uses: In Unani and Ayurvedic medicinal systems, the bark is quoted as acrid, bitter and pungent. Different parts of the tree are also utilized in reducing inflammation, piles and liver problems. It has proved useful in the treatment of fevers, asthma and coughs. The juice is applied in treating rheumatism. Myrica nagi with ginger is helpful as a rubefacient in cholera treatment. The bark juice is taken internally to treat catarrh, headaches, is applied externally to cuts and wounds. The oil extracted from flowers acts as a tonic and a remedy in headache and paralysis. The root is beneficial in the treatment of bronchitis, asthma, cholera and cough. Externally, the plant's aqueous extract is boiled to form a gelatinous mass, used as a poultice for sprains (a sudden or violent twist of the ligaments).

Biological Uses: The unripe fruit extract is also helpful as an anthelmintic. The volatile oil of the stem bark is a potent antimicrobial and antiviral agent. Non-aqueous (methanol and ethanol) extracts show antiasthmatic, anti-cancer, anti-diabetic, antiallergic, antimicrobial and anti-inflammatory activities. The plant also has a chemopreventive affect.

Chemical Constituents: The plant contains tannins (gallic acid and catechin), flavonoids, glycosides, terpenoids, steroids and volatile oils. The plant is also rich in minerals such as calcium, magnesium, potassium, phosphorus, manganese and zinc.

Distribution: Myrica esculenta is a large shrub/tree native to East Asian hills (Indian Himalaya), Bhutan, Nepal, Singapore, China and Japan.

Punica granatum

Aanar (Fruits, Flower and Annardana)

Latin Binomial	Punica granatum
Family	Punicaceae
English Name	Pomegranate
Urdu Name	Annar

Medicinal Uses: The pericarps and the bark of the deciduous, red flowering Punica granatum small tree are astringent, styptic (tendency to check bleeding), stomachic and anthelmintic in action. Animal studies show that pomegranate juice and pomegranate flower extract offer strong protection against atherosclerosis progression. Studies on humans, demonstrate a modest affect on blood pressure and inflammation reduction, and these are the reasons for adding pomegranate to a heart-healthy food list.

Traditional Uses: In Unani and Ayurvedic medicinal systems, Pomegranate is useful in treating piles, is a digestive aid and controls diarrhoea. The peel is suitable for the heart and blood vessels; the white membrane effectively stops diarrhoea, which is good for wounds, ulcers of the mouth and throat. The fruit also strengthens the brain, cleanses the body and blood from toxins. It is very effective in expelling worms from the intestines. The flower is used as a food supplement in treating diabetes mellitus. The Pomegranate seed oil is good for nourishing the skin and hair. The fruit kills parasites; it is specifically used for tapeworms, pinworms, roundworms and an excellent natural aphrodisiac (improves sperm count and semen quantity).

Punica granutam has been used in traditional Chinese medicines in treating ailments ranging from inflammation, rheumatism and a simple sore throat pain. In one study, people with hypertension significantly reduced blood pressure after consuming 5 ounces (150 ml) of pomegranate juice daily for two weeks.

Biological Uses: Extracts (methanol, ethanol, ethyl acetate and petroleum ether) of different parts of the plant possess antimicrobial, antivirus, antifungal, anti-inflammatory and anti-cancer (colon cancer) properties.

One of the most interesting areas of pomegranate research is on prostate health. Laboratory and animal studies have shown that the fruit's juice, peel and seed oil, all interfere with the spread of prostate cancer tumours. In men, prostate cancer is the second leading cause of cancer-related death in the U.S.A. Punicic acid, present in the seed oils of the plant, is a type of conjugated linoleic acid with potent biological effects. The plant's anticarcinogenic effect can be attributed to punicic acid and the metabolite conjugated linoleic acid. Pomegranate extract may inhibit breast cancer cells' reproduction, even killing some of them. However, the evidence is currently limited to laboratory studies. Pomegranate is three times more antioxidant than green tea.

Chemical Constituents: Pomegranate contains hydrolysable tannin catechins and prodelphinidin (is polymeric tannins composed of gallocatechin). The seed oil of Pomegranate contains punicic acid, palmitic acid, stearic acid, oleic acid and linoleic acid. The fruit is also a good source of minerals (potassium, calcium, phosphorus, iron, manganese and magnesium) and vitamins (B, C, K and E).

Distribution: India is the world's largest pomegranate producer in Asia, followed by Iran, Turkey, Spain, Tunisia, Morocco, Afghanistan, Pakistan and China. It is believed that the Iranian pomegranate is amongst the best, perhaps the best, in the world.

In Pakistan, it grows wild throughout the western range of Balochistan, Waziristan, Dir, Chitral, etc.

Punicic Acid ($C_{18}H_{30}O_2$)   Linoleic acid ($C_{18}H_{32}O_2$)

Quercus baloot

Shah-Baloot (Plant Parts and Fruits)

Latin Binomials	Quercus baloot/Quercus incana
Family	Fagaceae
English Name	Grey Oak
Urdu Name	Shah-Baloot

Medicinal Uses: The bark, leaves, seeds, seed cups and galls of the evergreen shrub are useful for medicinal purposes. The galls are produced as a result of insect damage. The fruit of Quercus baloot is astringent, desiccative (extreme dryness), antiseptic and antihaemorrhagic in action. The Oak species are used in many cultures' traditional medicine, being valued especially for their tannins. A decoction or infusion of the plant's bark is astringent, antiseptic, styptic and haemostatic. It is taken internally to treat acute diarrhoea, dysentery and haemorrhages.

Traditional Uses: In the Unani system of medicine, it is useful for treating vaginal discharge, prolapse (a condition in which organs fall), laxity (lack of strictness) and many other female genital disorders. The fruit may also be valuable as an injection for leucorrhoea. Externally, it is beneficial as a mouthwash in treating toothache or gum problems and is applied topically as a wash on cuts, burns, various skin problems, haemorrhoids, genital and anal mucosa inflammation. Extracts of the plant can be added to ointments to heal cuts.

Biological Uses: Various aqueous and non-aqueous extracts of the plant have antioxidant, antibacterial, antiviral, antiseptic, antifungal and antimicrobial properties.

Chemical Constituents: The plant contains tannins ((+)-catechin and (+)-gallocatechin, procyanidin), tannins, flavonoids, resin etc.

Distribution: Quercus baloot is native to Asia - Afghanistan, Pakistan (Swat, Hazara, Dir and Murree) and Northwest India.

Quercus infectoria

Mozu Sabaz (Plant Parts, Galls Dried and Fresh)

Latin Binomial	Quercus infectoria
Family	Fagaceae
English Name	Oak Galls
Urdu Name	Mazu

Medicinal Uses: The galls of Quercus infectoria small tree are astringent, desiccative (tendency to dry up) and antihaemorrhagic in action. Various properties of the gall have been reported, such as analgesic, antidote, anti-inflammatory, antiseptic, germicidal, astringent and wound healing.

Traditional Uses: The Oak gall is described in detail in ethnobotanical and classic Unani and Ayurvedic literature. The Oak galls help restore the elasticity of the uterine wall and in treating many inflammatory disorders. The decoction is mixed with vinegar and is used in the form of mouthwash. They are also used in Malay traditional medicine in treating wound infections after childbirth.

In the Indo-Pak subcontinent, galls are employed traditionally as dental applications, such as in the treatment of toothache and gingivitis. It has been widely used in East

Asia to treat infectious diseases, skin disorders and inflammatory ailments. In Korean medicine, galls are beneficial for their dysentery, anti-diarrhoea and anti-dermatitis proprieties. The fruit (acorn) of Oak species is a rich energy source, containing high amounts of carbohydrates, proteins, amino acids, lipids and sterols.

Biological Uses: The ethyl acetate extract of Quercus infectoria plant possesses the most potent cytotoxic activity towards cervical cancer cells. The manifestation of cytotoxic effects and cell death may be due to the presence of biologically active compounds such as tannins, alkaloids, flavonoids, saponins, terpenoids, phenols, etc.

Chemical Constituents: The gall comprises 50 to 70 per cent of the tannins known as gallotannic acid, a complex mixture of phenolic acid (polyphenols). The gall also contains gallic acid, ellagic acid, sitosterol, methyl-betulate, methyl- loeanolate, flavonoids and calcium oxalate.

Distribution: After the United States of America, where 90 species were found, the second most significant Oak diversity is found in China.

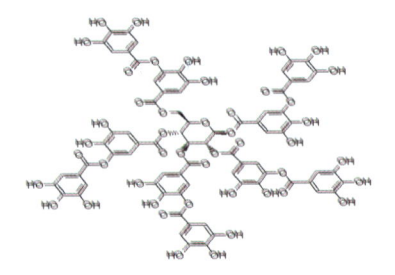

Gallotannic acid ($C_{76}H_{52}O_{46}$)

Rhus coriaria

Sumac (Seeds, Plant and Leaves in fall)

Latin Binomial	Rhus coriaria
Family	Anacardiaceae

English Name   Sumaq

Urdu Name   Sumac

Medicinal Uses: The barks and fruit of the deciduous, evergreen, small tree of Rhus coriaria are astringent, anti-diarrhoeal and antidiuretic in action.

Traditional Uses: In traditional Unani and Ayurvedic medicinal systems, the plant has helped treat diarrhoea, ulcer, haemorrhoids, bleeding, wound healing, haemoptysis (cough with blood), leucorrhoea, dieresis (excessive production of urine) and liver diseases. The powder of its bark is effective in cleaning the teeth. An infusion of the bark is helpful at the beginning of viral eye infections.

Rhus coriaria bark is braised in water and applied on the forehead for first-aid treatment in acute haemorrhage from the nostrils. A decoction of the fruit is prepared and administered orally to treat liver disease, diarrhoea and urinary system disorders. The leaves and the seeds are astringent, diuretic, styptic and act as a tonic. They are beneficial in the treatment of dysentery, haemoptysis and conjunctivitis. The seeds are eaten before a meal to provoke an appetite.

Jawarish-e-Tabasheer and Namak Shaikh-ur-Rais are popular Unani preparations that contain Sumaq as one of the ingredients in poly-herbal formulations.

Biological Uses: Some studies have shown that the Sumac plant has anti-cancer (antioxidant), antifungal and anti-inflammatory properties. Research has also shown that the alcoholic extract is effective against Gram-positive and Gram-negative bacteria. An aqueous fraction of fruit also shows antimicrobial activity against coliforms, Listeria. Monocytogenes. Methanolic extract of seeds has shown antidiabetic activity.

Chemical Constituents: The plant contains hydrolysable tannins, flavonoids, anthocyanine, terpenoids etc. The leaves and bark are rich in tannin and yield a yellow dye. A black dye is also obtained from the fruit. Leaves also contain monomeric flavonols (kaempferol, quercetin, myricetin and rutin) and dimeric flavonoids (agathisflavone, amentoflavone, hinokiflavone, and surnaflavone).

Distribution: Rhus coriaria is native to Southern Europe and Western Asia and grows in subtropical regions of the world such as East Asia, Africa and North America.

Rumex acetosa

Hammaz (Plant Parts, Leaves and Dried Roots)

Latin Binomial	Rumex acetosa
Family	Polygonaceae
English Name	Sorrel
Urdu Name	Hammaz

Medicinal Uses: The seeds, leaves and roots of the perennial, herbaceous Rumex acetosa plant are used for medicinal purposes. The plant is astringent, diuretic, febrifuge, exhilarant and antiscorbutic in action and is also a cardiac tonic. Rumex acetosa is a cooling drink, in all febrile conditions and can help correct scrofulous deposits. Its astringent qualities meant it was formerly used to stop haemorrhages and was applied as a poultice on cutaneous tumours. The juice and vinegar (sirka) are said to cure ringworm, while a decoction is made to cure jaundice, uncrated bowels and remove gravel and stone from kidneys. The plant is known to contain high amounts of potassium, a vasodilator. This mineral helps reduce the cardiovascular system's overall stress and relaxes the arteries and stress in veins.

Traditional Uses: In Unani and Ayurvedic medicinal systems, the seeds are roasted and pulverized and taken with water to treat diarrhoea and scorpion bites. The seeds are also effective in treating palpitation, stomach membrane inflammation, a burning sensation and irritation in the urethra. The decoction of the whole plant is helpful in treating an enlarged spleen and piles. A paste of the leaves is suitable for the gum and tooth affected by dental caries, in relieving pain and inflammation. The juice of the leaves is installed into the ears to treat ear pain.

Many traditional healers (Hakims and Ayurveda) of the Indo-Pak subcontinent recommend this herb to detoxify the kidney. The root is beneficial in treating diarrhoea. The extract of its leaves is also useful in producing a remedy that lowers inflammation from the body. The plant is also helpful in uterine bleeding. When applied to the skin, the leaves can directly cure rashes and skin irritation issues.

Biological Uses: The extract (aqueous and ethanol 30:70 per cent) shows protective activity against gastric ulcers. Biologically active ingredients in the plant are responsible for various activities, like anti-cancer antioxidant, antibacterial, antifungal and anti-inflammatory.

Chemical Constituents: The leaves mainly contain tannic acid and nitrogenous matter. The plant also has essential phytochemicals such as flavonoids, e.g., orientin, isoorientin, vitexin and isovitexin, vitamins like A, B_2, B_6, B_9 and C and minerals such as phosphorus, potassium, magnesium, calcium and iron.

Distribution: Rumex acetosa plant is native to Eurasia and the British Isles and is also grown in Asia, North America and Greenland.

Proanthocyanidin (Chemically they are Oligomeric Flavonoids)

Salix alba

Bed Mushk (Tree and Barks)

Latin Binomial	Salix alba
Family	Salicaceae
English Name	Willow White
Urdu Name	Bed Mushk

Medicinal uses: The bark of the deciduous Salix alba tree is an aphrodisiac, diuretic, febrifuge, astringent in action and is a heart tonic. An extract of fresh leaves is effective against bloody diarrhoea. It provides a temporary pain relief. The German Commission E Monographs, a therapeutic guide to herbal medicine, approved Salix Willow for diseases accompanied by fever, rheumatic ailments and headaches.

Traditional Uses: The bark of this plant is helpful in Unani and Ayurvedic medicinal systems, in febrile diseases of rheumatic or gouty origin, diarrhoea and dysentery. It is beneficial in dyspepsia and is connected with digestive organ disorders. The bark of the plant is valuable in healing acute diseases. An infusion of the leaves has calming effects and is helpful in the treatment of nervous insomnia. When added to bathwater, the infusion is of real benefit in relieving widespread rheumatism.

The aromatic water of the bark (Arq-e-Bede-Mushk) strengthens the heart, brain, liver and the stomach.

Biological Uses: The bark and its non-aqueous extract are anodyne, anti-inflammatory, antiperiodic and antiseptic in properties. The hydroalcoholic fraction of the bark shows intense antibacterial activities.

Chemical Constituents: The bark contains flavonoids, salicin, which the body converts into salicyl alcohol and subsequently to the known anti-inflammatory agent salicylic acid (a natural form of aspirin). It also contains proanthocyanidins (condensed tannins), known for their astringent and wound-healing properties.

Distribution: The White Willow tree is widely distributed throughout Europe, Asia Minor, Russia and China.

Saraca indica

Ashoka (Tree, Barks and Flowers)

Latin Binomial	Saraca indica/Saraca asoca
Family	Fabaceae/Leguminosae

English Name	Ashoka Tree	
Urdu Name	Ashoka	

Medicinal Uses: The bark of the evergreen, flowering Saraca indica tree is astringent, carminative, digestive, antiulcer in action and is used in uterine affections, dyspepsia and dysentery.

Traditional Uses: In Unani and Ayurvedic medicinal systems, the local application of Ashoka paste on the affected part helps relieve pain. The flowers are diuretic. An extract of the flowers is useful in treating haemorrhoids and dysentery. Saraca indica flowers can also cure scabies in children and various other skin diseases. Saraca indica flowers are considered a uterine tonic and are used in dysentery and diabetes. The seeds are helpful in the treatment of urinary discharges. The bark has natural detoxification properties that improve skin complexion (skin toner) and keeps the body free from toxins.

Ashoka is a prevalent medicinal herb in Ayurveda, where it is said to be particularly useful for treating a range of conditions related to the female reproductive system. It is a strong astringent, uterine sedative and is said to have a stimulating affect on uterine and ovarian tissue. The bark has a strong impact on the uterine muscles and is especially useful in treating uterine haemorrhages, menstrual cramps, menorrhagia and leucorrhoea. It is also beneficial in treating conditions such as haemorrhoids and internal bleeding. The plant is useful in central nervous system depressant activity.

Saraca indica plant helps manage all painful conditions, alleviating burning sensation and excessive thirst. Saraca is also useful in the management of inflammation of the lymph nodes.

Biological Uses: The extract of Ashoka shows antioxidant and antitumor activities, which indicates that the herbal preparation may have the potential to be used in complementary and alternative medicine, for breast cancer therapy. Alcohol extracts of both the flowers and the bark have shown antimicrobial activities. Both aqueous and alcoholic extracts of the bark have shown significant analgesic property. The plant's oxytocic activity is seen in rats and human isolated uterine preparations.

Chemical Constituents: The plant contains tannins, 'catechol,' cardiac glycosides, flavonoids, alkaloids, ergo sterols, fixed oil, resins and saponins. The bark also contains flavonoids and leucoanthocyanidins (flavan-3-4-diols).

Distribution: Saraca indica (Ashoka) is distributed throughout Pakistan, Burma, India and Sri Lanka.

Terminalia arjuna

Arjuna (Fruits, Leaves and Barks)

Latin Binomial	Terminalia arjuna
Family	Combretaceae
English Name	Arjun
Urdu Name	Arjuna/Arjun

Medicinal Uses: The bark of the large evergreen, deciduous Terminalia arjuna tree is astringent, expectorant, antiseptic, hyperlipidemic, antiasthmatic and alexiteric (a preservative against infectious diseases) in action and is a cardiac stimulant.

Traditional Uses: In Unani and Ayurvedic medicinal systems, Arjuna is beneficial in treating wounds, diarrhoea, dysentery, haemorrhages and ulcers. The Arjuna plant has been traditionally used in treating heart disease for centuries, yet its role in the treatment of heart diseases remains uncertain.

The plant is a good source of minerals, which helps prevent bone loss (osteoporosis) and improves bone mineral density. It reduces urination frequency, so it is valuable in polyuria (excessive urination) and in frequent urination.

The bark has an astringent action and it is helpful in the management of leucorrhoea. The juice of the bark is a valuable tonic. The juice from the leaves has been beneficial traditionally, in treating earache. Arjuna helps in thickening the serum and is the sperm essential for the ovum's proper fertilisation. It is also helpful in increasing sperm count.

Biological Uses: The extract of the bark (methanol) shows remarkable activity against various gram-positive and gram-negative bacteria, including Staphylococcus aureus. Ethanol extracts of the bark possess antioxidant and anti-diabetic activities.

Chemical Constituents: Arjun's bark contains tannins (terminic acid and arjunolic acid), triterpenoids, saponins, sugar, glycosides (arjunetin and arjunosides), flavons, resins and fixed oil. The Arjun root also contains cardiac glycoside, e.g. cardenolides.

Distribution: Terminalia arjuna plant is found in East Asia, Pakistan, India, Sri Lanka, Bangladesh and Myanmar. In Pakistan, the tree is planted throughout the plains, in gardens and as roadside trees.

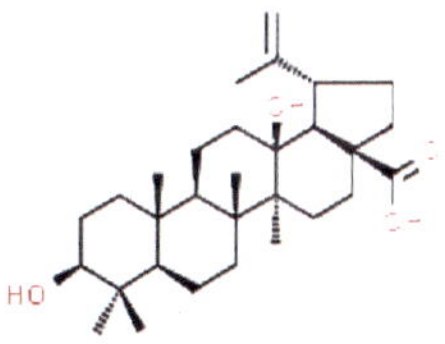

Terminic acid ($C_{30}H_{48}O_4$) 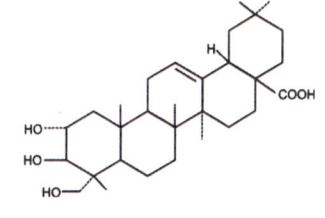   Arjunolic acid ($C_{30}H_{48}O_5$)

Terminalia belerica

Bahira (Tree, Dried and Fresh Fruits)

Latin Binomial	Terminalia belerica
Family	Combretaceae
English Name	Beleric myrobalan
Urdu Names	Bahira/Balilah

Medicinal Uses: The fruit of the large Terminalia belerica tree is astringent, digestive, laxative and antipyretic in action. The plant's dried pulp helps in the treatment of sore throat, cough, hoarseness and dyspepsia.

Traditional Uses: In the traditional herbal medicine of the Indo-Pak subcontinent (Unani and Ayurvedic), the ripe fruit is beneficial in treating diarrhoea and indigestion cases. The unripe fruit is helpful as a laxative in cases of chronic constipation. The seed oil of this herb is useful in skin disorders and premature greying of the hair. It also boosts hair growth and gives a black colour to the hair. The fruit is used internally, principally, in treating digestive and respiratory problems. The fruit is also valuable in hepatitis, asthma and piles. Some research shows that taking fruit with other herbs lowers pre-meal blood sugar levels in women, with diabetes. The ripe fruit is astringent and is antidiarrhoeal. A decoction of the fresh fruit is useful in cough. The seed oil is suitable for rheumatism. The gum of the bark is demulcent and purgative.

Externally, the fruit is helpful in making a lotion for sore eyes. The fruit is one of the ingredients of the famous 'Triphala,' of Unani and Ayurvedic medicine, along with the fruits of Phyllanthus emblica (amla) and Terminalia chebula (harr).

Biological Uses: The plant demonstrated multiple pharmacological and medicinal activities, such as being an antioxidant, antimicrobial and anti-diabetic. The methanol/aqueous extract has shown the highest antibacterial activity.

Chemical Constituents: The plant fruit contains tannins (gallic acid), anthraquinone, beta-sitosterol, flavonoids, alkaloids and volatile oils. The seeds contain cardenolides (a type of Steroid) and the bark contains arjungenin and glycosides, belleric acid and bellericosides.

Distribution: Continents where Terminalia belerica plant has been found, are Africa, Asia (Pakistan, India, Nepal, etc.), Australia and the United States. In Pakistan, it is planted in the sub-Himalayan tract, east of Rawalpindi, Sialkot and Azad Kashmir.

Arjungenin ($C_{30}H_{48}O_6$)   Bellericosides ($C_{36}H_{58}O_{11}$)

Terminalia chebula

Halila Siyah (Tree, Freah and Dried Fruits)

Latin Binomial	Terminalia chebula
Family	Combretaceae
English Name	Chebulic myrobalan
Urdu Names	Halila Siyah/Harr

Medicinal Uses: The fruit of the deciduous, flowering Terminalia chebula tree is astringent, digestive, laxative in action and is a brain tonic.

Traditional Uses: The plant is called the 'King of Medicine' in Tibit. It is always listed at the top of the Ayurvedic and Unani pharmacopeia lists because of its extraordinary healing power. It is effective in ailments associated with the brain, eyes, nose and ear. The fruit is beneficial in treating diarrhoea, piles and the enlargement of the spleen. The fruit is also an anthelmintic, an astringent when ripe, digestive, tonic and a laxative when unripe. It is frequently useful in treating upper respiratory tract infections that cause sore throats, hoarseness and coughs. Externally, the fruit helps make a lotion for sore eyes.

The seeds yield about 40 per cent of a clear yellow oil. It is used as hair oil and also in the manufacturing of soap. The bark is suitable for making dyes.

Biological Uses: The plant is known to possess multiple pharmacological and medicinal activities, such as being an antioxidant, antimicrobial, anti-diabetic, hepatoprotective and anti-inflammatory.

Chemical Constituents: Terminalia chebula contains hydrolysable tannins (pyrogallol, gallic acid and chebulic acid), purgative compounds like anthraquinones and fixed oils. The plant also has valuable constituents like flavonol glycosides, triterpenoids, coumarin conjugated with gallic acid called 'chebulin' and phenolic compounds.

Distribution: Terminalia chebula is native to South Asia and grows in Pakistan, India, Bangladesh, Egypt and Iran.

Note: It is an essential ingredient of 'Triphala (three fruits) in Unani and Ayurvedic Systems of Medicine.

Chebulic Acid ($C_{14}H_{12}O_{11}$)   Galic Acid ($C_7H_6O_5$)

Ziziphus jujuba

Unnab (Tree Parts, Fruits Fresh and Dried)

Latin Binomial	Ziziphus jujuba
Family	Rhamnaceae
English Name	Jujuba
Urdu Name	Unnab

Medicinal Uses: The fruit of the flowering Ziziphus jujuba tree or shrub is emollient, expectorant, laxative in action and is a blood purifier. The plant is both a delicious fruit and an effective herbal remedy.

Traditional Uses: In Unani and Ayurvedic medicinal systems, the fruit is useful for being anti-diabetic, sedative, anxiolytic (a herb used to reduce anxiety), expectorant, antiseptic and anti-inflammatory. The root is beneficial in treating dyspepsia. A decoction of the root and leaves helps to treat fevers. The root is made into a powder and applied to old wounds and ulcers.

The leaves are astringent and febrifuge. They are said to promote the growth of hair. The leaves' aqueous paste is applied externally, to relieve a burning sensation. The fruit of the wild plant is considered cooling, anodyne and is used as a tonic and employed as an antidote to aconite-poisoning.

The traditional healers of the Indo-Pak subcontinent use fresh leaves of the plant with cumin, 'Zeera' in Urdu (Cuminum cyminum), to treat urinary infections.

Based on traditional Iranian books, local traditional healers use the bark and leaf powder in curing wounds; and the root is suitable for treating dysentery. The fruit is widely applicable in Iran as an antitussive (a herb used to relieve cough), as a laxative and antihypertensive. It aids in weight gain, improves muscular strength and increases stamina.

It is prescribed as a tonic in Chinese medicine in strengthening liver function. The plant is widely used in China as a treatment for burns. Japanese research has shown that the Jujube increases immune-system resistance. The seed contains several medically active compounds and is hypnotic, sedative, stomachic and a tonic.

Biological Uses: The leaf and fruit extracts (methanol and ethanol) have antibacterial, anti-inflammatory, antiulcer and antispastic properties, whereas the ethyl acetate extract has antifertility activity. The lupane-type triterpenes show high cytotoxic activities.

Recent phytochemical studies of jujube fruits have shed light on their biological effects, such as anticancer, antiobesity, immunostimulating, antioxidant, hepatoprotective, and gastrointestinal protective activities. It also shows inhibition of foam cell formation in macrophages (**a phagocytic tissue cell of the immune system that may be fixed or freely motile).**

Chemical Constituents: The plant contains alkaloids, glycosides, flavonoids, saponins, resins and triterpene- saponins (jujubosides A, B). The juice of this plant is very rich in Vitamin C. The fruit of this plant is a rich source of Tannins.

Distribution: Ziziphus jujuba is native to China and grows in the cooler regions of Iran, India, Thailand, Malaysia, Australia and Africa. In Pakistan, Ziziphus jujube has been successfully cultivated in Hyderabad, Khairpur, Multan, Lahore and Sargodha.

Jujuboside A ($C_{58}H_{94}O_{26}$) and B ($C_{52}H_{84}O_{21}$)

Medicinal Plants
Plants containing Volatile Oils and Isoprenoids (Terpenoids)

Definition: As the name implies, they are volatile and do not leave a stain. They derive the odour and the flavour from the plant.

Properties of Volatile oils

1. They possess characteristic odours.

2. Most of them are optically active.

3. Volatile oils are immiscible in water.

4. They are soluble in alcohol and organic solvents.

5. They are lighter than water.

6. They have a high refractive index.

7. They are antiseptic, carminative and antispasmodic in action.

Phytochemistry

- Composition: Hydrocarbon/Oxygenated compounds.
- In some plants, the hydrocarbon is predominated (terpenes or Isoterpences), whereas oxygenated compounds (terpenoids) make up the bulk.

Isoprene

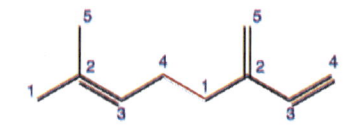

Isoprene Units

The plant synthesized isoprene by a non-mevalonate pathway. One of the two end products of methylerythritol phosphate (MEP0 pathway, dimethylallyl diphosphate (DMADP), is catalyzed by the enzyme isoprene synthase from isoprene. Carbon 1 is called the head of the molecule, carbon four is called the tail and carbon five is sometimes called the middle of the molecule.

Terpenes

Two isoprenes units = Monoterpene ($C_{10}H_{16}$)

Three isoprenes units= sesquiterpenes ($C_{15}H_{24}$)

Four isoprenes units= Biterpenes ($C_{20}H_{32}$)

Six isoprenes units= Triterpenes ($C_{30}H_{48}$)

Eight isoprenes units= Tetraterpenes

Isoprene Rule: The isoprene rule dictates how isoprene units are joined together in a head to tail configuration. The first molecule's tail joins the second molecule's head to form a larger unit. The simplest example is Myrcene.

Myrcene (the mother of all terpenes)

Classification of Volatile oils

Usually, volatile oils are classified according to the type of organic compounds.

Hydrocarbon: Examples: cubeb, limonene, turpentine oil- alpha and beta-pinene, myrcene and phellandrene.

Ketonic: Examples: fennel - fenchone, spearmint-carvone, camphor – (+)-(-) camphor and caraway-carvone, menthone and pulegone.

Phenolic: Examples: clove-eugenol, ajwan (ajwain)-thymol and thyme-thymol, carvacrol and chavicol.

Phenolic-Ether: Examples: fennel-anethol, nutmeg-myristicin, terpenes and anise-anethol

Oxide: Examples: Eucalyptus-Cineole, linalool, sclareol oxide.

Ester: Example: wintergreen (gaultheria)-methyl salicylate and mustard-allylIsothiocyanate.

Alcoholic: Examples: peppermint-menthol, coriander-linalool, rose-nerol, sandalwood-santalol and cardamom-borneol and nerol.

Aldehyde: Examples: bitter lemon peel-citral, sweet orange peel-citral, cinnamon-cinnamic aldehyde, lemon grass-citronellal and citronella-citronellal

Miscellaneous: Examples: allium-allicin-alliin

Extraction of Volatile Oils

Volatile oils are extracted by steam distillation, solvent extraction or mechanical means such as ecuelle and enfleurage techniques.

Hydro-distillation: - The method comprises water distillation, water and steam distillation and steam distillation.

(a) Distillation

(b) Steam Distillation

(c) Steam/Water Distillation

(d) Solvent Extraction

(e) Expression

(f) Enfleurage

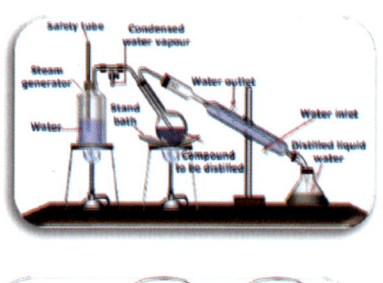

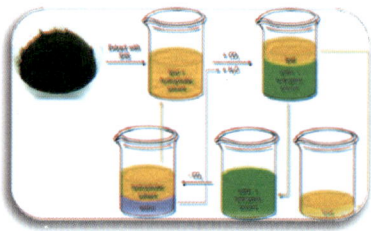

Acorus calamus

Waj-Turki (Rhizomes, Plant Parts and Flowers)

Latin Binomial	Acorus calamus
Family	Araceae/Acoraceae
English Name	Calamus/Sweet Flag
Urdu Name	Waj-Turki

Medicinal Uses: The rhizomes of the flowering Acorus calamus plant are aromatic, carminative, stimulant, anti-phlegmatic, gastritis and emetic, in action. They help remove the discomfort of flatulence, wind, colic and dyspepsia. They can increase appetite and aid in digestion.

The essential oil from the rhizome is valuable in perfumery and food flavouring.

Traditional Uses: The Unani and Ayurvedic practitioners of the Indo-Pak subcontinent have used the plant since time immemorial for diseases ranging from memory weakness to being used as an anthelminthic. The rhizome is useful in the nervous system diseases, ailment of the throat, diarrhoea and as an antitumor agent. A decoction of the rhizome is effective as a diuretic, emmenagogue (increases menstrual flow) and in stomach disorders. An infusion of the root can bring about an abortion, whilst chewing the root, alleviates toothache and it is also said to kill the taste of tobacco.

Chewing large amounts of leaves and/or roots may cause hallucinations due to the organic compound 'asarones,' which is an anticonvulsant agent.

Acorus calamus is also valuable externally in treating skin eruptions, rheumatic pains and neuralgia. In small doses, it acts as anthelmintic. However, if the dose is too large, it will cause nausea and vomiting. The plant's rhizome is beneficial for kidney and liver troubles, rheumatism and eczema. Calamus oil is suitable for inhalation. In

Ayurvedic medicine, Calamus is a vital herb and is valued as a 'rejuvenator' for the brain and nervous system and a remedy for digestive disorders. The rhizome pieces are tied around the belly for jaundice.

The Chinese also use this herb for speech development and recovery from stroke.

Biological Uses: The rhizome's non-aqueous extracts (ethanol and ethyl acetate) exhibited strong antimicrobial and antifungal properties. The leaves, rhizomes and essential oil of the plant possess several biological activities such as antispasmodic, anti-inflammatory, antioxidant and carminative. The pharmacological studies have also established numerous beneficial properties, including anti-cancer, antiulcer, antiallergic, anti-diabetic and radioprotective.

The anticancer property may be due to alpha and beta asarone (compounds of phenylpropanoid). The methanolic and acetone fractions of the rhizome show elevated antibacterial activity against five bacterial pathogens. The ethanolic fraction of the rhizome and saponins isolated from the extract exhibits significant hypolipidemic activity. On the contrary, the aqueous extract shows hypolipidemic property only at a dose of 200mg/kg.

Chemical Constituents: The rhizomes' odour and flavour are due to the presence of ketonic volatile oil. Major components of the oil are beta-asarone, alpha-asarone (a trans- isomer of asarone) γ.-asarone, calamene, calamenenol, calameone, α.-pinene, β.-pinene, camphene, p.-cymene, eugenyl acetate, eugenol, isoeugenol, methyl isoeugenol, calamol, azulene, eugenol methyl ether and linalool.

The rhizome also contains glycosides, flavonoids, triterpenoids saponins, steroids tannins, polyphenolic compounds and a bitter principle. The plant also has alkaloids and glucosides.

Distribution: Acorus calamus is native to Asia. It grows in northern areas of Pakistan, India, Central Asia, Southern Russia, Siberia and Europe.

Note: The Unani and Ayurvedic practitioners' are used rhizomes in the form of powder, balms, enemas, and pills and also in ghee preparations.

Alpha Asarone and Beta Asarone ($C_{12}H_{16}O_3$)

Allium cepa

Onion (Flower and Bulbs)

Latin Binomial	Allium cepa
Family	Liliaceae/Amaryllidaceae
English Name	Onion
Urdu Name	Piyaz

Medicinal Uses: The bulbs of Allium cepa plant are diuretic, expectorant, aphrodisiac, antiseptic, antibacterial and anti-inflammatory in action.

Externally, They are stimulant and rubefacient (redness of the skin). Although Onions are extensively used in cooking, they also have many more medicinal uses. A roasted onion is applied to tumours or earache to remove the pain and onions steeped in the alcohol produce a fluid extract given for gravel and dropsy.

Traditional Uses: In Unani and Ayurvedic medicinal systems, this plant's bulb is useful as an anthelmintic, diuretic, anti-inflammatory, antispasmodic, febrifuge (reduce fever), hypotensive, lithotriptic (for kidney stones) and a tonic for the heart. Fresh onion juice is an excellent first aid treatment for bee and wasp stings, bites, grazes or fungal skin complaints. When used regularly in the diet, it offsets tendencies towards angina, arteriosclerosis and heart attack. The topical application of Onion juice can reduce hair loss and increase hair re-growth on the scalp. Onion juice improves the blood circulation to the hair roots and scalp

The traditional healers (Hakims and Ayurveda) of the Indo-Pak subcontinent considered these bulbs as a demulcent, indolent ulcers, diarrhoea, high blood pressure, bile production and cholera. They also use seeds to increase semen and relieve dental worms and urinary diseases.

The Onion is one of the essential ingredients of poly-herbal Unani preparations such as Jawarish Zaruni, Labub-e-Kabir, Majun-e-Piyaz, Majun-e-Raig-Mahi, etc.

Biological Uses: Allium cepa has a high antioxidant activity associated with various pharmacological effects like anti-inflammatory, antibiotic and anticarcinogenic, mainly due to flavonoids. It is rich in sulphur, an essential element that kills or inhibits fungus infections. The Onion lowers the risk of colorectal (bowel, colon and rectal), ovarian cyst, renal cell, prostate, oesophageal, mouth and breast cancers.

Chemical Constituents: The Onion is a good source of Vitamin C, which helps build better and stronger immunity. The bulb also contains acrid (bitter or pungent) volatile oil, flavonoids, quercetin, polyphenols, sulphur compounds and minerals (calcium, phosphorus and iron). Studies have shown that quercetin presences in Onion protect against cataract (eye disease or safed motia) and cardiovascular diseases.

Distribution: China is the leading country in the production of Allium cepa, followed by India, the United States, Egypt, Iran and Pakistan. Pakistan is the seventh-largest producer of Onion in the world.

Quercetin ($C_{15}H_{10}O_7$)

Allium sativum

Lehsan (Bulbs and Flowers)

Latin Binomial   Allium sativum

Family	Liliaceae/Amaryllidaceae
English Name	Garlic
Urdu Name	Lehsan

Medicinal Uses: The perennial, flowering Allium sativum plant's bulbs are antiseptic, diaphoretic, diuretic, expectorant and stimulant in action. The syrup of garlic is very effective in asthma, cough, difficulty in breathing and chronic bronchitis, while the fresh juice is beneficial in easing tubercular consumption. It may be applied externally, as an ointment, lotion and as antiseptic or a poultice.

In 2002, the Journal of the National Cancer Institute (UK) reported a population-based study showing reduced risk of prostate cancer in men with a high dietary intake of Garlic and Onion. In seven studies evaluating Garlic consumption, those who ate raw and cooked garlic had the lowest risk of colorectal cancer.

Traditional Uses: In Unani and Ayurvedic medicinal systems, Garlic is a useful cardiac tonic, is useful in high blood pressure, rheumatism, asthma and stomach complaints. Garlic juice or the roasted bulb is also valuable as drops in otalgia (ear pain), for pain relief in the internal ear and locally applied to indolent tumours.

In the Ayurvedic medicinal system, garlic is suitable as a general health stimulant rather than a relief for diseases and for its effectiveness in improving the health of digestive, nervous, circulatory, respiratory and reproductive systems, whereas, in Unani medicine, the use of Garlic relieves intestinal infection, dysentery, arthritis and food poisoning. Moreover, Ayurveda recognizes onions and Garlic as blood purifiers. Furthermore, Garlic can prepare various Ayurvedic medicines, but Ayurveda does not support their excessive use.

A famous poly-herbal Unani medicine for hypertension known as 'Majun-Seer-Alvi-Khan' contains Garlic as an active ingredient.

Biological Uses: Garlic has a broad spectrum of action; not only is it antibacterial, antiviral, antifungal and anti-protozoal, but it also has beneficial effects on the cardiovascular and immune systems.

Garlic oil demonstrates significant antibacterial activity, particularly against methicillin-resistant (a narrow-spectrum antibiotic) Staphylococcus aureus.

Chemical Constituents: The bulbs of the Allium sativum plant contain hundreds of phytochemicals, including sulfur-containing compounds such as alliin, allicin, e-ajoene, diallyl sulphide etc. The plant also has other valuable constituents such as essential oils, sulphur compounds, flavonoids, vitamin C and minerals like calcium, magnesium, manganese, selenium and zinc.

Distribution: China is the leading country in the production of Garlic, followed by India, Thailand, Bangladesh, Egypt, South Korea, Russia and Ukraine. In Pakistan, Garlic is the second most widely cultivated crop after onion. It is grown throughout Pakistan and consumed by most of the people.

Alliin ($C_6H_{11}NO_3S_2$)   Allicin ($C_6H_{10}OS_2$)

Ajoene ($C_9H_{14}OS_3$)

Amomum subulatum

Ilaichi Kalan (Plant Parts, Fresh and Dried Fruits)

Latin Binomial	Amomum subulatum
Family	Zingiberaceae/Scitamineae
English Name	Greater Cardamom/Black Cardamom
Urdu Name	Ilaichi Kalan

Medicinal Uses: The fruit of the **perennial, herbaceous,** flowering Amomum subulatum plant is aromatic, appetizer, carminative, antiseptic and is astringent in action. They have an aromatic warming effect which is helpful in treating indigestion and flatulence. If chewed, they are said to be good for colic and headaches.

Traditional Uses: In Unani and Ayurvedic medicinal systems, large Cardamoms are helpful as a preventive and curative for throat troubles, congestion of lungs, inflammation of eyelids, digestive disorders and pulmonary tuberculosis treatment. The fruit is useful as an appetizer, a digesting agent, carminative and antispasmodic. It stimulates the heart and is beneficial as an expectorant. The seeds are also helpful as constituents of mouthwashes. A decoction of the seeds is useful in hiccups and as a gargle in affections of the teeth and gums. In asthma, oral intake of Greater Cardamom oil (10-20 drops) is valuable. The Cardamom with melon seeds (Cucumis melo of the Cucurbitaceae family) is a diuretic in gravel cases of the kidneys and in gonorrhoea.

The fruit of Amomum subulatum is a popular ingredient in Unani, mono and poly-herbal medicines, for example, Cardamom's aromatic water (Arq-e-Ilaichi) is useful in stomach disorders. A poly-herbal preparation known as Jawarish-e-Anarain is an effective remedy for loss of appetite (anorexia), nausea and vomiting also contains Cardamom seeds.

Externally, Cardamom oil helps tone the skin; it shrinks the pores and makes the face look tight and fresh.

Biological Uses: The non-aqueous extracts (methanol, acetone, carbon tetrachloride) of the fruit, possess antiseptic, antioxidant and antibacterial activities. The Leaf extract (methanol) showed good antimicrobial activity against Staphylococcus aureus. The aqueous and ethanol fractions of the fruit exhibit hypo-lipidaemic properties.

Chemical Constituents: The plant contains volatile oils, carbohydrates, flavonolds (alpinetin), tannins, flavones, glycosides and triterpenoids. The composition of the alcoholic essential oils of the large Cardamom is 1-8, Cineole (65 to 85 per cent), limonene (10 per cent) and a hydrocarbon monoterpene (3 to 5 per cent).

In France and America, the oil is also used in perfumery.

Distribution: Amomum subulatum is native to Arabia and Syria. The plant grows in Bhutan, Nepal, Bangladesh, China, India and Africa.

1-8, Cineole ($C_{10}H_{18}O$)   Alpinetin ($C_{16}H_{14}O_4$)

Anethum graveolens

Soya/ Shabbat (Plant, Fresh and Dried Seeds)

Latin Binomials	Anethum graveolens/Peucedanum graveolens
Family	Umbelliferae/Apiaceae
English Name	Dill
Urdu Name	Shabbat/Soya

Medicinal Uses: The fruit of the annual, yellow flowering Anethum graveolens herb is aromatic, stimulant, carminative and stomachic in action. It is usually useful as Dill-water, which is very good for children's flatulence or disordered digestion. The oil of Dill is suitable in medicine broadly, but it is also helpful in perfuming soap. It controls diabetes and insulin levels as it manages serum lipids and insulin levels in corticosteroid-induced diabetes.

Traditional Uses: In Unani and Ayurvedic systems, the Dill is beneficial as carminative, in loss of appetite, in flatulence, in liver and gall bladder complaints.

Traditional healers (Hakims and Ayurveda) of the Indo-Pak subcontinent also believe that chewing the seeds improves bad breath and stimulates milk flow in lactating mothers. It also cures urinary complaints, piles and mental disorders. Moreover, Dill is a preservative as it inhibits several bacteria like staphylococcus, streptococcus, Escherichia coli and pseudomonas.

The seeds of the plant are rich in Vitamin A; this Vitamin is a fat-soluble vitamin that maintains healthy vision, skin and immune functions. The presence of flavonoids in Dill act like antihistamines and are anti-congestive.

Biological Uses: The oil and non-aqueous extracts (methanol) of the Dill plant are antiseptic, antibacterial and anti-inflammatory.

Chemical Constituents: The Dill oil contains essential oils, e.g., carvone, limonene, dillapiole, piperitone, etc. The plant (root, leaves and stems) also has valuable bioactive constituents such as tannins, terpenoids, cardiac glycosides and flavonoids. Dill is a good source of micronutrients such as calcium, magnesium, phosphorus, manganese, iron and vitamins, like C, B_2, B_9 and A. The seeds are useful as an ingredient in gripe water, in relieving colic pain in babies and flatulence in young children.

Distribution: Anethum graveolens is believed to be a native to South-West Asia or South-East Europe. Anethum graveolens grows in South-West Asia is naturalized in Europe, in the Mediterranean, Russia and Central Asia.

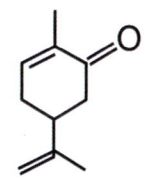

Carvone ($C_{10}H_{14}O$) 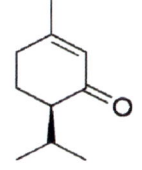   Piperitone ($C_{10}H_{16}O$)

Carum carvi

Zirah Siyah (Plant Parts Seeds and Flowers)

Latin Binomials   Carum carvi/Carum gracile

Family	Umbelliferae/Apiaceae
English Name	Black Caraway/Persian Cumin
Urdu Name	Zirah Siyah

Medicinal Uses: The fruit of Carum carvi plant is aromatic, carminative, digestive, stimulant and antispasmodic in action. It is widely used as a cordial to ease dyspepsia and hysteria.

Traditional Uses: The Caraway oil is applied to treat flatulence and stomach disorders. Distilled Caraway water (Arq-e-Zeera) is beneficial in easing colic in infants and an excellent children's medicine. The bruised fruit is used to eradicate pain in a bad earache and is valuable as a poultice in taking away bruises. It lessens the sagging of skin and aids in tissue regeneration.

The Caraway has a long history of use as a household remedy, especially for treating digestive complaints where its antispasmodic action soothes the digestive tract. Its carminative action relieves bloating caused by wind and improves the appetite.

The Caraway has been useful for centuries in traditional Asian, Unani and Ayurvedic medicine systems for gastrointestinal tract disorders. The seed is also said to increase breast milk production in nursing mothers. In tradition, infusion of the seeds is suitable as an eyewash. The Caraway is often used in combination with peppermint oil to relieve irritable bowel syndrome and indigestion symptoms.

In some South Asian countries, the seed helps treat failing vision and appetite loss. The Caraway oil has powerful antiseptic, antibacterial and antispasmodic activities. Carvone and limonene are two components present in Caraway oil and the oils have enormous effects on ageing symptoms and in clearing out wrinkles.

Biological Uses: The alcoholic extracts of the plant showed antibacterial, anti-diabetic, anti-inflammatory and antifungal activities, whereas the aqueous extract possesses the anticonvulsant property. The presence of limonene in Caraway oil is one of the essential oil constituents, is said to lower cholesterol and dissolve gallstones. The volatile oils of the seed can also help flush toxins out of the urinary tracts.

Chemical Uses: Carum carvi plant contains important biologically active constituents like flavonoids, isoflavonoids, glycosides, glucosides, alkaloids and phenolic compounds. It is an excellent source of minerals such as iron, copper, zinc, selenium, calcium, potassium, magnesium and manganese. The leaves are a rich source of vitamin B, C and iron.

The Caraway is widely used as a flavouring in cheeses and seed cakes.

Distribution: The Carum carvi is a native to Western Asia, Europe and North Africa. It is cultivated in Pakistan, India, Australia and many other parts of the world.

Carvone ($C_{10}H_{14}O$)   Limonene ($C_{10}H_{16}$)

Chenopodium album

Bathwa (Plant, Leaf and Seeds)

Latin Binomials	Chenopodium album/ Chenopodium ambrosioides
Family	Chenopodiaceae
English Name	White Goose Foot
Urdu Name	Bathwa

Medicinal Uses: The fast-growing annual Chenopodium album plant is anthelmintic, antispasmodic, carminative in action and helps in liver diseases.

Traditional Uses: This herb is popular in folk, Unani and Ayurvedic systems of medicine, in the form of teas, poultices and infusions for inflammatory problems, contusions (an injury) and lung infection. Externally, the aerial parts mixed with alcohol are beneficial in treating arthritis and rheumatism. A fine powder of the leaf is useful as a wash or poultice in bug bites, sunstroke, rheumatic joints and swollen feet, whilst a decoction is valuable for carious teeth. The stem juice is good for freckles, sunburn and bloody diarrhoea treatment. The traditional healers of the Indo-Pak subcontinent use the leaves in kidney diseases, hepatic disorder, spleen enlargement and urinary stones. The seeds are chewed in the treatment of urinary problems and are considered beneficial in spermatorrhoea. Seeds and leaves are anti-inflammatory and mildly laxative.

The famous Unani syrup known as 'Sherbet-e-Kasni' contains Chenopodium as one of the ingredients which is beneficial in relieving liver and spleen inflammation.

Biological Uses: Chenopodium album extracts have several pharmacological functions, which include anti-cancer, antiulcer, antiphlogistic, antirheumatic, anti-inflammatory and anti-diarrhoeal properties

Chemical Constituents: The Chenopodium contains a light-coloured essential oil with an unpleasant odour and a bitter, burning taste. The chief active constituent of the oil is ascaridole which is unsaturated terpene peroxide. The plant also contains valuable secondary metabolites such as flavonoids, saponins, terpenoids, sterols and alkaloids.

Distribution: Chenopodium album is a native to Europe and Western Asia. The plant is extensively cultivated and consumed in the Indo-Pak subcontinent as a food crop known as 'Bathu.' It also grows in Pakistan, Brazil, Germany, Denmark, Netherland and South Africa.

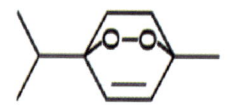

Ascaridole ($C_{10}H_{16}O_2$)

Cinnamomum camphora

Kafur (Leaves and Resin)

Latin Binomial		Cinnamomum camphora

Family	Lauraceae
English Name	Camphor
Urdu Name	Kafur

Medicinal Uses: The resin of a large handsome, evergreen Cinnamomum camphora tree is aromatic, sedative, anodyne, antispasmodic, rubefacient, carminative and antiseptic in action. It is useful in treating colds, chills, fevers, inflammatory complaints and severe diarrhoea. It is taken internally for hysteria, nervousness, neuralgia and is used as an excitant in heart failure cases due to infections, fever and pneumonia. Camphor is highly valuable in all irritations of the sexual organs. The wood and leaves are analgesic, antispasmodic, rubefacient and stimulant. Camphor oil is a common ingredient in pain relief medications, including topical analgesics. It may help treat muscle aches and pains while stimulating circulation by interacting with receptors on the sensory nerves.

Traditional Uses: An infusion of Camphor is suitable for treating lung diseases. Camphor balms and creams can be helpful in healing burn wounds. Camphor products may also be useful as a muscle rub. They may help in relieving muscle cramp, relieve spasms and stiffness. One study in mice found that Camphor leaves alleviated pathologic atopic dermatitis or eczema and helped in the treatment.

The essential oil is valuable in aromatherapy. It helps treat digestive complaints and depression. It is also helpful for its aromatic properties as an insect repellent and in various topical skin preparations.

Camphor is one of Unani and Ayurvedic medicine's essential ingredients, called 'Amrit-Dhara.' The resin helps produce Vicks VapoRub 'and' Tiger balm, which are helpful in relieving congestion and easing, cough and muscular pains.

A large dose of Camphor is harmful as it can cause vomiting, palpitations and convulsions due to their effects on the brain.

Biological Uses: Camphor essential oil (ketonic) has antiseptic, antibacterial, anti-inflammatory, insecticidal, antifungal, antirheumatic, antispasmodic, cardiotonic and analgesic properties.

Chemical Constituents: The essential oil contains linalool, cineol, thujene, beta-pinene, borneol, terpineol, camphene, etc.

Distribution: The Camphor tree is native to China, India, Mongolia, Japan and Taiwan and a variety of this fragrant evergreen tree is grown in the Southern United States (Florida). The tree of Cinnamomum camphora is widely grown in Taiwan, Japan, China, Pakistan (Hazara Distt, Abbottabad) and India.

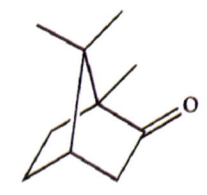

Camphor ($C_{10}H_{16}O$)

Cinnamomum cassia

Taj (Barks and Leaves)

Latin Binomial	Cinnamomum cassia
Family	Lauraceae
English Name	Chinese Cinnamon
Urdu Name	Taj

Medicinal Uses: The bark of the evergreen Cinnamomum cassia tree is carminative, aromatic, antiseptic, astringent and stimulant in action. It helps the body to fight infections and repair tissue damage. It is used as a local stimulant as a powder, and as infusion, generally combined with other herbs. Cinnamon prevents vomiting and nausea, relieves flatulence and diarrhoea.

By increasing insulin sensitivity, Cinnamon can lower blood sugar levels. It can also reduce risk factors of heart disease and has other impressive health benefits. The leafy twigs are used in the Orient to treat colds, influenza, fevers, arthritic and rheumatic complaints, angina, palpitations and digestive complaints.

Traditional Uses: The aromatic water (Arq-e-Darchini) of cinnamon is used in the Unani medicine system to stop vomiting, nausea and relieve flatulence and diarrhoea. The essential oil of the bark is used as a flavouring in toothpaste and as an incense. The dried and powdered bark is useful in commercial cosmetic preparations as a skin conditioner, hair conditioner, oral care, etc. Externally, the oil has absorbent and stimulant actions.

Biological Uses: The oil of Cinnamon cassia is carminative, antiseptic and antibacterial. Research shows it has a more substantial affect against Staphylococcus aureus. The crude fractions of different species of Cinnamomum exhibit significant antifungal, antiviral, anti-inflammatory, antioxidant, antiulcer, cytotoxic, antidiabetic, anodyne, hypolipidemic, antispasmodic, antiplatelet, immunostimulant, anaesthetic and sedative properties. The presence of polyphenols in Cinnamon can help tackle obesity. The bark also boots insulin production.

Chemical Constituents: There are approximately 35 components in Cinnamon oil. The Cinnamon bark oil contains a primary ingredient, cinnamaldehyde; other constituents include eugenol, eugenol acetate, cinnamyl acetate, cinnamyl alcohol, methyl eugenol, cinnamic acid, benzyl benzoate, linalool etc.

Distribution: Cinnamomum is native to South China. Indonesia is the leading producer of Cinnamomum cassia, followed by China, Vietnam and Sri Lanka.

Cinnamaldehyde (C_9H_8O)   Cinnamic acid ($C_9H_8O_2$)

Citrus x sinensis

Malta (Tree and Fruit)

Latin Binomial   Citrusx sinensis/Citrus limetta

Family	Rutaceae
English Name	Sweet Orange/Sweet Lemon
Urdu Name	Malta/Musambi/Mousammi

Medicinal Uses: The fruit of the evergreen Citrus x sinensis tree is aromatic, antiscorbutic (curing scurvy), refrigerant, antibilious and stimulant in action. It is useful as an astringent gargle in sore throats and for uterine bleeding after childbirth. A decoction of the lemon is an excellent antiperiodic drug and can replace quinine in malaria and reduce the temperature in typhoid fever. Lemon oil is a strong external rubefacient and has carminative and stomachic properties.

Traditional Uses: The Orange juice is good for jaundice and heart palpitations in Unani and Ayurvedic medicinal systems. An infusion of the leaves is taken internally to treat minor complaints such as biliousness, headaches and cold. The juice is added to various medicinal preparations, especially for diarrhoea, chest colds and fevers. It is mixed with oil and rubbed on the stomach to relieve the sagging muscles of the sexual organs. Lemon juice mixed with garlic (Allium sativum) and some water, is drunk for relief from snakebite. Lemon is a good source of Vitamin C. Research shows that eating fruits and vegetables rich in vitamin C, reduce heart disease and the risk of a stroke.

Products of the Citrus fruit such as essential oil and pectin of the fruit peel are valuable in cosmetic industries.

Biological Uses: It is widely applicable because of its antibacterial, anti-cancer, anti-diabetic, antifungal, anti-hypertensive, anti-inflammation, anti-lipidemia and antioxidant properties. Lemon oil has two important properties in skin disorders: - it is astringent and antimicrobial. These properties can potentially reduce inflammation and acne.

Chemical Uses: The plant contains valuable constituents such as alkaloids, carotenoids, coumarins, essential oils, flavonoids, flavanones, limonoids, phenolic acids and triterpenoids. Limonene, Linalool, citronellal and citronellol are the main constituents found in the essential oils from Citrus leaves and the fruit peel.

Distribution: The Orange is native to South Asia. India is the leading producer of Citrus sinensis (indica), followed by Mexico, China, Argentina, Brazil, Turkey and Pakistan. Due to the distinct aroma and delicious taste, Orange may be called a miracle fruit cultivated worldwide, especially in tropical and subtropical regions. In Pakistan, many varieties are widely cultivated in the Punjab, KPK and Sind.

Note: The Original habitat is unknown, possibly an introgressed hybrid of Citrus maxima x Citrus. Reticulate.

Citronellal ($C_{10}H_{18}O$)   Citronellol ($C_{10}H_{20}O$)

Coriandrum sativum

Kishneez/Dhanya (Leaves, Seeds and Flowers)

Latin Binomial	Coriandrum sativum
Family	Umbelliferae/Apiaceae
English Name	Coriander
Urdu Names	Kishneez/Dhanya

Medicinal Uses: The seeds of the flowering Coriandrum sativum herb are aromatic, stimulant, carminative and antiseptic in action. They have generally been used for gastrointestinal tract complaints as in dyspepsia, flatulence, vomiting and bilious affections. Coriander water was formerly used for windy colic.

Traditional Uses: In Unani and Ayurvedic medicinal systems, the seeds are used as carminative, diuretic and are used to prepare many household medicines for curing a cold, seasonal fever, nausea and stomach disorders. The paste of the green Coriander is helpful in headache. The powdered green Coriander helps alleviate the burning sensation and pain in diseases like inflammation caused by erysipelas (a bacterial infection) and in lymph nodes. The seeds are also useful as a poultice for ulcer and carbuncles (painful swelling under the skin). The fresh juice of the leaves is valuable as a gargle in sore throat and stomatitis. The Coriander oil is unique and is used internally to promote digestion, aromatically for relaxation, tropically for clear skin. It is traditionally beneficial as anti-inflammatory and analgesic.

The famous Unani preparations like Arq-e-Kishneez and Itrifal Kishnizi contain Coriander as one of the active ingredients.

Biological Uses: Extracts (non-aqueous) of the plant have antioxidant, antibacterial, anti-diabetic and antifungal properties. The oil possesses antiseptic, antioxidant and antimicrobial properties. The methanolic fraction of the Coriander seeds has a marked antispasmodic action.

Chemical Constituents: The seeds contain alcoholic volatile oils, e.g., linalool, dodecanal, dodecenal, etc. Other valuable components are alkaloids, phenols, flavonoids, tannins, sterols and glycosides. The plant is also a rich source of minerals like calcium, iron, potassium, magnesium, phosphorus, zinc and vitamins such as A, B_1, B_2, B_3 and C.

Distribution: Some of the important Coriander producing and exporting countries are India, China, Afghanistan, Indonesia, Iran, Turkey and Bulgaria. Although it is grown throughout the country, Pakistan is a comparatively a smaller Coriander producer.

Dodecanal ($C_{12}H_{24}O$)   Dodecenal ($C_{12}H_{22}O$)

Cuminum cyminum

Zirah Safaid (Herb Parts and Seeds)

Latin Binomial	Cuminum cyminum
Family	Umbelliferae/Apiaceae
English Name	Cumin
Urdu Name	Zirah Safaid

Medicinal Uses: The seeds of flowering Cuminum cyminum herb are stimulant, aromatic, carminative, antispasmodic and antiseptic in action.

Traditional Uses: In Unani and Ayurvedic medicinal systems, it is useful in several diseases of the digestive, respiratory and circulatory systems. It helps in the treatment of hoarseness of voice, dyspepsia, chronic diarrhoea and relieves hiccup. In powdered form, Cumin acts as a useful diuretic. It is still widely used in the Indo-Pak subcontinent in promoting other herbs' assimilation and improving liver function. The seeds are also valuable in treating insomnia, colds, fevers and improving milk production in nursing mothers.

The herb has been used externally as a poultice to relieve stitch and pains. In traditional Chinese medicine, Cumin is used in treating various diseases, including hypolipidemia, cancer and diabetes.

Biological Uses: The seed oil of Cumin is antiseptic, antibacterial, antioxidant and anti-inflammatory in action. Cumin seed has a distinctively strong flavour and is used in perfumery and for flavouring beverages.

Chemical Constituents: This plant's seeds contain aldehyde volatile oils, cuminaldehyde, cymene and terpenoids. Cumin seeds are nutritionally rich; they provide high amounts of fat (predominantly monounsaturated fat), protein and dietary fibre, vitamins B, E and several dietary minerals such as potassium, phosphorus, calcium, magnesium, iron and especially iron.

Distribution: An ancient spice, Cumin, is native to the Mediterranean Sea and Egyptian shores. Pakistan is one of the leading countries producing Cuminum cyminum, followed by India, Uzbekistan, Iran and Turkey.

Cuminaldehyde ($C_{10}H_{12}O$)

Cymbopogon martinii

Izkhir (Fresh and Dried Plant)

Latin Binomials	Cymbopogon martini/Cymbopogon jwarancusa
Family	Gramineae/Poaceae
English Name	Russ Grass
Urdu Name	Izkhir

Medicinal Uses: All above the ground parts of this plant are valuable medicinally. The plant Cymbopogon martinii is aromatic, antiseptic, carminative, stimulant, emmenagogue and diuretic in action.

Traditional Uses: In traditional medicinal systems (Unani and Ayurvedic) of the Indo-Pak subcontinent, the plant's decoction is useful in treating intestinal worms and diarrhoeal- dropsical affections and inflammation of the liver and spleen. The Cymbopogon is also beneficial in combination with other suitable herbs in treating rheumatism, hair loss, arthritis, lumbago and spasms. The paste of the plant's leaves and stem is rubbed externally over the area affected with scabies and in the discolouring of the skin. In Ayurvedic practices, the plant's oil is known as 'Rohisha' and is used in treating bronchitis, fevers and jaundice.

This plant is an essential ingredient of a famous Unani, poly-herbal, semisolid preparation known as 'Majun Dabid-ul-ward,' an effective remedy for jaundice, hepatitis, liver and spleen disorders.

Biological Uses: The oil known as 'Palmarosa' is antiseptic, anti-inflammatory, antiviral, antibacterial and antifungal. This oil is also known for its hydrating properties and can help prevent inflammation and dehydration. The Palmarosa essential oil is also reputed in benefitting stress relief, exhaustion, calming the mind, relieving muscle soreness and is a skin conditioner. Traditionally, the essential oil is used as a massage oil, as skin and body care lotion, as an agent for cleaning products, is also used in perfumery and making candles in many countries. The plant's therapeutic properties include antiseptic, antiviral, antifungal and antibacterial. The essential oils of Cymbopogon martinii have been studied and found to display a high anthelmintic activity against Caenorhabditis elegans (a transparent nematode).

Chemical Constituents: The plant contains alcoholic essential oil, rich in geraniol. Besides, flavonoids, coumarins, tannins and phenolic compounds are also present.

Distribution: The origin of Cymbopogon martini plant is from the Indo-Pak subcontinent and China but is now widely cultivated for commercial and essential oil production, in Australia and other countries.

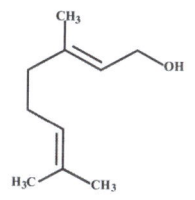

Geraniol ($C_{10}H_{18}O$)

Elettaria cardamomum

Ilaichi Khurd (Fruits and Flowers)

Latin Binomial	Elettaria cardamomum/Elettaria repens
Family	Zingiberaceae
English Name	Cardamom
Urdu Name	Ilaichi Khurd/Ilaichi Sabz

Medicinal Uses: The fruit of Elettaria cardamomum herb is aromatic, carminative antiemetic and stimulant in action. It has an aromatic warming effect which is useful in indigestion and flatulence. If swallowed, the fruit is good for treating colic and headaches. The Cardamom is used chiefly as a flavouring for cakes and liqueurs, etc.

Traditional Uses: In Unani and Ayurvedic medicinal systems, the plant is beneficial as a whole fruit, the seeds or ground seeds. The use of Cardamom checks nausea and vomiting. Powdered cardamom seeds boiled in tea water impart a delightful aroma to tea. It can be suitable as a medicine for scanty urination, diarrhoea, palpitation of the heart, exhaustion due to overwork and depression. Eating a Cardamom capsule daily with a tablespoon of honey improves eyesight, strengthens the nervous system and enhances a person's health.

The seed is taken internally to treat indigestion, nausea, vomiting, involuntary discharge of urine and pulmonary diseases with copious phlegm. The seed is chewed after meals to sweeten the breath. When taken with garlic, it helps to neutralize the garlic aroma. The powdered rhizomes are useful in treating colds. Elettaria cardamomum has a long-lasting reputation as an aphrodisiac.

In the Unani system of medicine, aromatic water (Arq-e-Elaichi) of the Cardamom is widespread in the use for restoring the stomach, poor digestion and diarrhoea. When taken with garlic, the seeds help to neutralize the garlic aroma.

Biological Uses: Cardamom oil is antiseptic, antibacterial, antispasmodic and stimulant. It is an essential constituent of perfumery. Cardamom capsules have moderate natural antioxidant properties due to phenol compounds such as quercetin, kaempferol and luteolin.

In one animal study, in which the researchers fed rats (rodents) a diet high in carbohydrate and fat, the rodents that also consumed Cardamom powder had a lower weight and better cholesterol than those that did not receive this supplement.

Chemical Constituents: The oil of the Cardamom fruit contains pinene, sabinene, myrcene, phellandrene, limonene, 1, 8-cineole, terpinene, p-cymene, terpinolene, linalool etc. The Cardamom is a good source of minerals like potassium, calcium and magnesium. The methanolic fraction of the grounded seeds also indicates the presence of flavonoids and glycosides.

Cardamom is an ingredient in betel nut (Paan) chewing and popular chewing gum in the Indo-Pak subcontinent, Mexico and Guatemala.

Distribution: Elettaria cardamomum plant is native to India, Burma and Sri Lanka and is cultivated in Brazil, Vietnam, Tanzania, Indonesia, Sri Lanka and South Asia. India was the world's largest cardamom producer from ancient times until about 1980, when Guatemala surpassed India.

Note: Cardamom is the third most expensive spice in weight, after saffron and vanilla. It is a crop that wild animals do not destroy.

Luteolin ($C_{15}H_{10}O_6$)   Phellandrene ($C_{10}H_{16}$)   Sabinene ($C_{10}H_{16}$)   Cineole ($C_{10}H_{18}O$)

Eucalyptus obliqua

Safayda (Tree and Leaves)

Latin Binomial	Eucalyptus obliqua
Family	Myrtaceae
English Name	Eucalyptus
Urdu Name	Safayda/Yukaliptus

Medicinal Uses: The oil of the large evergreen Eucalyptus oblique tree is aromatic, antiseptic, antispasmodic and stimulant in action.

Traditional Uses: In Unani and Ayurvedic medicinal systems, its fresh leaves are used as a gargle to relieve sore throat, sinusitis and bronchitis. The oil is useful as an antiseptic and stimulant gargle; it increases the heart's action and is said to have some antimalarial properties. Eucalyptus is beneficial internally in pulmonary tuberculosis, scarlet, typhoid and intermittent fevers. The oil is also used as an inhalant to clear catarrh; however, in large doses, it can irritate the kidneys, depress the nervous system, possibly stop respiration and breathing. Eucalyptus oil vapour appears to act as a decongestant when inhaled.

Biological Uses: Eucalyptus leaves and fruit significantly inhibit the grown of gram-positive (Staphylococcus aureus and Bacillus subtilis) and gram-negative (Escherichia coli and Streptococcus sp) bacteria. The oil also shows antifungal activity. Researchers have found that Eucalyptus oil could enhance the immune system phagocytic (cell that protects the body) response to pathogens in a rat model (phagocytises is a process where the immune system consumes and destroys foreign particles).

Chemical Constituents: The oil contains 1, 8-cineole, alpha-terpineol, cinole, limonene, myrcene, sclareol oxide and pinene and these are the major components of essential oil Eucalyptus oblique. The eucalyptus tree also contains biologically active constituents such as flavonoids, tannins, oleo-resins, terpenoids and volatile oils. Eucalyptus oblique is the principal source of Eucalyptus oil worldwide.

Distribution: Most Eucalyptus obliqua species are native to Australia, Brazil, Pakistan, India, China, South Africa and Portugal. It has been successfully grown throughout the plains and in the hills of Pakistan.

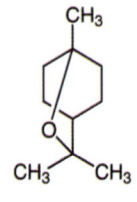

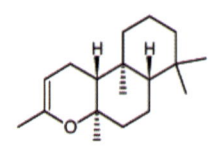

Cineole ($C_{10}H_{18}O$)   Sclareol oxide ($C_{18}H_{30}O$)

Foeniculum vulgare

Badiyaan/Sonuf (Herb and Fruits)

Latin Binomial	Foeniculum vulgare
Family	Umbelliferae
English Name	Fennel

Urdu name   Badiyaan/Sounf

Medicinal Uses: The seeds, roots and leaves of this plant are used for medicinal purposes. The fruit of the flowering Foeniculum vulgare herb is aromatic, carminative, digestive and stimulant in action. The herb is principally employed in purgatives to allay their tendency in griping and the fruit forms an ingredient of the compound liquorice powder. In addition to medicinal uses, fennel is helpful as a food flavouring, in toothpastes, soaps, perfumery, in air fresheners etc.

Traditional Uses: In Unani and Ayurvedic medicinal systems, it is an aromatic gastric stimulant, clears the organ from obstructions, particularly the digestive tract, thoracic (relating to the thorax) region, liver, spleen and kidneys. An infusion of the root is useful in treating urinary disorders. Many herbalists and complementary healthcare practitioners (Hakims and Ayurveda) recommend Fennel tea in regulating blood sugar.

In Popular traditional medicine, the aromatic water of Fennel (Arq-e-Badiyaan), acts similarly to Dill water in correcting infant flatulence. Fennel is one of the popular ingredients of many mono and poly-herbal Unani preparations, e.g. Arq, Jawarish, Sharbet and Ruh-e-Badiyaan.

Biological Uses: The essential Fennel oil is often extracted from the fully ripened and dried seed for medicinal uses, though it should not be given to pregnant women. The essential oil is antibacterial, antiseptic, anti-inflammatory, carminative and stimulant. The fatty oil obtained from the seed has antimicrobial properties. Phenolic compounds isolated from the plant are antioxidant in activity. Fennel oils show antiseptic, anti-inflammatory, anti-diabetic, antibacterial and antioxidant properties.

Chemical Constituents: The main compounds of volatile oils are trans-anethole, fenchone, limonene and estragole. Fennel provides essential micronutrients such as Vitamin C, calcium, magnesium, potassium and manganese. In Pakistan, Fennel is conventionally grown without fertilizer.

Distribution: Foeniculum vulgare is one of the most widely used herbal plants, globally.

Anethole ($C_{10}H_{12}O$)   Fenchone ($C_{10}H_{16}O$)   Estragole ($C_{10}H_{12}O$)

Juniperus communis

Abhal (Tree, Leaves and Fruits)

Latin Binomial	Juniperus communis
Family	Cupressaceae
English Name	Juniper
Urdu Name	Abhal/Aarar

Medicinal Uses: All parts (fruit, leaves, stems, oil and wood) of Juniperus communis are used for medicinal purposes.

The small evergreen tree of Juniperus is diuretic, astringent, corrosive, emmenagogue and carminative in action. The juniper oil obtained from the ripe berries is stomachic, diuretic, carminative and is used to treat indigestion, flatulence and kidney and bladder diseases. The primary use of Juniper is in treating dropsy (oedema) and in aiding other diuretic herbs in easing the condition.

Traditional Uses: In the Unani system of medicine, this shrub is chiefly helpful as a diuretic. The aerial parts are beneficial for treating acute and chronic cystitis, albuminuria, catarrh of the bladder, renal suppression, leucorrhoea and amenorrhea. The fruit is valuable as an antiseptic, stimulant, disinfectant and for treating chronic kidney disease, painful swelling and infantile tuberculosis. The bark is useful in managing gonorrhoea, respiratory affections, diabetes and skin disorders. The oil is carminative, antiseptic, antibacterial and anti-inflammatory. Steam inhalation of the plant is helpful in treating bronchitis. The bark of Juniperus is beneficial in asthma, pulmonary blennorrhoea, arthritis, abdominal disorders and skin affections.

Biological Uses: The plant has been reported to have anti-inflammatory, antifungal, hepatoprotective, antioxidant, antihypercholesterolemic, anti-diabetic and anti-hyper-lipidemic (lipid in the blood) activities. The essential oil has antimalarial property.

Chemical Uses: The oil chiefly consists of alpha-pinene, β-pinene (acintene), Sabinene, β- limonene, myrcene etc. The plant also contains flavonoids, flavones, terpenoids, monoterpenoids, sesquiterpenoids, steroids, glycoside, volatile oils, tannins and resins. The leaves are a rich source of terpenoids.

Distribution: These circumboreal species occur across North America, Europe, northern Asia and Japan.

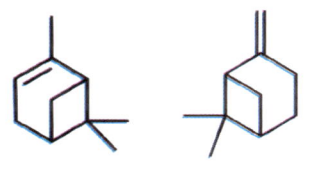

α-Pinene ($C_{10}H_{16}$)   β-Pinene ($C_{10}H_{16}$)

Juniperus oxycedrus

Jangli Abhal (Tree Parts and Dried Fruits)

Latin Binomial	Juniperus oxycedrus
Family	Cupressaceae
English Name	Cade Juniper
Urdu Name	Jangli Abhal

Medicinal Uses: The Fruit and oil of Juniperus oxycedrus tree are widely applicable in traditional folk medicine in treating various infectious diseases, like chronic eczema, several other skin diseases, hyperglycaemia, obesity, tuberculosis, bronchitis and pneumonia. The Juniper is beneficial in digestive problems, including upset stomach, intestinal gas (flatulence), heartburn, bloating and appetite loss. The fruit is also helpful in treating urinary tract infections.

Traditional Uses: In Unani and Ayurvedic medicinal systems, the Juniper fruit is valuable as a tonic, sudorific (causing sweat), stomachic, diuretic, emmenagogue and carminative. The nuts are useful in the treatment of gonorrhoea and leucorrhoea. The juice of the barries and its oil has disinfectant property. Some people apply fruit (berries) directly to the skin for wounds and for pain in the joints and muscles.

The plant yields an essential oil, 'oil of Cade' used externally in treating skin diseases such as psoriasis and chronic eczema. It is useful in diabetes, high blood pressure and the common cold if taken orally. Juniperus oxycedrus oil is suitable as a fragrance component in soaps, detergents, creams, lotions and perfumes. Care should be taken in using this oil internally.

Biological Uses: The pharmacological investigations reveal that the plant extracts (aqueous, methanol, ethanol and dichloromethane) possess antimicrobial, hypotensive, cytotoxic, analgesic anti-inflammatory, smooth muscle relaxant and hypoglycaemic effects. The methanol fraction of ripe barriers (fruit) of the plant is antioxidant in nature. The oil is antimicrobial, antiparasitic and antiseptic.

Chemical Constituents: The Juniperus, is a plant of the Cupressaceae family and contains manoyl oxide, pentadecan-2-enone 6Z, abietatriene, abieta-8, 11, 13-triene-7-one, cubebol, epi-torilenol and alpha-cadinol. The plant also contains essential biologically active compounds like flavonoids, flavones, terpenoids, monoterpenoids, steroids, sesquiterpenoids, volatile oils, tannins and resins. The leaves also contain terpenoids.

Distribution: Juniperus oxycedrus is a native to the Mediterranean region from Morocco to Portugal and it is also cultivated in France, Iran, Lebanon and Indo-Pak subcontinent.

Cubebol ($C_{15}H_{26}O$)   Epi-Torilenol ($C_{15}H_{24}O$)

Lactuca serriola

Kahu (Plant Leaves and Seeds)

Latin Binomial	Lactuca serriola/Lactuca sativa
Family	Compositae/Asteraceae
English Name	Lettuce
Urdu Name	Kahu

Medicinal Uses: The whole plant is valuable medicinally. The seeds of the evergreen Lactuca serriola herb are aromatic, anodyne, mildly diaphoretic and diuretic in action. They are used to ease irritable coughs, as a sedative and for dropsy to induce sleep and in easing colic.

The seed extract is useful against phlegmatic cough, asthma, bronchitis and palpitation. Lactuca serriola can help manage neurosis, anxiety, rheumatic pain and dry cough. The whole plant helps in treating stomach issues and stimulates the digestive process. It is known to enhance the appetite and reduce inflammatory tendencies. Internally, the plant is a remedy in treating insomnia, anxiety, neuroses, hyperactivity in children, dry coughs, whooping cough, rheumatic pain, etc.

The seed acts as an anodyne and promotes lactation and externally sap in treating warts. Lactuca serriola plant can eliminate toxins due to minerals in it.

Traditional Uses: The Lettuce seeds are a prevalent ingredient in Unani and Ayurvedic medicines and help manage insomnia, neurosis (mild mental disorders), anxiety, rheumatic pain and dry cough. Lettuce oil (Roghan-e-Kahu) is a beneficial Unani medicine for insomnia.

Biological Uses: Extracts (non-aqueous) of the plant possess antiseptic, antimicrobial and antioxidant activities. Aqueous leaf fraction exhibits the highest analgesic and anti-inflammatory properties, followed by methanol and methanol-chloroform extracts. The ethyl acetate fraction of the plant demonstrates neuroprotective action.

Chemical Constituents: The seeds contain volatile oil, flavonoids, alkaloids, coumarins, tannins, bitter substance lactucopicrin and a sesquiterpene lactone. The oil is rich in thymol, durenol, pinenes and alpha-terpinene. The plant is also a good source of micronutrients such as vitamins B_1, B_3, B_6 and minerals like calcium, phosphorus, selenium, iron and magnesium.

Distribution: Lactuca serriola is native to Europe, Asia and North Africa and has become naturalized at other places as well. China is the leading producer of Lactuca, followed by the United States, India, Spain, Italy, Japan and Turkey. In Pakistan, the plant is found on the lower hills of Azad Kashmir, Punjab, Khyber Pakhtunkhwa, Balochistan and the hills on the west side of the Indus in Sindh.

Lactucopicrin ($C_{23}H_{22}O_7$)

Laurus nobilis

Hab-el-Ghar (Tree, Leaves and Fruits)

Latin Binomial	Laurus nobilis
Family	Lauraceae
English Name	Sweet Bay/Bay Leaf
Urdu Name	Hab-el-Ghar

Medicinal Uses: The leaves of the evergreen Laurus nobilis tree or large shrubs are aromatic, carminative, stimulant, diuretic and a nerve tonic. The fruit is antiseptic, aromatic, digestive, narcotic and stimulant. The fruit is valuable in making carminative medicines and inducing abortion. Recent scientific studies have shown that Laurus nobilis leaves have many benefits and help eliminate many serious health problems and illnesses, like heartburn, constipation and in regulating bowel movement. The leaves also convert triglycerides to monosaturated fats **(hypertriglyceridemic)**. A decoction of the leaves is anti-diabetic in action.

Traditional Uses: In Unani and Ayurvedic medicinal systems, the leaves are useful in treating many ailments, particularly as an aid to digestion, bronchitis, influenza and regulating bowel movement. The fruit and leaves are usually applicable in treating hysteria, amenorrhoea, flatulent colic, etc. A decoction of the leaves helps eliminate bad cholesterol, reduces triglycerides and treats urinary organs and dropsy problems. It is also handy in colds, flu and severe cough as it is a rich source of vitamin C. Vapours of boiled leaves and inhalation of the steam is good in getting rid of phlegm and in reducing the cough's severity. The aqueous extracts of the Laurel fruit and leaves are beneficial in herbal medicine as an astringent agent and to treat several neurological, dermatological and urological disorders. Besides, the Laurel essential oil is currently used in folk medicines for treating different health problems, such as rheumatism and dermatitis. It is also used in massage therapy and aromatherapy.

In Iranian folk medicine, the essential oil obtained from the leaves has been helpful in rheumatic pains, epilepsy, neuralgia, Parkinsonism and muscular convulsion.

The leaves are highly aromatic and can be used as an insect repellent. The dried leaves protect stored grain, beans etc., from weevils (beetles of the Curculionoidea family).

Biological Uses: The essential oil from the leaves has narcotic, antibacterial and fungicidal properties. The oil also possesses antioxidant activity. The leaves protect the heart from seizures and strokes as they contain cardiovascular protective compounds. Laurus nobilis lowers blood sugar. The oils produced demonstrate antimicrobial activity against some highly susceptible strains of pathogenic and spoilage bacteria and yeasts. The anticonvulsant effect can be due to methyl eugenol, eugenol and pinene present in the essential oil of Laurus nobilis.

The methanol extract is rich in phenols, flavonols and flavonoids. These biologically active compounds are significantly more active and potent against cancer cells.

Chemical Constituents: The plant is rich in acids such as caffeic acid, quercetin, eugenol and other biologically active substances (polyphenols) that prevent the growth of cancer cells in the body.

Distribution: Laurus nobilis is native to the southern Mediterranean region and is cultivated mainly in Europe and the USA, as an ornamental and medicinal plant.

Note: Indian Bay leaf Cinnamomum tamala (tezpat) of the Lauraceae family differs from Laurus nobilis (Hab-el-Ghar) with leaves, which are shorter and light to medium green in colour, with three veins running the length of the leaf.

Lavandula x stoechas

UstuKhuddos (Field and Flowers)

Latin Binomial	Lavandula x stoechas
Family	Labiatae/Lamiaceae
English Name	Lavender
Urdu Name	UstuKhuddus

Medicinal Uses: All above the ground parts of the flowering Lavandula x stoechas plant are used for medicinal purposes. Lavendula x stoechas is aromatic, carminative, stimulant, anti-phlegmatic and nervine in action. The essential oil, when taken internally, is refreshing as a tonic against faintness, heart palpitations, giddiness and colic. It raises the spirits, promotes the appetite and dispels flatulence. When the oil is applied externally, it relieves toothache, neuralgia and rheumatism. Its tea is often drunk as a digestive aid after meals and it is a mild diuretic.

Externally, the plant and its oil are also beneficial for wounds, ulcers, sores and valuable oil for massage. When rubbed into the temples, the essential oil helps calm headaches and migraines.

The oil is principally valuable in the perfumery industry. For example, lavender oil is used in soap making and perfumery.

Traditional Uses: In the Unani system, the plant is known as 'Jaroobee-e-Dimagh,' which means 'broom of the brain' because it removes, black bile from the brain and helps in strengthening and improving the intellect. The plant is extensively used in the treatment of migraines and epilepsy. Both dried flowers and plant, are useful in the Unani system of medicine. Lavendula is the chief ingredient of a famous, poly-herbal Unani medicine, called 'Itrifal UstuKhddus,' which helps treat neuralgic, neuromuscular pains due to cold, melancholy and even retains the original hair colour through long term regular use.

Lavender is commonly used for anxiety, stress and insomnia. It is also beneficial in treating depression, dementia, pain after surgery and many other conditions. The plant also has positive effects on wounds, in urinary tract infections, against eczema and has analgesic, sedative and antiseptic properties. In the Palestinian tradition, the decoction of the areal part of lavender is valuable in treating migraine and epilepsy. It is considered an expectorant, antispasmodic, carminative, stimulant, deobstruent and wound healing agent in Turkey. In countries such as Morocco, Algeria and Tunisia, Lavandula x stoechas is mentioned in the traditional pharmacopoeias in treating headaches, depression, diabetes, inflammatory and rheumatic diseases. In Persian, it is called 'Ossghodus' and an infusion of the leaves is beneficial as anticonvulsant, as a sedative and is antispasmodic.

Biological Uses: The ethanolic extract of the plant is anti-inflammatory and antioxidant. The flowers and the essential oil derived from them are anti-asthmatic, antiseptic, antispasmodic, antifungal and antibacterial. The anti-diabetic activity of the essential oil of Lavandula x stoechas revealed a protective effect against hyperglycemia and oxidative stress. The oil also has cytotoxic properties.

Chemical Constituents: The Lavender oil contains linalool, linalyl acetate, cineol, pinene, limonene and tannin. The plant also contains constituents such as sterols, flavonoids, terpenoids, volatile oils, steroids, glycosides, tannins, resins and minerals like aluminium, calcium, iron, magnesium, potassium and strontium. The leaves are also rich in terpenoids.

Distribution: It is native to the Old World from Cape Verde to Canary Islands, Southern Europe to Northern and Eastern Africa, the Mediterranean, Southwest Asia and Southeast Asia.

Linalyl acetate ($C_{12}H_{20}O_2$)

Matricaria chamomilla

Babuna (Fresh and Dried Flowers)

Latin Binomial	Matricaria chamomilla
Family	Compositae/Asteraceae
English Name	Chamomile
Urdu Name	Babuna

Medicinal Uses: The flowers and roots of the annual Matricaria chamomilla plant are aromatic, stimulant, stomachic, anti-inflammatory and antispasmodic in action.

Chamomile is perhaps the most commonly used European herb in herbal medicine today. An infusion of chamomile tea is a highly effective remedy for hysterical and nervous problems. This plant has a powerful soothing and sedative affect which is harmless. Chamomile has long been used as a sedative to counter anxiety and to promote sleepiness, even in ancient times. It is said to aid digestion, if taken after a meal. A decoction of the flowers helps relieve morning sickness, such as in pregnancy and as a gargle in treating mouth sores and gingivitis. The ulcer-protective properties are also established in German Chamomile. Externally, it can be applied alone or combined with other herbs to relieve pain, swelling and inflammation.

Traditional Uses: In the Chinese medicinal system, Chamomile has been useful for centuries as anti-inflammatory, antioxidant and mildly astringent.

In Unani and Ayurvedic medicine, the plant helps treat psoriasis, eczema, motion sickness, heartburn and stomachache. The plant is valuable in herbal medicine for a bad stomach, for skincare and as a gentle sleep aid. An infusion of the flowers is taken internally, as anodyne, anti-inflammatory, antiseptic, antispasmodic and carminative.

The flowers are also beneficial externally, in treating wounds, sunburn, burns, haemorrhoids, mastitis and leg ulcers (stasis ulcers). In addition to pharmaceutical uses, the oil is extensively applicable in perfumery, cosmetics, aromatherapy and the food industry.

Biological Uses: An extract (ethanol) and the oil of the plant have antispasmodic, antibacterial, sedative and antiallergenic properties. The oil can be considered a potent antibacterial agent and an antioxidant. Chamomile is also popular for alleviating inflammation of the mouth and skin. In a study of patients with chronic mouth ulcers, a remarkable 82 per cent rated Chamomile extract as very effective in relieving pain.

Chemical Constituents: The plant contains volatile oils, mainly of the sesquiterpenes, flavonoids and lactones. The major components of Chamomile oil are α-bisabolo oxide, chamazulene, (E)-En-in-dicycloether, α-bisabolone oxide, n-octanal, α-bisabolol oxide B, 1, 8-cineole (3.85 per cent), α-terpineol and germacrene. The plant also contains terpenoids, flavones, flavonols, flavanone, coumarins, phenolic compounds, a small amount of resins and tannins.

Distribution: Matricaria chamomile has originated from Europe (Germany) and western and South Asia (Pakistan, India and Sri Lanka) and is also found in Australia and North America. In Hungary, it grows abundantly in poor soil and it is a source of income for the poor inhabitants of these areas.

Chamazulene ($C_{14}H_{16}$)   Bisabolol oxide ($C_{15}H_{26}O_2$)

Mentha x piperita

Pudina (Leaves and Plant)

Latin Binomials	Mentha x piperita/Menthe arvensis
Family	Labiatae/Lamiaceae
English Name	Peppermint
Urdu Name	Pudina

Medicinal Uses: The green leaves of the rhizomatous upright, perennial Mentha x piperita plant are aromatic, stimulant, antispasmodic, carminative, refrigerant and stomachic in action. These leaves help treat flatulence, menstrual pains, diarrhoea, nausea, depression-related anxiety, muscle pain, common cold and indigestion. The oil alleviates sickness and nausea.

Peppermint tea can ward off colds and influenza at an early stage, can calm heart palpitations and is also used to reduce the appetite. Externally, Peppermint oil is extensively applicable in both medicine and commerce. It is good in the treatment of dyspepsia, flatulence, colic and abdominal cramps.

Traditional Uses: In the Indo-Pak subcontinent, Mentha x piperita is useful as a stimulant, carminative, antipyretic, antispasmodic and is remedial in infantile troubles. A decoction of the leaves helps relieve hiccups, bronchitis and control vomiting during pregnancy. Menthol is an analgesic and is thus beneficial in reducing pains such as headaches, muscle aches and inflammation. The aromatic water of the Peppermint (Arq-e-Pudina) is generally applicable as a carminative, raising body temperature and inducing perspiration.

In France, the plant is considered to be a powerful stimulant. In Turkey, the hot extract is used between meals can relieve gastrointestinal complaints. In China, various parts of the plant are used in treating sores, rashes, headache, red eyes and mouth ulcers. In the USA, the odour of the Peppermint serves as a stimulant for the central nervous system. In Spain, it is considered hypotensive.

Mentha x piperita oil is one of the most popular and widely used essential oils. It is used in oral preparations such as toothpaste, dental creams, mouthwashes, chewing gums and cough drops. The fresh green leaves of Mentha x piperita are also blended to create bittersweet 'Pudina-Ke- Chatney ' (mint sauce).

Biological Uses: The plant's oil and non-aqueous fractions of the plant have antibacterial, antimicrobial and antiproliferative properties. The aqueous extract of the leaves also appears to be antibacterial in action. The ethanolic and aqueous extracts of the root, stem and leaves possess anti-allergic and anti-inflammatory activities due to the presence of polyphenols, flavonoids and the essential oil. **The essential oil in the leaf is antiseptic, though it is toxic in large doses.** It has also been reported that the root's non-aqueous extract is less antibacterial in effect than the leaf and stem fractions.

Chemical Constituents: Peppermint oil is composed primarily of menthol and menthone and several other minor constituents, including menthofuran, 1, 8-cineole and limonene. The plant also has beneficial bioactive compounds like alkaloids, flavonoids, steroids, tannins and phenols.

Distribution: This plant is indigenous to Europe and the Middle East. The plant is now widely spread and cultivated in many world regions. In Pakistan, these plants are found in the Punjab, Azad Kashmir, Khyber Pakhtunkhwa and Baluchistan.

Note: Mentha × piperita, also known as Mentha balsamea wild, is a hybrid mint, which is a cross between water mint and spearmint.

Menthol ($C_{10}H_{20}O$)   Menthone ($C_{10}H_{18}O$)

Myristica fragrans

Jaifal/Javatri/Bisbasa (Dried and Fresh Seeds)

Latin Binomial	Myristica fragrans
Family	Myristicaceae
English Name	Nutmeg
Urdu Name	Jaifal/Bisbasa/Jozbuwa/Jawatri

Medicinal Uses: The seeds of the evergreen Myristica fragrans tree are carminative, stomachic, stimulant, antiseptic and aromatic in action.

Traditional Uses: In Unani and Ayurvedic medicinal systems, the powdered kernel helps relieve flatulence, vomiting, colic, gastrointestinal complaints like dyspepsia, diarrhoea and nausea. Externally, the seeds are useful in treating toothache, rheumatic and abdominal pains; they are an irritant and a weak local anaesthetic. The seed of the nutmeg is rich in essential oils. It is a bitter, astringent, spicy herb that acts as a warming digestive tonic. It controls vomiting and relaxes spasms. The oil of this plant is aphrodisiac. When applied externally, it has an anti-inflammatory effect. The Nutmeg essential oil is valuable as a natural flavouring agent and as a perfume in the cosmetic industry.

The Nutmeg seed forms a constituent of many Unani poly-herbal, medicinal tonic preparations, e.g. Hab-e-Ambe -Momyiai, Majun Seer Alvi Khan, Laboob-e-Kabir and Maul-ul-Laham.'

Biological Uses: The extracts (aqueous-ethanol) of the plant possess antimicrobial and antioxidant activities. The oil extracted from the seeds has hypoglycaemic, antibacterial, antimicrobial, anti-inflammatory, anti-cancer and memory-enhancing properties.

Chemical Constituents: Nutmeg contains volatile oil (5 to 15 per cent), phytosterol, starch and colouring matter. The most important constituent of the volatile oil is myristicin, elemicin and eugenol. Nutmeg also contains fixed oils, solid at ordinary temperature, known as nutmeg butter and flavonoids, resins, tannins, terpenoids, phenolic compounds, minerals like potassium, magnesium, iron, phosphorus, copper, zinc and manganese.

Distribution: Myristica fragrans, the tree, is native to Indonesia. It is widely grown across Southern China, Malaysia, Taiwan, India and Sri Lanka.

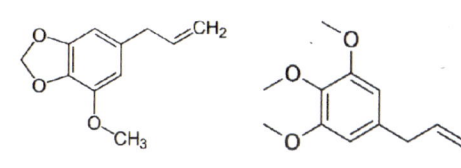

Myristicin ($C_{11}H_{12}O_3$)   Elemicin ($C_{12}H_{16}O_3$)

Origanum marjorana

Mirzanjosh (Plant and Flowers)

Latin Binomial	Origanum marjorana
Familly	Labiatae/Lamiaceae
English Name	Common Marjoram
Urdu Name	Mirzanjosh

Medicinal Uses: The leaves of the flowering Origanum marjorana plant are aromatic, stimulant, carminative and emmenagogue in action. When extracted from the leaves, the essential oil, oleo Majorana, makes an excellent external application for sprains, bruises and internally, acts as an emmenagogue. Common Marjoram is widely used in cooking and aids the digestion of food.

Traditional Uses: In Unani and Ayurvedic medicinal systems, the leaves are used as a general tonic. The herb is an effective detergent for abnormally produced catarrh in the brain. It is taken internally to treat bronchial complaints, tension, headaches, insomnia, anxiety, minor digestive upsets and painful menstruation.

It has been useful in Morocco as an antihypertensive plant. In Iran, Origonum is beneficial in treating various diseases in traditional and folklore medicines, including gastrointestinal, ocular, respiratory, cardiac, rheumatologic and neurological disorders. Italian villages evidenced the traditional use of the infusion of the leaves Origanum to treat stomach pain, neuralgia and even a sedative.

In Turkey, the essential oil is used in treating asthma, indigestion and headache. In Egypt, the leaves are a remedy for cold and chill. The essential oil is valuable in aromatherapy. It is a muscle relaxant.

Biological Uses: In modern medicine, a wide range of pharmacological activities, including antioxidant, cardio-protective, anti-platelet, gastro-protective, antibacterial and antifungal, anti-inflammatory, antitumor and antiulcer inhibitory activities, have been reported from the use of this plant. The ethanolic fraction and the oil of Origanum also show anticholinesterase activity.

Chemical Constituents: The essential oil obtained by steam distillation contains terpinen-4-ol, terpineol, terpinene, cis-sabinene hydrate, linalool and several other compounds.

Distribution: Sweet marjoram is endemic to the Island of Cyprus but is cultivated worldwide as a culinary herb.

Note: The *in-vivo* acute toxicity test demonstrated a large margin of safety of this plant.

Terpinene-4-ol ($C_{10}H_{18}O$)

Origanum vulgaris

Sa'atar (Plant, Leaves and Flowers)

Latin Binomial	Origanum vulgaris
Family	Labiatae/Lamiaceae
English Name	Marjoram
Urdu Name	Sa'atar

Medicinal Uses: All above the ground parts of the plant and its oil, are useful for medicinal purposes. The perennial, flowering Origanum vulgaris plant is aromatic, carminative, stimulant diaphoretic in action and mildly tonic. It is beneficial in producing sweat, to bring out the measles spots, relieve spasms and is colic and dyspeptic when used as a warm infusion. The oil has been used externally as a rubefacient. The dried herb may be utilized as a hot poultice for swelling, rheumatism and for colic, while an infusion of the fresh plant will ease a nervous headache.

Traditional Uses: In Unani and Ayurvedic medicinal systems, the plant has a beneficial effect on the digestive and respiratory systems and is also used to promote menstruation. The leaves and stems are antispasmodic, carminative, diaphoretic, emmenagogue, stimulant and stomachic. Origanum is useful internally in treating colds, influenza, mild feverish illnesses, indigestion, stomach upsets and painful menstruation. A few drops of the essential oil put on cotton wool and placed in the hollow of an aching tooth, frequently relieves the toothache. This plant is one of the best natural antiseptics because of its high thymol content.

In Turkey, the flowering branches and the leaves are prepared as infusions and used for treating cold, flu, headache and toothache.

The essential oil is valuable in aromatherapy. However, the oil is harmful for pregnant women.

Biological Uses: The extracts of the plant and its oil possess antimicrobial, antifungal, antioxidant, anti-inflammatory, anti-cancer, anti-mutagenic and anti-parasitic activities. The antiparasitic effect of Origanum oil may be due to the presence of phenolic compounds (thymol and carvacrol) that interact with the permeability of the cytoplasmic cell membrane. The oil also stimulates spermatogenesis.

Chemical Constituents: The essential oils (carvacrol and thymol) are the major components of Marjoram. The plant also contains flavonoids, tannins, phenolic acids (polyphenols), phenolic glycosides, resins, terpenoids and steroids.

Distribution: It is native to Northern Europe and is cultivated commercially. The plant is widely distributed in the fields of China and some central Asian countries.

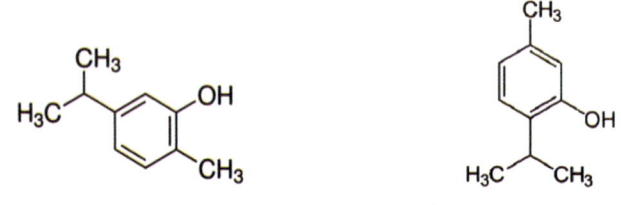

Carvacrol ($C_{10}H_{14}O$)   Thymol {Isopermic with Carvacrol} ($C_{10}H_{14}O$)

Pimpinella anisum

Anisun (Shrub Parts and Fruits)

Latin Binomial	Pimpinella anisum
Family	Umbelliferae/Apiaceae
English Name	Anise
Urdu Name	Anisun

Medicinal Uses: The fruit of the herbaceous, flowering Pimpinella anisum herb is aromatic, carminative, stimulant, stomachic and pectoral in action. When taken internally, the seeds expel tapeworms. Locally, the oil is applied to the head in headache and the abdomen in flatulence and intestinal colic.

Traditional Uses: In Unani and Ayurvedic medicinal systems, the fruit of Pimpinella is useful in treating dyspepsia, flatulence, diarrhoea, carminative, dropsy and is an expectorant. The tea of the seeds is suitable in colds and cough. The plant is beneficial as a stimulant to sexual drive and a strong decoction of the seeds can be applied externally to stimulate breast-milk production.

Externally, it is helpful in treating infestations of lice, scabies and as a chest rub in cases of bronchial disorders. Anise is used internally for treating whooping cough, flatulence, colic-like pain, digestive, menstruation disturbances, liver disease and tuberculosis in folk medicine.

In Iran, Anise seeds are also used as an analgesic in migraine and as carminative, aromatic, disinfectant and diuretic. In some traditional Iranian texts, Anise is mentioned for melancholy, nightmare and also in the treatment of epilepsy and seizure.

Aromatic water (Arq-e-Anisun) of Anise is used as carminative, stomachic and to relieve spasms of involuntary muscles. In homoeopathic, Anise is valuable in shoulder pain and lumbago.

Biological Uses: The Anise oil is antiepileptic, antirheumatic, antibacterial, antiseptic, antioxidant and antispasmodic. An aqueous-methanol extract (50:50 per cent) and methanol extract of the seeds, exhibits antibacterial and anticonvulsant properties.

The aqueous suspension possesses antiulcer activity. Since the oil is antimicrobial and has germ-killing qualities, it will help get rid of flu brought on because of microbes. Few reports show that certain chemicals in Anise may have estrogen-like effects and so affect the human body in relation to menstruation and menopause.

Chemical Constituents: The plant contains phenols, flavonol, flavones, phenolic glycosides and monomeric anthocyanins (are the water-soluble vacuolar pigments). The principal constituent of Anise oil is trans-anethole and γ-himachalene. Anise seeds are a good source of many essential B-complex vitamins such as pyridoxine (B_6), niacin (B_3), riboflavin (B_2) and thiamine (B_1).

The seeds are also an essential source of minerals like calcium, copper, potassium, iron, manganese, magnesium and zinc. Antioxidant vitamins such as vitamin C and A can also be found in the spice.

Distribution: Pimpinella anisum is a native to Egypt and is also cultivated in Greece, Rome, the Middle East, South-West Asia and Africa. Pimpinella diversifolia is also found in Pakistan, northern India and Afghanistan.

Note: Aniseed oil is harmful in dermatitis and inflammatory or allergic skin conditions.

γ -Himachalene ($C_{15}H_{24}$)

Pinus palustris

Sanobar/ Cheer (Tree, Cones and Needles)

Latin Binomial	Pinus palustris
Family	Pinaceae
English Name	Pine
Urdu Name	Sanobar/Cheer

Medicinal Uses: The oil and oleo-resin of the Pinus palustris tree are stimulant, rubefacient, aromatic, diuretic in action and a remedy for gonorrhoea. The oil is beneficial as an inhalant for bronchitis and laryngitis and is also effective against ulcers and abscesses. It acts as a vermifuge in chronic ulcers. It is suitable for fumigation in scrofula (tuberculosis infection of the lymph nodes in the neck) and dries the affected sites.

Traditional Uses: In Ayurvedic and Unani systems of medicine, the leaves, the bark, the oil and resin of this tree are useful for medicinal purposes. It reduces inflammation and detoxifies circulatory channels and early ageing symptoms. The decoction of the bark of the tree helps skin hydration and reduces skin pigmentation when taken orally as a nutritional supplement or if applied locally. The oil is beneficial externally, in liniment plasters, poultices, herbal steam baths and inhalers. It is useful in treating various skin complaints, wounds, sores, burns and boils, etc. It is a valuable remedy for kidney and bladder complaints. An infusion of the dried buds is suitable as an eyewash. The branches are helpful in herbal steam baths as a treatment for muscular pains.

Biological Uses: The leaf extracts (methanol and ethanol) possess antiseptic, anti-inflammatory and antimicrobial activities. The oil is also antibacterial in nature.

Chemical Constituents: The Pine oil consists mainly of alpha-terpineol and other cyclic terpenes alcohols. The plant also contains constituents like glycosides, flavonoids, essential oils, tannins, resins and terpenoids.

Distribution: Pinus palustris is a native to the United States and is now cultivated in Asia, Africa, Austria, South Africa and Australia. In Lahore, pine trees were introduced during the British era when they were planted in the Lawrence Garden. It is now a widespread plant in the different parts of Pakistan.

Note: Cosmetic products are useful as an antiseptic, anti-ageing, as a moisturizer and UV protector as they mostly contain an extract of leaves and the needles of the Pine tree. The favourite dry fruit, 'Chilgoza,' is fruit of Pinus gerardiana tree which is also known as Chilgoza Pine.

Piper cubeba

Kabab Chini (Leaves, Dried and unripe Fruits)

Latin Binomial	Piper cubeba
Family	Piperaceae

English Name		Cubebs
Urdu Name		Kabab Chini

Medicinal Uses: The fruit of the evergreen, climbing Piper cubeba shrub is aromatic, carminative, anti-inflammatory, antiseptic and antibacterial. It is beneficial in treating gleets and gonorrhoea. The Cubebs are administered as single (mono-herbal) or in compound preparations for cleaning and procuring antiseptic effects. The Cubeb berry is effective in easing the symptoms of chronic bronchitis.

Traditional Uses: Piper Cubeba fruit is mentioned in Unani and Ayurvedic pharmacopoeias/formularies as a valuable herb for treating cough, swelling, dysmenorrhoeal, erectile dysfunction and indigestion. In the classical Unani literature, the plant has also been mentioned in detail and various actions such as diuretic, lithotriptic, antiseptic, kidney tonic and nephroprotective have been attributed to this plant. Although several other effects are known to be possessed by this herb, it often helps in urogenital disorders.

The plant's stem has several uses, such as being useful in rheumatic pains, muscular aches and fever. A cold extraction of the Piper cubeba fruit is suitable for urinary tract infections.

Unani physicians use a paste of the Cubeb berries externally on male and female genitals to intensify sexual pleasure during coitus. They also use powdered fruit to treat dysentery, syphilis, abdominal pain and asthma.

The modern use of Cubeb in England is for treating gonorrhoea, where its antiseptic action is of much value. The Cubeb oil is antiseptic, carminative, diuretic and a stimulating expectorant. In Chinese medicine, Cubeb is valuable for its warming property.

Biological Uses: The oil of Cubeb possesses antiseptic, antibacterial, antifungal, anti-cancer and anti-inflammatory properties. The extracts (water-ethanol-methanol) of plant chiefly have antiseptic, antioxidant and antimicrobial activities.

Chemical Constituents: The plant principally possesses complex mixtures of monoterpenes and sesquiterpenes. The oil contains sabinene, abinene, beta-elemene, caryophyene or beta-Caryophyllene, epi-cubebol and cubebol.

Distribution: It is mainly grown in Java and Sumatra; hence it is called Java pepper.

Caryophyllene (C$_{15}$H$_{24}$)   Cubebol (C$_{15}$H$_{26}$O)

Pterocarpus santalinus

Sandal Surkh (Tree and Woods)

Latin Binomial	Pterocarpus santalinus
Family	Papilionaceae/Fabaceae
English Name	Red Sandal
Urdu Name	Sandal Surkh

Medicinal Uses: The wood of the fast-growing (when young) Pterocarpus santalinus tree is diaphoretic, sedative, anti-inflammatory, antiseptic, analgesic in action and a general tonic. Based on its ethnomedicinal and traditional use, the plant was screened for analgesic, anti-inflammatory and antioxidant activities. An extract of the wood is helpful in commercial cosmetic preparations and the wood powder helps as a skin conditioner in commercial cosmetic preparations.

Traditional Uses: In Unani and Ayurvedic medicinal systems, Pterocarpus is commonly used as an antiseptic, wound healing agent and as an acne treatment. A decoction of the fruit is a remedy which acts as an astringent tonic in chronic dysentery. The powdered wood helps in controlling bleeding, bleeding piles and inflammation. It is also beneficial for treating skin diseases, bone fracture, leprosy, spider poisoning and scorpion sting. Internally, the syrup of the wood acts as a cardiac tonic. The powdered wood is brewed as tea which helps in treating chronic dysentery and is also used in treating diabetes and boosting the immune system. The wood paste is suitable as a cooling, external application for inflammations, ophthalmia, sore eyes and headache. Pterocarpus santalinus is one of the common ingredients in mono-herbal (Khamira Sandal) and poly-herbal Unani medicines such as 'Dawa-ul-Misk, Majun-e-Ushba, Arq Maul-Juban,' etc. The wood is also an ingredient in many medicinal oils and pharmaceutical preparations.

Biological Uses: The oil of Pterocarpus santalinus showed antioxidative, anti-diabetic, antimicrobial, anti-cancer, anti-inflammatory actions and has protective affects on the liver, gastric mucosa and nervous system. The angiogenic (the formation of new blood vessels) activity of the plant may be attributed to the phytoconstituents present in the extract.

Chemical Constituents: The plant contains flavonoids, alkaloids, triterpenoids, phenolic compounds, saponins, tannins and glycosides. The oil of Sandal contains alpha-bisabolol (monocyclic sesquiterpene alcohol), squalene, cedrol, propanoic acid, spathulenol and heptacosane.

Distribution: Pterocarpus santalinus is endemic to South India. Various Pterocarpus species are widely distributed throughout the world. This tree is valued for the rich red colour of its wood.

Note: This tree should not be confused with the aromatic Santalum album (sandal safaid).

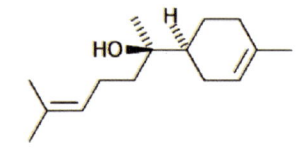

Bisabolol/Levomenol ($C_{15}H_{26}O$)

Pyrethrum indicum

Aqarqara (Roots and Flowers of two different Species)

Latin Binomial	Pyrethrum indicum/Anacyclus pyrethrum
Family	Compositae/Asteraceae
English Name	Pyrethrum
Urdu Name	Aqarqara

Medicinal Uses: The root of the flowering Pyrethrum indicum plant is aromatic, carminative, antiphlegmatic, stimulant, bitter and digestive in action and a cardiac tonic. The pyrethrum works very effectively on the male reproductive system and improves sexual potency. The herb may also enhance testosterone levels in males, improve libido, enhance sperm count and helps infertility problems.

Traditional Uses: Traditional healers (Hakims and Ayurveda) of the Indo-Pak subcontinent recommend using Pyrethrum (Aqarqara) as an aphrodisiac and in spermatogenic actions. As per Ayurvedic theories, Anacyclus Pyrethrum roots act as libido stimulant for men. These influence the secretion of androgens and increase their production. Alkyl-amide and the principal alkaloid in the Pyrethrum root increases testosterone production in the animal model.

The root powder is mixed with mustard oil and is used in treating pyorrhoea. The leaves are depurative. The flowers help treat skin boils, swelling, inflammation of the throat, eyes, cervix, eczema, itchiness of the skin and hypertension. An essential oil obtained from the plant contains terpene, chrysanthenone, which is useful in Parkinson's disease. In China, the root is a remedy for migraine and eye ailments. In combination with black pepper, it helps in treating gonorrhoea.

Biological Uses: The plant and its oil have antiseptic, insecticidal, antibacterial and antifungal properties. The aqueous and methanol extracts of the plant exhibit anti-inflammatory, antioxidant and antinociceptive activities.

Chemical Constituents: This plant's root contains essential oils (monoterpenes), fatty amides, anacyclin, pellitorine, tannins, Inulin, resin, lactones, amides and volatile oils. The Pyrethrum flowers also contain volatile oils, e.g., trans-chrysanthemumic acid, decanoic acid and nerolidol. The plant comprises of valuable biologically active constituents like flavonoids, alkaloids (pellitorine), tannins, phenolic compounds, triterpenes, sterols and resins. The root is rich in alkaloids, while the aerial parts are a good source of tannins and flavonoids.

Distribution: The Pyrethrum indicum is cultivated in Kenya, Tanzania, East Asia, China and Japan. The plant is native to Pakistan, India and the Arabian countries.

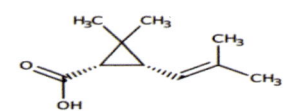

Chrysanthemic acid ($C_{10}H_{16}O_2$)

Decanoic acid ($C_{10}H_{20}O_2$)

Rosa x damascena

Gul-e-Surkh

Latin Binomials	Rosa x damascena/Rosa indica
Family	Rosaceae
English Name	Rose
Urdu Name	Gul-e-Surkh/Gulab

Medicinal Uses: The petals and oil of the deciduous flowering Rosa x damascene plant are aromatic, demulcent, astringent, mild laxative and refrigerant in action.

Traditional Uses: In the Unani system of medicine, Rose petals have been useful for centuries. It is described in detail in ethnobotanical and classical Unani literature, owing to its various therapeutic actions, such as a laxative, an analgesic, exhilarant, demulcent and astringent. A decoction of the plant's root is helpful as a cough remedy to ease cough in children.

The most therapeutic effects of Rosa damascena in ancient medicine, include treating abdominal and chest pain, strengthening the heart and treating menstrual bleeding and digestive problems. The Rose oil heals depression, grief, nervous stress and tension. The vapour therapy of the rose oil helps in some allergies, headaches and migraine.

Aromatic water (Arq-e-Gulab) of the Rose petals is used worldwide and is a proper remedy for irritating eyes and dry skin. The Rose's main products are essential oil, Rosewater, 'Gulkand' (a herbal formulation useful in constipation), Rose tea and petals.

Biological Uses: Rosa damascena extracts have a broad spectrum of biopharmacological activity like antiseptic, antifungal, hypoglycemic, antidepressant, anti-inflammatory, analgesic, antioxidant and antimicrobial.

Chemical Constituents: The plant contains alcoholic essential oil (pale yellow), e.g., citronellol, geraniol, nerol and phenyl ethyl alcohol, etc. The roots have kaempferol-3-O-galactoside, whereas cyanidin, kaempferol, quercetin, flavonoids, saponins, phenolic compounds and alkaloids are also found in the plant. The Rose plant is also a rich source of micronutrients such as phosphorus, potassium, sodium, calcium, zinc, magnesium, manganese, iron, boron and vitamins like A, B_3, C, D and E.

Distribution: Rosa damascene is cultivated in Asia, Europe, Africa, Australia, the United States and other countries.

According to a survey, in Punjab, Pakistan, 1,300 acres of land is used for Rose flower crop, which is 68 per cent of Roses' total area in Pakistan.

Note: The rose is the national flower of the United States and also the Maldives and the United Kingdom.

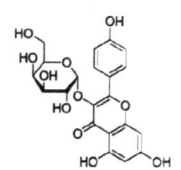

Kaempferol-3-O-galactoside ($C_{21}H_{20}O_{11}$) 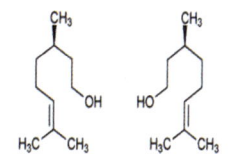   Citronellol ($C_{10}H_{20}O$)

Santalum album

Sandal (Woods and Fruit)

Latin Binomial	Santalum album
Family	Santalaceae
English Name	Sandalwood
Urdu Name	Sandal Safaid

Medicinal Uses: All parts of the plant are used medicinally. Santalum is one of the most precious trees in the world. The wood of the evergreen Santalum album tree and its oil is aromatic, analgesic, antiseptic, diuretic in action and also a cardiac tonic. The oil is given internally for treating chronic mucous conditions, e.g. bronchitis and inflammation of the bladder. It is also helpful in treating chronic cystitis, gleets and gonorrhoea.

Traditional Uses: In Unani, Ayurvedic and traditional Chinese medicinal systems, Sandalwood and its oil products are used to treat dysentery, stomach ache, gonorrhoea, skin diseases and anxiety. The wood is pulverized into a paste and applied to local inflammation on boils, skin diseases and the forehead in fever. A decoction of the wood is given in genitor-urinary infections. It is also beneficial as an astringent for the bowels and acts as an aphrodisiac. The wood paste in milk, is a remedy for leucorrhoea and thirst. The wood, root, bark and leaves of the plant are beneficial for treating liver diseases like jaundice and liver enlargement. Its fruit is edible.

The oil is used in aromatherapy to lessen tension, anxiety and it is also considered a sexual stimulant, in folk traditions. The syrup from an infusion of the wood is effective in treating palpitation, tachycardia and stomach irritation. The paste made from wood can improve skin complexion, stop burning sensation and clear apparent wounds.

Biological Uses: The extract of Sandalwood (oil) shows antimicrobial, antioxidant, anti-inflammatory, anti-cancer, antispasmodic, antifungal and antiseptic activities. The hydro-alcoholic extract of the leaves of Santalum album shows significant hepatoprotective properties. The Biologically active compound 'santalols' (α-Santalol a sesquiterpene) are reported to have depressant effects on the central nervous system (CNS), demonstrating implications in patients having sleep disorders.

A recent study revealed that saponins in the leaves of the plant are responsible for haemolytic activities in the blood. The non-aqueous (petroleum-ether) fraction of the Sandalwood possesses antihyperglycemic and antihyperlipidemic effects.

Chemical Constituents: The Sandal wood oil contains sesquiterpenes (alcoholic volatile oils); terpenoic acid, terpenoids and the major constituents in the plant's essential oil are alpha-beta-santalol. The wood contains essential oils, tannin, resin, phytosterols, vitamin E, etc.

Distribution: It is native to the Indo-Pak subcontinent. They are cultivated in Indonesia, Pakistan, Sri Lanka, Malaysia, the Philippines and Australia. In Pakistan, Santalum album is grown in Karachi, Sind and Sambrial, Punjab.

α-and β-santalol ($C_{15}H_{24}O$)

Syzygium aromaticum

Qaranful/Long (Plant parts and Dried Buds)

Latin Binomials	Syzygium aromaticum/Eugenia aromatic
Family	Myrtaceae
English Name	Clove
Urdu Name	Loung/Qaranful

Medicinal Uses: The evergreen Syzygium aromaticum tree buds are antiseptic, carminative, analgesic and stimulant in action. It is beneficial for treating nausea, vomiting, flatulence and dyspepsia in the form of a powder or an infusion. The volatile oil contains medicinal properties and it is anti-inflammatory, antioxidant, antiseptic, antibacterial and a local irritant. The Clove oil is classed as a flavour stimulant, commonly employed as a toothache remedy. Clove oil can also reduce the signs of ageing, wrinkles and sagging skin. Apply the clove oil daily onto the skin to see visible results. As a natural hair conditioner, one drop of Clove oil and one drop of olive oil, apply this solution to damp hair and leave it on for 10-15 minutes.

Traditional Uses: The Clove is widely used in Unani, Ayurvedic, Chinese and Western herbal medicines and is considered warm, aromatic, carminative, useful in the treatment of toothache and as an aphrodisiac in treating male sexual disorders. Chewing cloves regularly for at least six weeks or more can reduce hypertension. Massaging clove oil on the belly helps the uterus in contracting during childbirth. The flower buds are chewed to freshen up the breath or ease a toothache. The intake of cloves is very much effective in the treatment of cholera. Its frequent use in teeth problems makes it an ingredient in popular toothpaste and mouth fresheners. In Chinese medicine, Cloves are considered acrid, warm and aromatic.

The FDA now believes that there is not enough evidence indicating that Clove oil or eugenol is effective in toothache or other types of pain and that more research is needed.

Biological Uses: Clove and Clove oil possess antifungal, antibacterial, antiviral and anti-inflammatory activities. In low concentrations, it is also an antioxidant. The presence of eugenol and acetyl eugenol are found to be more potent than aspirin in inhibiting platelet aggregation (antithrombotic). The hydro-alcoholic fraction of the dried Clove buds showed favourable bone preserving efficacy. The oil of the plant possesses anticarcinogenic and antimutagenic potential because of its substantial free radical scavenging property.

Chemical Constituents: The oil contains eugenol, eugenyl acetate, caryophyllene and flavonoids (eugenin, kaempferol, rhamnetin and eugenitin), β–caryophyllene, vanillin stigmasterol, gallic acid and triterpenoids like oleanolic acid.

Distribution: Syzygium aromaticum is native to Indonesia. The plant is commercially harvested in Pakistan, Indonesia, India, Sri Lanka, Madagascar and Tanzania.

Eugenol ($C_{10}H_{12}O_2$)   Eugenol acetate ($C_{12}H_{14}O_3$)

Thymus vulgaris

Hasha (Fresh and dried Plant)

Latin Binomials	Thymus vulgaris/Thymus serpyllum
Family	Lamiaceae
English Name	Wild Thyme
Urdu Names	Hasha/Jangli Pudina

Medicinal Uses: All above the ground parts of the shrub are valuable for medicinal purposes. The evergreen, flowering Thymus vulgaris plant is antiseptic, antispasmodic, carminative, digestive, laxative, anti-phlegmatic and anthelmintic in action. It is very rich in essential oils and these are the active ingredients responsible for most of the medicinal properties. The fresh herb, in syrup, forms a safe cure for whooping cough, as an infusion of the dried herb. The infusion is also beneficial for treating catarrh, sore throat, colic and cold. Thyme may also improve liver function and acts as an appetite stimulant.

Traditional Uses: In Unani and Ayurvedic medicinal systems, Wild Thyme is used as a potent diuretic, helping the kidneys improve urine frequency and volume. Thyme is beneficial in the treatment of sore throat due to its powerful antiseptic properties and also as an astringent, disinfectant, anthelmintic and is carminative. The plant helps improve liver function and acts as an appetite stimulant. The plant is a stimulant and expectorant in action on the respiratory system. As a gargle, Thyme helps laryngitis, inflammation and is antiseptic. The plant has an antioxidant affect. Thus, regular use of this herb improves individual body cell health and therefore prolongs the body life. Thyme with honey and lukewarm water, act as an antispasmodic, in general, and in facial paralysis as well.

Externally, it is a remedy for rheumatism, arthritis and fungal infections. Thymus vulgaris helps in skin issues like oily skin, acne, dermatitis and in bug bites. It is also helpful in preventing the hardening of the arteries, treating toothache and treating urinary tract infections and dyspepsia.

The Thyme oil may cause allergic reactions, like irritation of the skin and irritation of the mucous membranes.

Biological Uses: The Thyme oil is antifungal, antioxidant and antibacterial. It is valuable in the bad odour of the mouth (halitosis). It is also beneficial in killing harmful worms present in the gut. An aqueous extract of the plant has antifungal property. The plant, in large quantity, acts as an ecbolic (herb induces contractions of the uterus).

Chemical Constituents: Thyme contains ketonic volatile oils, thymol, flavonoids, phenolic acids, tannins, saponins and resin traces.

Distribution: Thymus vulgaris is native to Southern Europe and grows from the Western Mediterranean to Southern Italy, Asia and North Africa.

Thymol ($C_{10}H_{14}O$)   Alpha and beta Santalol ($C_{15}H_{24}O$)

Tanacetum umbelliferum

Bozedan (Flowers and Roots)

Latin Binomials	Tanacetum umbelliferum/Tanacetum vulgare
Family	Asteraceae
English Name	Pellitory
Urdu Name	Buzedan

Medicinal Uses: The roots of the perennial, flowering Tanacetum umbelliferum tree are anthelmintic, stimulant, emmenagogue, aphrodisiac in action and a general tonic. It is primarily useful in expelling worms in children. It is employed in hysterical complaints, nervousness, low spirits and is a general tonic. A decoction helps ease coughs, wheezing and difficulty in breathing. An earache is relieved by a cold infusion, while a tincture of the plant reduces the pain and swelling caused after an insect or vermin bites.

Traditional Uses: In traditional systems (Unani and Ayurvedic) of medicine, the plant helps prevent or ease migraines or headaches. A warm infusion is diaphoretic, emmenagogue and beneficial in treating intermittent fever, gout and suppressed menstruation.

The seeds are reputed to be most efficient in expulsion of worms. The cold infusion will help recover from exhausting diseases like dyspepsia, in small doses. Some traditional healers use this plant to start menstruation and abortion; others use it for kidney problems, tuberculosis, fever and hysteria. In Central and South America, the plant has been used in treating kidney pain, stomach ache, morning sickness and colic. In Mexico, it is used as an antispasmodic and as a tonic to regulate menstruation. In Venezuela, it is used in treating earaches and as an antidote for the overindulgence of opium.

Biological Uses: When given in small doses, the presence of the essential oil in the plant has helped in epilepsy. The antioxidant property of this plant's root may be due to flavonoids. The oil is poisonous and has antibacterial, antiviral and antimicrobial properties.

Chemical Constituents: The herb's primary constituents are the essential oils known as oleum tanaceta, flavonoid, glycosides, luteolin, tanetin and apigenin. Besides, a bitter amorphous principle, 'tanacetin', occurs chiefly in the flowers.

Distribution: Tanacetum umbelliterum is indigenous to Europe and also grows in many countries, e.g., Austria, Belgium, France, Germany, Pakistan, India and China.

Tanetin ($C_{18}H_{16}O_7$)   Tanacetin ($C_{15}H_{20}O_4$)

Teucrium chamaedrys

Hussain Booti/Kalpura (Plant Parts and Flowers)

Latin Binomial	Teucrium chamaedrys/Teucrium stoksianum
Family	Labiatae/Lamiaceae
English Name	Germander
Urdu Name	Hussain Booti/Kalpura

Medicinal Uses: The whole plant is useful for medicinal purposes. The flowering Teucrium chamaedrys plant is aromatic, antirheumatic, diaphoretic, diuretic, aperients and stimulant in action. Dating back to the sixteenth century, the plant has the reputation of a specific cure for gout. It is useful as a tonic in treating intermittent fevers and uterine obstructions and a decoction of the fresh herb is good against asthmatic afflictions and coughs.

Teucrium chamaedrys containing capsules and teabag preparations are approved as weight loss remedies in France, although their active ingredient and precise action mechanism remain unknown.

Traditional Uses: The expressed juice of the plant is taken for obstructions of the viscera, while the herb is beneficial for treating jaundice, as a vermifuge, for ulcers, for continued headaches and cramps. Due to its diuretic properties, it helps treat weak stomachs and lack of appetite. The plant aids in weight loss and is a common ingredient in tonic wines. It is used externally as an astringent infusion on the gums and in treating wounds. Some herbalists use this plant in amenorrhoea, leucorrhoea and chronic bronchitis. It is declared to be of much value in treating whooping cough and the powder has been used to cure nasal polyps.

Several Teucrium species are used in Iranian folk medicine as a medicinal plant. In Yemeni folk medicine, it is useful as antispasmodic and as an insect repellent. However, it is seldom used in Unani and Ayurvedic treatments.

Biological Uses: The oil of Teucrium possesses antimicrobial, antiviral, anti-mycotic, antioxidant, anti-parasitic and insecticidal properties.

Chemical Constituents: The dark-brown essential oil is the plant's main constituent. These oils have sesquiterpenes such as caryophyllene, caryophyllene oxide, germacrene, D, alpha-humulene, alpha-muurolene (E) beta-farnesene and the monoterpene carvacrol. The plant also contains some beneficial biologically active ingredients like iridoid, phenylethanoid glycosides, flavonoids, terpenoids and some phenolic compounds.

Distribution: The Teucrium chamaedrys plant is native to the Mediterranean region of Europe and North Africa and the Middle East as far east as Iran.

Note: Some caution is essential when using this plant internally; it may cause liver damage.

Vetiveria zizanioides

Khas (Fresh and Dried Roots)

Latin Binomials	Vetiveria zizanioides / Andropogon squarrosus
Family	Gramineae/Poaceae
English Name	Cuscus Grass/Khas-Khas Grass
Urdu Name	Khas

Medicinal Uses: The flowering Vetiveria zizanioides plant roots are a cardiac tonic, aromatic, exhilarant, diuretic and astringent in action.

Traditional Uses: In Unani and Ayurvedic medicinal systems, this plant is used for treating fever, weak digestion and metabolism. The root is beneficial in traditional medicine in the Far East (Malaysia, Indonesia and Thailand) and in West Africa. It is known as Khas-Khas and is extensively used as a cooling agent, as a tonic and a blood purifier. The plant helps in treating many skin disorders and has a calming effect on the nervous system.

Biological Uses: The plant's oil is known as 'Vetiver oil. 'It improves the alertness of the brain and also demonstrates anti-anxiety effects. The oil exhibits its ability against Gram-positive bacteria, especially Staphylococcus aureus. Extracts (methanol and ethanol) possess antibacterial, antioxidant, antiglycemic and anti-inflammatory activities. The ethanol extract and hexane fraction exhibit potent anti-Mycobacterium (anti-tuberculosis) activity.

Chemical Constituents: The plant contains volatile oils, beta-vetispirene, khusimol, vetiselinenol, tannins, flavonoids, sterols, saponins, phenolic compounds and resin.

Distribution: Vetiveria zizanioides is native to South Asia and is cultivated in Pakistan (widely distributed in all provinces of Pakistan), India, Bangladesh and Burma. It is grown for its oil, mainly in Haiti, West Java, India, Russia, China and Brazil

Note: The roots of Vetiveria zizanioides are useful in making 'Khas-Khas' mats. During summer, making these mats help cool the air; they also help make a syrup known as 'Sherbet-e-Khas. The essential oil from the roots is valuable in perfumery.

Beta-Vetispirene ($C_{15}H_{22}$)   Khusimol ($C_{15}H_{24}O$)

Vetiselinenol ($C_{15}H_{24}O$)

Viola odorata

Gul-e-Banafsha (Fresh and dried Flowers)

Latin Binomials	Viola odorata/Viola indica
Family	Violaceae
English Name	Violet Flowers/Viola
Urdu Name	Banafsha

Medicinal Uses: The flowers of the herbaceous, perennial Viola odorata plant, also known as 'sweet violet,' are expectorant, mildly laxative, aperients, anti-inflammatory, diaphoretic (inducing perspiration) and antibacterial in action. A recent study shows that the violet syrup is significantly more effective than a placebo, in reducing and suppressing intermittent asthma-caused cough, in children aged between 2 and 12 years.

Traditional Uses: The rhizome of the plant is strongly emetic, purgative and has violent effects when administered; the seeds also have purgative and diuretic actions. The flowers possess expectorant properties and have long been used in treating cough. It is traditionally very much effective in jaundice. The whole plant is anti-inflammatory, diaphoretic, diuretic, expectorant and laxative in its properties. The seeds are diuretic and purgative. The tea of the flowers is soothing.

Externally, it is useful in treating mouth and throat infections. In France, Viola syrup is helpful as a cough remedy. The plant has been prescribed against cancerous growth in the Chinese medicinal system.

This is a popular medicinal plant of Unani and Ayurvedic medicinal systems. Violet flowers are one of the most popular ingredients of Unani poly-herbal preparation, known as 'Joshanda.' (word Joshanda is derived from Persian words 'Josh and anidan' {Andah}, **which means boiling).**

The essential oil from the flowers is valuable in aromatherapy in treating bronchial complaints, exhaustion and skin problems. The leaves are edible.

Biological Uses: The flowers showed antiseptic, antibacterial and antioxidant activities due to volatile oils. The aqueous extract of the plant revealed the presence of anthocyanine. The extract of leaves is antioxidant and antibacterial. The methanolic extract of the plant and various fractions, including chloroform, ethyl acetate, *n*-hexane and aqueous fractions, possess significant antimicrobial activities against S. Typhi, E. coli, B. subtilis, S. flexeneri and P. aerogenes. The extract of all the aerial parts of Viola odorata shows antitumor activity.

Chemical Constituents: Essential oils contain butyl-2-ethyl hexyl phthalate, linalool, benzyl alcohol, alpha-cadinol and viridiflorol. The plant also has important bioactive constituents such as alkaloids (violine), phenolic glycosides, saponins, flavonoids, steroids, tannins, salicylic acid (so-called natural aspirin) and triterpenoids.
Distribution: The plant is native to Europe (Norway, Portugal, Ukraine and Greece, etc.) and Asia (Pakistan, Iran and India). It has been introduced into North America and Australia.

Butyl-2-Ethylhexyl phthalate ($C_{20}H_{30}O_4$)   Viridiflorol ($C_{15}H_{26}O$)

Terpenoids

According to modern definition, Terpenoids, also known as isoprenoids, are hydrocarbons of plant origin; the general formula $(C_5H_8)_n$ applies to their oxygenated, hydrogenated and dehydrogenated derivatives.

There are many different classes of naturally occurring compounds. Terpenoids also form a group of naturally occurring compounds that occur in plants. A few of them have also been obtained from other sources. Terpenoids are volatile substances that give plants and flowers their fragrance. They occur widely in the leaves and fruits of higher plants: conifers, citrus and eucalyptus.

The term 'terpene' is given to the compounds isolated from turpentine, a volatile liquid isolated from the pine tree. The simpler mono and sesquiterpenes are the chief constituents of the essential oils obtained from the particular plant and tree sap and tissues. The di and triterpenoids are not steam volatile. They are obtained from plant and tree gums and resins. Tertraterpenoids form a separate group of compounds called 'Carotenoids.'

The term 'terpene' was initially employed to describe a mixture of isomeric hydrocarbons of the molecular formula $C_{10}H_{16}$, in the essential oils obtained from plants and tree' sap and tissue. But there is a tendency to use the more general term 'terpenoids,' including hydrocarbons and their oxygenated derivatives. However, some authors use the term terpene these days to represent terpenoids.

Classification of Terpenoids according to the 'Number of Rings'

(a) Acyclic Terpenoids: They contain an open structure.
(b) Monocyclic Terpenoids: They contain one ring in the structure.
(c) Bicyclic Terpenoids: They contain two rings in the structure
(d) Tricyclic Terpenoids: They have three rings in the structure.
(e) Tetracyclic terpenoids: They contain four rings in the structure.

Phytol ($C_{20}H_{40}O$)

Vitamin A (Bicyclic)

Tri-Terpenoid

Tetra-Terpenoid

Terpenoids: In addition to all compound groups mentioned in this book, there is a tremendous range of other Isoprenoids (Terpenoids) available in nature. Most of them are essential as medical agents and valuable in an alternative system (Unani and Ayurvedic) of medicine.

Artemisia absinthium

Afsanteen (Fresh and Dried Plant)

Latin Binomials	Artemisia absinthium/Artemisia vulgaris/Artemisia annua
Family	Compositae/Asteraceae
English Name	Wormwood
Urdu Name	Afsanteen

Medicinal Uses: The leaves of the herbaceous, perennial, flowering Artemisia absinthium plant are aromatic, a bitter tonic, anthelmintic, antipyretic, antiseptic, stomachic and antiperiodic in action. Artemisia (wormwood) has always been associated with a very bitter taste.

Artemisia has its monograph published by the European Medicines Agency (EMA). Based on a well-established use, It is recommended to use the raw material in temporary loss of appetite, mild dyspepsia and gastrointestinal disorders. German Pharmacopoeia has also mentioned a tincture from the herb. However, the Artemisia herb is not mentioned in the latest edition (10th) of the European Pharmacopoeia.

Traditional Uses: In modern herbal medicine and traditional Unani, Ayurvedic and homoeopathic, Artemisia is useful as a bitter tonic in stimulating the appetite and clearing liver and gall bladder disorders. The leaves help lower the body temperature and the flowers help treat the stomach and worm infections. Artemisia tincture is valuable as a tonic and as a digestive aid. The plant is beneficial as a base for preparing ointments and balms, for use on the skin. The Wormwood herb is suitable for treating jaundice, constipation, obesity, enlargement of the spleen (splenomegaly) and for treating anaemia. Besides, the herb is used in making tea to facilitate pregnant women during labour and to treat leukaemia and sclerosis. In traditional Chinese medicine, the plant is used in cancer therapy.

Biological Uses: The plant extracts (aqueous, methanol and ethanol) exhibit several pharmacological activities such as antimicrobial, anti-cancer, antiviral, anti-inflammatory, hypoglycemic and hepatoprotective. The antioxidant activity of the herb can be attributed to several phenolic compounds. The herb contains volatile oil and a bitter principal called 'absinthin' (a triterpene lactone). Artemisia absinthium has tremendous anti-inflammatory, antioxidant, antimicrobial effects; It also appears to affect the gastrointestinal tract and urinary system. Aqueous extracts also have antioxidant and analgesic properties, whereas the ethanolic fraction is hepatoprotective and antiviral. The oil is a potent anti-inflammatory. It is also known that most of the therapeutic properties of this plant are due to the presence of 'thujone,' which is a major, bioactive component of the essential oil. Wormwood also expels the parasitic worms, particularly roundworms and threadworms.

Chemical Constituents: The main substances responsible for the herbs' biological activity are the essential oil, bitter sesquiterpenoid lactones, flavonoids, other bitterness-imparting compounds, azulene (an isomer of naphthalene), phenolic acids, tannins and lignans. A Chinese medicinal plant, Artemisia annua, has provided a new class of highly effective antimalarials due to the presence of an endoperoxide sesquiterpene lactone, 'artemisinin.'

Distribution: Artemisia is native to Europe but has been naturalised in Canada and the United States. It grows in Europe, Africa and Asia. A high-quality Artemisia absinthium is growing in Azad Kashmir, Pakistan.

Note: Based on Wormwood's essential oil, a very popular alcoholic drink, 'absinthe' was made in the 19th century, which is an intoxicant whose excessive consumption leads to irreversible damage to the central nervous system. The plant is poisonous if used in a large quantities and prolonged use has a detrimental effect.

Long considered a hallucinogen and potential poison, Wormwood was banned in the United States for nearly a century, from 1912 until 2007. It is now legally available in the United States. The herb should not be used during pregnancy and should be administered for a short period.

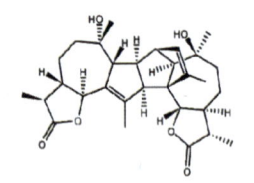

Absinthin ($C_{30}H_{40}O_6$) 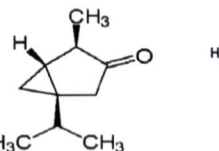 Thujone ($C_{10}H_{16}O$) 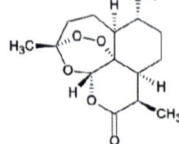 Artemisinin ($C_{15}H_{22}O_5$)

Achras sapota

Chikoo (Tree Parts and Fruits)

Latin Binomials	Achras sapota/Manilkara zapota
Family	Sapotaceae
English Name	Chicoo
Urdu Name	Chikoo

Medicinal Uses: The fruit of the evergreen, flowering Achras sapota tree relieves stress, ulcer, indigestion and diarrhoea. The presence of vitamin C enhances the immune system to counter colds and viruses. Chicoo contains insoluble fibre that assists in passing of the stool bulk through the body. Anaemia is caused due to iron deficiency and this plant is rich in iron.

Traditional Uses: The presence of bioactive compounds in Achras sapota may find practical applications in traditional medicines (Unani and Ayurvedic), such as antidiarrhoeal, haemostatic which is a remedy for haemorrhoids. The crushed seeds help prevent oedema due to diuretic property. A decoction of the bark and fruit is beneficial in fever and diarrhoea. A paste of the flowers and fruit prevents respiratory disorders. The fruit is eaten as a remedy for indigestion and it is also an antispasmodic agent. Chikoo is helpful in pregnancy due to its high micronutrients content.

In Indonesia, the flowers of the Achras are one of the ingredients of a powder rubbed on the women's body after childbirth. In Mexico, seeds are used for kidney stones and in rheumatism. In Cuba, an infusion of the seed is used as an eyewash. In Cambodia, tannin from the bark is used for fever and diarrhoea.

Biological Uses: The stem bark extracts (methanol) show antifungal and antitumor activities. The antitumor property may probably be due to the presence of saponins. The leaf aqueous and non-aqueous extracts exhibit analgesic and anti-inflammatory properties. The hepatoprotective effect of the fruit is based on its potent antioxidant property, due to flavonoids. The tyrosinase (rate-limiting enzyme) and elastase effect have been seen in the fruit's methanolic extract. Research studies suggest that tannins possess astringent properties and are shown to have a potential in antiviral, antibacterial and antiparasitic effects. The presence of phytochemical constituents like saponin, sapotin (a bitter crystalline glucoside) and the bitter sapotinine in the seed of Achras sapota, have an anti-diabetic effect.

Chemical Constituents: The fruit contains sugar, ascorbic acid, iron, calcium, potassium, copper, zinc, protein and carotenoids. Apart from the nutritional components, Chikoo juice shows potential antioxidant activity. The plant (leaves, root, bark and fruit) contains terpenoids, e.g., erythrodiol (pentacyclic triterpenes), alkaloids, fixed oils, saponins, phenolic compounds, glycosides, flavonoids and tannins. The bark is also rich in saponins, sapotin and fixed oils.

Distribution: Achras sapota is a long-lived, evergreen tree native to Southern Mexico, Central America and the Caribbean. It is grown in a large quantity in Pakistan, India, Thailand, Malaysia, Bangladesh and Indonesia.

Erythrodiol ($C_{30}H_{50}O_2$)

Careya arborea

Baokhumba (Tree, Fruit and Flower)

Latin Binomial	Careya arborea
Family	Myrtaceae/Lecythidaceae
English Name	Wild Guava/Slow Match Tree
Urdu Name	Baokhumba

Medicinal Uses: The fruit, leaf and bark of the deciduous, flowering Careya arborea tree, are useful for medicinal purposes. The fruit is astringent, demulcent and antipyretic in action. The bark is demulcent, is antipyretic and also a skin tonic

Traditional Uses: In Unani and Ayurvedic medicinal systems, the fruit is valuable in treating coughs and colds. An infusion of the bark is beneficial in cold and fever. The leaves are used in filarial (a threadlike parasitic nematode worm) colic, loose motions and ulcers.

The bark has been applied medicinally for relieving oedema. The powder of the bark mixed with honey, is effective in treating piles and its milk is taken orally to treat dysentery. The bark juice and the flower sepals are astringent, mucilaginous and applied internally to treat earache. An astringent gum that exudes from the fruit and stems, helps diarrhoea and dysentery. A decoction of the fruit promotes digestion and cures anorexia (loss of appetite).

In Ayurveda, Careya arborea is one of the most essential medicated water components known as 'Vethuvellam,' used by women to take a bath after delivery, to overcome body weakness.

Biological Uses: Extracts (methanol) of the aerial parts of the plant exhibit antiseptic, antibacterial and antioxidant properties. The antioxidant property may be attributed to the presence of flavonoids and flavones present in the plant. The methanolic extract of the bark shows antidiarrhoeal activity. Ethyl acetate, ethanol and hexane fractions of the fruit possess excellent antibacterial activities against Escherichia coli, Salmonella typhimurium, Listeria monocytogenes, Staphylococcus aureus and Staphylococcus epidermidis. The ethanol and methanol fractions of the stem bark have analgesic antiulcer and CNS depressant properties.

Chemical Constituents: The plant contains triterpenoid lactone, e.g., careyagenolide, steroids, phenols, saponins, flavonoids and tannins. The bark also contains piperine alkaloids and is a rich source of tannins. The seeds of Careya are regarded as poisonous.

Distribution: Careya arborea is native to Pakistan, India, Afghanistan and China.

Centella asiatica

Barhami Boti (Plant, Stems and Leaves)

Latin Binomial	Centella asiatica
Family	Umbelliferae/Apiaceae
English Name	Indian Pennywort

Urdu Name   Barhami Buti

Medicinal Uses: The herbaceous, perennial, flowering Centella asiatica plant is exhilarant, diuretic, astringent and a local stimulant in action. The Centella is a brain tonic due to its broad beneficial neuroprotective activity; besides this, various other effects such as anti-inflammatory, antiproliferative, anti-cancer, antioxidant, antiulcer and wound healing, have been reported.

Traditional Uses: Centella asiatica is a valued herb in Unani and Ayurveda medicinal systems for various ailments like asthma, skin disorders, ulcers and leucorrhoea treatment. It is also useful for improving memory, treating leprosy, dropsy, elephantiasis and stomach disorders. The whole plant is alterative, cardio-depressant, hypotensive, a weak sedative and a tonic. The leaf extract is taken orally to cure dysentery and improve memory power. Externally, the herb is applied to a range of skin conditions and wounds, haemorrhoids and rheumatic joints.

The traditional Chinese medicine Centella asiatica herb is beneficial in dysentery, diarrhoea, vomiting, jaundice and scabies. It was historically known as the 'Snow Plant' for its cooling properties. In Brazil, it is used for treating elephantiasis and leprosy. In Nepal, this herb is used traditionally in rheumatism, indigestion, leprosy and poor memory. The decoction of the leaves is applied to cure leprotic wounds. In Malaysia, the tea of the plant is taken in hypertension, diarrhoea and urinary tract infections.

Biological Uses: An aqueous extract of the herb shows significant learning and memory affects. An alcoholic fraction of the whole plant shows antiprotozoal activity against Entamoeba histolytica (an anaerobic parasitic amoebozoan) and possesses cardioprotective, antidepressant, antioxidant and antileprotic properties. The powder of Centella asiatica is found to have anti-cancer affects on skin cancer.

Chemical Constituents: The plant contains triterpenoid saponin, glycosides like asiaticoside, centelloside and madecassoside, etc. Glycosides are predominantly present in the leaves as compared to the root. The plant also has valuable biologically active constituents such as indole alkaloids (vinblastine, vincristine, vinleurosine, etc.), essential oils, flavonoids, tannins, amino acids and minerals like calcium, magnesium, sodium and potassium and vitamins, like B and C.

Distribution: Centella asiatica is indigenous to the Indian subcontinent, Southeast Asia and wetland regions of the Southeastern United States.

Asiaticoside ($C_{48}H_{78}O_{19}$)

Crocus sativus

Zafran (Flowers and Styles)

Latin Binomial	Crocus sativus
Family	Iridaceae
English Name	Saffron
Urdu Name	Zafran

Medicinal Uses: The dried stigma and tops of the flowering Crocus sativus plant styles are aromatic, carminative, diaphoretic, emmenagogue and stimulant in action. The herb is useful as a diaphoretic herb for children and can also benefit female hysteria, absent or painful menstruation and stop chronic bleeding of the uterus in adults.

Traditional Uses: Saffron is used commonly in the Unani system of medicine for treating flatulent, colic, spasmodic asthma and as a tonic. The styles and stigmas are anodyne, antispasmodic, aphrodisiac, appetizer, carminative, sedative diaphoretic, stimulant emmenagogue and expectorant.

The traditional healers (Hakims and Ayurveda) of the Indo-Pak subcontinent recommended Saffron in curing chronic diseases such as asthma, arthritis, skin diseases and spasmodic disorders. It is also helpful in treating sleep problems, cancer, hardening of the arteries and depression.

Biological Uses: Saffron is antioxidant, antiseptic and antibacterial in action due to volatile oils and other important organic compounds. The results both *in vivo* and *in vitro* show that this compound could be an excellent antitumour agent. Another study involving 14 individuals indicated that the oral administration of crocetin (apocarotenoid dicarboxylic acid), might decrease the effects of physical fatigue in healthy men.

Chemical Constituents: The plant contains a carotenoid compound called crocetin. Picrocrocin is a colourless monoterpene glycoside and precursor of Saffron aroma components.

Distribution: It is believed that Crocus sativus originated in Iran. However, Greece and Mesopotamia (Turkey, Iraq, Syria and Kuwait) have also been suggested as the possible region of the origin of this beautiful plant. Crocus sativus is the most expensive spice known.

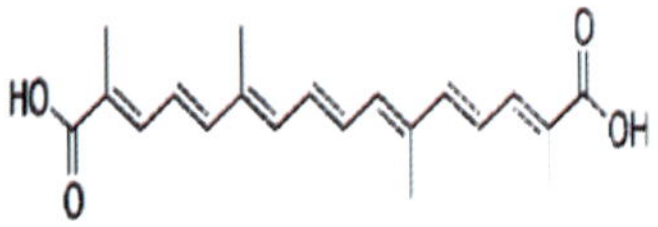

Crocetin ($C_{20}H_{24}O_4$) 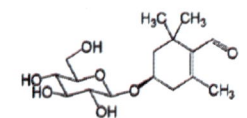 Picrocrocin ($C_{16}H_{26}O_7$)

Cyperus rotundus

S' ad Kufi/Nagar-Motha (Plants and Rhizomes)

Latin Binomial	Cyperus rotundus
Family	Cyperaceae
English Name	Nut Grass
Urdu Name	S' ad Kufi/Nagar-Motha

Medicinal Uses: The rhizomes of perennial Cyperus rotundus plant tubes are aromatic, antiulcer, attenuant (herbs that dilute the fluid), alternative and diuretic in action. Cyperus rotundus is a pungent bitter-sweet herb that relieves spasms and pain, mainly in the digestive system and uterus. The roots and tubers are analgesics.

Traditional Uses: According to the traditional healers (Hakims and Ayurveda) of the Indo-Pak subcontinent, the rhizomes are astringent, diaphoretic, diuretic, aromatic, antispasmodic, carminative, sedative, stimulant, tonic and antibacterial. They are useful internally in treating digestive problems. The rhizomes part of the plant is one of the oldest known medicinal parts in treating dysmenorrhoeal and menstrual irregularities. An infusion is effective in relieving fever, diarrhoea and dyspepsia. The plant is beneficial in the treatment of cervical cancer.

In Asian countries, the rhizomes of Cyperus rotundus are used as traditional folk medicines in treating stomach, bowel disorders and inflammatory diseases. In Western parts of Kenya, Cyperus rotundus and Typha latifolia are used in treating infectious diseases. An aromatic oil of the plant is analgesic and is made of perfumes.

Biological Uses: The extracts (ethanol) of rhizomes possess antibacterial, tranquillizing, antioxidant and anti-cancer properties. The methanolic fraction is antidiarrhoeal. Several other pharmacological and biological activities, including anti-inflammatory, anti-diabetic, cytoprotective, antimicrobial, cytotoxic, anticandida, antipyretic and analgesic, have been reported for this plant. The petroleum ether extract and essential oil of Cyperus rotundus are said to possess analgesic properties.

Chemical Constituents: The plant contains sesquiterpenes, essential oils, such as cyperene, humulene, zierone, campholenic aldehyde, alkaloids, flavonoids, tannins, steroids and glycosides.

Distribution: Cyperus rotundus is native to Africa, Europe and South Asia (Pakistan, India, Bangladesh and Sri Lanka).

Note: Cyperus rotundus plant is rated 8th amongst 250 potential antifertility plants in China.

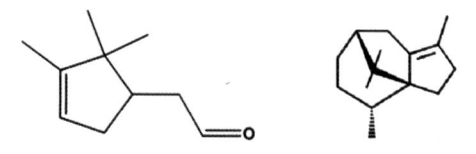

Alpha-Campholenic aldehyde ($C_{10}H_{16}O$)   Cyperene ($C_{15}H_{24}$)

Delphinium denudatum

Jadwar (Plant, Roots and Flowers)

Latin Binomial	Delphinium denudatum
Family	Ranunculaceae
English Name	Delphinium
Urdu Name	Jadwar

Medicinal Uses: The root of the flowering Delphinium denudatum plant is antiphlegmatic, digestive, astringent and stimulant in action. The powdered root is a popular folk remedy for the treatment of epilepsy. It is a remedy in the treatment of sleeping problems.

Traditional Uses: Delphinium, an important herb used in the Unani system of medicine, is regarded as deobstruent, a purifier of impurities, especially from the cephalic region. The roots are valuable in treating fever, skin disease, cough, piles, leucorrhoea and fungal infections. It is an antidote for poisons, is a cardiac tonic and a tonic for vital organs. Its decoction helps nervous disorders, whereas its pills or tablets are valuable in cardiac and brain weakness. It is also used as a sedative.

The Indo-Pak subcontinent's traditional healers recommend its use in treating mania, migraine, paralysis, epilepsy, pain and as an antidote for snakebite and scorpion sting. A paste of the root is useful in the treatment of toothache. They also recommend treating fungal infections, dysuria, calculi, jaundice and nervous problems with this plant.

Famous Unani, poly-herbal preparations known as 'Khamira-e-Jadwar, Hab-e-Jadwar, Hab-e-Jawahar and Jawahar-Mohra are some tonic formulations of the Delphinium.

Biological Uses: The aqueous and alcoholic extract of the root showed antianxiety activity, whereas the plant's methanolic extracts possess antipyretic, antioxidant, antimicrobial and anticonvulsant properties.

Chemical Constituents: The root contains diterpenoid alkaloids vilmorrianone, panicutine, isotalatizidine and triterpenoids, flavonoids, phenolic compounds and other alkaloids and sterols.

Distribution: Delphinium denudatum is native to the Indo-Pak subcontinents and is also found on the outer range of the Western Himalayas and Nepal.

Vilmorrianone ($C_{23}H_{27}NO_5$)   Panicutine ($C_{23}H_{29}NO_4$)

Daucus carota

Gajar (Fruits and Plant)

Latin Binomial	Daucus carota
Family	Apiaceae
English Name	Carrot
Urdu Name	Gajar/Guzar

Medicinal Uses: The fruit of the flowering Daucus carota is a tonic for vital organs; the plant is aromatic, expectorant, stimulant, aphrodisiac and diuretic in action.

Traditional Uses: In the traditional medicinal system (Unani and Ayurvedic), it is beneficial for eyesight, in treating cough, asthma and burning sensation in urine. A decoction of the seeds and roots of the carrot, in recommended doses, acts as a stimulating diuretic and emmenagogue. An infusion of the leaves has helped counter cystitis, kidney stone formation and in diminishing stones. The Carrot leaves have a significant amount of porphyrins that stimulate the pituitary gland and increase sex hormones. The raw root is a suitable remedy for threadworms. The seed oil is used in treating diarrhoea, dysentery, indigestion and in menstrual pain.

The Daucus plant forms a constituent of many Unani poly-herbal general and kidney tonics like Labub-e-Kabir, Jawarish-e-Zaruni, Arq-e-Guzar, etc.

Biological Uses: The plant is a rich source of natural antioxidant products. The seed oil exhibits antifungal, hepatoprotective, antioxidant, antiulcer, cholesterol-lowering and antibacterial activities. The phytochemicals in the Daucus carota plant (polyphenols, carotenoids, polyaclyterenes and vitamin C) reduce the risk of cardiovascular and cancer diseases. The methanol fraction of Daucus carota seeds also significantly reduces low-density lipoprotein (LDL cholesterol) serum levels.

Chemical Constituents: The Carrot is a high-quality pro-vitamin A source. Every 100 grams contains 850ug, which is 95 per cent of the daily value (DV). There are two types of carotenoids present in carrots, namely, carotenes and xanthophylls. The leaves have a significant amount of porphyrins (heterocyclic macrocycle organic compounds that bind metals to form complexes).

Distribution: The plant is native to Europe and South Asia. The plant was probably cultivated in Persia and was originally cultivated for its leaves and seeds.

In Pakistan, Daucus carota is grown on an area of 14 thousand hectares during the year 2017-18 and its production was 242 thousand tonnes. World production of Carrot is estimated to be about 27.5 million tonnes per year on an area of 9,90 thousand hectares.

Porphyrins

Euphorbia thymifolia

Dudhi Khurd (Plants)

Latin Binomial	Euphorbia thymifolia
Family	Euphorbiaceae
English Name	Euphorbia Small/Thyme-leaved Euphorbia
Urdu Name	Dudhi Khurd

Medicinal Uses: The Euphorbia thymifolia plant is useful in treating asthma, bronchitis, hay fever and digestive problems. Externally, the plant is also suitable in treating affections of the skin and mucous membranes, including measles, warts, scabies, ringworm, thrush, fungal afflictions and an antiseptic in treating wounds, sores and conjunctivitis.

Traditional Uses: In Unani and Ayurvedic medicinal systems, the seeds and leaves of the plant are useful as oral powder in treating metrorrhagia, bleeding piles, spermatorrhoea and leucorrhoea. The decoction is used in urinogenital disorders, particularly, in gonorrhoea and shows benefits in treating syphilis. The plant has a reputation as an analgesic in treating severe headaches, toothache, rheumatism, colic and pains during pregnancy. Euphorbia is beneficial as an antidote, pain relief of scorpion stings and snake bites.

Traditional healers (Hakims and Ayurveda) of the Indo-Pak subcontinent recommend the juice of the plant in dysentery, abdominal pain, leaf poultice for treating swelling, boils and a decoction of the root to improve breast milk quantity.

Biological Uses: The leaf extract of the plant showed strong antioxidant potential. The *in-vivo* studies show that Euphorbia has anti-diarrheal and anti-rotaviral activity. The extract shows the antibacterial effects of flavan-3-ol.

Chemical Constituents: The plant contains triterpenoids, phytosterols, tannins, alkaloids, cardiac glycosides, steroids, polyphenols, saponins and flavonoids.

Distribution: Euphorbia thymifolia is native to tropical America and is now widely distributed throughout the tropics and subtropics. It is widespread in West Africa and the Indian Ocean islands and advancing into eastern and southern Africa. The plant grows in Punjab and other parts of the country, Pakistan.

Note: However, the plant should not be used without expert guidance since large doses cause gastrointestinal irritation, nausea and vomiting.

flavan-3-ols   anthocyanidins

Flavan-3-ol ($C_{15}H_{14}O_2$) and a water soluble pigment

Euphorbia hirta

Dudhi Kalan (Plant, Leaves and Flower of different Species)

Latin Binomial	Euphorbia hirta
Family	Euphorbiaceae
English Name	Small Euphorbia/Asthma Plant
Urdu Name	Dudhi Kalan

Medicinal Uses: All above the ground parts of the flowering Euphorbiahita hirta are useful for medicinal purposes. The plant is antiasthmatic, pectoral, demulcent and antispasmodic in action. It is also an effective remedy in cough, coryza, respiratory disorders and often beneficial in female disorders. A decoction of dry herbs is helpful in skin diseases. An extract of the whole plant is useful against acute and chronic dysentery, colic and worms in children. Euphorbiahita hirta is sometimes also called the asthma plant.

Traditional Uses: In Indo-Pak subcontinent, Euphorbiahita hirta plant helps against syphilis. It acts as a demulcent and proves helpful in cardiac complaints, for example, angina, temporary rise in blood pressure due to flatulence, indigestion and dyspepsia. The stem, taken internally, is well-known for treating asthma, bronchitis and other lung complaints. The plant is also used as a diuretic in treating urogenital diseases, such as kidney stones, menstrual problems, sterility and venereal diseases. An ointment made from the plant can be applied directly to the skin on boils, wounds, burns, rashes and other marks.

Biological Uses: The plant of Euphorbia hirta possesses anti-inflammatory, anthelmintic, antiasthmatic, sedative, antispasmodic, diuretic and antifungal properties. The plant's methanolic extract exhibits antimalarial properties and its aqueous extract shows antioxidant and antidiarrhoeal activities.

An aqueous fraction of the whole plant acts as antiamoebic and antispasmodic. The powdered herb shows galactogenic property. An ethanolic extract of the aerial parts shows significant hepatoprotective activity. Euphorbiahita hirta, at a dose of 50mg/kg, reduces sperm motility and sperm count.

Chemical Constituents: Euphorbia hirta (above the ground parts) plant contains triterpenoids, steroids, coumarins and diterpenes. A glycoside formed from the flavonoid quercitrin and deoxy sugar rhamnose shows remarkable antidiarrheic activity. The plant also contains gallic acid, euphorbin A, B, C, D, shikimic acid, and tinyatoxin, an analogue of the neurotoxin

Distribution: Euphorbia hirta is native to the Indo-Pak subcontinent. It is a hairy herb that grows in open grasslands, roadsides and pathways.

Note: In modern medicine, plants occupy a significant place as a raw material for some essential drugs.

Quercitrin ($C_{21}H_{20}H_{11}$) Tinyatoxin ($C_{36}H_{38}O_8$)

Gymnema sylvestre

Gurmar Buti (Fresh and Dry Leaves)

Latin Binomial	Gymnema sylvestre
Family	Asclepiadaceae
English Name	Gymnema Plant
Urdu Name	Gurmar Buti

Medicinal Uses: The leaves of the woody, climbing, flowering Gymnema sylvestre shrub are hyperglycemic, absorbent, abrasive and antidotary in action.

Traditional Uses: In Unani and Ayurvedic medicinal systems, Gymnema leaves and extracts help treat diabetes, eye diseases, allergies, constipation, cough, obesity and viral infections. It is also valuable for treating hepatosplenomegaly, amenorrhea, jaundice, dyspepsia, haemorrhoids, intermittent fever and leucoderma.

The leaf extract of the plant is also suitable as a single preparation (decoction) for symptomatic relief of diabetes mellitus. One of the most important biologically active constituents in Gymnema sylvestre plant is gymnemic acid, which helps suppress sweetness by blocking the sugar receptors.

Traditional healers (Hakims and Ayurveda) of the Indo-Pak subcontinent recommend this plant in the treatment of malaria, jaundice, amenorrhoea, renal, vesicle and asthma. Furthermore, in traditional medicines, different parts of the plant (alone or in combination) such as roots, stems and leaves have been used as a cardiotonic, digestive, diuretic, stimulant and uterine tonic. Gymnema sylvestre (an infusion of the leaf) has traditional uses in the treatment of asthma, eye complaints and snake bites.

Biological Uses: Methanolic and aqueous extracts of the leaves possess antioxidant, aphrodisiac, antimicrobial and anti-diabetic activities, whereas ethanolic extracts reduce blood glucose levels up to 43 per cent. The plant leaves are also helpful as a single preparation (decoction) for symptomatic relief of diabetes mellitus. The chloroform, ethanol and hexane fractions of the dried leaves show antibacterial activity.

Chemical Constituents: Gymnema sylvestre contains volatile oils, triterpene glycosides known as gymnemic acids, phenolic compounds, gymnema-saponins, anthraquinone and a polypeptide 'gurmarin.' Gurmarin is a highly specific sweet taste suppressing protein that is isolated from the Gymnema sylvestre plant. It contains thirty-five amino acids.

Distribution: Gymnema sylvestre is native to Asia, China, Indonesia, Malaysia, Sri Lanka, and the Arabian Peninsula.

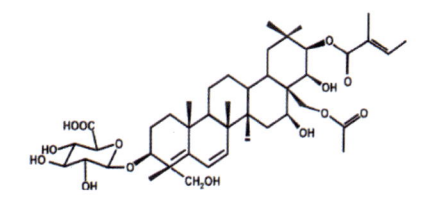

Gymnemic acids ($C_{43}H_{66}O_{14}$)

Lagenaria siceraria

Kaddu (Leaves, Fruits and Flower)

Latin Binomial	Lagenaria siceraria/Lagenaria Guineensis
Family	Cucurbitaceae
English Name	White Gourd
Urdu Name	Kaddu

Medicinal Uses: The fruit of the annual, running or climbing, flowering Lagenaria siceraria plant has been known since ancient times for its curative properties for treating various ailments, including jaundice, diabetes, piles, skin diseases and hypertension. Lagenaria siceraria is a vegetable food, also used as traditional medicine.

It is reported to have hepatoprotective, diuretic, cardioprotective, antioxidant, antistress, antiulcer, antihyperlipidemic, sedative, analgesic, emetic and anti-inflammatory properties.

Traditional Uses: In the Unani and Ayurvedic medicinal systems, the fruit juice of this plant helps treat jaundice, cough, asthma, vomiting and blood disorders. The fruit juice is also helpful in treating constipation. The fruit pulp is beneficial as an emetic, sedative, purgative, cooling, diuretic, antibilious and pectoral.

The flowers are an antidote to poison. The stem bark and rind of the fruit are diuretics. The seed is vermifuge. The extracts of the plant have shown antibiotic activities. The leaf juice is widely used for treating baldness. A poultice of crushed leaves of Lagenaria siceraria can be applied to the head to treat headaches.

The seed helps treat aching teeth, gums, boils, etc. In China, three grams (seeds) a day is used as a single treatment for diabetes mellitus. The pulp is also eaten with vinegar or made into curry and used in sweets.

Biological Uses: Although cucurbitacins are highly toxic compounds and their biological activities are often close to their poisonous dose level, they possess immense pharmacological potentials, like their effectiveness against inflammation, cancer, atherosclerosis, hepatoprotective, antibacterial, antihyperlipidemic and diabetes. Methanolic fraction of the fruit also shows antihyperglycemic activity.

Chemical Constituents: A wide range of chemical compounds, including sterols, terpenoids, triterpene hydrocarbon (cucurbitacin) flavonoids and saponins, vitamin C, have been isolated from the species. The plant is also a good source of minerals such as calcium, phosphorus, iron, sodium, iodine, potassium, sulfur and magnesium. Phytochemical analysis of the edible portion of the fruit shows a good source of glucose and fructose.

Distribution: Lagenaria siceraria is probably native to tropical Africa and cultivated in Asia, Africa, Europe, Australia, etc. It is grown throughout Pakistan.

Cucurbitacin-A ($C_{32}H_{46}O_9$)

Mallotus philippinensis

Kamela (Plant Parts and Fruits)

Latin Binomial	Mallotus philippinensis
Family	Euphorbiaceae
English Name	Kamala
Urdu Name	Kamela

Medicinal Uses: Mallotus philippinensis tree is anthelmintic, vermifuge and purgative in action. The powder and hair of the fruit kill and expel tapeworms from the body. It is a quick and an active purgative herb, causing griping and nausea. It is used externally for parasitic affections of the skin like scabies, ringworm and herpes.

Traditional Uses: According to Ayurveda, the leaves are bitter, cooling and an appetizer. In the Unani system of medicine, the fruit is useful as a diuretic. A decoction of the leaves is beneficial in the treatment of diarrhoea. The root scraping is chewed with a betel nut (Areca catechu) mixture, as a contraceptive.

The plant also helps in promoting the healing of ulcers and wounds. The whole plant helps treat the skin's parasitic affections like scabies, ringworm and herpes. The fruit and bark of Mallotus philippinensis are suitable for medicinal purposes, in treating stomach ulcers and tapeworm. The fibrous bark is helpful in making rope and artificial fur.

Histopathological studies suggest the antihepatotoxicity (herb used in chronic liver disease) activity of the plant.

Biological Uses: Various non-aqueous (methanol) fractions of the bark and fruit possess antioxidant, hepatoprotective, antituberculosis and anti-cancer activities. The presence of 'rottlerin' in the plant has been shown to possess antitumour, antioxidant and anti-inflammatory activities.

Chemical Constituents: The bark of Mallotus contains betulin (triterpene) and friedelin (triterpenoids), the fruit contains rottlerin (a coloured resin), fixed oil, bitter glucoside, gallic acid (tannin) and mallotoxin (polyphenols). The plant comprises triterpenoids, tetranortriterpenoids, phenolic compounds, flavonoids, cardenolides and coumarins.

Distribution: Mallotus philippinensis is native to the Philippines and has a wide natural distribution, from the western Himalayas, India, Sri Lanka, southern China and throughout Malaysia to Australia.

Melia azedarach

Neem (Seeds, Leaves and Fruits)

Latin Binomials	Melia azadirachta/Azadirachta indica
Family	Meliaceae
English Name	Margosa/Indian lilac
Urdu Name	Neem

Medicinal Uses: All parts of Melia azadirachta tree are used for medicinal purposes. The plant is a valuable blood purifier, alternative, antiseptic, emetic and cathartic in action. The root and the bark are useful as anthelmintic, vermifuge, cathartic and an emetic for intermittent fevers and dysentery.

The fruit is beneficial in treating haemorrhoids, intestinal worms, urinary tract disorders, bloody nose, phlegm, wounds and leprosy. Some people apply 'Neem' directly to the skin to treat head lice, skin diseases, injuries, skin ulcers, as a mosquito repellent and as a skin softener. Inside the vagina, Margosa (Neem) oil is helpful for birth control. Melia oil is valuable in cosmetology in common skin diseases-eczema, scabies and ringworm infection. It is useful in herbal oil, hair tonic and nail oil in European countries.

Traditional Uses: Traditional healers (Hakims and Ayurveda) of the Indo-Pak subcontinent use the plant's bark as antidiarrhoeal, the stem in asthma and the root for insect bites, malaria, antiseptic, anthelmintic, depurative etc. The fruit is purgative and emollient. The bark is bitter and astringent. A decoction is applied externally to haemorrhoids. Leaf teas help treat malaria, peptic ulcers, pain and intestinal worms. It is one of the most important detoxicates in Ayurvedic medicine and a potent febrifuge.

The Neem oil is a powerful spermicidal and can be beneficial as an inexpensive birth control method. In addition, Neem ingredients are valuable in Ayurveda, Unani, Homeopathy and modern medicine in treating many infectious, metabolic or cancerous diseases.

Biological Uses: The plant's biological and pharmacological activities can be attributed to different parts of the plant and the extracts of these display antispasmodic, antioxidant, anti-cancer, antiviral and antifungal activities. Other properties include antiulcer, spermicidal, anthelmintic, anti-diabetic, antiimplantation, immunomodulating, molluscicidal (snail baits), insecticidal, antifeedant and insect repellent effects.

Chemical Constituents: Melia azadirachta plant contains many bitter limonoids (triterpenoids), including nimbin, nimbibin, salannin and triterpenoids, tannins, flavonoids, etc. and essential oils. The bark contains tannins, margosin and azadarin. The oil contains margosic acid.

The insecticidal activity of the Melia plant is due to the presence of limonoids. The Fruit and seeds are a good source of Neem oil and tetranortriterpenes.

Distribution: Melia azadirachta is native to the Indo-Pak sub-continent. It is typically grown in Iran, Bangladesh and Myanmar. It is found in Sind, Southern Punjab and lower Balochistan, in Pakistan.

Note: Melia azadirachta tree should not be confused with the Azadirachta trees of the same family but a distinct genus.

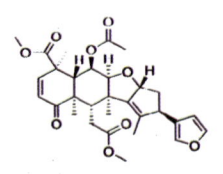

Nimbin (C$_{30}$H$_{36}$O$_9$)

Salannin (C$_{34}$H$_{44}$O$_9$)

Saussurea lappa

Qust (Plant, Freah and Dried Roots)

Latin Binomial	Saussurea lappa
Family	Compositae/Asteraceae
English Name	Coctus/Indian Coctus/Kuth
Urdu Name	Qust

Medicinal Uses: The root of the flowering Saussurea lappa plant is carminative, stimulant, expectorant, anti-inflammatory in action and a tonic for the vital organs.

Traditional Uses: Saussurea lappa is traditionally known as a potent plant for its medicinal uses in different indigenous systems of medicine. It is popularly known as the 'Qust' root in Urdu. It is beneficial because of its antiulcer, anticonvulsant, anti-cancer, hepatoprotective, antiarthritic and antiviral activities. In Unani and Ayurvedic medicinal systems, its roots are useful in treating fevers, skin diseases, headache, asthma, inflammatory diseases and stomach problems. It is also valuable in treating diseases of the liver and kidney. The powder of the dried root of the plant is the principal ingredient in an ointment for ulcers; it is also a hair wash. Saussurea lappa roots and root stalks are helpful in toothache.

In Ayurveda, the root is used to improve complexion, cure leucoderma, itching, ringworm, vomiting, scabies and epilepsy. It flushes out toxins which make this plant an effective remedy for gout. The oil extracted from Saussurea lappa's roots is known as 'Costus oil,' which is suitable for preparing hair oil and high-quality perfumes. Costus oil is intensely aromatic, viscous, is pale yellow to brownish in colour and is valuable in treating leprosy.

It is a superior herb in Chinese medicine and is aromatic stomachic, vermifuge and fragrant. Saussurea lappa is useful for treating asthma, chest pain, abdomen pain, indigestion, vomiting, and diarrhoea.

Biological Uses: Non-aqueous fractions of this plant's root show various biological activities such as anti-cancer (breast, prostate, oral and gastric cancers), anti-inflammatory, antiulcer, antioxidant, antispasmodic, hypoglycemic and antiviral. The petro-ether fraction of the root is beneficial for asthma and bronchitis. The ethanolic plant extract also has an antimicrobial effect against gram-positive and gram-negative bacteria.

Chemical Constituents: Cactus roots contain sesquiterpenes and sesquiterpene lactones; other compounds include glycosides, anthraquinones and saussureamins. Phytochemical compounds are isolated from this plant, such as costunolide, isodihydrocostunolide, cynaropicrin, etc. An essential oil present in the root is intensely aromatic.

Distribution: Saussurea lappa flowering plant is native to the Indo-Pak subcontinent, Central Asia and China. In Pakistan, it is a wild plant in Azad Kashmir and Kaghan valley.

Costunolide a sesquiterpene lactone ($C_{15}H_{20}O_2$)

Taxus wallichiana

Talishpatar/Zarnab (Fruirs, Leaves and Bark)

Latin Binomials	Taxus wallichiana/Taxus baccata
Family	Taxaceae
English Name	Silver Fir/Yew
Urdu Name	Talishpatar/Zarnab

Medicinal Uses: The bark and leaves of Taxus wallichiana tree are carminative, expectorant, anti-cancer, antirheumatic, abortifacient and astringent in action.

Traditional Uses: In Unani and Ayurvedic medicinal systems, the traditional healers (Hakims and Ayurveda) have used the bark and leaves for treating common cold, cough, fever and pain. The infusion of the leaves exerts abortifacient activity and is the cause of poisoning. They also use its bark and leaves in steam baths to treat rheumatism and the paste made from its bark is used to treat fractures and headaches. Extracts from the tree are also valuable in medicinal hair oils. In Pakistan, a decoction of the stem is useful in treating tuberculosis. Young shoots of the plant are used in Ayurveda to prepare a tincture to treat headache, giddiness and bradycardia.

Biological Uses: The extracts (methanol, chloroform and petro-ether) of the root possess anti-cancer, antibacterial, anxiolytic, anti-inflammatory and antifungal activities. The crude extracts (methanol, ethanol and acetone) of the plant parts also exhibit an inhibitory effect on bacteria (Gram+ve and Gram-ve) and fungi. The plant oil is an antioxidant used in perfumery preparations and insect repellent formulations.

Chemical Constituents: The bark contains diterpene alkaloids, flavonoids, quercetin, myricetin, flavonols and flavones. The diterpene pseudo-alkaloid exhibit significant anti-cancer activity (breast cancer, lung cancer and ovarian cancer). Taxus wallichiana has mainly been exploited for its leaves and bark, which are used to produce the anti-cancer drug 'Paclitaxel' or similar chemicals. The leaves and bark have been harvested commercially from the wild, as a source of the anti-cancer drug taxol. Taxol is a diterpenoids alkaloid. The bark is a good source of tannins.

Distribution: The tree of Taxus wallichiana is native to South East Asia and is similar to a plant (species) growing further East in China, Taiwan, Vietnam and the Philippines. Palas valley (KPK) is considered as one of the diversity zones in Pakistan.

Note: Modern research has shown that the plant contains taxol' in its shoots. Taxol has shown an exciting potential as an anti-cancer drug, particularly in treating ovarian cancers. This plant is also mentioned under 'Plants with Anti-cancer properties, page 444).'

Taxol ($C_{47}H_{51}NO_{14}$)

Tephrosia purpurea

Sarphoka (Dried, Fresh Plant and Flowers of two different Species)

Latin Binomial	Tephrosia purpurea
Family	Papilionaceae/Fabaceae
English Name	Yellow Thistle
Urdu Name	Sarphoka

Medicinal Uses: All parts of the plant, including the roots, are valuable for medicinal purposes. The flowering plant of Tephrosia purpurea is aromatic, anthelmintic, alexiteric, antipyretic in action and a blood purifier.

Traditional Uses: In Unani and Ayurvedic medicinal systems, the plant is useful in treating leprosy, ulcers, asthma, tumours, liver, spleen, heart and blood diseases. The traditional healers of the Indo-Pak subcontinent also use a decoction of the roots in dyspepsia, diarrhoea, rheumatism, urinary disorders, gonorrhoea and skin diseases. It is known to be an effective herb for liver cirrhosis treatment. The roots are bitter and anthelmintic. The pounded leaves decoction is a remedy against snakebite. The fruit extract is useful in relieving body pains and inflammation problems. The pulverized roots, when used as smoke, are suitable in alleviating asthma and cough.

The whole plant forms a constituent of the famous Unani poly-herbal 'blood purifier' preparation known as Naqua-e-Shahtarah.

This plant's anti-diabetic properties help maintain a healthy blood sugar level. It is regarded as effective cure against enduring chronic disorders, itching, scabies and pimples. Antipyretic and analgesic properties of this herb are quite valuable for treating fever.

Biological Uses: The non-aqueous extract of the plant shows excellent anti-cancer activity. The plant extracts (ethanol and methanol) possess antioxidant, antimicrobial, anti-inflammatory, antileprosy, antiviral and antiulcer properties. The seed fraction (aqueous) demonstrates antihyperglycaemic activity. The root is bitter and its decoction is useful as a nematicide (herbs to kill nematode worms) for treatment against larvae that cause lung disease. Aqueous and methanol (80 per cent) fraction exhibits protection against castor oil-induced diarrhoea in mice.

Chemical Constituents: The plant contains terpenoids, rotenoids, flavones, flavanones, saponins, sterols, volatile oils and fixed oil. In some plant species, flavonoids like pongamol, semiglabrin, lanceolatins A and B are the dominating constituents. Purpurin (trihydroxyanthraquinone) is also present in the root.

Distribution: Tephrosia purpurea is native to the Indo-Pak sub-continent and China. The plant species are also grown in Iran, Jordan, Oman, Egypt, Ethiopia, Sudan etc.

Pongamol ($C_{18}H_{14}O_4$)   Lanceolatin B ($C_{17}H_{10}O$)   Purpurin ($C_{14}H_8O_5$)

Valeriana hardwickii

Taggar/Asarun (Flowers and Roots)

Latin Binomial	Valeriana hardwickii
Family	Valerianaceae/Caprifoliaceae
English Name	Valerian
Urdu Name	Taggar/Asarun

Medicinal Uses: The root of the herbaceous, perennial, flowering Valeriana hardwickii plant is antispasmodic, stimulant, antidiarrhoeal, diuretic in action and a cephalic tonic. The plant is valuable in all nervous debility cases, irritation and hysterical affections; it is firmly nervine without any narcotic effects. It is also beneficial as a tonic for the urogenital organs and mainly useful as a diuretic.

The results from multiple studies indicate that the Valeriiana hardwickii plant when taken, may reduce the time it takes for a person to fall asleep and help one sleep better. Although valerian is reasonably safe, its side effects such as headache, dizziness, stomach problems may occur. This plant's root may help minimize hot flashes, commonly affecting women during menopause. The exact mechanism of action is unknown since Valerian doesn't directly influence hormone levels. The crude extract of the rhizomes and roots of Valeriana fauriei may have therapeutic potential for treating obesity.

The Valeriana species are now listed in the European and United States pharmacopoeias. These are also sold as a diet supplement in the USA and are one of the highest-selling natural medicines in Europe and the USA.

Traditional Uses: In the traditional medicine system (Unani and Ayurvedic) of the Indo-Pak subcontinent, the plant roots help treat ulcers, convulsions, asthma, jaundice, seminal weakness, cardiac debility, skin diseases, leprosy and are helpful also in sleep enhancement. These are also suitable for the treatment of rheumatism and low blood pressure.

The juice of the fresh plant is a narcotic, in insomnia and anticonvulsive in epilepsy. The powdered root or leaves are used as a poultice to treat boils. Externally, it is also valuable in treating eczema, ulcers and minor injuries.

The plant is a popular ingredient of many poly-herbal semi-solid Unani preparations such as Majun-e-Ushbah, Jawarish-e-Jalinus, Jawarish-e-odd-Shirin and Majun Murraweh-ul-Arwah. Moreover, it is a conventional sedative medicine in Brazil, and is also anticonvulsant, with hypnotic effects and anxiolytic activity.

Biological Uses: The plant possesses various biological activities, such as being antioxidant, antiulcer, anti-inflammatory, antibacterial, anti-cancer, anticonvulsive, anti-Parkinson's and anti-Alzheimer's disease. The hydro-methanol extract (30:70 per cent) of a root possesses antidiarrhoeal activity.

Chemical Constituents: The yellowish-green essential oil showed high content of oxygenated sesquiterpenes. The major constituents are valeracetate, bornyl acetate, methyl linoleate, cuparene and α-cedrene. The plant also possesses important valepotriates (a class of indole alkaloids) and is a good source of flavones or flavone glycosides, sesquiterpenoids glycoside, bakkenolid type sesquiterpenoids, phenolic compounds and terpenoids.

Distribution: Valeriana hardwickii is indigenous to Pakistan, India, Burma, Sri Lanka and China.

Note: The fresh root of the Valeriana plant is about three times as effective as its roots dried at 40°C, while temperatures above 82° destroy the active constituents in the root.

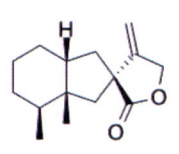

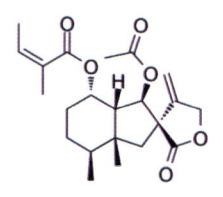

Bakkenolide A (C$_{15}$H$_{22}$O$_2$) and B (C$_{22}$H$_{30}$O$_6$)

Valeriana officinalis

Baalchar (Plant, Roots and Flowers of Different Species)

Latin Binomial	Valeriana officinalis/Valeriana jatamansi
Family	Valerianaceae/Caprifoliaceae
English Name	True Valerian
Urdu Name	Baalchar/Sumbal-at-Teeb/Bile-Lotan

Medicinal Uses: The roots of the perennial, flowering Valeriana officinalis herb are aromatic, stimulant, carminative, diuretic, antispasmodic in action and a potent nerve tonic. These may be helpful in all nervous debility and irritation cases as these are not a narcotic. The fresh root juice is valuable as a narcotic in insomnia and an anticonvulsant in epilepsy. The plant's oil is beneficial against cholera and strengthens eyesight and is valuable in insomnia.

The British Herbal Pharmacopoeia describes Valerian as a sedative, mild anodyne, hypnotic, spasmolytic, carminative and hypotensive as indicated for hysterical states, excitability, insomnia, hypochondriasis, migraine, cramp and rheumatic pain. An alcoholic extract of Valerian for dandruff treatment has been mentioned as well as the use of Valerian for treating sores and pimples.

The European Medicines Agency has approved the health claim that Valeriana can be used as a traditional herbal medicine in relieving mild nervous tension and as an aid in sleep. In Brazil, it has been valuable in conventional medicine for its sedative, anticonvulsant, hypnotic effects and anxiolytic activity. A clinical trial of valerian and lemon balm improves sleep in children under twelve.

Traditional Uses: In Unani and Ayurvedic medicinal systems, Valeriana officinalis is beneficial both externally and internally, and is one of the principal herbs used against insomnia. Externally, the root extract with other herbs helps remove freckles due to its detersive action. It is also used internally in traditional Chinese medicine and in Japanese medicine as a sedative, antispasmodic and antidepressant. In the United States, it is mainly sold as a sleeping aid, while in Europe, it is useful in conditions of restlessness, tremors and anxiety.

Traditional healers (Hakims and Ayurveda) of the Indo-Pak subcontinent regarded this plant's root as applicable against neurosis, hysteria and epilepsy. It also helps in treating digestive problems and urinary tract infections. The decoction of the roots of the plant is given in treating abdominal pain and the cold infusion of the roots is useful in treating fever.

In homoeopathy, the mother tincture of Valeriana officinalis is used in hysteria, over-sensitiveness and nervous affections.

Valeriana officinalis plant's root forms a constituent of many poly-herbal Unani medicinal preparations like 'Itrifal Ghudaddi, Majun-e-Jalali, Majun-e-Ushbah, Jawarish-e- Jalinus, Labub-e-Kabir, etc.

Biological Uses: The oils and extracts of the plant possess antiseptic and antibacterial activities. Valeriana officinalis exhibit a broad spectrum of biological and pharmacological properties, like antimicrobial, anticancer, antirheumatic, sedative, anxiolytic, tranquillizing, hepatoprotective, anticonvulsant and as neuroprotective. The anti-inflammatory, antioxidant, antiviral and lipid-lowering properties may be due to the presence of furostanol steroidal saponin and flavonol glycosides. The extracts and essential oils of the Valeriana officinalis plant were shown to exhibit strong peripheral and weak central antinociceptive effects.

Chemical Constituents: Due to its strong musky, earthy odour, Valeriana officinalis root is an important ingredient in natural incenses and perfumes, where it is useful as a fixative. The herb's scent is released when it is dried, which is caused by isovaleric acid, also known as 3-methylbutanoic acid. Actinidine is a monoterpenoid pyridine alkaloid with a cyclopenta pyridine structure, in the plant's yellowish-green to brownish-yellow essential oil.

Actinidine (iridoid, a type of monoterpenoid) is a compound that can attract cats; the plant is also called 'Billie-Lotan' in Urdu. Valeriana contains sesquiterpenoids, triterpenoids, alkaloids, pyridine derivatives, e.g., valerianine, actinidine, chatinine, shyanthine, pentanoic acid, essential oils, esterified iridoid-monoterpenes, didrovaltrate (an iridoid monoterpenoid) and flavonoids. Two new pharmacologically active compounds are also isolated from the Valeriana plant, such as orivalerianol (sesquiterpene) iridoid, monovalerianester-A (aglycone of kanokoside A).

The herb is a rich source of Isovaleric acid, hesperidin and linarin, which act as antioxidants. The level of valerenic acids can be highly variable based on the age of the plant. The rhizome of the plant also contains cyclopentapyrans, valepotriates, valtrate and a terpene glycoside 'valerosidatum.'

Distribution: Valeriana officinalis is a perennial plant native to Europe, Western Asia and South Asia. The plant has become naturalized in Canada and the southern United States. The Valerian of commerce consists of rhizomes and roots, collectively called roots.

The plant is distributed in temperate forest areas of Pakistan from Waziristan, Kurrum agency, Swat, Dir, Hazara in Khyber Pakhtunkhwa, Murree Hills in Punjab and Azad Kashmir. In 1973/74, approximately 350 tonnes of Valeriana worth Rs four million were exported from Karachi to different countries worldwide.

Note: Although valerian is thought to be reasonably safe, side effects such as headache, dizziness, stomach problems, or sleeplessness may occur. The plant contains compounds that induce a depression of the central nervous system. Care should be taken while using this herb with other depressants like alcohol, benzodiazepines, barbiturates, opiates and antihistaminic drugs.

Pregnant or nursing women must not take Valeriana officinalis without medical advice because of the possible risks to the fetus or infant.

Still, Valerian is considered safe by the U.S. Food and Drugs Administration (FDA) and is gentler than synthetic drugs, such as benzodiazepines and barbiturates.

Valerianine (C₁₁H₁₅NO)   Actinidine (C₁₀H₁₃N)   Isovaleric acid (C₅H₁₀O₂)

Didrovaltrate (C₂₂H₃₂O₈)   Valerosidatum (C₂₁H₃₄O₁₁)

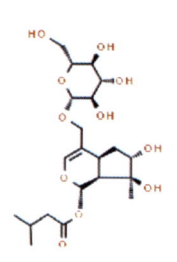

Furostanol Saponins   Kanokoside C (C₂₇H₄₂O₁₇)

Medicinal Plants
Plants with Anti-cancer Properties

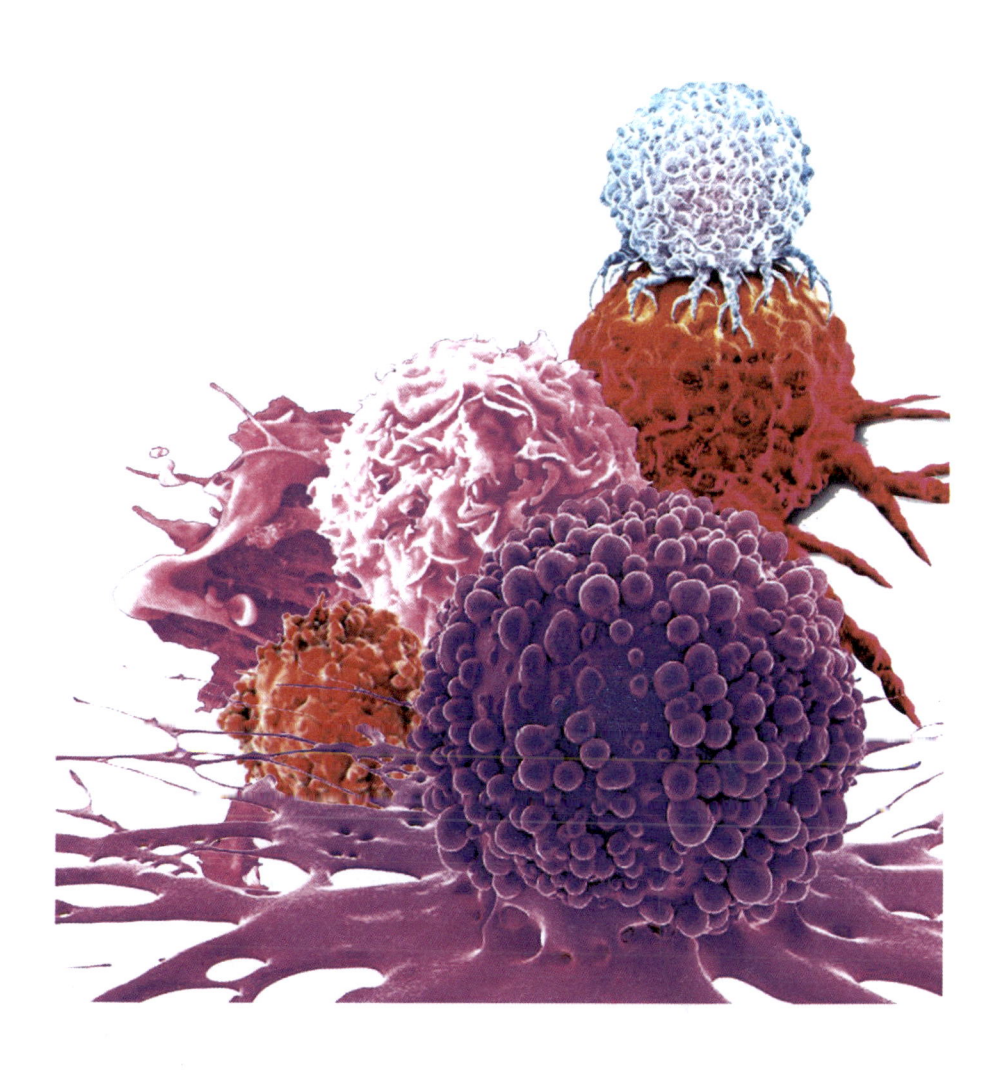

Important Note:

Scientific evidence suggests that cancers are not an inevitable consequence of ageing but are preventable diseases. The evidence in this chapter indicates that herbs may be the factors in our diet that may lower cancer risk and affect tumour behaviour. Many herbs can reduce cancer cell spread and growth. Current research is limited to test-tube, animal (*In vitro* and *In vivo*) and observational studies. More studies are needed to understand how these Medicinal herbs may directly affect human cancer development. In the meantime, it's a safe bet that herbs or a diet rich in whole foods, paired with a healthy lifestyle, will improve many aspects of human health.

Cancer

Cancer is the uncontrolled growth of cells anywhere in the body.

Types of Cancer

The major types of cancer are melanoma, carcinoma, sarcoma, lymphoma and leukaemia. Carcinomas, are the most commonly diagnosed cancers, that originate in the skin, breast, pancreas and other organs and glands. Lymphoma is a cancer of the lymphocytes. Leukaemia is the cancer of the blood. It does not usually form solid tumours. Sarcoma arises in the bone, muscle, fat, blood vessels, cartilage or other soft or connective tissues of the body. They are relatively uncommon. Melanomas are cancers that arise in the cells that make skin pigment.

Symptoms of Cancer

Cancer symptoms and signs depend on the specific type and grade of cancer, although general signs and symptoms are not precise. For example, in patients with various cancers: can be fatigue, weight loss, pain, skin changes, change in bowel or bladder function, unusual bleeding, persistent cough or voice change, fever, lumps or tissue masses.

Antioxidants and Cancer Prevention

Antioxidants are substances that may protect cells from damage caused by unstable molecules known as free radicals. Free radicals can lead to cancer. Antioxidants interact with and stabilise free radicals and prevent some of the damage free radicals otherwise might cause. Considerable laboratory evidence from chemical, cell culture and animal studies indicate that antioxidants may slow or possibly prevent cancer development. However, information from recent clinical trials is less clear. In recent years, large-scale, randomised clinical trials have reached inconsistent conclusions.

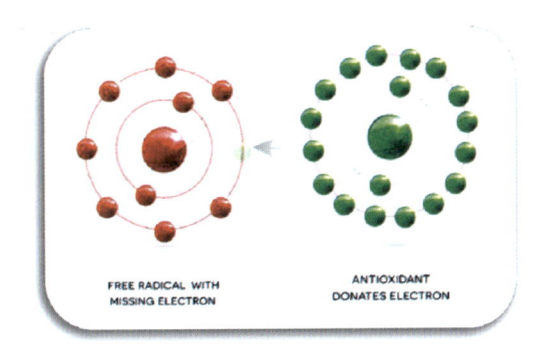

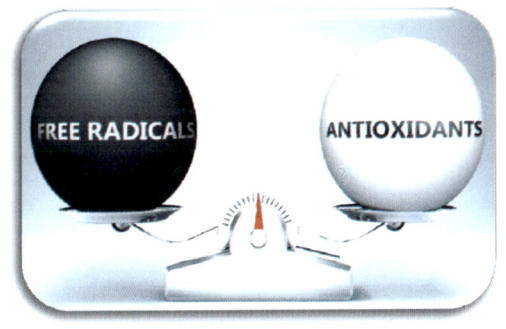

Oxidative stress occurs when an oxygen molecule splits into single atoms with unpaired electrons, which are called free radicals

Phenols

The term phenol refers to many chemical compounds found in plants. These chemicals make up the active substances in many plants. They are responsible for controlling the activity of a range of enzymes and cell receptors, thus protecting the plant from bacterial and fungal infections and UV radiation damage. Phenols, having such protective properties and high antioxidant profiles, have caught scientists' attention **and those people searching for good health.**

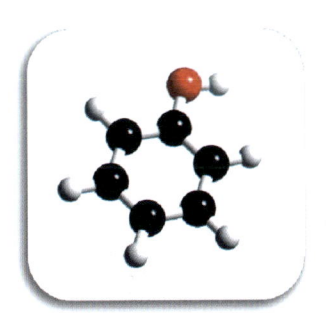

Phenol

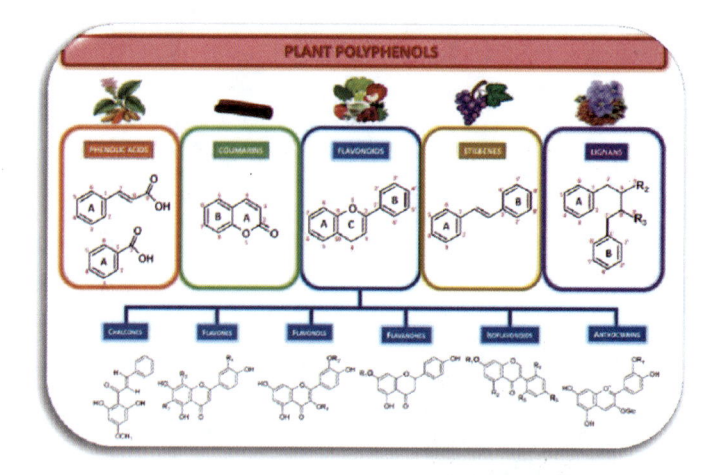

(Phenolic Acids, Coumarins, Flavonoids, Polyphenolic amides)

Plants with Anti-cancer Properties

Since the beginning of human history, plants have been useful for medical purposes are the basis of modern medicine. Most chemotherapeutic drugs for cancer treatment are identified and isolated from plants or their synthetic derivatives. The diversity in natural compounds makes it a rich source for discovering and studying biological activities to overcome several diseases. Approximately 60 per cent of drugs, currently used for cancer treatment, are isolated from natural products and the plant kingdom has been the most significant source. This chapter focuses on the promising natural medicinal plants that possess anti-cancer (anticarcinogens) properties.

Actaea racemosa

(English: Black Cohosh) - (Urdu: Kawhush Alsawda)

Actaea racemosa or Cimicifuga racemosa, of the Ranunculaceae family, is among the most frequently cited agents used by breast cancer patients during their radiotherapy and chemotherapy. It is a shrub-like plant commonly seen in the Eastern forests of North America. It has been used for centuries by Native American herbalists for health issues like menopausal symptoms, pre-menstrual discomfort and dysmenorrhoea and it induces abortion and numerous other problems.

Allium sativum

(English: Garlic) - (Urdu: Lehsan)

Garlic is still used globally to treat various diseases and cancer, as a natural remedy. Allium sativum, belongs to the Amaryllidaceae family, and is also called 'Poor Man's Treacle'. It contains allicin (diallyl-thiosulfinate). Fresh garlic contains an amino acid called alliin. When the clove is crushed or chopped, an enzyme, alliinase, is released. Alliin and alliinase interact to form allicin, which is considered a major biologically active garlic component. Allicin is a compound that has been shown to kill cancer cells in multiple test-tube studies. A study of 470 men showed that a higher intake of garlic was associated with a reduced prostate cancer risk.

Another study found that people who ate lots of garlic and fruit, deep yellow vegetables, dark green vegetables and onion, were less likely to develop colorectal tumours. However, this study did not isolate the effects of Garlic. Benefits have been found in garlic regarding cancers of the stomach, colon, oesophagus, pancreas, breast, prostate and in some cases, up to a 50 per cent reduced risk, have been found. There is also some preliminary evidence that garlic might play a role in cancer treatment.

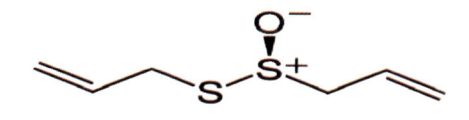

Allicin (Organo-sulfur compound) **($C_6H_{10}OS_2$)**

Aloe barbadensis

(English: Aloe)- (Urdu: Ailwa)

Aloe barbadensis, of the Asphodelaceae family, has been around for centuries. The earliest known references to its medicinal uses was from the ancient Egyptians, who also used it for skin problems. Aloe barbadensis contains a compound called anthraquinone, which has impressive anti-cancer effects. Despite the lack of substantial evidence, aloe products are promoted in cancer patients, especially for use against radiation-induced skin toxicity. Aloctin A, isolated from the leaves of Aloe arborescens, has mitogenic, anticancer and antitumour activities.

Artemisia absinthium

(English: Wormwood)- (Urdu: Afsanteen)

Artemisia absinthium, of the Asteraceae family, contains the compound Artemisinin. This compound has a positive effect on cancer cells and on malaria, along with numerous viruses, including hepatitis B and C. Artemisia annua, a different species of Artemisia, is also a rich source of antioxidant flavonoids that are thought to play an essential role in potentiating the effects of artemisinin drugs, against cancer. Artemisia absinthium extract has anti-cancer effects mediated via the apoptotic pathway in human breast cell lines.

Absinthin ($C_{30}H_{40}O_6$)   Thujone ($C_{10}H_{16}O$)   Artemisinin ($C_{15}H_{22}O_5$)

Berberis aristata

(English: Barberry)- (Urdu: Rasout)

Berberis aristata, of the Berberidaceae family, is a helpful herbal medicine. According to Ayurvedic and Unani medicinal systems, Rasaut (extract) is an effective treatment for liver tumours. A study shows that when berberries are administered in high doses to cancer patients, the alkaloid present in berberries, known as berberine, kills cancer cells *in vivo* trials. In another study, the alcoholic extract of Berberis aristata, possessing tumour inhibitory activity, in the later stages of cancer, is very encouraging and may be due to its composite nature. Berberis aristata methanolic extract has also significantly increased anti-cancer activity in breast cancer cell lines. Therefore, it may be postulated that the plant extract would help pharmacological applications, in breast cancer treatment.

Berberine ($C_{20}H_{18}NO_4+$)

Boswellia glabra

(English: Frankincense)- (Urdu: Loban)

Boswellia glabra, of the Burseraceae family, contains pentacyclic terpenoid, boswellic acid that suppresses viability and stimulates cell death among cancer cells (in this case, human pancreatic cancer cells). Human pancreatic cancer cells seem to be sensitive to Frankincense essential oil distillate fractions, with higher-molecular weight compounds. Various anti-cancer research studies and published data reports on the safety of Boswellia glabra, show that 'boswellic acids' could be used to treat colon cancer, pancreatic cancer, brain tumour, leukaemia and prostate cancer.

Boswellic acid ($C_{30}H_{48}O_3$)

Camellia sinensis

(English: Tea)- (Urdu: Chayi)

Camellia sinensis, of the Theaceae family, contains polyphenolics which are recognised to have anti-mutagenic and anti-cancer actions. The most abundant polyphenol in green tea is Epigallocatechin-3-gallate, which focuses on pre-clinical and clinical research in various health settings. These compounds have substantial free radical scavenging activity and protect cells from DNA damage, caused by reactive oxygen species. Tea polyphenols have also been shown to inhibit tumour cell proliferation and induce apoptosis in laboratory and animal studies. In other studies, tea catechins inhibit angiogenesis and tumour cell invasiveness and modulate the immune system function. Some evidence from animal studies, suggests that tea has a protective effect against stomach and colon cancers. The threat of cancer, in several organs, is diminished by using green and black tea or their primary catechins. Furthermore, studies have also found that green tea also shields the body from the harmful effects of radiation. Although tea's potential beneficial effects have been attributed to tea polyphenols' intense antioxidant activity, the precise mechanism of tea is that it might help prevent cancer, has not been established.

Catharanthus roseus

(English: Catharanthus)- (Urdu: Sada-Bahar)

Researchers have examined Catharanthus roseus, of the Apocynaceae family, a plant well known for producing the antitumor compounds classified as Terpenoid Indole alkaloids. Various intermediary compounds are created during metabolising terpenoid Indole alkaloids (TIAs). They travel across different cells, finally arriving at the idioblast (isolated plant cell that differs from neighbouring tissues), or laticifer (elongated secretory cell) found in the leaves and/or stems of plants producing latex cells where they are stored. However, it was still unclear how each compound moved among cells.

Vinblastine is an antitumour alkaloid used in treating Hodgkin's disease. Vincristine is a compound and is used to treat leukaemia, in children.

Vinblastine (C₄₆H₅₈N₄O₉)   Ajmalicine (C₂₁H₂₄ON₂O₃)   Reserpine (C₃₃H₄₀N₂O₉)

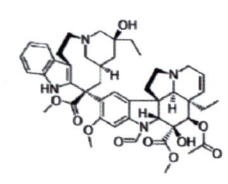

Vincristine (C₄₆H₅₆N₄O₁₀)

Crocus sativus

(English: Saffron)- (Urdu: Zafran)

Crocus sativus, of the Iridaceae family, contains a carotenoid compound called crocetin. The results of studies done, both *in vivo* and *in vitro*, show that this compound could be a potent anti-tumour agent. Saffron, was found in another study, to inhibit skin cancer in mice. Crocin (water-soluble yellow-red pigments) has been considered an essential anti-cancer agent in saffron, that plays a role in gene expression and apoptosis in cancer cells.

Crocetin (C₂₀H₂₄O₄)   Crocin (C₄₄H₆₄O₂₄)

Curcuma longa

(English: Turmeric)- (Urdu: Haldi)

Curcuma longa, of the Zingiberaceae family, imparts a rich yellow colour to food. The root and rootstock, or rhizome, of the plant, contains curcumin, which is considered to be the active ingredient. Its anti-mutagenic action and cancer inhibition activity is attributed to its phenolic constituents. Turmeric has been shown to curb the progress of breast, lung, stomach and skin malignancies. Its antioxidant, bright yellow 'curcumin' (diferuloylmethane), is a successful anti-inflammatory agent in humans and slows down cancer development by averting toxic eicosanoid production such as prostaglandin E2. This anti-cancer outcome has been established in all the phases of tumour growth.

Furthermore, studies have revealed that Curcuma longa inhibits nitrosamine production, enhancing the body's natural antioxidant functions. Numerous researches also advocate that curcumin hampers cancer initiation and encourages its deterioration. Laboratory studies support that, curcumin interferes with several important molecular pathways involved in cancer development, growth and spread. Simultaneously, researchers report that Curcumin inhibits the formation of cancer-causing enzymes in rodents.

Curcumin (**a diarylheptanoid**) ($C_{21}H_{20}O_6$)

Cyclea peltata

(English: Ink Berry)- (Urdu: Paatha)

Cyclea peltata, of the Menispermaceae family, in the current study, assesses the immune-modulatory, anti-cancer and antioxidant activity of a single fraction. A yellow active fraction was isolated using ethyl acetate: methanol (1:4). The fraction gave a good yield and its water-soluble sample has indicated the presence of two compounds in the fraction. The phytochemical analysis showed the presence of flavonoids. The fraction exhibits immune-modulatory potential since it stimulates the proliferation of lymphocytes and macrophages. The nitrite generation in macrophages is also an indication of macrophages' activation. Hence, this fraction can be further purified, identified and developed into an active drug molecule for immunity-related diseases. The plant contains bebeerine, a member of isoquinolines and a bisbenzylisoquinoline alkaloid.

Bebeerines ($C_{36}H_{38}N_2O_6$)

Glycyrrhiza glabra

(English: Liquorice)- (Urdu: Mulaithi)

The roots of Glycyrrhiza glabra, of the Leguminosae family, contain polyphenols that encourage apoptosis (automatic death) in cancer cells. Liquorice regulates hormones from the adrenal glands and reduces stress chemicals. Chronic stress often triggers the growth of cancer cells. According to a study, Liquorice root stops breast cancer cell proliferation, in humans. Glycyrrhizin is the most potent ingredient in Glycyrrhiza (mulaithi).

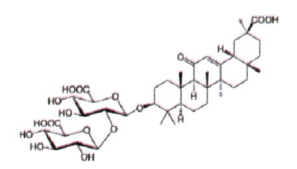

Glycyrrhizin ($C_{42}H_{62}O_{16}$)

Hemidesmus indicus

(English: Sarsaparilla)- (Urdu: Ushbah)

Hemidesmus indicus, of the Asclepiadaceae family, is a plant found in South Asia. It is used in Unani/ herbal preparations. A few studies appear to investigate its anti-cancer potential. Scientific data indicates that 'Ushbah Magrabi' induces immunogenic (denoting substances able to produce an immune response) cell death in human tumour cells and suggests its potential relevance in innovative cancer immunotherapy protocols

Maytenus ilicifolia

(English: Espinheira-Santa)- (Urdu: Asbynhyra Santaan)

Maytenus ilicifolia or Maytenus aquifolia, of the Celastraceae family, contains bioactive compounds inhibiting the four cancer cell-line growth, in a dose-dependent manner. Besides, the Maytenus has revealed a more robust, proliferation inhibitory effect, suggesting that the plant compounds could exhibit a favourable anti-lung cancer and anti-cervical cancer effect. However, the Maytenus compound had low cytotoxicity in the human normal epithelial cell lines.

The Maytenus compound has significant anti-cancer activities against human-lung cancer cells and HeLa cells (immortal cell line) *in vitro* and *in vivo,* highlighting an anti-cancer medicine. Lupane ($C_{30}H_{52}$) and quinine methide (C_7H_6O), deserve special mention for presenting important biological activities.

Rheum emodi

(English: Cascara Sagrada)- (Urdu: Rewand-Chini)

Rheum emodi, of the Polygonaceae family, became the most common active ingredient in over-the-counter laxatives until the FDA banned it in May 2002. Cascara

sagrada is used today, by traditional healers, naturopaths and health-minded individuals to cleanse the colon of toxic matter.

Research indicates that Cascara sagrada increases vitality and protects against colon cancer. The modern study shows that aqueous and methanolic extracts of the rhizome of Rewand emodi (rhabarberone), might be a potential source for anti-cancer metabolites that can be mustered to develop effective cancer drugs.

Rhabarberone/Aloe emodin ($C_{15}H_{10}O_5$)

Ruta graveolens

(English: Garden Rue)- (Urdu: Berg-e-Sadab)

The Ruta graveolens, of the Rutaceae family, was reported to have constituents, including flavonoids, rutin, alkaloids (arborinine and evoxanthine), graveoline, coumarins and essential oils. While the pro-oxidant activity of Berg-e-Sadab may be due to psoralens, the actual ingredient responsible for Ruta graveolens extract's antitumor activity, is not known at present. However, one report has suggested that furanoacridones are suitable candidates for anti-cancer drug development.

Psoralens ($C_{11}H_6O_3$)   **Arborinine ($C_{16}H_{15}NO_4$)**

Solanum miniatum

(English: Black Night Shade)- (Urdu: Anbul Saalab/Mako)

The juice from Solanum miniatum, of the Solanaceae family, has been used to treat cancers, tumours and warts. References to its use have appeared in the literature of many countries. The active tumour-inhibitory compound has recently been identified as the steroid glycoside beta-solamarine.

Beta-Solamarine ($C_{45}H_{73}NO_{15}$)

Taxus wallichiana

(English: Common Yem)- (Urdu: Zarnab)

Taxus wallichiana,[5] of the Taxaceae family, contains Taxol, renamed Paclitaxel and sold under the trademark Taxol, which is the most successful anti-cancer agent developed from trees. The alkaloid – natural product Taxol was isolated for the first time from the bark of Taxus brevifolia and is now characterized as part of the National Cancer Institute (NCI) screening program at Research Triangle Institute (RTI). Together with baccatins III (is a tetracyclic diterpenoid), the natural product Taxol is isolated at a low level from needles, seeds and the bark of Taxus brevifolia. The yield quantity varies with genotype tissue, season, environmental factors, endophytes and culture conditions, storage condition and extraction techniques. The poor solubility and limited supply hampered the quality yield.

Paclitaxel ($C_{47}H_{51}NO_{14}$)   Baccatins ($C_{31}H_{38}O_{11}$)

Note: Paclitaxel is a tetracyclic diterpenoid compound, isolated originally from the bark of the evergreen Taxus brevifolia, the Pacific Yew tree of the Taxaceae family. It is a mitotic inhibitor used in cancer chemotherapy. Taxus wallichiana is a medium-sized tree species of Asia, ranging from Afghanistan through the Himalayas to the Philippines

Vaccinium myrtillus

(English: Bilberry)- (Urdu: Neeli-Berry)

---

[5] A. Hussain, Z. K. Shinwari et al, (2013), 'In vitro Callogenesis and Organogensis in Taxus wallichiana, Department of Biotechnology, Quaid-i-Azam University Islamabad Pakistan.

Vaccinium myrtillus[6] of the Ericaceae family (bilberry, also known as European blueberry), effectively inhibits the growth of leukaemia, colon and breast carcinoma cell lines in humans and also decreases the number of intestinal adenoma in rats. The growth-inhibitory and cytotoxic activity of the bilberry fruit extract is evident on cancer cells. It is likely attributed to phenolic pigments, the anthocyanins, as bilberry fruit is among the richest natural sources of flavonoids. The consumption of blue berries is the predominant means of anthocyanin (are water-soluble vacuolar flavonoids) ingestion. Anti-cancer effects of Vaccinium myrtillus fruit extract on breast tumour cells, are probably independent on estrogen receptor expression. The growth of estrogen-responsive and unresponsive cell lines is suppressed.

Anthocyanins (Basic Structure)

Viscum album

(English: Mistletoe)- (Urdu: Amar-Bail)

The Viscum album plant of the Santalaceae family, is also known as Mistletoe. Research done on humans, suggests that mistletoe reduces symptoms and improves life quality. For example, a study published in the European Journal of Cancer, found that mistletoe reduces chemotherapy's side effects in lung cancer patients.

In the year 2013, a study published in Evidenced Based Complimentary Alternative Medicine found that cancer patients with advanced tumours, were able to tolerate higher doses of gemcitabine (a chemotherapy drug used to treat the malignant tumour) with the addition of mistletoe. Among well described and most biologically

---

[6] W.Kalt and D.Dufour (1997), HortTechnology July-September 7(3).

active components in the plant are lectins and viscotoxins, which play an essential role in the treatment of cancer because of their apoptotic and cytotoxic effects[7].

Note: The gemcitabine brand and other names Gemzar and Infugem ($C_9H_{11}F_2N_3O_4$) is a prescription medicine used to treat cancer symptoms such as pancreatic, non-small cells lung, breast, bladder and ovarian cancers. Chemically it is pyrimidine nucleoside 2', 2'- difluoro-2-deoxycytidine.

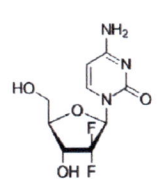

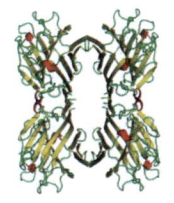

Gemcitabine ($C_9H_{11}F_2N_3O_4$)   Lectins (Proteins that binds to Carbohydrates)

Vitis vinifera

(English: Grapes)- (Urdu: Angoor)

The antioxidant activity of Vitis vinifera of the Vitaceae family, seed extracts are highly dependent on extraction solvent and temperature. The most abundant individual polyphenolic compound is catechin, making 45.11 per cent of the total phenolic content, followed by epicatechin, procyanidin B2 ($C_{30}H_{26}H_{12}$), gallic acid, gallocatechin, epicatechin gallate. Recent scientific studies have identified some grape varieties, with high antioxidant activities and have shown that their high antioxidant potential might be due to their phenolic and flavonoid contents. The aqueous extracts of Vitis vinifera seed and peel also strongly indicate a potent cytotoxic effect on skin cancer cell lines.

---

[7] J. Nazaruk and P. Orlikoski, Natural Product research, (2016), Vol.30, Issue 4, Page 373.

Catechin ($C_{15}H_{14}O_6$)

Procyanidin B2 ($C_{30}H_{26}H_{12}$)

Zingiber officinale

(English: Ginger)- (Urdu: Adrak)

The active ingredient of Zingiber officinalis of the Zingiberaceae family, is gingerol. Pharmacological experiments show that ginger might inhibit tumour growth in human beings. Researchers have found that gingerol causes cancer cell death, reduces inflammation and improves immune function. Research also indicates that gingerol might offer protection from colon cancer as well. It has also been reported that ginger extract may have a chemotherapeutic affect in treating liver cancer. A National Cancer Institute (UK) study found that if patients took 0.5 to 1.0 g of ginger for three days, before and after chemotherapy, along with antinausea medications, nausea was reduced by an additional 40 per cent.

Medicinal Plants in Holy Scriptures

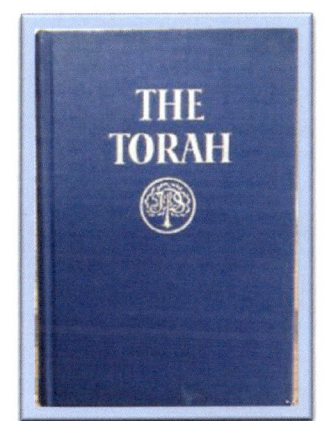

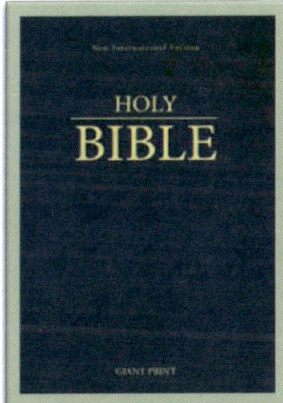

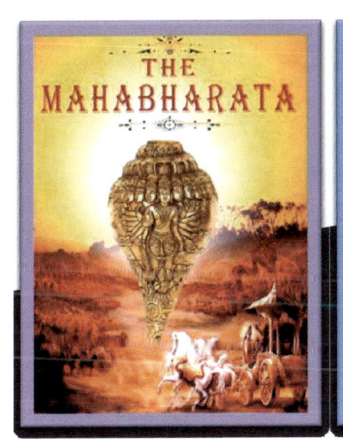

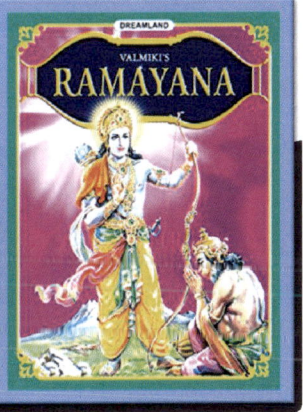

Medicinal Plants in Holy Scriptures

Alkaloids

Conium maculatum (Urdu Name: Qonyun)

The Hebrew word 'rosh' is variously translated as Hemlock by Jewish scholars. The Poison Hemlock 'Conium maculatum' of the Apiaceae family is mentioned three times in The Bible (Deuteronomy 32:32 - 33), (Lamentations 3:19 - 20) and (Matthew 27:33 - 34).

Hyoscyamus niger (Urdu Name: Ajwain-e-Khurasani)

Hyoscyamus aureus (Henbane) of the Solanaceae family is mentioned once in The Bible and the plant is identified with the Hebrew word 'shikrona'(Joshua 15:11).

Mandragora officinarum (Urdu Name: Mardum Giyah)

In Hebrew, Mandrake is 'dudaim' meaning 'love plant' and is mentioned three times in The Bible (Genesis 30:14 - 15), (Songs of Solomon 7:13) and (Issachar 1:3 - 5). However, some Jewish scholars believe that the plant is mentioned only in Genesis and the Song of Solomon.

Papaver somniferum (Urdu Name: Afiyun)

The common Poppy, Papaver rhoeas of the Papaveraceae family is mentioned twice in The Bible as a field flower (Isaiah 40:6 - 8) and (I Peter 1:24 - 25).

Piper longum (Urdu Name: Filfil Daraz)

Piper longum is mentioned once in the Indian epic, Ramayan (3.11 .74).

Sida cordifolia (Urdu Name: Beej-Band)

The Mallow plant is mentioned once in The Bible **(Job 6:6 - 7), but that is Malva** sylvestris (Beej-Band or Loofa in Urdu) **of the Malvaceae family.**

Carbohydrates

Citrus x aurantifolia (Urdu Name: Nibu)

The Citrus tree is mentioned once in The Bible, but that is Citrus medica (Chakotra in Urdu) of the Rutaceae family (II Kings 4:39 - 40).

Ficus carica (Urdu Name: Anjeer)

There is a chapter in the Quran named after the Fig tree. In The Holy Quran, the Fig is mentioned in Surah At-Tin's first verse (95: 1).

"By the Fig and the Olive; and by the Mount Sinai"

The Fig is also mentioned three times in The Bible. It is the first fruit to be mentioned by name in The Bible, in Adam and Eve's story (Genesis 3:6 - 7), (Song of Solomon 222: 13) and (Matthew 24:32).

The Ficus tree is mentioned twice in the Indian epic, Ramayan (3.73.3) and (4.1.79) and on one occasion in the great epic, Mahabharata (VII 153: 24).

Musa acuminate (Urdu Name: Kela)

The Banana is mentioned in The Holy Quran as one of the fruits of paradise (56: 29).

Phoenix sylvestris (Urdu Name: Khajur)

In The Holy Quran, Dates are mentioned at several occasions (6: 141), (13: 7), (16: 11), (16: 67), (17: 91), (18: 32), (19: 25), (2: 19), (26: 148), (36: 34), (50: 10), (55: 11), (55: 68) and (80: 29).

The date palm is one of the Holy Land's most ancient fruit trees and it is mentioned twice in The Bible and the tree identified as Phoenix dactylifera of the Palmae family (Psalms 92:1 2 - 14) and (John 12:12 - 13). The plant is also cited once, in the Indian epic, Ramayan. (3. 15. 16).

Triticum aestivum (Urdu Name: Gundum)

The word 'Grain' is mentioned at several occasions in different verses of The Holy Quran (2:261), (6: 59), (6:95), (6:99), (21:47), (31:16), (36:33), (50:9), (55:12), (78:15) and (80:27).

The Bible has mentioned it twice and the plant is identified as 'Triticum durum' of the Poaceae family (Deuteronomy 8:8) and (I Kings 5:10 - 11).

Vitis vinifera (Urdu Name: Angoor)

The word(s) Grape appears eight times in The Holy Quran (6:99), (12:49), (13:4), (16:11), (16:67), (17:91), (23:19) and (80:28).

The words 'grapes and vines' are mentioned three times in The Bible (Deuteronomy 8:7-8), (Amos 9:13) and John (15:1 - 2)

'Noah was the first tiller of the soil. He planted a vineyard (Genesis, 8:20).'

Apis mellifera (Urdu Name: Shahed) (Biological Origin)

The sixteenth Sura of the Holy Quran is An Nahl (The Honey Bees). Honey is mentioned twice in The Holy Quran, described as a healing source, (16:68) and (47:15).

"The description of the Paradise promised to the righteous is that in it are rivers of fresh water, rivers of milk that never changes in taste, rivers of wine delicious to drink, and rivers of pure honey." (Sura Mohammod 47-15)

Honey is also mentioned several times in The Bible. For example, in one of The Bible verses, Honey was a symbol of good health for Samuel (one of Hazrat Noah's sons in The Hebrew Bible (Exodus 3:6 - 8), (1 Samuel 14:24 - 27), (Genesis 43:11), (Proverbs 24:13), (Matthew 3:1 - 4) and (Revelation 10:7 - 11).

Fixed Oils

Eruca sativa (Urdu Name: Jarjir)

In The Bible, the plant is mentioned as 'oroth.' In Arabic, it is called 'Jarjir and in the Talmud, it appears as 'gargir.' Eruca sativa of the Brassicaceae family is mentioned once in The Bible (II Kings 4:39 - 40).

Gossypium herbaceum (Urdu Name: Binola)

White cotton, the Hebrew 'Karpas,' is mentioned only once in The Bible (Esther 1:5 - 6).

The Cotton tree is also mentioned on one occasion in the Indian epic, Ramayan, but that is a red cotton tree named Bombax ceiba (Shalmali in Hindi and Urdu) of the Malvaceae family (4. 1 . 82).

Linum usitatissimum (Urdu Name: Alsi)

Flax seeds are cited twice in The Bible and the plant is identified as Linum usitatissimum of the Linaceae family. (Exodus 9:31) and (John 19:40).

"Now the Flax and the barley were ruined, for the barley was in the ear, and the Flux was in the bud" (Exodus 9:31).

Olea europaea (Urdu Name: Zaitoon)

The word 'Olive' is mentioned six times in The Holy Quran (6:99), (6:141), (16:11), (24:35), (80:29) and (95:1).

"He causes the crops therewith to grow for you, and olives, and date palms, and grapevines, and all the fruits. Surely, in that, there is a sign for a people who ponder." (Sura Nahl).

The Olive is also mentioned twice in The Bible (Judges 9:8 - 9) and (Romans 11:17 - 18).

Prunus amygdalus (Urdu Name: Badam)

Almond is mentioned twice in The Bible (Numbers 17:18) and Ecclesiastes 12:5). The Hebrew word 'shaked' (meshukadim) also appears as an almond tree or its branch and fruit in the Bible. The term 'Almond shaked' is used three times in one verse of Exodus (25: 33 - 34). Genesis (30:37) gives the name 'luz' to the almond tree.

Ricinus communis (Urdu Name: Arand)

The Castor plant is mentioned once in The Bible and identified as Ricinus communis of the Euphorbiaceae family (Jonah, 4:6 - 7).

"Then the Lord providing a leafy plant and made it grow up over Jonah (a Prophet in the Hebrew Bible and The Quran, Dhul-Nūn Alaihis salam in Arabic, Sura-Anbiya, Verse 87) to give shade for his head to ease his discomfort, and Jonah was very happy about the plant." (Jonah, 4:6 - 7).

Glycosides

Aloe barbadensis (Urdu Name: Ailwa)

The Aloes are mentioned twice in The Bible besides Myrrh and Cassia (Psalms 45:8) and (John 19:39 - 40).

Brassica nigra (Urdu Name: Rai)

In Arabic, the mustard seed is called 'Khardal.' The seed has been mentioned twice in The Holy Quran (21:47) and (31:31-16). "So no one shall be wronged in the least. Even if it (a deed) is to the measure of a mustard seed, We will bring it forth, and We are enough to take account."(Sura Al-Anbya 21:47).

The Greek word 'Sinapis;' is undoubtedly Mustard. Mustard is not quoted in The Torah (Old Testament), but it is often referred to in The Mishnah (the first part of the Talmud). The Brassica nigra seed is mentioned three times in The New Testament (Mark 4:30 - 32), (Matthew 13:31) and (Luke 14:19).

Cassia fistula (Urdu Name: Amaltaas)

Cassia fistula of the Caesalpiniaceae family is cited three times in the Indian epic, Ramayan (3.73.3), (4.1.73) and (4.40.56) and on one occasion in the great epic, Mahabharata (XIII 54. 5).

Cassia senna (Urdu Name: Senna Makki)

The 'Burning Bush' is mentioned twice in The Bible (Exodus 3:2 - 4) and Acts (7:30). Jewish scholars believed that the Senna was the plant. Some scholars also believe that, as there is no hint in the Hebrew text that the 'Sneh' was a thorny bush and also no plants in the Sinai or anywhere else are not consumed when burnt, 'Sneh' may be identified linguistically only.

In The Torah (3:2) and Bible (7:30 - 33), the word 'Bush' is used, whereas, in The Quran (28:30), it is a tree. The Arabic translation of Tree is 'shajar.' The literal meaning of 'shajar' is joint or attached. One may allude to husband and wife as 'shajar' because they are connected to each other. The Bush in The Bible and the Tree in the Quan are attached to the ground. According to Muhammad Asad, 'Tree referred to in The Quranic version is obviously identical to the burning 'Bush' of The Bible (The Massage of The Quran, DarAl-Andalus Gibraltar, 1980, Page 593).

Cinnamomum zeylanicum (Urdu Name: Darchini)

The much-discussed identification of the biblical 'kinnamon' as Cinnamomum has been clarified and confirmed by various scholars.

Cinnamon is mentioned two times in The Bible, along with myrrh, aloes and frankincense (Proverb 7:17 - 18) and (Revelation 18:12 - 13). Moreover, The Lord spoke unto Moses, saying,

"Take the finest spices of liquid myrrh five hundred shekels (1 shekel= 11.4grams) and of sweet-smelling cinnamon half as much" (Exodus 30:22 - 25).

Cinnamon is also mentioned four times in the Indian epic, Ramayan (3.15.17), (3.73.4), (4.1.78) and (4.1.83).

Citrullus colocynthis

Citrullus colocynthis of the Cucurbitaceae family is mentioned in Sura As -Saffat.
"Is this the better welcome or the tree of Zaqqum?" (Sura Al-Saffat 37:62)

Echinops echinatus (Urdu Name: Barham Dandi)

In The Bible, the words' thorns' and 'barriers' each are mentioned once and the Jewish scholars believed that the plant is one of the Echinops' species (Echinops viscosus) of the Asteraceae family (Judges 8:7) and (Judges 8:16).

Morus alba (Urdu Name: Shahtut)

Various spices identified as 'Morus nigra' of the Moraceae family are mentioned three times in The Bible (Isaiah 40:20), (I Maccabees 6:34) and (Luke 17:5 - 6). For mulberry words, *'sycamine'* is mentioned in Luke and *'mesukan'* is used in Isaiah.

Rubia cordifolia (Urdu Name: Majith)

Rubia cordifolia is mentioned once in the Indian epic, Ramayan (4.1.82).

Ruta graveolens (Urdu Name: Sadab)

The plant 'Rue,' Ruta chalepensis of the Rutaceae family, appears once in The Bible, under its Greek name 'Peganon' (Luke 11:42).

Symplocos racemosa (Urdu: Lodh Pathani)

The Symplocos racemosa plant is mentioned twice in the Indian epic, Ramayan (4.1.79) and (4.43.13).

Saponins

Trigonella foenum-graeum (Urdu Name: Methi)

The Prophet Muhammad (peace and blessings be upon him) spoke about the healing properties of fenugreek (Helba) in the 7th century. His (PBUH) statement: 'Heal yourself with 'Helba!' clearly indicates the healing properties of this plant (Zaad-ul Ma'ad by Ibn e Qayyim[8] (d. 1350 AD).

Gums and Mucilage

Acacia arabica (Urdu Name: Gond Kiker)

The Gum tree is mentioned once in The Holy Quran, but that is Gum Acacia (Mimosa arabica of the Mimosaceae family). Some scholars believe it was a banana tree; regardless of the nature of the Tree, Acacia[9] is thought to be the Tree of Bai'at Rizwan (Pledge of Allegiance (Al-Fath 48:18).

The Acacia wood and the Hebrew word 'shittim' for Acacia each, is mentioned once in The Bible Joshua (2:1). The plant is identified as Acacia raddiana of the Fabaceae family.

The Lord said to Moses: (Exodus 25:1). "Have them make an ark of acacia wood — two and a half cubits long, a cubit and a half wide and a cubit and a half high." (Exodus 25:10).

Acacia is also mentioned in the great epic, Mahabharata at one occasion (VII. 153.24).

---

[8] Shams al-Dīn Abū 'Abd Allāh Muḥammad ibn Abī Bakr ibn Ayyūb al-Zur'ī l-Dimashqī l-Ḥanbalī known as Ibn e Qayyim was a student of Taqī ad-Dīn Aḥmad ibn Abd al-Halim ibn Abd al-Salam al-Numyri al-Ḥarrānī simply known as Imam Ibn Taymiyya (d. 1328 AD). Ibn Taymiyya was a Syrian scholar, theologian, jurist, reformer and moralist. His declarations of faith 'Hamawiyya' and 'Wasitiyya' earned him prison with his student Ibn e Qayyim. Another famous disciple of Ibn Taymiyya was Ibn Kathir (Abu al-Fiḍā 'Imād Ad-Din Ismā'īl ibn 'Umar ibn Kathīr al-Qurashī Al-Damishqī D. 1373 AD), a Syrian theologian and historian of 'Mumluk era').

[9] Ahmad Y. al-Hassan and Donald R.Hill, Technology-An Illustrated History, page 206.

Aegle marmelos (Urdu Name: Bail-l-Giri)

This plant is mentioned three times in the Indian epic, Ramayan (4.1.78), (3.11.74) and (1.24.15) and once in the great epic, Mahabharata (III.174.23).

Bambusa arundinacea (Urdu Name: Banslowchan)

The plant is mentioned twice in the great epic, Mahabharata (XIII. 109.47) and (II. 48.2) and on one occasion in Ramayan (3.15.21).

Cordia latifolia (Urdu Name: Sapistan)

The Cordia plant is mentioned twice in the Indian epics, Ramayan (4.1.81) and (4.42.7) and at one occasion in Mahabharata (XIII. 54.4).

Linum usitatissimum (Urdu Name: Alsi)

Flax was the most important plant fibre in Biblical times because it was used to make linen. The Linum usitatissimum plant is mentioned twice in The Bible (Exodus 9:31) and (John 19:40).

The 'Fine linen' (Esther 1:5 - 6), mentioned in The Bible, has been satisfactorily proved to have been spun from Flax. It was the plant to which the plague of hail (thunderstorm of hail and fire) proved so disastrous.

Ocimum basilicum (Urdu Name: Faranj-Mushk)

Ocimum basilicum plant is mentioned once in The Holy Quran's Sura Ar-Rehman (55:12 - 13). The plant is also mentioned once in the Indian epic, Ramayan (3.15.18).

Resins

Alhagi maurorum (Urdu Name: Taranjebin)

The plant is mentioned three times in The Holy Quran as a sweet Manna source (2:57), (7:160), (20:80). "We sent down manna and quails upon you: Eat of the good things wherewith We have provided you" (2:57).

Boswellia glabra (Urdu Name: Loban)

The plant is mentioned three times in The Bible (Exodus 30:34-35), (Matthew 2:10 - 11) and (Luke 1:8 - 10).

Commiphora molmol (Urdu Name: Murr)

According to the Hadith of Hazrat Muhammed (PBUH), narrated by Abu Nuaim on Abban bin Saleh bin Anas's[10] (795 A D) authority, Muhammad (PBUH) said, 'Fumigate your houses with mugwort, myrrh and thyme' (Kanz al-Ummal Fee Sunan wa al Af' al 28 316).

Myrrh, a resin, is mentioned twice in The Bible and it is connected with the birth and crucifixion of Jesus (Hazrat Essa Alaihis salam ibn Maryam bint Imran, Christians called him as Joachim), (Psalm 45:8) and (Matthew 2:11).

Ferula galbaniflua (Urdu Name: Jawashir)

Galbanum, a gum resin, is mentioned twice in The Bible as one of the four Holy incense ingredients (Exodus 30:34) and (Ecclesiasticus 24: 14 - 15).

'When God listed offerings for the Tabernacle (House of worship), He included spices for the fragrant incense' (Exodus, 25:6).

Garcinia morella (Urdu Name: Usarah-e-Rewand)

Garcinia is mentioned three times in the Indian epic, Ramayan (3.15.16), (4.40.56) and (4.42.11).

Pinus roxburghii (Urdu Name: Behroza)

The Pine plant is mentioned twice in The Bible (I Kings 6:23, 31) and Nehemiah 8:15).

Pistacia lentiscus (Urdu Name: Mastaghi)

The Tree of Mastic is mentioned twice in The Bible (Genesis 35:4) and Joshua 24:26). Several Biblical stories are connected with the Pistacia palaestina.

"So they gave Jacob (Hazrat Ya'qūb bin Hazrat Isḥāq bin Hazrat Ibrāhīm Alaihis salam) all the foreign gods they had and the rings in their ears and Jacob buried them under the Oak at Shechem[11] (Genesis 35:4).

---

[10] Mālik ibn Anas, in full Abū 'Abd Allāh Mālik ibn Anas ibn al-Ḥārith al-Aṣbaḥī, he is the author of one of the highly respected and the oldest surviving compendia of the Islamic law book 'Al Muwatta'.

[11] Nablus is a city on the West Bank, 65 km north of Jerusalem. Neapolis, along with most of Palestine was conquered by the Muslims under Khalid ibn al Walid (d. 642 AD) a general of Rashidun (al-Khilāfah ar-Rāšidah, 632-661 AD) army of Hazrat Umar Ibn Khattab (d. 644 AD) in 636 AD, after the Battle of Yarmouk (August 636 AD).

Commiphora stocksiana (Urdu Name: Balsan)

Balsam, a resin plant, is mentioned once in The Bible. (Song of Solomon 5:1). In the Talmud, Balsam appears as an ointment (Keritot 5b), a highly praised Jericho (a city in Palestine) product.

Liquidambar orientalis (Urdu Name: Maya Ambar Desi)

The famous German biblical scholar Paul Anton de Lagarde[12] (1872 - 1891 AD) accepted that the Greek name 'Storax' derives from the Hebrew word 'Tzore.

' The balsam-resin is mentioned twice in The Bible (Genesis 37:25 and Jeremiah 8:22) and the plant is identified as an exclude of the Liquidambar orientalis tree of the Hamamelidaceae family.

Tannins

Acacia catechu (Urdu Name: Katha)

Acacia is mentioned once in the epic, Ramayan (3.5.18).

Bauhinia variegate (Urdu Name: Kachnar)

The plant is mentioned once in the Indian epic, Ramayan (4.1.80). It is also cited at one occasion in the great epic, Mahabharata (VII. 153. 24).

Butea monosperma (Urdu Name: Palas)

Butea monosperma is one of the sacred trees worshipped in India and it is mentioned three times in the Indian epic, Ramayan (4.1.75), (4.1.82) and (3.15.18).

Lawsonia inermis (Urdu Name: Mehndhi)

Henna is not mentioned anywhere in The Holy Quran. However, its use is referred to several times in the Hadith literature 'Sayings of The Prophet Muhammad (PBUM), (Musnad Ahmad Ibn Hanbal, Vol. 1, P. 99), (Abu Dawood), (Ibn Majah, Sahih, vol. 2, P. 519) (Sahih Muslim), etc.

---

[12] Paul de Lagarde was a German biblical schlor and orietalist , some time regarded as one of the greatest orietalists of the 19th century.

Henna is mentioned once in The Bible. "My beloved is to me a cluster of henna blossoms from the vineyards of En Gedi" (Songs of Solomon 1:14).

Lawsonia inermis is also cited on one occasion in the Indian epic, Ramayan (4.1.82).

Punica granatum (Urdu Name: Annar)

The Pomegranate fruit is mentioned three times in The Quran (6:99), (6:141) and (55:68).

"And He is The (One) Who has brought into being gardens trellised and untrellised and the palm-trees and plantation of different crops and the olives and the pomegranates" (Sura Al An'am: 141).

The plant (fruit) is also mentioned twice in The Bible (Numbers 13:23) and (Song of Solomon 4:3). "When they reached the Valley of Eshkol, they cut off a branch bearing a single cluster of grapes. Two of them carried it on a pole between them, along with some pomegranates and figs" (Numbers 13:23).

Quercus baloot (Urdu Name: Shah-Baloot)

The Hebrew word 'allon' with many citations in The Bible, should generally be translated as 'Oak,' mentioned three times in The Bible (Genesis 35:8), (Hosea 4:13) and (Amos 2:9).

Salix alba (Urdu Name: Bed Mushk)

Willow (Salix) is also acknowledged in Psalms (137:1-2) in the same verses as

"By the river of Babylon,[13] we sat and wept when we remembered Zion. We hanged our harps upon the Willows in the midst thereof."

Saraca indica (Urdu Name: Ashoka)

The plant is mentioned several times in the Indian epic, Ramayan (3.11.74), (4.1.79),. It is also mentioned at one occasion in the great epic, Mahabharata (XIII. 54.4).

---

[13] Noah's great-grandson, Nimrod, was the first mighty man of the Bible (Genesis 10:10) and the Bible says "Babel was one of the towns that encompassed the beginning of Nimrod's kingdom in the land of Shinar." (Present- day Iraq).

In Ramayan, the plant is mentioned in the garden of Ashoka trees where Hanuman, son of Vayu, first met Sita, daughter of Bhumi.

Terminalia arjuna (Urdu Name: Arjuna)

The hero of the famous epic, Mahabharata 'Arjuna' (meaning shinning), was named after this Tree because of its protective effects. The plant is mentioned once in the Indian epic, Ramayan (1.24.15).

Terminalia belerica (Urdu Name: Bahira)

This Tree, in Sanskrit, is Bibhita and Bibhitaka (fearless), is avoided by the Hindus of Northern India, who will not sit in its shade as it is supposed to be inhabited by demons. The plant is mentioned once in the great epic, Mahabharata (IX. 36.58).

Ziziphus jujube (Urdu Name: Unnab)

Jujube is mentioned twice in the Holy Quran (34:16) and (53:12 - 15).

The plant Ziziphus spina-christi of the Rhamnaceae family is mentioned three times in The Bible (Judges 9:14 - 15), (Matthew 27:27) and (John 19:5).

It is believed locally to be the very Tree from which Jesus' Crown of Thorns was made. However, in some books, the plant was Euphorbia milii of the Euphorbiaceae family.

Ziziphus jujube is also cited once in the Indian epic, Ramayan (1.24.16) and three times in the famous epic, Mahabharata (III.174.23), (VII. 153.24) and (IX. 36.58).

Volatile Oils

Allium cepa (Urdu Name: Piyaz)

The Onion is mentioned once in The Holy Quran with other plants, cucumber, wheat and lentils (2:61).

"O Moses, we can never endure one (kind of) food. So call upon your Lord to bring forth for us from the earth its green herbs and its cucumbers and its garlic and its lentils and onions."

The Onion is cited only on one occasion in The Bible, only in the passage quoted, where the longing of the Israelites of the Exodus, for remembered foods, is articulated (Numbers, 11:5 - 6).

Allium sativum (Urdu Name: Lehsan

Garlic is widely known as 'Thum' or 'Fum' in Arabic. The Arabic word 'Foomiha' has been used in The Holy Quran. Garlic is mentioned just once, in The Quran (2:61).

The translation of the Hebrew word 'Shumim' is garlic and is mentioned on one occasion in The Bible. (Numbers 11:5 - 6).

"We remember the fish we ate in Egypt at no cost—also the cucumbers, melons, leeks, onions and garlic. But now we have lost our appetite; we never see anything but this manna!" (Numbers 11:5 – 6).

Anethum graveolens (Urdu Name: Shabbat)

Dill is mentioned once in The Bible, in the New Testament, together with mint and Cumin (Matthew 23:23). In post-biblical literature, dill is named 'Sheveth,' which is identical to its Arabic name 'sabth.'

Carum carvi (Urdu Name: Zirah Siyah)

The Hebrew word 'Kamon' as Cumin is similar to the Arabic 'Kemun' and is mentioned once in The Bible with Mint and Dill (Matthew 23:23).

Cinnamomum camphora (Urdu Name: Kafur)

The plant identified as Dryobalanops camphora of the Dipterocarpaceae family is mentioned once in The Holy Quran

'The virtuous shall drink from a cup tempered with camphor water' (Surah Al-Insan: 76: 5).

Cinnamomum cassia (Urdu Name: Taj/Darchini)

Cassia oil was a precious perfume, one of the Holy oil ingredients used to anoint the Tent of the congregation' (Tabernacle) and the High Priest Aaron (Hazrat Harun, younger brother of Hazrat Musa) and his sons (Eleazar, Abihu, Nadab and Ithamar).

Cinnamon is mentioned three times in The Bible and the plant is identified as Cinnamomum cassia of the Lauraceae family (Exodus 30:24), (Job 42:14) and Psalms (45:7 - 8).

"And He called the name of the first Jemimah and the name of the second Keziah; and the name of the third Keren-happuch" (Job 42:14). Job[14] (Hazrat Ayub Alaihis salam) is a prophet in Islam and is mentioned in The Quran.

Coriandrum sativum (Urdu Name: Kishneez)

The Bible tells us that the famous heavenly bread, of the Israelites in the desert the manna was like the seeds of Coriander and it is mentioned once in The Bible (Exodus 16:31).

Cuminum cyminum (Urdu Name: Zirah Safaid)

The plant is mentioned once in The Bible (Matthew 23:23). The Nigella sativa of the Ranunculaceae family, known as Black Cumin, is also mentioned on one occasion in The Bible (Isaiah 28:27).

Juniperus communis (Urdu Name: Abhal)

The Eastern Savin tree, identified as Juniperus excels of the Cupressaceae family, is mentioned three times in The Bible (I Kings 9:11), (Ezekiel 27:3 - 5) and (Zechariah 11:1 - 2).

O Tyre, you have said, "I am perfect in beauty." "Your borders are in the heart of the seas; your builders made perfect your body. They made all your planks of 'fir' from Senir; They took a 'Cedar' from Lebanon to make you a mast. (Ezekiel 27:3 - 5).

Valeriana officinalis (Urdu Name: Baalchar)

Nardostachya jatamansi, a genus of Valeriana of the Valerianaceae/Caprifoliaceae family (spikenard), is mentioned three times in The Bible (Song of Solomon 1:12), (Mark 14:3) and (John 12:3) ***Also mentioned on Page 496.

---

[14] The Hebrew Book of Job is part of Ketuvim (the third and the final section contains thirteen books of the Hebrew bible 'Tanakh') of the Jewish Bible. Not much is known about Job based on the Masoretic text of the Jewish Bible.

Mentha piperita (Urdu Name: Pudina)

Mentha plant Mentha longifolia of the Lamiaceae family is mentioned once in The Bible along with dill and Cumin (Matthew 23:23).

"Woe to you, teachers of the law and Pharisees, you hypocrites! You give a tenth of your spices-Mint, Dill and Cumin" (Matthew 23:23).

Pinus palustris (Urdu Name: Sanobar)

Branches of a Pine tree are mentioned twice in The Bible and the plant species, identified as Pinus halepensis, of the Pinaceae family (I Kings 6:23,31) and (Nehemiah 8:15).

" Go out of the hills and bring branches of olive, wild olive, myrtle, palm and other leafy trees to make booths, as it is written(Nehemiah 8:15)."

Pterocarpus santalinus (Urdu Name: Sandal Surkh)

Red Sandal is mentioned once in the Indian epic, Ramayan (3.73.5).

Rosa damascene (Urdu Name: Gul-e-Surkh)

People call this plant the Flower of Prophet Mohammad (PBUH) because they believe it has a pleasant aroma that reminds them of Prophet Mohammad (PBUH).

The Rose's prominent symbolic place in Judaism, comes from Solomon's Biblical Song. (2:1).

The Hebrew word 'vered,' which can be identified with the Rose, is mentioned only in post-biblical literature, several times in the Talmud. However, a 'Rose plant' is mentioned at one occasion in The Bible. The plant is identified as Rosa Phoenicia of the Rosaceae family (Ecclesiasticus, 24:14).

Santalum album (Urdu Name: Sandal Safaid)

The plant is mentioned twice in the Indian epic, Ramayan. (3.15.18) and (4.1.82).

"Lord Krishna and Lord Balarama, on their way to the Vrishni (an ancient Vedic clan) Kingdom, came across a dwarf named Kubja (a hunchbacked woman of Mathura, Uttar-Pradesh, India) carrying a paste of Sandalwood" (Bhagavata or history devotees of Vishnu).

Terpenoids

Artemisia absinthium (Urdu Name: Afsanteen)

The Hebrew word 'Laanah' appearing eight times in The Bible has educed much dispute because there is no linguistic or contextual evidence that 'Laanah' is a bitter plant. Yet, its identification with wormwood is strongly supported by many Jewish scholars.

Artemisia herba-alba (Wormwood) of the Asteraceae family is mentioned twice in The Hebrew Bible.

"O you turn justice to Wormwood (sour) and cast down righteousness to the earth" (Amos 5:7).

Therefore this is what the Lord Almighty says concerning the prophets:

"Behold, I will feed them with wormwood and give them poisoned water to drink" (Jeremiah 23:15).

Butea monosperma (Urdu Name: Palas)

Butea tree is one of the sacred trees worshipped in India. Hindus traditionally use a bright yellow to a deep orange-red dye called 'Kesari' to mark the forehead. The plant is mentioned three times in the Indian epic, Ramayan (4.1.75), (4.1.82) and (3.15.18).

"On the mountainsides, Soumitri (Palas), all over fully flowered are the exquisite Kimshuka trees." (Kishkindha Kanda Sarg 1.75).

Crocus sativus (Urdu Name: Zafran)

Saffron is mentioned once in the Biblical love poem, 'The Song of Solomon' (4:13 - 14), along with henna, calamus and cinnamon.

" Your shoots are an orchard of pomegranates with all choicest fruits, henna with nard, nard and saffron, calamus and cinnamon, with every kind of incense tree, with myrrh and aloes and all the finest spices." (The Song of Solomon' 4:13)

Crocus sativus has also mentioned in Talmudic (the book of Jewish Laws) texts.

There is no reference to saffron in The Holy Quran, but Islamic traditions (Hadith, statements or actions of Prophet Muhammad PBUH) include the plant frequently due to its medical, esthetic and edible properties.

The word 'Saffron' appear twelve times in twelve Hadiths in 'Sahih Al-Bukhari' (the book complied by Persian Islamic scholar Muhammed Ibn Ismail al-Bukhari, also known as Imam Bukhari[15] (d. 870 AD, 256 AH).

Lagenaria siceraria (Urdu Name: Kaddu/Louki)

Lagenaria siceraria fruit is mentioned in The Quran, which says,

"And We caused a gourd plant to grow wisdom" (37:146).

The plant 'Bottle Gourd' (Louki in Urdu and Delaath in post-biblical literature) is identified as Lagenaria siceraria of the Cucurbitaceae family. It is cited on one occasion in The Torah (Joshua 15:37 - 38).

"Zenan, Hadashah, Migdal-gad, Dilean[16], Mizpeh, Joktheel, Lachish".

"And The Lord God prepared a gourd and made it to come over Jonah, that might be a shadow over his head, to deliver him from grief" (Jonah 4:6).

Although there are some differences, the basic story of Jonah (Hazrat Yunus Alaihis salam) is very similar in both books (The Torah and The Quran). The tenth Sura of The Holy Quran is al- Yunus. The book of Jonah is a book of Nevi'im (Prophets) is the second main division of the Hebrew Bible, 'Tanakh[17].'

Note: Some Jewish scholars believed that the plant was Ricinus communis (Arand in Urdu) of the Euphorbiaceae family.

---

[15] From Bukhara, a city of Khurasan at that time, now in Uzbekistan.
[16] The town-name of 'Dilean' is undoubtedly derived from 'delaath' a term occurring in post-biblical literature for the 'Bottle Gourd.

[17] Books of the Tanakh, Torah (Five Books), Nevi'im (Ninteen books) and Ketuvi (Eleven Books).

Historical Facts of the Medicinal Plants

Alkaloids

Achillea millefolium (Urdu Name: Biranjasif)

Achillea refers to Achilles[18] (he was a hero of the Trojan War), using the species to treat his fellow soldier's wounds during the War. The word millefolium refers to its 'many leaves' or 'thousand leaves.' It is a promising plant, bringing good luck and fortune, in the Chinese tradition.

Aconitum napellus (Urdu Name: Bichnag)

During the ancient Roman period (753 BC 476 AD) of European history, the plant was often used to kill criminals and enemies. By the end of the period, it was banned and anyone growing Aconitum napellus was liable for death sentence. Aconitum was well known in antiquity. Medea (an ancient Greek tragedy) is supposed to have murdered her son with it. It is also reported that Aristotle, a Greek philosopher (d. 322), died of aconite poisoning.

Adhatoda vasica (Urdu Name: Bansa)

The famous ancient Indian saying, 'No man suffering from phthisis (pulmonary tuberculosis) needs despair as long as the Vasaka plant exists.'

Areca catechu (Urdu Name: Supari)

In the Indo-Pak subcontinent, Betel quid chewing is at least 2,000 years old, whereas tobacco was introduced around the sixteenth century. Areca nut found its place in the social and cultural functions of the Indo-Pak subcontinent. The betel nut's presence was a must in the ceremonial social and cultural functions, as betel nuts were believed to increase prosperity. The nut was offered to guests, along with a betel leaf, as a mark of respect.

Areca nut is also one of South Asia's famous chewing gum ingredients called Paan. In the Indo-Pak subcontinent, Areca catechu is the fourth most widely used substance after tobacco, alcohol and caffeine, affecting approximately 20 per cent of the world's population.

---

[18] The warrior Achilles is one of the great heroes of Greek mythology. According to legend, Achilles was extraordinarily strong, courageous and loyal, but he had one vulnerability-his 'Achilles heel'.

Atropa belladonna (Urdu Name: Luffah)

The beauty tonic of this herb was used to dilate women's pupils, a look and practice that was seen as fashionable at that time. From this popularity as a cosmetic, the Atropa (Deadly Nightshade) established its formal name, 'Atropa belladonna,' meaning 'Beautiful Lady' in Italian, where 'Atropos' is the name of the Greek goddess of fate and destiny also known as Moirae. The names of Moirae are 'Clotho,' the spinner, 'Lachesis,' the allotter and 'Atropos,' the inflexible.

The Romans used Belladonna as a biological weapon to contaminate their enemy food reserves. The Nightshade has been a killer of kings, emperors and warriors throughout history, as Macbeth (1793 - 1873 AD), King of Scotland, was laid to rest in the hand of the Deadly Nightshade. The wives of Roman emperors Augustus (23 BC) and Claudius (10 BC) poisoned them with atropine, an alkaloidal component found in belladonna.

In Shakespeare's (d. 1616) play, Macbeth, the Scottish army defeats the Danes by contaminating their liquor supply with belladonna, inducing deep, unconscious sleep and murdering them in their unfortunate state.

During World War II (1939-1945 AD), the Germans invented a deadly, odourless nerve gas and the only antidote to its paralysing effects turned out to be the atropine (Tropane alkaloids).

Belladonna is also one of the ingredients of the famous strong poison, Aqua Tofana.

Berberis aristata (Urdu Name: Rasaut)

Berberry has played a prominent role in herbal healing for more than 2,500 years. Rhazes (d. 925 AD) was the first to introduce the medicinal properties of Berberis aristata and considered its use to be helpful for human beings. The plant is also mentioned in Ibn al Baytar's (d. 1248 AD) treatise Jâmi mufradat al-adwiya wa-'l-aghdiya.

Camellia sinensis (Urdu Name: Chaey)

Tea, likely originated in the Yunnan region, during the Shang dynasty (China) as a medicinal drink.

A Tea plantation in India was introduced in the early 19th century by Robert Bruce (d. 1824 AD), a Scottish gentleman and Maniram Dewan (d. 1858 AD), a nobleman from Assam.

Tea culture is defined by how Tea is made and how people interact with Tea and the aesthetics surrounding Tea drinking. Tea is one of the popular drinks in Pakistan and it is referred to as Chaey. There are many 'Chaey Khanas' (Tea houses) in Pakistan for cultural and social gatherings.

Cephaelis ipecacuanha (Urdu Name: Arq-uz-Zahab)

Ipecacuanha is one of the oldest medicinal plants known to man. In Portuguese, the word 'i-pe-Kaa-guene' (means' road-side-sick' making plant). The plant is mentioned in the famous Ibn Sina's (d. 1037 AD) book Al-Qanoon Fi at-Tibb[19].

Ipecacuanha was known to Europe by the mid 17th century. Nicholas Culpeper (1616 - 1654 AD). An English botanist, herbalist and physician, compared Ipecacuanha to the herb Atriplex hortensis (Orach, English) of the Amaranthaceae family in his book, 'Complete Herbal & English Physician,' published in 1653 AD.

Cinchona officinalis (Urdu Name: Cinchona)

From the 17th century, when the Cinchona plant was introduced into Western medicine, up to the middle of the 20th century, Quinine from Cinchona, was the only effective remedy for malaria.

Claviceps purpurea (Urdu Name: Argot)

St. Anthony's was famous as Anthony the great (d. 365 AD). St. Anthony Fire (SAF) is an illness brought on by the ingestion of fungus-contaminated Rye grain, causing ergot poisoning (egotism). It has recently been postulated that the victims were often thought to be witches during the dark ages. St. Anthony of Egypt, is considered the patron saint of undertakers, gravediggers and cemetery workers because he sold everything he owned and lived in a tomb, at the start of his life's work.

---

[19] Al Qanun Fi Al-Tibb (The Canon of Medicine) was translated into Latin towards the end of the twelfth century CE, and became a reference source for medical studies in the universities of Europe until the end of the seventeenth century. Saint Albert Magnus the great (1280 AD) of Cologne, Germany, owes everything to Ibn-e-Sina.

An outbreak of violent hallucinations among hundreds of residents of Pont St. Esprit in 1951 in the south of France, has also been attributed to egotism. Seven people died.

Coffea arabica (Urdu Name: Kofi)

There is a well-known saying, 'Coffee is a beverage that puts one to sleep when not drunk.' The word coffee entered the English language in 1582, via the Dutch word Koffie, borrowed from the Ottoman Turkish (Khilafat-e-Usmania) word Kahve, which was borrowed from the Arabic 'Qahwah.'

Colchicum autumnale (Urdu Name: Suranjan-e-Shireen)

The Colchicum, also known as Autumn crocus, has a long history as poison. Greek slaves were known to eat the plant to make them sick and even commit suicide.

Conium maculatum (Urdu Name: Qonyun)

Because of its association with the death of Socrates 399 BC (Suqraat in Urdu), Hemlock is one of the most recognised botanicals in ancient medicine. Ancient populations were very aware of Hemlock and its poisonous nature.

Datura stramonium (Urdu Name: Dhaturah)

History states that the herb was taken by Apollo's[20] priests (one of the twelve Olympians) at Delphi in Ancient Greece, to assist them in their prophecies.

In India, the sadhus and yogis smoked the leaves and seeds mixed with 'Ganja' (Cannabis indica). The plant was highly sacred as a powerful aphrodisiac. Powdered seed in butter, was applied topically to invigorate the male genitalia.

In England, Datura stramonium was considered a plant that aided witches in their ill-doings during the witch's time and the wizard hunt. It was exceedingly dangerous to grow Stramonium in one's garden, as it was said to confirm the household's supernatural powers.

Doronicum hookeri (Urdu Name: Darunaj Aqrabi)

Rhizomes of this plant look like the tail of a scorpion named 'Aqrabi' in Arabic.

---

[20] Apollo, sometimes called Phoebus Apollo, was the god of sun, light, harp, music and more. He was often portrayed as being bardic in nature, with a lyre and he was the twin brother to Diana (Greek: Artemis), goddess of the moon and archery. He is served by the Nine Muses.

Erythroxylum coca (Urdu Name: Coca)

For the Andean people (the Andes Mountains of South America), the Coca plant is essential for religious and cultural reasons. Analysis of mummified human remains from Northern Chile, indicate the use of Coca as early as 1000 BC.

Hyoscyamus niger (Urdu Name: Ajwain-e-Khurasani)

The references to this plant are found in 'Arabian Nights[21]' (Alf Laylah wa Laylah) and Anglo-Saxon work on medicine.

The wives of the Roman emperors, Augustus and Claudius, used Hyoscyamus niger (deadly Nightshade) to murder a large number of Romans.

Fumaria officinalis (Urdu Name: Shahtarah)

The great scholar and polymath Abu Rayhan Al-Biruni[22] (973 - 1048 AD) mentioned this plant in his book 'Ketāb al-ṣaydana fi'l tibb'(book of pharmacy in medicine). The formulation of the aromatic water (Arq) of the whole plant of Fumaria is mentioned in Encyclopedia Iranica. There is a long history of usage of this plant by native South Americans, as a stimulant tonic.

Lobelia inflate (Tambahu Jangli)

The plant was used as a traditional medicinal plant by the Cherokee, Iroquois, Penobscot and other indigenous peoples of the United States. The Cherokee burned the foliage as a natural insecticide to smoke out the Mycetophilidae family's flying insects.

---

[21] Is collection of folk tales of Afro-Euro-Eurasian countries complied in Arabic during the Islamic golden age. The work was collected over many centuries by various authors about Shahryar (The King) and Scheherazade (King's wife). This frame story, for the entirety of the work, is the common thread among each edition of Arabian Nights.

[22] Mathematician, Astronomer, physicist, geographer, historian and physician Abu Rehan Muhammad Ibn Ahmad alias Al-Biruni, Latinized as Aliboron, was Iranian, is originally from Khiva (is a city in Uzbekistan). Al-Biruni is considered in the domain of natural science. He left an excellent historical account of India in his book 'Tarikh Al-Hind' (History of India), Kitāb al-ṣaydanah (Pharmacology) etc.

Mandragora officinarum (Urdu Name: Mardum Giyah)

In the past, they often made mandrake into amulets (Taweez) which were believed to bring good fortune and cure sterility. According to superstitious ideas, prevalent people who pulled up this root would go to hell and the mandrake root would scream as it was pulled from the ground, killing anyone who heard it. Thus, people tied the roots to an animal's body and then used the animal to remove the roots from the soil.

Mitragyna speciosa (Urdu Name: Qartum)

The leaves and the plant stigmas resemble a bishop's mitre (ceremonial headdress of bishops).

Nicotiana tabacum (Urdu Name: Tambaku)

From South America, the plant Nicotiana passed to Central America and the Caribbean (from 1500 to 500 BC). The plant is now native to the Caribbean, where the indigenous peoples were the first to use and cultivate it.

Smoking tobacco has probably been responsible for more deaths than any other herb.

Papaver somniferum (Urdu Name: Afiyun)

Stone age alchemy (an ancient branch of philosophy) is the reference to the use of Opium. Morphine was named after a Greek god, 'Morpheus–god[23] of sleep or the god of dreams.'

Peganum harmala (Urdu Name: Harmal)

The smoke of the Peganum harmala seeds is traditionally used in Iran as both a disinfectant and for all kinds of rituals against the evil eye and bad luck. In Turkey, dried capsules from the plant are strung and hung in homes or vehicles to protect against the evil eye'.

---

[23] Morpheus was known as the god of dreams. He shaped and formed the dreams, through which he could appear to mortals in any form. The name, mprphine, which derives from Morpheus was coined in 1805 by German apothecary Adolf Serturner (d. 1841 Ad).

A red dye extracted from seeds of Peganum is used in Turkey and Iran for colouring carpets. Since 2005, the possession of the seed, the plant itself and the alkaloids, are illegal in France. In Finland, the plant is officially listed as a medicinal plant.

Pilocarpus jaborandi (Urdu Name: Jhalar)

Dr Coutinho (d. 1874 AD) sent the plant to Europe from Pernambuco, Brazil, hence the name Pernambuco jaborandi or Pilocarpus jaborandi. Later, Louis-Édouard Byasson (1870 - 1911 AD) in 1895, showed its alkaloidal nature and further, Gerrard and Hardy isolated the main alkaloid pilocarpine. This alkaloid has been used in glaucoma for a hundred years.

Piper longum (Urdu Name: Filfil Daraz)

Piper longum is one of the famous ingredients of one of Pakistan's national dishes called 'Na'hari' (special spicy beef curry). Nahari is a stimulant and a home remedy for cold and rhinorrhoea.

Piper nigrum (Urdu Name: Kali Mirch)

During the Siege of Rome (410 AD), pepper was so highly priced that it was used as a currency form. Black peppercorns were found stuffed in Ramses II's (Ramses who raised Moses) nostrils placed there as part of the mummification rituals shortly after his death in 1213 BCE.

Rauwolfia serpentina (Urdu Name: Asroal)

It is a plant with a fascinating history. It found its place in the literature of Charaka, as early as 300 BC, who mentioned it by its Sanskrit name 'Sarpgandha.' The aroma of this vegetation repelled snakes. According to others, the plant's roots look like a snake, but both assumptions are unrealistic and unfounded. The more appropriate reason for this name is its therapeutic value in snake-bitten victims. There is popular folklore and belief that before fighting with a cobra, the mongoose (nevla) first chews its leaf to gain strength. There is also a belief that it serves as an antidote when its leaves are ground, made into a paste and applied to the snake-bitten victim's toes. It was also used as a medicinal cure for madness and aptly named Pagal-ki-Dawa (Medicine for the Insane) in the Indo-Pak subcontinent.

The legendary Hakim Ajmal Khan (my great-grandfather) of Delhi, was a renowned Unani physician, a respected politician and a great philanthropist. He founded the

Tibbiya College in Delhi to promote advanced learning and research in Unani medicine.

As part of bringing Unani Medicine and the other indigenous traditional healing systems of India into the modern world, Hakim Ajmal Khan recognised the vital importance of laboratory research and clinical trials, in proving traditional Unani's therapeutic efficacy of Ayurvedic medicinal herbs. Perhaps the best-known example is his collaboration with the chemist, Dr Salimuzzaman Siddiqui[24], to chemically isolate and analyse the indigenous Unani and Ayurvedic herb's active constituent Rauwolfia, whose Latin binomial is Rauwolfia serpentina, of the Apocynaceae family.

The work of a great chemist led to discovering the modern drug Ajmaline. Salimuzzaman Siddiqui named the antiarrhythmic agent 'ajmaline' in honour of his mentor Hakim Ajmal Khan. In addition, Salimuzzaman Siddiqui named some other Rauwolfia alkaloids after Hakim Ajmal Khan, namely, ajmalicine, isoajmaline and neoajmaline. Other very important indole alkaloids are reserpine and yohimbine.

Rauwolfia serpentina, the generic name, was given in honour of a French Botanist and a well-known sixteenth-century German Physician, traveller and author Leonhard Rauwolf Augsburg (d. 1596 AD). Rauwolf is famous for his 'Luxurious book Herbarium' containing information of plants from the Near East.

Scopolia carniolica (Urdu Name: Scopolia)

Scopolia carniolica was first described by the Swedish botanist Cari Linnaeus (d. 1778 AD) and named in honour of the Austrian physician Giovanni Antonia Scopoli (d. 1788 AD) Hyoscyamus scopolia.

Strychnos nuxvomica (Urdu Name: Kuchla)

Cleopatra (69 - 30 BC), daughter of Ptolemy Auletes (*ca* 117 - 50 BC), supposedly investigated the seeds to search for perfect suicidal poisons. She had prisoners and slaves swallow the seeds to see how quickly they would die. Death was fast enough, but Cleopatra was disturbed by the convulsions and distorted facial features Indole alkaloid produced. She wanted her beauty preserved even after death and finally decided to commit suicide by allowing an asp (Egyptian cobra) to sting her.

---

[24] Dr Salimuzzaman Siddiqui MBE, HI, FRS (1897-1994 AD) must be one of the few scientific personalities of the twentieth century to lay genuine claim to being a true Renaissance man. His early university education was in philosophy, a subject for which he retained a lifelong passion.

Tylophora indica (Urdu Name: Anantmul)

The plant's general medicinal uses have been incorporated as an official drug in the Bengal pharmacopoeia of 1884, by an Irish Physician, W. B. O'Shaughnessy (1809 - 1889). He also introduced Cannabis sativa to Western medicine.

Wrightia tinctoria (Urdu Name: Inderjo Shirin)

The name of this plant, 'Wrightia,' is after the Scottish physician and botanist William Wright (1735 - 1818). Wright was a joint founder of the Royal Society of Edinburgh in 1783.

Carbohydrates

Avena sativa (Urdu Name: Jau)

Avena sativa has been used as a food and fodder since ancient times (1000 BC).

Beta vulgaris (Urdu Name: Chuqandar)

Jews traditionally eat Beetroot on Rosh Hashanah (their New Year) as it embodies the hope that all enemies will be removed in the New Year.

Ficus carica (Urdu Name: Anjeer)

Ficus carica is the Tree under which Gautama Buddha (d. *c.* 483 or 400 BCE) is believed to have attained enlightenment.

Ipomoea paniculata (Urdu Name: Bidari-Kand)

According to Archaeologists, prehistoric remnants of sweet Potato proves that it has been used in Polynesia (the largest country in Polynesia is New Zealand) from about AD 1000 to AD 1100 carbon-14 dating (the half-life of Carbon-14 is 5730 years).

Musa acuminate (Urdu Name: Kela)

In Hindu culture, the Banana is regarded as a symbol of fertility and prosperity. The leaves and fruit are used in many festivals and ceremonies and placed at a house's entrance on special occasions, especially in marriages and Satyanarayana (worship of the Hindu god Visnu) pooja.

Oryza sativa (Urdu Name: Chawal)

Oryza sativa grains are used to mark the forehead along with saffron at many social and Hindu religious occasions such as Diwali, Akshay Tritiya, Raksha Bandhan etc. It is also considered a symbol of prosperity. Rice milk is a form of milk that is non-dairy; therefore, it is often recommended for lactose intolerant and vegan people. It is believed that rice milk is lighter than cow's milk; however, it may not be as nutritious as cow's milk. During the second Indo-China war (1955 - 1975 AD), Vietnam's mothers fed infants with rice milk.

Solanum tuberosum (Urdu Name: Aalu)

The species of Solanum are considered native to Central and South America. The Potato was cultivated for over 2,000 years by the Inca people before becoming a popular staple food in Europe in the 18th century.

It is a myth that Potatoes make you fat; the oil and the butter used with it, are the real culprits.

Tamarindus indica (Urdu Name: Imli)

This Tree is mentioned in the Indian Brahmasamhita scriptures between 1200 and 200 BC and in Buddhist sources from 650 CE.

The name 'Tamarind' is derived from the Arabic' Tamar-u'll' Hind because the fruit pulp resembles dried dates (Phoenix sylvestris). It is therefore called the Tamere-Hindi or 'Date of India.

Triticum aestivum (Urdu Name: Gundum)

Naked wheat (Triticum aestivum) was found in Roman burial sites ranging from 100 BCE to 300 CE.

Vitis vinifera (Urdu Name Angoor)
This prehistoric wine was most likely made from wild grapes, as the domestication of grapevines did not begin until around 5000 B.C. However, Sumerian texts[25] from 3000 B.C. contain some of the first written accounts of both grapes and wine.

---

[25] The Sumerian language remained in official and literary use in the Akkadian (the first ancient empire of Mesopotamia) and Babylonian empires.

The colourful grape harvesting and winemaking scenes decorate many Egyptian tomb walls, revealing Vitis vinifera's importance in ancient Egypt and in the afterlife by at least 2700 B.C. Seven hundred years later, sailors of Phoenician (ancient Semitic-speaking thalassocratic civilization) transported grapevines across the Mediterranean to Greece. From there, grapes and grape growing spread to Europe and the rest of the world.

Fixed Oils

Cocos nucifera (Urdu Name: Nariyal)

In India, fruits are offered to the gods and goddesses in temples. The branches are used in many religious ceremonies and festivals such as Satyanarayan puja, anniversaries etc. Due to its perceived purity, coconut milk is used to wash the faces of the dead as their bodies are prepared for funerals to clear the deceased person's mind, so they can peacefully travel to the next life.

'The Mutiny of the Bounty,' is supposed to have been triggered by the British Royal Navy, Vice Admiral William Bligh's (1754 - 1817 AD) harsh punishment for the theft of coconuts from the ship's store. The famous British drama film based on 'The Bounty,' directed by R. Donaldson, was released worldwide in 1984.

Elaeis guineensis (Urdu Name: Tarr)

In Judaism, the lulav, a closed frond of the date palm, is part of the festival of Sukkot[26] (Feast of the Tabernacles). A palm branch was awarded to the victorious athletes, in ancient Greece.

In Christianity, the palm branch is associated with Jesus' Triumphal Entry on Palm Sunday (A moveable feast that falls on the Sunday before Easter). In Thailand, palm sugar is still made traditionally by collecting the sweet sap from the cut flower buds of coconut palm trees.

Eruca sativa (Urdu Name: Jarjir)

In the ancient world, the Romans and the Egyptians considered Eruca sativa to be a potent aphrodisiac used to 'restore vigour to the genitalia.'

---

[26] Commonly called the 'Feast of Tabernacles' or in some translations the 'Festival of Shelters' and known also as the' Feast of Ingathering' a bibilical Jewish holiday, celebrated on the 15th day of the seventh month (Tishrei).

Gossypium herbaceum (Urdu Name: Binola)

Cotton wicks are made from the Indian cotton plant, the most popular and commonly used wick in India to light an oil lamp to attain every good fortune.

Helianthus annuus (Urdu Name: Suraj-Mukhi)

In Greek, 'Helios' means sun and 'Anthos' means flower, thus the name Sunflower.

Because of the myth of Clytie (a water nymph) and Apollo (one of the Olympian gods), the Sunflower most commonly means, adoration and loyalty. In China, people associate Sunflowers with long life, good fortune and vitality.

Sunflowers also symbolise worship and faithfulness in various religions because they resemble the sun, which is associated with spiritual knowledge and the desire to seek light and truth. Sunflower is the national flower of Russia and the state flower of Kansas, USA

Linum usitatissimum (Urdu Name: Alsi)

Ancient Egyptians made fine linens from flax fibre. It represents personal holiness and suggests that the person clothed in this linen is in a condition suitable to approach God. One of the synonyms for a priest wearing this linen ephod (an article of clothing and an object of worship in ancient Israelite culture), was closely connected with oracular practices and priestly ritual.

Olea europaea (Urdu Name: Zaitoon)

So popular were the tree and fruit that, apart from the daily diet, the oil was used in holy ointments for kings and priests and the anointing (rub with oil) the sick, for lighting at homes and in Temples. The Olive oil and wine were closely linked in the Greco-Roman civilisation because of similarities in their transformation processes and their importance in the economy, including daily life and trade, religious rites and art.

Prunus amygdalus

Historically, almond oil had been used in Ancient Chinese, Ayurvedic and Greco-Persian schools of Medicine to treat dry skin conditions such as psoriasis and eczema. The Egyptian Queen, Cleopatra, who was famous for her beautiful skin, hair and body, is also said to have included almonds in both her diet and skincare regime.

The tree has always been a favourite, and in Shakespeare's time, as John Gerard (1545-1612 AD) tells us, Almond trees were 'in our London gardens and orchards in great plenty.' There are many references to it in our early poetry. Edmund Spenser (1552-1599 AD) alludes to it in the Fairy Queen. William Shakespeare (1564-1616 AD) mentions it only once, very casually, in Troilus and Cressida.

Sesamum indicum (Urdu Name: Til)

Sesamum indicum seed is one of the oldest oilseed crops known, domesticated well over 3000 years ago.

Zea mays (Urdu Name: Makai)

Around 4,500 years ago, maize began to spread to the north, first cultivated in what is now the United States, at several sites in New Mexico and Arizona, about 4,100 years ago. For western civilisation, the Zea mays story began in 1492 AD when Columbus's men discovered this new grain in Cuba.

Glycosides

Barosma betulina (Urdu Name: Buchu)

The Buchu plant was introduced by the colonists at the Cape to Europe (European-Asian sea route). It was known as the 'Noble Tea' as only the rich could afford it. Bales of Buchu were found in the cargo of the famous ship 'Titanic' (sank April, 1912 AD).

Caesalpinia bonduc (Urdu Name: Karanjwa)

A different species of this plant known as 'Caesalpinia pulcherrima' is the national flower of the Caribbean island of Barbados. In Ayurvedic, the plant is called 'kuberakshi,' meaning eyes of 'Kuber' also known as Kuvera, the Hindu God for wealth.

Cichorium intybus (Urdu Name: Kasni)

The ancient Greek used it as a community medicine and called it 'friend of the liver.' It also produces industrial raw material called inulin, which is used for fructose production.

Cinnamomum zeylanicum (Urdu Name: Darchini)

In ancient times, it was used to flavour Roman wine. In Rome during the 1st century AD, cinnamon was at least 15 times more expensive than silver and centuries later, it was still costly. Only the very wealthy in medieval Europe could afford this costly spice, for which the demand was high and supply low.

A desire to monopolize the cinnamon trade prompted European expansion into Asia in the 16th and 17th centuries. Eventually, cinnamon became more widely available and affordable. Today, it adds a spicy flavour to whiskey, to liquor and is added to hot wine in some countries, during the cold winter months.

Citrullus colocynthis (Urdu Name: Indrain Talkh)

The colocynth's characteristic small seeds appear in several Egyptian, Libyan and near Eastern sites from about 4000 years BC.

Croton tiglium (Urdu Name: Jamal-Gotta)

It was introduced to the Western world in the 16th century, by the Dutch.

Digitalis purpurea (Urdu Name: Zehar-al-Kashatabeen)

Digitalis was one of the many herbal remedies used by the ancient Romans. Digitalis, is derived from the foxglove plant. Digitalis purpurea, is mentioned in writings as early as 1250. A Welsh family, known as the Physicians of Myddfai (a small village in Carmarthenshire, Wales), collected various herbs and digitalis was included in their prescriptions. Although its use for the treatment of heart failure has been traced back to 10th century Europe, digitalis was not widely used for this indication until its scientific investigation by British physician William Withering (1741 - 1799), which became public in the late 1700s.

Gentiana lutea (Urdu Name: Kiraal)

The name Gentian is derived from the name of a king who first identified the plant and was healed by it. His name was Gentius[27]. Dioscorides (the Greek physician d. 90 AD) believed that king Gentius (d. after 167 BC) identified the properties of this plant and used the plant root in 167 BC for the incidence of Plague. Al-Razi and Avicenna

---

[27] Gentius was the last king of Illyria. He was the son of the Illyrian king Pleuratus II, of the tribe of the Labeates. He had his capital at Scodra (Republic of Albania).

both mentioned this plant in their book Al-Havi and Al-Qanoon, respectively. The contents of these books are based on their observations and their scientific experiments.

Ginkgo biloba (Urdu Name: Aljunaka)

The Ginkgo is the world's oldest living tree, a species whose existence can be traced back to over 250 million years. Thus, the Ginkgo is referred to as a living fossil by Charles Darwin[28] (1809 - 1882). The Chinese called Ginkgo seeds 'jinxing,' meaning 'silver apricot.' In Japan, where ginkgo was introduced, 'yin-hsing' is thought to have become corrupted into Gingkyo. Ginkgo leaves and seeds have been used in traditional Chinese medicine since the 15th century and probably were used much earlier in folk medicine.

Morus alba (Urdu Name: Shahtut)

The Mulberry is also grown for rearing silk around many of the villages between Jerusalem and Nablus (Shechem) and often covers the terraced hillside.

Apart from its worldwide medicinal uses, Morus alba (wood) has been traditionally used for making Iranian bowl-shaped musical instruments, known as Persian Tanbur.

Rhamnus purshiana (Urdu Name: Kasikarana)

Spanish conquerors exploring the Pacific Northwest in the 1600s came across many Native Americans. In Spanish, it is called the Sacred Bark. It was the most widely used laxative herb on the planet. In the mid-1900s, demand for cascara began to decline as other products came on the market.

Rheum emodi (Urdu Name: Rewand Chini)

The word Rhubarb was derived from the Latin words' Rha and Barb', which means River and Barbarian Land. The Romans imported it from a barbaric land across the 'Rha' river and the plant became Rhabarbarum. Rheum emodi was also documented in the traditional Chinese book on materia media 'The Shen Nong Ben Cao Jing.

---

20 Charles Darwin is believed to be the first proponent of the evolutionary theory. However, philosopher and prose writer Abu Uthman Amr ibn Bahr known as al Jahis (d. 869 AD) was the originator of idea of evolution through his famous work 'Kitab al Hayawan' an encyclopedia of animals in seven volumes composed in honour of Ibn-al Zyaat (d. *ca.* 847 AD) viazir of the Abbasid caliph. John William Draper (1811-1882 AD), a contemporary of Darwin, called it the 'Mohammadan Theory of Evolution.'

Smilax glabra (Urdu Name: Chob Chini)

Smilax glabra has been widely used since ancient times. The drug and instructions for its use were spread westward from China by traders of all nationalities from 1535 onwards. The demand became global before being replaced mainly in Europe by supplies of various American Smilax species, known collectively as 'Sarsaparilla.'

In Chinese, the plant is known as 'Jin Gang Ten.' For centuries, indigenous people worldwide used the root of the sarsaparilla plant to treat joint problems like arthritis and for healing skin problems. Sarsaparilla was later introduced into European medicine and eventually registered as a herb in the United States Pharmacopoeia (USP) to treat syphilis.

Strophanthus hispidus (Urdu Name: Kombe)

Strophanthus hispidus was used since the historic period. The latex and seeds were used as arrow poisons in the savanna zone of Africa. For the first time in West Asia, the plant was noticed by a French man in 1775 AD.

Urginea indica (Urdu Name: Jangli Piyaz)

The oldest written about this plant dates back to 1500 BC. The ancient Egyptians discovered its use against oedema, emesis and cough. The ancient Romans used the extract of the bulbs as a cardiotonic.

The genus name Urginea, derived from an Arabian tribe, Ben Urginea, was coined by a German botanist Adolphe Steinheil (1810 - 1839 AD), who identified seven species. John Lindley (1799 - 1865 AD) placed this genus under the tribe Scillea.

Vanilla planifolia (Urdu Name: Fanilana)

Vanilla was utterly unknown in the Old World before Hernan Cortes (1485 - 1547 AD), a Spanish conquistador, arrived in Mexico. Spanish explorers, arriving on Mexico's Gulf Coast, gave vanilla its current name in the early 16th century.

Portuguese sailors and explorers brought vanilla into Africa and Asia later that century. The name vanilla is derived from the Spanish word, which means 'little pod.'

Saponins

Achyranthes aspera (Urdu Name: Charchitah)

The juice of this plant is a potent ingredient for a mixture of wall plasters, according to the Samarāṅgaṇa Sūtradhāra, which a Sanskrit treatise is dealing with Śilpaśāstra (Hindu science of art and construction). In India, Shiva pooja is performed with Chaff Flower leaves. Achyranthes aspera leaves are one of the twenty-one leaves used in the Ganesh pooja.

Asparagus racemosus (Urdu Name: Satawar)

In Hindi, asparagus is 'Shatavari,' meaning a woman with a hundred husbands. Asparagus racemosus is being used from Pre-Vedic times and mentioned in Ayurvedic literature. Ayurveda systems were originated in India around 5000 years ago.

Glycyrrhiza glabra (Urdu Name: Mulaithi)

Evidence of liquorice's use is widespread in ancient cultures. For example, archaeologists found bundles of liquorice root sealed inside the 3,000 year-old tomb of Tutankhamen, presumably so that in his afterlife, the Egyptian king could brew 'mai sus,' a sweet drink, still enjoyed in Egypt today.

The liquorice history continues from being used in cough medicine to candy in Italy, France, Germany and England. Many liquorice development examples through the 19th century abound that remind us of its current use.

Liquorice is one of the ingredients of meetha (sweet) 'Paan' (betel leaf) in the Indo-Pak subcontinent and Indonesia, Malaysia, the Philippines, Nepal, etc.

Gynostemma pentaphyllum (Urdu Name: Jayawjulan)

This Chinese plant 'Jiaogulan' is documented in history that goes back to the Ming Dynasty (1368 - 1644 AD), when it was harvested for food.

The medical history of this lesser-known herb goes back to 1578 AD. A renowned herbalist, Li Shi-Zhen, included a sketch and description of Jiaogulan in his classical book, 'Compendium of Materia Medica.' He described the herb's usefulness in treating hematuria (blood in the urine), oedema, pain of the pharynx, tumours and psychological trauma.

Panax ginseng (Urdu Name: Jenseng)

Ginseng has been called the 'king of herbs,' the Root of Heaven and the Wonder of the World. The species name 'ginseng' comes from the Chinese word 'rensheng,' which means 'human,' as ginseng root resembles the human body.

Polypodium vulgare (Urdu Name: Bisfaij)

The Arabic name of Bisfaij is 'Azra's-ul-Kalb,' which means dog's tooth, an illusion to the toothed appearance of the leaves. Its Hindi name is 'Khangaali,' which means multiple legs.

Gum and Mucilage

Acacia arabica (Urdu Name: Gond Kiker)

The Acacia wood was used to construct the Ark of the Testimony or Ark of the Covenant (a gold-covered wooden box made up of Acacia).

Cochlospermum gossypium/Cochlospermum religiosum
(Urdu Name: Gond Katira)

The name religiosum derives from the fact that the flowers are used as temple offerings. The plant is grown near temples in India, due to its bright yellow flowers, which are used as offerings to gods and for aesthetics. Cochlospermum religiosum is also used as a tree for achieving enlightenment.

Abelmoschus esculentus (Urdu Name: Bhendi)

The exact origin of Abelmoschus esculentus is unknown, but it is probably originated somewhere around Ethiopia and was cultivated by the ancient Egyptians by the 12th century BC. The Okra was previously included in the genus Hibiscus. Later, it was designated to Abelmoschus.

Aegle marmelos (Urdu Name: Bail-I-Giri)

This tree is considered to be sacred by Hindus. It is associated with the Lord Shiva[29] as the Lord is pleased when people offer its leaves and fruits to the Lord.

Althaea officinalis (Urdu Name: Khatmi)

Marsh mallow's medicinal use dates back 2,000 years. Hippocrates (460 - 370 BC), the father of medicine, used marshmallows to remedy bruises and blood loss. Arabian doctors created a poultice from the leaves to treat inflammation. The genus Althaea is a Greek term that means 'heal' or stimulating the body's own healing abilities.

Ocimum basilicum (Urdu Name: Faranj-Mushk)

Basil has religious significance in the Greek Orthodox Church, where it is used to sprinkle as Holy water. The plant is also a sacred herb in the Hindu religion. In Hindu houses, Tulsi is the protecting spirit of the family. The British, at one time, used Ocimum basilicum (Tulsi) as a substitute for a Bible upon which the Indians would take an oath in a court of law. Jewish people used it for strength during fasting. In Italy, it is used as a symbol of love. In France, it is called an herb of the royal; however, a group of Europeans thinks that it symbolises Satan.

In Europe, Basil is placed in a dead's hands to ensure a safe journey. The ancient Egyptians and ancient Greeks believed it would open the gates of heaven for a person passing on. In India, they place it in the dead's mouth to ensure they reach God.

Resins

Boswellia glabra (Urdu Name: Loban)

The combination of Boswellia glabra and Commiphora molmol (myrrh) has been documented in the ancient Egyptian prescription collection of Papyrus Ebers (written in c. 1550 BC) to treat wounds and skin ulcers.

Commiphora molmol (Urdu Name: Murr)

Myrrh was used by the ancient Egyptians and Natron (a mixture of carbonate,

---

[29] The scriptures state, that the leaf, represents the three eyes of Lord Shiva. As Lord Shiva was very fond of Bilva leaves.

bicarbonate, chloride and sulfate of sodium) in embalming mummies. Myrrh was burned during ancient Roman funerals to mask the smell emanating from charring corpses. The Roman Emperor Nero[30] burned a year's worth of myrrh at the funeral of his second wife, Poppaea Sabina (30 - 65 AD).

Curcuma longa (Urdu Name: Haldi)

Curcuma longa (Kumkum in Hindi) is considered an essential herb in Hinduism as it is a cultural identity of any married Hindu woman. It forms an inseparable part of her life. Since ancient times, Kurkum 'bindi'[31] (a colour dot worn on the centre of the forehead) on the forehead, is a must for married women.

Turmeric paste is used to adorn the statues or 'murtis' of the God. For example, Lord Vishnu loves to be decorated with Haldi.

The 'Haldi' ceremony is called 'Mayun' in the Indo-Pak subcontinent and is usually organised by the bride and the groom's house, either a day before or on the morning of the wedding day. The ceremony is all about applying Turmeric paste on the bride and the groom's face, neck, hands and feet by their loved ones. The ceremony is marked by the enactment of folk songs and dance performances.

Dorema ammoniacum (Urdu Name: Ushaq)

The gum resin is also called 'agasyllon,' 'criotheos' and the Romans call it 'gutta.' In the first century, it was first documented by the famous Greek physician, pharmacologist and botanist, Pedanius Dioscorides (*ca* 40 to 90 AD) in his five volumes book The 'De Materia Medica' (Pharmacopoeia of Medicinal Plants).

Ferula foetida (Urdu Name: Hiltit)

Alexander III of Macedon (Sikander-e-Azam) introduced this plant into Europe after returning to North-Eastern ancient Persia. In ancient Rome, Asafoetida was stored in jars and pine nuts (chilgoza), alone were used to delicate flavour dishes.

Ipomoea hederacea (Urdu Name: Kaladana)

One of the species of plants known as 'Morning Glory' is used in religious rituals and ceremonies from ancient times and even today. The ritual contains many elements,

---

[30] Nero (37 - 68 AD). was the fifth Roman emperor after Claudia (d. 54 AD), Caligula (d. 41 AD), Tiberius (d. 37 AD) and Augustus (d. 14 AD). The month of August was named to honor Augustus Caesar.
[31] The word bindi' stems from the Sanskrit word bindu, which means drop or particle.

including the names given to the plants, such as 'Seeds of the Virgin,' 'Holy Mary Herb,' and 'Virgin's Cloak,' also known as 'Virgin of Guadalupe[32].

Ipomoea purga (Urdu Name: Jalapah)

The plant is named 'John the Conqueror' (son of an African king in the Congo and fiancé of Devil's daughter 'Lilith'), a folk hero from African-American folklore. He was sold as a slave in America. The famous root of the plant symbolizes enduring courage, love and success.

Plantago ovata (Urdu Name Ispagol)

The common name for Plantago ovata in India is Isabgol, which comes from the Persian words 'Isap' and 'ghol,' meaning 'horse ear.' The name aptly describes the peculiar shape of psyllium seeds. The word psyllium comes from the Greek word meaning 'flea' and refers to the tiny seeds. Each plant can produce up to 15,000 (approx) seeds.

Pistacia lentiscus (Urdu Name Mastagi)

Chios, one of the largest islands in the Eastern Mediterranean, became internationally known during the 13th century due to the production of the Pistacia lentiscus of the Anacardiaceae family.

After the island was conquered by Sultan Suleiman (1494 - 1566 AD), the magnificent of the Ottoman Empire (Khilafat-e-Usmania) in 1566, following a period of almost two centuries of Genoa rule (1346 to 1566), the valuable product of Chios Mastic constitutes one of the monopolies of the Ottoman State.

Tannins

Emblica officinalis (Urdu Name: Amla)

According to a belief in the ancient Indian mythology, this is the first Tree created in the Universe.

---

[32] In Roman Catholicism, Virgin of Guadalupe makes her apperance before St. Juan Diego in 1531. He was born in the year 1474 near Mexico City.

Lawsonia inermis (Urdu Name: Mehndhi)

The earliest civilizations which used henna are Babylonians, Assyrians, Sumerians, Semites, Ugaritics and Canaanites. In ancient Egyptian times, even mummies wore henna designs and it is documented that Cleopatra VII (69 - 30 BC), daughter of Ptolemy Auletes, used henna for decorative purposes.

In South Asian countries, the most popular traditions are the Mehndi (henna) night, where the bride, the family, relatives and friends celebrate the wedding to come.

In Islamic countries, Muslim men have particular customs for dyeing their beards, whereas women are encouraged by religion to colour their nails and fingers red with Henna to display femininity.

Punica granatum (Urdu Name: Annar)

Steeped in history and romance, pomegranate is native to the mountainous region, including northern Iraq and northwest Iran. Sumerian cuneiform records reveal that pomegranates have been cultivated in the Middle East since approximately 3000 B.C.

In Egyptian art and mythology, the pomegranate symbolized abundance and unity. In early Christian, Jewish and Islamic artistic traditions, the fruit represented blood, death and life renewal. According to Greek mythology, Persephone, the goddess Demeter's daughter, makes the mistake of eating pomegranate seeds in the underworld and is eternally bound to that place for a part of every year.

The Romans named the fruit Punica granatum, or 'seeds from Carthage,' possibly because the Phoenician city in North Africa was a source of fine pomegranates in the ancient world.

The plant is also mentioned in Buddhist and Chinese arts. It has been a symbol of health, fertility and rebirth, as mentioned in many cultures.

Quercus intectoria (Urdu Name: Mazu)

The earliest evidence of the acorns of Quercus infectoria tree as foodstuff dated back to the late Mesolithic era,[33] and is found in Western Europe as well. The oak is a symbol of strength and endurance and it is chosen as the national Tree of many countries.

---

[33] Also called middle Stone Age era, an ancient cultural stage that existed between the Paleolithic old stone age.

In England, the oak has been a national symbol since at least the sixteenth century, often used by Shakespeare, to confer heritage and power. Today, in England, the oak remains a symbol of the nation's history, traditions and countryside beauty.

Saraca indica (Urdu Name: Ashoka)

The Asoka tree is considered sacred throughout the Indian subcontinent, especially in India, Nepal and Sri Lanka. In India, married Hindu women eat the flower buds of Saraca indica on 'Ashok Shasti Day' to guard their children against grief and sorrow. Likewise, people who have a mental disorder are advised to take a bath under the Ashok tree's shade.

Terminalia arjuna (Urdu Name: Arjuna)

The hero of the famous epic, Mahabharata was named after this tree because of its protective effects. The plant is also mentioned once in Ramayan (4.1.81).

Hamamelis virginiana (Urdu Name Hamamelis virginiana)

The witch of hazel is likely to have been derived from the Anglo-Saxon 'wych,' meaning 'pliant' or 'bendable.' It refers to Hamamelis virginiana's traditional use as a source of forked branches used as divining rods, or witching sticks, to locate underground sources of water or precious minerals.

Volatile Oils

Anethum graveolens (Urdu Name: Shabbat)

Dill has been found in the tomb of Egyptian Pharaoh Amenhotep II (seventh Pharaoh of the 18th Dynasty of Egypt), dating to around 1400 BC.

The genus name Anethum is derived from the Greek word 'aneeson or aneeton,' which means strong-smelling.

Chenopodium album (Urdu Name: Bathwa)

Napoleon Bonaparte (1769 - 1821 AD) relied on Chenopodium plant seeds to feed his troops during lean times.

Cinnamomum camphora (Urdu Name: Kafur)

The name of the genus Cinnamomum comes from the Ancient Greek word 'Kinnamomom,' which means spice. The Greeks borrowed the word from the Phoenicians[34], indicating that they traded with the East earlier. Cinnamon is recorded in Sanskrit, the Old Testament and in Greek medicinal works and was used by Egyptians in early 1485 BC for embalming purposes. In Arabic, it is Kafur.

Citrus x aurantifolia (Urdu Name: Nebu)

In addition to medicinal uses, some thoughts are linked with the belief that limes drive evil spirits away. In Hinduism, lemons are used in Durga or Kali Puja.

Eucalyptus oblique (Urdu Name: Safayda)

Eucalyptus oblique plant was described in 1788 by French botanist L' He'ritier (1746 - 1800 AD) from specimens collected in 1777 AD, by plant collector David Nelson (d. 1789 AD), at Adventure Bay (a town in Tasmania established in 1798 by the British).

Juniperus communis (Urdu Name: Abhal)

It is also known that this plant's branches and berries were burned in a temple as a part of purification ceremonies.

Lactuca serriola (Urdu Name: Kahu)

Ancient Egyptians thought lettuce to be a symbol of sexual prowess and a promoter of love and childbearing in women. The Romans likewise claimed that it increased sexual potency. In contrast, the ancient Greeks connected the plant with male impotence.

Laurus nobilis (Urdu Name: Hab-el-Ghar)

The Laurus nobilis tree has long been known as a symbol of honour.

Lavendula x stoechas (Urdu Name: UstuKhuddus)

During Roman times, Lavendula flowers were sold for a hundred 'denarii' (the standard Roman silver coins) per five hundred grams, which was about the same as a

---

[34] Semitic-speaking civilization 2500 BC.

month's wages for a farm labourer or fifty haircuts from the local barber. The plant is known as 'Romero Santo,' meaning sacred Rosemary in Spain.

Mentha piperita (Urdu Name: Pudina)

The name comes from Minthe, a nymph in Greek mythology who had the misfortune of being loved by Hades, god of the underworld and subsequently was turned into an insignificant little plant by Hades's jealous wife. According to the story, Hades tried to make it up to Minthe by sweetly scenting her small, green leaves. While several mints have been cultivated since the ancient Egyptians' time, peppermint is a relatively newcomer. However, being a natural hybrid of two other mint species, it was discovered in England in 1696.

Piper cubeba (Urdu Name: Kabab Chini)

Abū Ḥanīfa al-Nuʿmān b. Thābit RUA (d. 767) and poet Hakim Momin Khan Momin (d. 851) described in their books' Kitab-Al-Nabat'[35] (book of plants) and 'Tohfat-ul-Mominin' respectively, that the aroma of Piper cubeba (Cubebs) is very much similar to that of the Tree Myrtus communis (Hab-ul-Aas).

In the famous book of 'Alf Laylah wa-Laylah' (One Thousand and One Nights), compiled in the 9th century, Piper cubeba is mentioned as a remedy for infertility.

Pyrethrum indicum (Urdu Name: Aqarqara)

In Japan, the plant symbolises the Emperor and the imperial family. In Australia, on Mother's Day, which falls in May, people traditionally wear a white chrysanthemum when the flower is in season. The plant is cultivated around the world for nearly 150 years. Kenya is accounting for about 80 per cent of the world production.

Rosa damascene (Urdu Name: Gul-e-Surkh)

People call this plant 'Flower of Prophet Mohammed (PBUH)' because they believe it has a pleasant aroma that reminds them of Prophet Mohammad (PBUH). Among Muslims, the Rose is sometimes chosen for use in marriages or funerals.

In Christianity, red roses stand for love or as a sign of Christ's blood. Buddhists see the rose flower as an expression of spiritual joy. The Rose's prominent symbolic

---

[35] Kitab al-Nabat is a monumental work on the knowledge of plants available up to the author's time - a landmark in the history of botany (present day Pharmacognosy).

place in Judaism comes from the biblical Song of Solomon or Canticle of Canticles. In Hinduism, the chief Hindu prayer rites are called 'Puja,' which means 'the flower act.'

In tradition, rose water was scattered at weddings to ensure a happy marriage. This is a symbol of love, purity and is also used to aid meditation and prayer.

The Rose is the national flower of the United States, the Maldives and the United Kingdom.

The War of the Roses (1455 – 1485), in English history, was a series of bloody civil wars for the throne of England, between two competing royal families: the House of York (White Roses) and the House of Lancaster (Red Roses). Red roses are also often considered a universal symbol of love. On the other hand, white has always been a symbol of purity.

Santalum album (Urdu Name: Sandal Safaid)

In Indian culture, the Tree is regarded with special reverence. It has been used as an object in ritualistic offerings and in the ointment to aid beauty. People have a strong spiritual association with Sandalwood and it is burnt at weddings and funerals. Sandalwood is used today in modern-day Buddhist practice.

Syzygium aromaticum (Urdu Name: Loung)

Archaeologists found Cloves within a ceramic vessel in Syria and the evidence dating the find, is to within a few years of 1721 BCE.

In many Asian countries, Clove buds called 'Loung,' are inserted in the ear after piercing.

Thymus vulgaris (Urdu Name Hasha/Jangli Podina)

The ancient Etruscans (civilization of ancient Italy) and Egyptians used thyme oil for embalming their dead. Many early cultures associated thyme with death and the minute, pale purple flowers were thought to provide a resting place for the souls of those who had died. The ancient Greeks burned Thyme as part of funeral rites, as incense in temples and as a fumigant to chase insects from houses. But they also believed that the herb had the power to instil courage.

Thyme's genus name may be derived from the Greek word for either 'courage' or 'to fumigate.' The link to courage, however, followed thyme to England when the

Romans introduced it there. During the Middle Ages, ladies of the court presented their brave knights with scarves embroidered with a sprig of thyme.

Viola odorata (Urdu Name: Banafsha)

The Greek word for violet is 'Lo.' Lo is a character in Greek mythology and the daughter of King Argos, whom Zeus (God of the sky, lightning, thunder, law, order and justice) loved. However, Zeus was concerned that Hera would discover their affair, so he turned 'Lo' into a cow and then created the sweet-scented flowers that we now know as violets, for her to eat.

Terpenoids (Isoprenoids)

Artemisia absinthium (Urdu Name: Afsanteen)

The origin of the word 'Artemesia' is probably from the Greek goddess 'Artemis.' In Hellenistic (300 to 30 BC) culture[36], 'Artemis' was the forest's hunt and protector's goddess. She was the wife and sister of Mausolus, ruler of Caria. When Mausolus (son of Hecatomnus) died, he was buried in a massive tomb dedicated to his memory.

The Mausoleum at Halicarnassus (one of the Seven Wonders of the Ancient World) is still present at Bodrum in modern-day Turkey. Unfortunately, the Mausoleum was probably destroyed by an earthquake between the 11th and 15th centuries.

The French word 'mausolée' (maqbara) is derived from the Mausoleum at Halicarnassus, the grave of King Mausolus or Maussolos.

In the famous William Shakespeare's play 'Romeo and Juliet' Act 1, Scene 3, Juliet's childhood nurse said, 'For I had then laid Wormwood to my dug' meaning that the nurse had weaned Juliet, then aged three, by using the bitter taste of Wormwood on her nipple.

Crocus sativus (Urdu Name: Zafran)

Crocus sativus documented history is authenticated in a seventh-century BC Assyrian/Arameans botanical treatise compiled under Ashurbanipal, the Neo-Assyrian Empire's king.

---

[36] Ancient Greek culture or ideals (323-33 BC), is the imitation or adoption of ancient Greek language, thought, customs, art, etc..

Greeks and Romans used this plant as perfume and it is also mentioned in the Chines 'Materia Medica' from the 1550s.

The Saffron plant is mentioned in one of the oldest medical texts in the Islamic world, known as Ferdous al-Hekma fil-Tibb[37] (Paradise of Wisdom), by the pioneer of medical deontology, Ali Rabban Tabri[38] (d. 870 AD). His famous student was Zakariya Ar-Razi[39] (Rhazes, d. *Ca.* 925 AD).

According to Hindu religion, Lord Krishna[40] used to put Tilak (a mark on the forehead) with Saffron daily.

Valeriana officinalis (Urdu Name: Baalchar)

Valerian has been used as a medicinal herb since at least the time of ancient Greece and Rome. Hippocrates (*ca.* 460 - 370 BC) described its therapeutic uses and in the 2nd century, Galen (Jalinus in Urdu, d. *ca.* 210 BC) prescribed Valerian for insomnia.

In medieval Sweden, the plant was sometimes placed in the groom's wedding clothes to ward off the envy (when you want something that someone else has) of the elves (human-like supernatural in folklore).

An herbal compound containing Valeriane officinalis was given to civilians during the Second World War to reduce stress caused by repeated air raids and to minimise health damage.

The derivation of the genus name, 'Valeriana,' is unclear. It may have been named for the German physician and botanist Valerius Cordus (1515-1544 AD). Others believe that the name is derived from the Latin word 'valere' meaning 'to be in health.' The seventeenth-century astrological botanist Nicholas Culpeper (1616-1654 AD) thought the plant was 'under the influence of Mercury and therefore hath a warming faculty.'

---

[37] Is the first 'medical compendium' written independently in the Arabic language in the year 850 A D Translated in Urdu by Hakeem Rasheed Ashraf Nadvi.

[38] He should not be confused with Abu Jafar Ibn Jarir Muhammod At-Tabari (d.923 AD). He was a great Muslim scholar and considered a great Muslim historian. Tabri was born in Amul, the capital of Tabaristan, Iran. He belonged to a wealthy local Iranian family. He memorized The Quran at the age of seven. At-Tabari came to Baghdad to listen to the lectures of Ahmad ibn Hanbal (d. 855 AD), but Ahmad ibn Hanbal died before he arrived. In Baghdad, he founded his own school of Jurisprudence. He named the school "Jaririya" after his father. His famous Islamic encyclopaedia of history, 'Tarikh ar-rusul val-muluk,' (history of Prophets and Kings) has been recognized as invaluable for many reasons.

[39] Ar Razi: From the city of Rayy, also spelt Rey, formerly one of the greatest cities of Iran, near Tehran.

[40] According to the tale, Lord Krishna was born in the Yadava clan of Mathura (City in Uttar Pradesh, India), to Queen Devaki and her husband, King Vasudeva also known as Ānakadundubhii.

*** (From Page 463) Valeriana is thought to be referred to as spikenard in the Bible (Mark 14:3, John 12:3 and Songs of Solomon (1:12, 4: 14 - 13),

"The Marry* took about a pint of pure nard, an expensive perfume, she poured it on Jesus's feet and wiped his feet with her hair." However, this plant is not mentioned in books 'Plants of The Bible' (Michael Zohary), 'Bible Plants' (F. N. Hepper) and 'Medicinal Herbs of The Bible' (J. A. Duke).

*Marry Magdalene[41] was a witness to the crucifixion of Jesus and its aftermath. She was one of the first people to learn his Resurrection.

---

[41] All four canonical Gospels of the New Testament (Matthew, Mark, Luke and John) noted Marry Magdalene's presence at Jusus's Crucifixion, but only the Gospel of Luke discussing her role in Jesus's life and ministry, listing her among "Some women who had been healed of evil spirits and infirmities" (Luke 8: 1-3)

Index of Therapeutic action

Adenocarcinoma: A cancer that forms in mucus-secreting glands throughout the body.

Alexipharmic: An antidote against poison or infection.

Alexiteric: A preservative against infectious diseases.

Alopecia: Loss of hair or baldness.

Alterative: A medicine or treatment which works by changing processes within the body rather than by evacuating something.

Alzheimer's: A progressive neurologic disorder causes the brain to shrink (atrophy) and brain cells to die.

Amenorrhoea: An abnormal absence of menstruation.

Analgesic: Acting to relieve pain.

Anaphylaxis: An extreme allergic reaction.

Anodyne: A painkilling drug or medicine.

Anthelmintic: A preparation used to destroy parasitic worms.

Antibacterial: Anything that destroys bacteria or suppresses their growth or ability to reproduce.

Antimicrobial: A substance that kills or inhibits the growth of microorganisms such as bacteria, fungi and algae.

Antioxidant: A substance that retards deterioration by oxidation, especially of fats, oils and foods.

Antipyretic: This prevents or reduces fever

Antispasmodic: A medication that relieves, prevents, or lowers the incidence of muscle spasms, especially those of smooth muscle such as in the bowel wall.

Antitubercular: An action against tuberculosis.

Aperient: A mildly laxative substance.

Aphrodisiac: An agent (such as a food or drug) that arouses or is held to arouse sexual desire.

Apoptotic: A type of cell death in which a series of molecules steps in a cell lead to its death.

Aromatherapy: A method of treatment using fragrant essential oils.

Arrhythmia: A condition in which the heart beats with an irregular rhythm.

Arthritis: A disease-causing painful inflammation and stiffness, of the joints.

Ascariasis: Ascariasis is an infection of the small intestine caused by Ascaris lumbricoides, a roundworm species.

Asthma: A respiratory condition marked by spasm attacks in the lungs' bronchi, causing difficulty in breathing. It is usually associated with an allergic reaction.

Astringent: Causing a contraction of skin cells and other body tissues.

Atherosclerosis: A process of progressive thickening and hardening of the walls of the medium-sized and large arteries resulting from fat deposits on their inner lining.

Atrabilious: Melancholy or irritable.

Atrophy: Washing of the body parts due to lack of use.

Beriberi: Beriberi is a disease in which the body does not have enough thiamine (vitamin B1).

Boil: A painful swelling with a puss-filled core, caused by bacterial infection of the skin and subcutaneous tissues.

Bronchitis: An inflammation of the mucous membrane, in the bronchial tubes, with a spasm of coughing.

Burns: A type of injury to the skin, or other tissues, caused by heat, cold, electricity, chemicals, friction, or radiation (like sunburn).

Calculus: A stone formed, within the body.

Carminative: A relieving flatulence (gases in the stomach).

Catarrh: An excessive discharge of mucous in the nose or throat.

Catarrh: An excessive discharge of mucous in the nose or throat.

Cathartic: A substance used for purgation.

Chilblain: A round, itchy inflammation of the skin.

Chorea: A disorder of the nervous system.

Cirrhosis: A disease of the liver.

Colitis: An inflammation of the lining of the colon.

Conjunctivitis: An inflammation of the mucous membrane.

Croup: A group of diseases characterized by swelling.

Cystitis: An inflammation of the urinary bladder caused by infection and accompanied by painful urination.

Cytostatic: Tending to retard cellular activity and multiplication.

Dandruff: Loose scales of dry, dead skin, shed from the scalp.

Debility: Weakness.

Decoction: A water extract of plants or herbs, made by boiling and filtering.

Delirium: A mental disorder typified by confusion.

Demulcent: Relieving inflammation or irritation.

Depurative: A substance that purifies.

Desiccative: Extreme dryness.

Diaphoretic: A drug inducing perspiration.

Diarrhoea: An illness in which the body's solid waste is more liquid than usual and comes out of the body more often.

Digestive debility: A weakness of the digestive system.

Diphtheria: A severe infections disease caused by the bacterium.

Diuretic: A drug that increases the flow of urine.

Dropsy: Oedema (a condition when an excess of watery fluid collects in the body's tissues).

Dysentery: A disease characterized by severe diarrhoea with mucus and blood passage and usually caused by infection.

Dysmenorrhoea: A painful menstruation.

Dyspepsia: Indigestion.

Eczema: A chronic or recurrent inflammatory skin disease, that usually begins in the first few years of life or at any stage.

Emetic: Causing vomiting.

Emmenagogue: A substance that restores the menstrual flow.

Emollient: A substance, especially medicine, that softens the skin and cures it when sore.

Epilepsy: A neurological disorder.

Erysipelas: A skin disease characterized by large raised red patches on the face and legs.

Expectorant: A medicine that promotes the secretion of sputum through the air passages and is used primarily to treat coughs.

Febrifuge: A medicine used to reduce fever.

Fistula: An abnormal opening between two hollow organs.

Flatulence: The presence of excessive amounts of gas in the stomach or intestine.

Freckle: A small flat brown spot on the skin.

Galactagogue: A food or drug that promotes the flow of a mother's milk.

Gallstones: Stones of varying composition those form in the gall bladder.

General debility: General weakness.

Germicidal: A **substance** that kills harmful microorganisms.

Gleets: A discharge due to chronic gonorrhoea.

Gonorrhoea: A venereal disease involving inflammatory discharge from the urethra or vagina.

Gout: A disorder caused by an imbalance of uric acid in the body.

Gravel: Small stones formation in the urinary tract.

Haemoptysis: The coughing up blood.

Haemorrhages: A heavy discharge of blood from the blood vessels.

Haemorrhoid: Dilated (enlarged) veins in the walls of the anus and sometimes around the rectum.

Haemostatic: A process to prevent and stop bleeding.

Hepatic: Of or relating to the liver.

Hepatoprotective: Protecting the liver.

Hepatosplenomegaly: It is a condition that causes swelling and enlargement of the liver and spleen.

Herpes: A virus disease of the skin characterized by the formation of blisters.

Histamine: A compound released by cells in response to injury and allergic and inflammatory reactions, causing muscle contraction and capillary dilation.

Hydrophobia: An extreme or irrational fear of water.

Hyperlipidemic: Having an excess of lipid (for example, cholesterol) in the blood.

Hypertension: High blood pressure is when your blood pressure, the force of your blood pushing against the walls of your blood vessels, is consistently too high.

Hyperthyroidism: An overactive thyroid gland.

Hypothyroidism: An underactive thyroid gland.

Hysteria: A type of neurosis that is difficult to define and in which a range of symptoms may occur.

Inflammation: A process by which the body's white blood cells and the things they make, protect you from infection from outside invaders, such as bacteria and viruses.

Jaundice: A yellow staining of the skin and sclera (the whites of the eyes) by abnormally high blood levels of the bile pigment, bilirubin.

Kalemia: Potassium in the blood.

Latex: An opaque or milky fluid produced by many plants.

Leucoderma: A disease in which the pigment is lost from areas of the skin, causing whitish patches, also known as vitiligo.

Leucorrhoea: A whitish, viscid discharge from the vagina.

Lumbago: A pain in the lower back.

Malaisa: A general feeling of discomfort, illness.

Melancholy: A feeling of pensive sadness, typically with no apparent cause.

Migraine: A severe and throbbing headache, usually with pain on one side of the head and accompanied by nausea and disorder of the eyesight.

Mole: A small, dark brown, slightly raised mark on the skin caused by a high melanin concentration.

Mucilage: A viscous or gelatinous solution extracted from plants, used in medicine (to soothe inflammation) and adhesives.

Mydriatic: A substance causing the dilation of the pupil of the eye.

Nephritis: An inflammation of the kidney.

Nervine: A medicine used to calm the nerves.

Neuralgia: A chronic pain condition that affects the trigeminal nerve, which carries sensation from your face to your brain.

Nociception: The sensory nervous system's process of encoding noxious stimuli. In nociception, intense chemical, mechanical, or thermal stimulation of sensory nerve cells called nociceptors, produce a signal that travels along a nerve fibre chain via the brain's spinal cord.

Nodulocystic: A severe form of acne.

Oedema: An accumulation of fluid in the body.

Otalgia: Pain in the ear.

Oxytocic: Inducing contraction of the uterine smooth muscle.

Pectoral: A medication for disorders of the chest or the lungs.

Perennial: A woody or soft-stemmed plant that lives for more than two years.

Periodical: Recurring at regular intervals.

Pharyngitis: Sore throat.

Phlegm: The thick viscous substance produced in the nose and throat, especially when one has a cold.

Plaster: A soft, semi-solid preparation usually medicated, spread on gauze and placed on the skin over the affected area.

Pleurisy: An inflammation of the pleurae, causing pain when breathing. Pleura is the membrane lining the thorax and enveloping the lungs, in humans and other mammals.

Pneumonia: An infection that inflames your lungs' air sacs (alveoli). The air sacs may fill up with fluid or pus, causing symptoms such as a cough, fever, chills and giving trouble in breathing.

Poultice: A soft, moist mass of material consisting of flour, herbs, etc., applied with a cloth to the body to relieve inflammation.

Prolapse: A moving down of an organ.

Pruritus: A severe itching of the skin.

Psoriasis: A skin disease that causes red, itchy, scaly patches, most commonly on the knees, elbows, trunk and scalp.

Pyorrhoea: An inflammation of the sockets of the teeth usually leading to the loosening of the teeth.

Refrigerant: A drug or an herb that provides a sensation of coolness or reduces fever.

Resolvent: A drug or an agent that is able to stop inflammation and reduce swelling.

Rheumatism: Any disease marked by inflammation and pain in the joints, muscles or fibrous tissue.

Rhinitis: An inflammation of the mucous membrane of the nose caused by a viral infection or an allergic reaction.

Rickets: A disease affecting children that involves a deficiency of vitamin D.

Rubefacient: A substance that causes redness of the skin.

Sciatica: A pain in the sciatic nerve.

Sclerosis: An abnormal hardening of body tissue.

Scorbutic: Relating to scurvy which is a disease caused by deficiency of vitamin C, characterized by swollen bleeding gums and the opening of previously healed wounds.

Seborrhoea: A chronic inflammatory disease of the skin characterized by the accumulation of scales of the greasy skin.

Sedative: A substance having a soothing effect and usually causing sleep.

Sinusitis: An inflammation or swelling of the tissue lining the sinuses.

Stimulant: A substance that activates or excites the function of the body's organs or senses.

Stomachic: Promoting the appetite or assisting indigestion.

Strangury: A painful condition of blockage or irritation, at the base of the bladder.

Styptic: A substance that stops bleeding by causing the contraction of blood vessels.

Sudorific: A drug that causes sweating.

Syphilis: A sexually transmitted venereal disease causing infection of the genitals and eventually travels to the bones, muscles and the brain.

Thrombosis: A local coagulating or clotting of the blood in a part of the circulatory system.

Thymoleptic: An herb that favourably modifies mood.

Toxin: A poisonous substance produced by bacteria in a living or dead plant, or animal body.

Tuberculosis: A group of infections caused by the bacillus.

Tyrosinase: An oxidizing enzyme occurring in plant and animal tissues.

Ulcer: An open sore on an external or internal surface of the body caused by a break in the skin or the mucous membrane may bleed or produce poisonous matter.

Varicose: Veins that have become stretched, distended and twisted.

Vermifuge: A medication for driving worms out of human or animal bodies; an anthelmintic drug.

Vitiligo: See leucoderma.

Wart: A small, complex and benign growth on the skin caused by a virus.

Whooping cough: An infectious disease caused by the bacterium.

Bibliography

1. **A. Hannan, A. Saeed and U. Shafi,** Pharmacognosy and Materia Medica for Estern Medicine, (2013), Faculty of Eastern Medicine, Hamdard University, Karachi, Pakistan.
2. **A. N. Kalia,** Textbook of Industrial Pharmacognosy (2017), Printed by India Binding House, Noida, UP, India.
3. **Anonymous,** British Pharmacopoeia, (1998) Market Towers, 1- Nine Elms lane, London 5W8 5 NQ, United Kingdom
4. **Anonymous,** Forest And Environment Species, Punjab Forest Department, 24, Copper Road, Lahore, Pakistan.
5. **Anonymous,** National Formulary of Unani Medicine 1st Edition, (1981), Government of India, Ministry of Health and Family Welfare (Department of Health), New Delhi-110011, India.
6. **Anonymous,** Pharmacopoeia of India 2nd Edition, (1970) Ministry of Health, Government of India, Delhi, India.
7. **Anonymous,** Physicochemical Standards of Unani Formulations (1987), Central Council For Research In Unani Medicine, Ministery of Health and Family Welfare, Government of India, New Delhi, India.
8. **Anonymous,** The Ayurvedic Pharmacopoeia of India, 1st Edition, Part-1, Volumes 1, 2, 3, 4, 5 and 6 (2005), Ministry of Health and Family Welfare, Government of India, New Delhi, India.
9. **Anonymous,** The Siddha Pharmacopoeia of India, 1st Edition, Part-1, Vol.-1 (2011), Ministry of Health and Family Welfare, Government of India, New Delhi, India.
10. **Anonymous,** The Unani Pharmacopoeia of India 1st Edition. Part-1, Volume 1, 2 and 3 (2007), Department of AYUSH, Ministry of Health and Family Welfare, Government of India, New Delhi, India.
11. **Anonymous,** The Wealth of India, (1950), Council of Scientific and Industrial Research, Delhi, India.
12. **G.E.Trease and W. C. Eva,** Pharmacognosy (1985), Printed in Great Britain by the Alden Press, Oxford.
13. **Ibn al-Baitar,** Al-Jami li-Mufradat al-Adviya wa al-Aghziya, (1985), CCRUM, New Delhi, India
14. **James A. Duke,** Hand Book of Medicinal Plants, 2nd Edition (2002), CRC Press LLC, 2000 N.W. Corporate Blvd., Boca Raton, Florida 33431, USA.

15. **K. Usmanghani, A. Saeed and M. T. Alam,** Indusyunic Medicine (1997), Department of Pharmacognosy, Faculty of Pharmacy, University of Karachi-75270, Pakistan.
16. **K. Usmanghani,** Herbal Medicine Industry in Pakistan (2000), A- 952, Block H, North Nazimabad, Karachi-74700, Pakistan.
17. **K.H.C. Baser, G.Honda and W. Miki,** Herb Drugs and Herbalists in Turkey, (1986), Institute for the Study of Languages and Cultures of Asia and Africa, Tokyo University, Tokyo.
18. **K.M. Nadkarni,** Indian Materia Medica (1982), Popular Prakashan Pvt, Ltd, Bombay, India.
19. **K.R. Kirtikar and B.D. Basu,** Indian Medicinal Plants (1933), Lalit Mohan Basu, Allahabad, UP, India.
20. **L. Gordon,** A Country Herbal (1984), Peerage Brook, Publishers, 59, Grosvenor Street, London W1, England.
21. **M. A. Khan,** The Compendium of Muslim Civilization (2019), Ajmal Publications, Plot No 155, Kot Lakhpat, Lahore, Pakistan.
22. **M. Amirthalingam,** Plant Diversity in The Valmiki Ramayana (2013), C.P. Environmental Education Centre-1, Eldams Road, Alwarpet, Chennai, India.
23. **M. Awais,** 10-Medicinal Plants of Pakistan (2008), Institute of Pharmacy, The Faculty of Mathematics and Natural Sciences, The University of Oslo, Norway.
24. **M. Ikram, S.F. Hussain,** Compendium of Medicinal Plants (1978), Pakistan Council and Industrial Research, Peshawer, Pakistan.
25. **M. Kabiruddin,** (2017), Mukhzan-al-Mufradat (2017), Usman Publication, Urdu Bazaar, Lahore, Pakistan.
26. **M. Said,** Hamdard, Pharmacopoeia of Eastern Medicine 2nd Edition, (1970), The Time Press, Sadar, Karachi.
27. **M. Zohary,** Plants of The Bible (1982), Cambridge University Press, Cambridge, England.
28. **M.Ali,** Textbook of Pharmacognosy 2nd Edition (2000), Neekunj Printing Press, Delhi, India.
29. **M.H. Awan, (2019),** Kitab-ul- Mufaradat Al-Marouf Khawas-ul-AAdvia (2016), Sheikh Ghulam Ali and Sons, 199, Circular Road, Anarkali, Lahore-54000, Pakistan.
30. **M.K. Hossain, I.Sobhan, M.K.Alam, N.A.Khan,** Selected Medicinal Plants of Chittagong (2011), IUCN, Bangladesh Country Club, House No-11, Road 138, Gulshan-1, Dhaka-1212, Bangladesh.
31. **M.S. Khan,** An Introduction to Islamic Medicine (2016) 5th Edition, 446, East Park Road, Leicester, England.

32. **N. A. Bloch,** Great Books of Islamic Civilization (1989), Pakistan Hijra Council, Islamabad.
33. **NajmulGhani,** Khazain-al Adviya (1971), Noval Kishore, Lucknow, Utter Pradesh (UP), India.
34. **P Pietroni,** Alternative Medicine (1991), Reader's Digest Associated Limited Berkeley Square House, London W 1X 6Ab, England.
35. **P. Frederic,** Agnes and J. McBrewster, (2010), Oxford & IBH Publishing Co, 113-B Shahpur Jat, New Delhi 110049, India.
36. **R.C. Wren and R.W. Wren**, Potter's New Cyclopaedia of Botanical Drugs and Preparations (1975), Health Science Press, Hengiscote, Bradford.
37. **R.L. Johnson and S Foster,** Healing Herbs (2012), Published by the National Geographic Society, 1145 17th Street N.W., Washington, D.C. 20036
38. **R.N. Chopra, I.C. Chopra and B.S. Varma,** (1969) Supplement to Glossary of Indian Medicinal Plants, Council of Scientific and Industrial Research, New Delhi, India.
39. **S. Ahsan and Rohma** (2008), Contribution Of Medieval Arab-Muslim Scientists To Botany And Agriculture, PhD. Thesis, Department of Islamic Studies, Aligarh Muslim University Aligarh, India.
40. **Sharif. Khan (Hakim),** Taleef-e-Sharifi (1301 AH), Matba Kishore Darussalam, Delhi, India.
41. **V. Sodhi,** Ayurvedic Herbs (2014), New Leaf Distribution Company, 401, Thornton Road, Lithia Springs, Georgia, USA.
42. **W.C. Evans, G.D. Trease and D.Evans,** Pharmacognosy (2002), W.B. Saunders, Edinburgh, Scotland, United Kingdom.

Index of Latin Binomials

A

Abelmoschus esculentus, **242**, 243, 485
Acacia arabica, **233**, 234, 301, 456, 485
Acacia catechu, **301**, 302, 459
Acacia nilotica, 233
Acacia senegal, **239**, 240
Acalypha indica, **139**, 140, 141
Achillea millefolium, **10**, 11, 468
Achras sapota, **398**, 399, 400
Achyranthes aspera, **208**, 209, 484
Aconitum heterophyllum, 12
Aconitum napellus, **12**, 13, 468
Acorus calamus, **333**, 334
Actaea racemosa, **432**, 433
Adhatoda vasica, **14**, 15, 468
Adiantum capillus veneris, 134, **141**, 142
Aegle marmelos, **244**, 457, 486
Agathosma betulina, 145
Alexandrine senna, 152
Alhagi maurorum, **261**, 262, 282, 457
Allium cepa, **335**, 461
Allium sativum, **336**, 337, 348, 433, 462
Aloe barbadensis, 434
Aloe vera, **143**, 144
Alpine galangal, **262**, 263, 264
Alpine officinarum, 263
Althaea officinalis, **245**, 246, 247, 486
Amomum subulatum, **338**, 339
Amygdalus communis, 178
Andropogon squarrosus, 391

Anethum graveolens, **340**, 341, 462, 490
Anogeissus Latifolia, 235
Apis dorsta, 103, 104
Apis mellifera, **103**, 104, 452
Arachis hypogaea, **109**, 110
Areca catechu, **15**, 16, 415, 468
Artemisia absinthium, **396**, 398, 434, 465, 494
Artemisia annua, 396, 397, 434
Artemisia vulgaris, 396
Asparagus adscendens, **209**, 210
Asparagus officinalis, 211
Asparagus racemosus, **211**, 212, 484
Atropa belladonna, 5, **17**, 18, 37, 48, 67, 124, 469
Avena sativa, **82**, 83, 476
Azadirachta indica, 176, 272, **416**

B

Bambusa arundinacea, **247**, 248, 457
Barosma betulina, **145**, 480
Batatas paniculata, 88
Bauhinia variegate, **302**, 303, 459
Berberis aristata, **19**, 20, 435, 469
Beta vulgaris, **83**, 84, 476
Bombax ceiba, **236**, 237, 453
Boswellia glabra, **264**, 265, 436, 457, 486
Brassica juncea, 146, 147
Brassica nigra, 135, **146**, 147, 454
Butea frondosa, 303
Butea monosperma, **303**, 304, 305, 459, 465

C

Caesalpinia bonduc, 135, **148,** 149, 301, 480
Calamus draco, 273
Camellia sinensis, **21,** 22, 436, 469
Careya arborea, **400,** 401
Carissa carandas, 301, **305,** 306
Carum carvi, **341,** 342, 343, 462
Carum gracile, 341
Cassia angustifolia, 87, 134, **152,** 153
Cassia fistula, 134, **150,** 151, 153, 301, 454
Cassia senna, 87, 134, **152,** 153, 454
Catharanthus roseus, 9, **23,** 437
Centella asiatica, 401
Centella asiatica, **401,** 402
Cephaelis ipecacuanha, **25,** 470
Cheiranthus cheiri, **154,** 155
Chenopodium album, **343,** 344, 490
Chenopodium ambrosioides, 343
Cichorium endivia, 156
Cichorium intybus, 135, **156,** 157, 480
Cinchona officinalis, **27,** 470
Cinnamomum camphora, **344,** 345, 346, 462, 491
Cinnamomum cassia, **346,** 347, 462, 463
Cinnamomum tamala, 134, **157,** 158, 364
Cinnamomum zeylanicum, 134, **158,** 159, 160, 455, 481
Citrullus colocynthis, 135, **160,** 161, 455, 481
Citrus limetta, 347
Citrus sinensis, **347**
Citrus x aurantifolia, **85,** 86, 451, 491
Claviceps purpurea, 9, **29,** 30, 116, 470

Cochlospermum gossypium, 123, **237,** 238, 239, 251, 485
Cochlospermum religiosum, 237, 485
Cocos nucifera, **111,** 478
Coffea arabica, **30,** 32, 471
Colchicum autumnale, **32,** 33, 471
Colchium luteum, 32
Commiphora molmol, **266,** 267, 458, 486
Commiphora mukul, **267,** 268
Commiphora myrrha, 266
Commiphora stocksiana, **291,** 292, 459
Conium maculatum, **34,** 35, 450, 471
Convoluvlus scammonia, **268,** 269
Copaifera langsdorffii, **270,** 271
Coptis teeta, **36,** 37
Cordia dichotoma, 249
Cordia latifolia, **249,** 457
Coriandrum sativum, **349,** 463
Crataeva marmelos, 244
Crocus sativus, **403,** 404, 438, 465, 494
Croton tiglium, 134, **162,** 163, 481
Cuminum cyminum, **350,** 351, 463
Curcuma longa, 134, **271,** 272, 273, 439, 487
Cycas revoluta, 251
Cycas sphaerica, **251,** 252
Cydonia vulgaris, 256
Cymbopogon jwarancusa, 352
Cymbopogon martini, **352,** 353
Cymbopogon martinii, **352,** 353
Cyperus rotundus, **404,** 405

D

Daemonorops draco, **273,** 274
Datura stramonium, 5, **37,** 38, 48, 471
Daucus carota, **407**

Delphinium denudatum, **406,** 407
Dendrocalamus strictus, 247
Digitalis purpurea, 134, **164,** 165, 481
Dioscorea brevipes, 165
Dioscorea sylvatica, **165,** 166, 167
Dorema ammoniacum, **274,** 275, 276, 487
Doronicum hookeri, **39,** 40, 471
Drimia indica, 199
Dryopteris chrysocoma, **276,** 277

E

Echinops echinatus, 134, **167,** 168, 455
Elaeis guineensis, **112,** 478
Elettaria cardamomum, **353,** 354
Elettaria repens, 353
Emblica officinalis, 301, **306,** 307, 488
Eruca sativa, **113,** 114, 452, 478
Erythroxylum coca, **41,** 42, 472
Eucalyptus obliqua, **355,** 356
Eugenia aromatic, 385
Euphorbia hirta, **410**
Euphorbia thymifolia, **409,** 410
Exogonium purge, 285

F

Ferula assafoetida, 277
Ferula foetida, 260, **277,** 278, 487
Ferula galbaniflua, **279,** 280, 458
Ferula jaeschkeana, 279
Ferula persica, **280,** 281
Ferula szovitsiana, 280
Ficus carica, **87,** 88, 451, 476
Filix-Mas, 276
Foeniculum vulgare, **356**
Frangula purshiana, 184
Fraxinus ornus, **281,** 282

Fumaria officinalis, **42,** 43, 44, 472

G

Galipea officinalis, **44,** 45
Garcinia cambogia, 283
Garcinia morella, **283,** 458
Gentiana lutea, **169,** 170, 481
Ginkgo biloba, 134, **170,** 171, 482
Glycyrrhiza glabra, **212,** 213, 441, 484
Gossypium herbaceum, **115,** 116, 452, 479
Guilandinia bonduc, 135, 148
Gymnema sylvestre, **412,** 413
Gynostemma pentaphyllum, **214,** 215, 484

H

Hamamelis virginiana, **307,** 308, 309, 490
Helianthus annuus, **117,** 118, 479
Hemidesmus indicus, 207, **216,** 217, 441
Holarrhena antidysenterica, **46,** 47
Hyocymus scoplia, 66
Hyoscyamus niger, 5, **48,** 49, 67, 450, 472

I

Ipomoea hederacea, **284,** 285, 487
Ipomoea paniculata, **88,** 89, 90, 476
Ipomoea purge, **285,** 286, 488
Ipomoea turpethum, **286**

J

Juniperus communis, **358,** 463, 491
Juniperus oxycedrus, **359,** 360

Justicia adhatoda, 14

L

Lactuca serriola, **361,** 362, 491
Lagenaria siceraria, **413,** 414, 466
Laurus nobilis, **362,** 363, 364, 491
Lavandula x stoechas, **364,** 365
Lawsonia alba, 309
Lawsonia inermis, **309,** 310, 459, 460, 489
Linum usitatissimum, **118,** 119, 453, 457, 479
Liquidambar orientalis, **292,** 293, 459
Lobelia inflata, **49,** 50
Lobelia nicotianiefolia, 49

M

Mallotus philippinensis, **415,** 416
Mandragora officinarum, **51,** 52, 450, 473
Manilkara zapota, 398
Matricaria chamomilla, **366**
Maytenus ilicifolia, **442**
Melia azedarach, **416**
Melilotus indicus, 172
Melilotus officinalis, **172,** 173
Mentha x piperita, **368,** 369
Mimosa catechu, 301
Mitragyna speciosa, **52,** 53, 473
Morus alba, 134, **173,** 174, 175, 455, 482
Morus indica, 173
Musa acuminata, **90,** 91
Myrica esculenta, **311,** 312
Myrica nagi, 311
Myristica fragrans, **370,** 371
Myroxylon balsamum, **293,** 294, 295

Myroxylon pereirae, **295,** 296

N

Nephrodium filix-mas, 276
Nicotiana tabacum, **54,** 55, 473

O

Ocimum basilicum, **252,** 253, 457, 486
Ocimum sanctum, 252
Olea europaea, **120,** 121, 453, 479
Operculina turpethum, **286,** 287
Origanum majorana, 371
Origanum marjorana, **371**
Origanum vulgaris, 373
Oryza sativa, **92,** 93, 477

P

Panax ginseng, **217,** 218, 485
Panax quinquefolium, 217
Papaver somniferum, **55**
Pedalium murex, **219,** 220
Peganum harmala, **57,** 58, 473
Pernambuco jaborandi, 59, 474
Peucedanum graveolens, 340
Phoenix dactylifera, 94, 451
Phoenix sylvestris, **94,** 95, 451, 477
Phyllanthus emblica, 306, 324
Picrorhiza kurroa, **175,** 176
Pilocarpus jaborandi, **59,** 60, 474
Pimpinella anisum, **374,** 376
Pinus longifolia, 288
Pinus palustris, **376,** 377, 464
Pinus roxburghii, **288,** 289, 458
Piper cubeba, **377,** 378, 492
Piper longum, 8, **61,** 62, 273, 450, 474
Piper nigrum, 8, **63,** 64, 149, 273, 474

Pistacia lentiscus, **289**, 290, 458
Plantago decumbens, 254
Plantago ispaghula, 254
Plantago ovata, **254**, 255, 488
Polygala senega, 140, **220**, 221
Polygonum bistorta, 134, **177**, 178
Polygonum viviparum, 134, 177
Polypodium vulgare, **222**, 223, 485
Prunus amara, **178**, 179
Prunus amygdalus, **122**, 123, 135, 453, 479
Prunus armeniaca, **180**, 181
Prunus laurocerasus, 181
Prunus serotina, **181**
Psoralea corylifolia, 135, **182**, 183, 184
Pterocarpus santalinus, **379**, 380, 464
Punica granatum, **312**, 460, 489
Pyrethrum indicum, **380**, 381, 492
Pyrus cydonia, **256**, 257

Q

Quercus baloot, 301, **314**, 315, 460
Quercus incana, 314
Quercus infectoria, **315**, 489
Quillaja brasiliensis, 224, 225
Quillaja saponaria, **224**, 225

R

Rauwolfia serpentina, **64**, 65, 66, 475
Rhamnus purshiana, **184**, 185, 482
Rheum emodi, 87, **186**, 442, 482
Rheum officinale, 186
Rhus coriaria, **316**, 317
Ricinus communis, **124**, 125, 453, 466
Rosa indica, 382
Rosa x damascena, **382**
Rubia cordifolia, **188**, 189, 455
Rumex acetosa, **318**, 319
Ruta graveolens, 134, **189**, 190, 443, 455

S

Saccharum bengalense, 95
Saccharum officinarum, **95**
Salix aegyptiaca, 191
Salix alba, **319**, 320, 460
Salix purpurea, 135, **191**
Salmalia malabarica, 236
Santalum album, 380, **383**, 384, 464, 493
Saponaria officinalis, **225**, 226
Saraca asoca, 320
Saraca indica, **320**, 321, 322, 460, 490
Saussurea lappa, **418**, 419
Scopolia carniolica, **66**, 67, 68, 475
Senegalia senegal, **239**, 240
Sesamum indicum, **125**, 126, 480
Sida cordifolia, **68**, 69, 450
Smilax china, 192, 193
Smilax glabra, 134, **192**, 193, 483
Solanum miniatum, **444**
Solanum tuberosum, **97**, 98, 477
Sterculia urens, **240**, 241, 242
Strophanthus hispidus, 134, **194**, 195, 483
Strychnos nuxvomica, **70**, 71, 475
Swertia chirata, 135, **196**, 197
Symplocos chinensis, 198
Symplocos racemosa, 134, **197**, 198, 199, 456
Syzygium aromaticum, **385**, 386, 493

T

Tamarindus indica, **98**, 100, 301, 477

Tanacetum umbelliferum, **388,** 389
Tanacetum vulgare, 388
Taxus baccata, 420
Taxus wallichiana, **420,** 421, 444, 445
Tephrosia purpurea, **421,** 422
Terminalia arjuna, **322,** 323, 461, 490
Terminalia belerica, **323,** 324, 461
Terminalia chebula, 300, 301, 324, **325,** 326
Teucrium chamaedrys, **390,** 391
Teucrium stoksianum, 390
Theobroma cacao, **126,** 127
Thymus serpyllum, 387
Thymus vulgaris, **387,** 388, 493
Tiglium officinale, 162
Tinospora cordifolia, **71,** 72
Trigonella foenum-graecum, **229,** 230, 456
Triticum aestivum, **100,** 101, 451, 477
Tylophora indica, 26, **73,** 74, 476

U

Urginea indica, 134, **199,** 483
Urginea maritima, 134

V

Vaccinium myrtillus, **445,** 446
Valeriana hardwickii, **423,** 424
Valeriana officinalis, **425,** 426, 427, 463, 495
Vanilla planifolia, **200,** 201, 483
Vetiveria zizanioides, **391,** 392
Viola indica, 393
Viola odorata, **393,** 394, 494
Viscum album, **446**
Vitis vinifera, **101,** 102, 103, 447, 452, 477, 478

W

Wrightia rothii, 75
Wrightia tinctoria, **75,** 76, 476

Z

Zanthoxylum armatum, 135, 202, 203
Zea mays, **128,** 129, 480
Zingiber officinale, **448**
Ziziphus jujuba, **326,** 327, 328

INDEX OF ENGLISH NAMES

A

Acacia, 234
Aconite, 12
Almond, 122
Aloe, 143
Angostura, 44
Anise, 374
Apricot, 180
Arjun, 322
Asafoetida, 278
Ashoka Tree, 321
Asparagus, 211
Asthma Plant, 410
Autumn Crocus, 32
Axle Wood tree, 235

B

Bael Fruit, 244
Balsam, 291
Bamboo Manna, 247
Banana, 90
Basil, 253
Bay Berry, 311
Bay Leaf, 362
Beetroot, 84
Beleric myrobalan, 323
Belladonna, 17
Berberry, 19
Betel Nut, 15
Bistorta, 177
Bitter Almond, 178
Bitter Oleander, 46

Black Caraway, 341
Black Cardamom, 338
Black Pepper, 63
Bonduc Nut, 148
Box Myrtle, 311
Buchu, 145
Butea tree, 304

C

Cade Juniper, 359
Calamus, 333
Caltrops Large, 219
Caltrops Small, 227
Camel thorn, 261
Camel's Foot Tree, 302
Camel's Thistle, 167
Camphor, 345
Cape Periwinkle, 23
Cardamom, 353
Carrot, 407
Cascara, 184
Cascara Sagrada, 162
Casplan manna, 261
Cassia Pod, 150
Castor, 124
Catechu, 301
Chaff-Flower, 208
Chamomile, 366
Chebulic myrobalan, 325
Chicoo, 398
Chicory, 156
China Root, 192

Chinese Cinnamon, 346
Chir Pine, 288
Chirata, 196
Chittem Bark, 184
Chocolate Tree, 126
Cinchona Bark, 27
Cinnamon, 159
Cinnamon leaves, 157
Citrus, 86, 348, 349
Clove, 385
Coca, 41
Coconut, 111
Coctus, 418
Coffee, 30
Colchicum, 32
Colocynth, 160
Common Marjoram, 371
Copaiba, 270
Coral Swirl, 46
Coriander, 349
Corn, 128
Cotton seeds, 115
Cotton Tree Gum, 230
Country Mallow, 68
Crescent Lignum, 172
Croton, 162
Cubebs, 378
Cumin, 351
Cuscus Grass, 391
Cycas, 251

D

Date, 94
Datura, 37
Deadly Nightshade, 17
Delphinium, 406
Dill, 340

E

Earth Smoke, 42
Endive, 156
Ergot, 29
Eucalyptus, 355
Euphorbia Small, 409

F

Fennel, 356
Fenugreek, 229
Fig, 87
Filix-Mas, 276
Flame-of-the-Forest, 304
Flaxseeds, 118
Flea Seeds, 254
Flowering -Ash, 281
Foxglove, 164
Frankincense, 264
Fumitory, 42

G

Galangal, 263
Galbanum, 279
Gamboge, 283
Garden Asparagus, 209
Garlic, 337
Gentian, 169
Germander, 390

Ginkgo, 170
Ginseng, 217
Golden Shower, 150
Golden Thread Root, 36
Grapes, 102
Greater Cardamom, 338
Grey Oak, 314
Guggul, 267
Gum Foetida, 278
Gurjo, 71
Gymnema Plant, 412

H

Hemlock, 34
Henbane, 48
Henbane bell, 67
Henna, 309
Honey, 104

I

Inderjo Sweet, 75
Indian acalypha, 139
Indian Coctus, 418
Indian gooseberry, 306
Indian ipecac, 73
Indian Ipecac, 25
Indian Jalap, 286
Indian lilac, 416
Indian Olibanum, 264
Indian Pennywort, 401
Indian Squill, 199
Indian Tobacco, 49
Ipecacuanha, 25

J

Jaborandi, 59
Jalap, 285
Jesuit's bark, 27
Jiaogulan, 214
John's Root, 285
Jujuba, 326
Juniper, 358

K

Kamala, 415
Karanda, 305
Karaya Gum, 241
Karukum, 272
Key Lime, 85
Khas-Khas Grass, 391
Kratom, 52
Kuth, 418

L

Lady Fingers, 243
Lavender, 364
Lemon, 85
Leopards Bane, 39
Lettuce, 361
Linseed, 118
Liquorice, 212
Lobelia, 49
Lodh Tree, 198
Long leaf Indian Pine, 288
Long Pepper, 61

M

Madder, 188
Maidenhair, 141

Malabar-nut, 14
Male Fern, 276
Mandrake, 51
Manna Ash, 281
Margosa, 416
Marjoram, 373
Marshmallow, 246
Mastic, 289
Meadow Saffron, 32
Melilot, 172
Mulberry, 173
Mustard Black, 146
Myrrah, 266

N

Nut Grass, 404
Nutmeg, 370
Nux Vomica, 70

O

Oak Galls, 315
Oat, 82
Okra, 243
Olive, 120
Onion, 335
Opium, 56
Orchid Tree, 302

P

Palm, 112
Peanut, 109
Pellitory, 388
Peppermint, 368
Periwinkle, 23
Persian Cumin, 341
Peru Balsam, 295

Pharbitis Seeds, 284
Picrorhiza, 176
Pine, 376
Polypody, 222
Pomegranate, 312
Potato, 97
Psoralea, 183
Psyllium Husk, 254
Pyrethrum, 381

Q

Quillaia bark, 224
Quince Fruit, 256
Quince Seeds, 256

R

Rauwolfia, 64
Red Sandal, 379
Rhubarb, 186
Rice, 92
Rocket, 114
Rose, 382
Rue, 190
Russ Grass, 352

S

Saffron, 403
Sagapenum gum
 Kundal, 280
Sak, 280
Salmalia gum, 236
Sandalwood, 384
Sarsaparilla, 216
Scammony, 269
Scopolia, 67
Sebestan Plum, 249

Senega, 220
Senna, 152
Sesame, 125
Silver Fir, 420
Slow Match Tree, 400
Small Euphorbia, 410
Snakeroot, 220
Soap Wort, 226
Sorrel, 318
Spogel, 254
Squill, 199
Sterculia Gum, 241
Stone Apple, 244
Storax, 292
Stramonium, 37
Strophanthus, 194
Sudan Gum, 239
Sugar cane, 95
Sumaq, 317
Sunflower, 117
Sweet Almond, 122
Sweet Bay, 362
Sweet Flag, 333
Sweet gum, 292
Sweet Lemon, 348
Sweet Orange, 348
Sweet Potato, 88
Syrian Rue, 57

T

Tamarind, 98
Tea, 21
Thorn Apple, 37
Thyme-leaved
 Euphorbia, 409
Tinospora, 71
Tobacco, 54

Tolu Balsam, 294
Tragacanth, 238
True Valerian, 425
Turmeric, 272
Turpeth, 286
Tylophore, 73

V

Valerian, 423
Vanilla, 201
Vasaka, 14, 468
Viola, 393
Violet Flowers, 393

W

Wallflower, 154
Wheat, 100
White Goose Foot, 343
Wild Cherry Bark, 181
Wild Guava, 400
Wild Thyme, 387
Wild Yam, 166
Willow, 191
Willow Barks, 191
Willow White, 319
Witch-hazel, 308

Wormwood, 396

Y

Yarrow, 10
Yellow Thistle, 421
Yew, 420

Z

Zanthoxylum, 202

Index of Urdu Names

A

Aalu, 97
Aarar, 358
Abhal, 358
Adrak, 448
Afiyun, 56
Afsanteen, 396, 434, 465, 494
Ailwa, 143, 434
Ajwain-e-Khurasani, 48
Aklil-Ul-Mulik, 172
Aljunaka, 170
Alkayna alnibah, 27
Alkina, 27
Alkubiba, 270
Alsi, 118
Alssahiruh Hazil, 308
Amaltaas, 150
Amar-Bail, 446
Amla, 306
Anantamul, 216
Anantmul, 73
Anbul Saalab, 444
Angoor, 101, 102, 447, 452, 477
Angusturaan, 45
Anisun, 374
Anjbar, 177
Anjeer, 87
Annar, 312
Antmool, 73
Anub-us-Saa'lab, 17
Aqaqia, 234
Aqarqara, 381
Arand, 124
Arghut, 29
Arjun, 322
Arjuna, 322
Arosa, 14
Arq-uz-Zahab, 25
Asal, 104
Asalas-Soos, 213
Asarun, 423
Asbynhyra Santaan, 442
Ashoka, 321
Aspand, 58
Asqeel, 199
Asroal, 65
Atees, 12
Azraqi, 70

B

Baalchar, 425
Babchi, 183
Babuna, 366
Badam, 122
Badam Talkh, 178
Badiyaan, 357
Bahira, 323
Bail-I-Giri, 244
Balilah, 323
Balsan, 291
Banafsha, 393
Banafsha Shab-boo, 114
Bansa, 14
Banslowchan, 247
Baokhumba, 400
Barham Dandi, 167
Barhami Buti, 402
Bathwa, 343
Batshu, 145
Bed Mushk, 191, 319
Beej-Band, 68, 450
Behi, 256
Behidana, 256
Behroza, 288
Berg-e-Sadab, 443
Bhendi, 243
Bichnag, 12
Bidari-kand, 88
Bile-Lotan, 425
Binola, 115
Biranjasif, 10
Bisbasa, 370
Bisfaij, 222
Buchu, 145
Buzedan, 388
Byru Bilisam, 295

C

Chaliya, 16
Charchitah, 208
Chawal, 92
Chayi, 21, 436
Cheer, 376
Cheery, 181
Chikoo, 398
Chiraita, 196
Chob Chini, 192
Chocolate Tree, 126
Choti Candan, 65
Chuqandar, 84
Coca, 41

D

Damm-ul-Akhwain, 274
Darchini, 159
Darhald, 19
Darunaj Aqrabi, 39
Dhanya, 349
Dhaturah, 37
Dhava, 235
Dudhi Kalan, 410
Dudhi Khurd, 409

E

Ealakat Satirikyula, 241
Easal, 104

F

Fanilana, 201
Faranj-Mushk, 253
Farfeeran, 283
Filfil Daraz, 61

G

Gajar, 407
Ganda Behroza, 279
Ganna, 95
Gasol, 226
Ghatti Gond, 235
Gilu, 72
Ginkgo, 170
Gokhru, 227
Gokhru Klaan, 219
Gond Jawasa, 281
Gond Katira, 238
Gond Kiker, 234
Gugal, 267
Gulab, 382

Gul-e-Surkh, 382
Gundum, 100
Gurmar Buti, 412
Guzar, 407

H

Hab-el-Ghar, 362
Habul-ul-Neel, 284
Haldi, 134, 271, 272, 439, 487
Halila Siyah, 325
Hammaz, 318
Hanzal, 160
Harmal, 58
Harr, 325
Hasha, 387
Henna, 309
Hiltit, 278
Hing, 278
Hussain Booti, 390

I

Ilaichi Kalan, 338
Ilaichi Khurd, 353
Ilaichi Sabz, 353
Imli, 98
Inderjo Shirin, 75
Inderjo-Tulkh, 46
Indrain Talkh, 160
Ispaghul, 254
Izkhir, 352

J

Jadwar, 406
Jaifal, 370
Jalapah, 285

Jamal-Gotta, 162
Jangli Abhal, 359
Jangli Piyaz, 199
Jangli Pudina, 387
Jarjir, 114
Jau, 82
Jawashir, 279
Jawatri, 370
Jayawjulan, 214
Jenseng, 218
Jhalar, 59
Jozbuwa, 370

K

Kabab Chini, 378
Kabab-e-Khandan, 202
Kachnar, 303
Kaddu, 413
Kafi, 30
Kafur, 345
Kahu, 361
Kaiphal, 311
Kakronda, 305
Kaladana, 284
Kali Mirch, 63
Kalpura, 390
Kamela, 415
Kangi Palm, 251
Kapas, 115
Karanjwa, 148
Kari-patta, 157
Kasikarana, 184
Kasni, 156
Katan, 118
Katha, 301
Katira, 238
Kela, 90

Medicinal Plants — Urdu Names

Khajur, 94
Khar-e-Khask, 227
Khas, 391
Khatmi, 246
Khayar Shanber, 150
Kher, 239
Khopra, 111
Khubani, 180
Khulanjan, 263
Khurma, 94
Kiraat, 169
Kishmish, 102
Kishneez, 349
Koka Darakht, 126
Kombe, 194
Kuchla, 70
Kuka, 41
Kundal, 280
Kunder, 264
Kunjad, 125
Kuppi, 139
Kuthi, 176

L

Lehsan, 336, 337, 433, 462
Loban, 264, 436, 457, 486
Lodh Pathani, 198
Loofa, 68, 450
Loung, 385
Luffah, 17

M

Maar Beekh, 220
Majith, 188
Makai, 128
Mako, 444
Malta, 348
Mamiran, 36
Mardum Giyah, 51
Mastaghi, 289
Maya Ambar Desi, 293
Mazu, 315
Mehndhi, 309
Methi, 229
Mirzanjosh, 371
Mochrus, 236
Mong-Phali, 109
Mousammi, 348
Mulaithi, 212, 213, 441, 484
Muqil, 267
Murr, 266
Musambi, 348
Musli Safaid, 210

N

Nagar-Motha, 404
Nariyal, 111
Neeli-Berry, 445
Neem, 416
Niazbo, 253
Nibat Alkarz, 181
Nibu, 85

P

Paatha, 440
Palas, 304
Panbah Dana, 115
Pershiaoashan, 141
Peru Ka Gond, 295
Piplamul, 61
Piyaz, 134, 199, 335, 461, 483
Post Cascara, 184
Post Cinchona, 27
Pudina, 368

Q

Qahua, 30
Qaranful, 385
Qartum, 52
Qonyun, 34
Quillaia Ke Chaal, 224
Qust, 418

R

Rai, 146
Rasout, 19, 435
Ratalu, 166
Rewand Chini, 186
Rewand-Chini, 442

S

S' ad Kufi, 404
Sa'atar, 373
Saban Ka Poda, 226
Sadab, 190
Sada-Bahar, 23, 437
Safayda, 355
Sago Balm, 251
Sahtaraj, 43
Sak, 280
Sandal Safaid, 384
Sandal Surkh, 379
Sanobar, 376
Sapistan, 249
Saqmunia, 269

Sarkhas, 276
Sarpagandha, 65
Sarphoka, 421
Satawar, 211
Satawari, 211
Sat-e-Behroza, 288
Sat-e-Gilu, 72
Sat-e-Rumi, 72
Senna Makki, 152
Sennai Iskandaria, 152
Shabbat, 340
Shah-Baloot, 314
Shahed, 104
Shahtarah, 43
Shahtut, 173
Shaqaqul Misri, 210
Shaqar Qand, 88
Shukran, 34
Sibr, 143
Silaras, 293
Skubulia Karnywlyka, 67
Soap Plant, 226
Sounf, 357
Soya, 340
Sumac, 317
Sumbal-at-Teeb, 425
Supari, 16
Suraj-Mukhi, 117
Suranjan-e-Shireen, 32

T

Tabasheer, 247
Taggar, 423
Taj, 346
Talishpatar, 420
Tambahu Jangli, 50
Tambaku, 54
Tamir Hindi, 98
Tamir Hindium, 98
Tara-Mira, 114
Taranjebin, 261
Tarbud, 286
Tarr, 112
Tesu, 304
Tezpat, 157
Tez-patta, 157
Thandi Booti, 141
Thiubruma Alkakaw, 126
Til, 125
Todri Surkh, 154
Tolu Ka Gond, 294
Tubut, 286
Tulsi-Jangli, 253
Turanjbin, 281

U

Unnab, 326

Usarah-e-Rewand, 283
Ushaq, 275
Ushbah, 216, 441
UstuKhuddus, 364

V

Vanilla, 201

W

Waj-Turki, 333
Waylad Yam, 166

Y

Yukaliptus, 355

Z

Zafran, 403, 438, 465, 494
Zaitoon, 120
Zarishk, 19
Zarnab, 420, 444
Zehar-al-Kashatabeen, 164
Zirah Safaid, 351
Zirah Siyah, 342

Index of Plant Family

A

Acanthaceae, 14
Acoraceae, 333
Altingiaceae, 292
Amaranthaceae, 83, 208
Amaryllidaceae, 335, 336
Anacardiaceae, 289, 316
Apiaceae, 34, 275, 278, 279, 280, 340, 341, 349, 351, 401, 407
Apidae of Order Hymenoptera (Z/O), 103
Apocynaceae, vii, 9, 23, 26, 46, 64, 65, 75, 136, 194, 216, 301, 305, 437, 475
Araceae, 333
Araliaceae, 217
Arecaceae, 15, 94, 111, 112, 273
Asclepiadaceae, 73, 216, 412
Asparagaceae, 199, 209, 211
Asphodelaceae, 143
Asteraceae, 10, 39, 117, 156, 167, 361, 366, 381, 388, 396, 418, 434, 455

B

Berberidaceae, 19
Bombacaceae, 236
Boraginaceae, 249
Brassicaceae, 114, 115, 146
Burseraceae, 264, 266, 267, 291
Buxaceae, 238

C

Caesalpiniaceae, 98, 148, 150, 152
Campanulaceae, 49
Caprifoliaceae, 423, 425
Caryophyllaceae, 226
Chenopodiaceae, 83, 343
Clavicipitaceae, 29
Clusiaceae, 283
Cochlospermaceae, 238
Colchicaceae, 32
Combretaceae, 235, 322, 323, 325
Compositae, 10, 39, 156, 167, 361, 366, 381, 396, 418
Convolvulaceae, 88, 269, 284, 285, 286
Cruciferae, 114, 146, 154
Cucurbitaceae, 160, 214, 413
Cupressaceae, 358, 359
Cycadaceae, 251
Cyperaceae, 404

D

Dioscoreaceae, 165
Dryopteridaceae, 276

E

Erythroxylaceae, 41
Euphorbiaceae, 124, 139, 162, 306, 409, 410, 415

F

Fabaceae, 98, 109, 152, 172, 212, 229, 234, 239, 261, 270, 293, 301, 302, 304, 320, 379, 421
Fagaceae, 314, 315
Fumariaceae, 42

G

Garcinia morella, 283
Gentianaceae, 169, 196
Ginkgoaceae, 170
Gramineae, 247, 352, 391
Guttiferae, 283

H

Hamamelidaceae, 292, 308
Hypocreaceae, 29

I

Iridaceae, 403

L

Labiatae, 364, 368, 371, 373, 390
Lamiaceae, 253, 364, 368, 371, 373, 387, 390
Lauraceae, 157, 159, 344, 346, 362
Lecythidaceae, 400
Leguminosae, 183, 270, 293, 295, 320
Liliaceae, 32, 143, 192, 199, 209, 211, 335, 336
Linaceae, 118
Lobeliaceae, 49
Loganiaceae, 70
Lythraceae, 309

M

Malvaceae, 68, 115, 126, 236, 241, 242, 245
Meliaceae, 416
Menispermaceae, 71
Mimosaceae, 234
Moraceae, 87, 173

Musaceae, 90
Myricaceae, 311
Myristicaceae, 370
Myrtaceae, 355, 385, 400

N

Nitrariaceae, 57

O

Oleaceae, 120, 281
Orchidaceae, 201

P

Palmae, 15, 94, 111, 273
Papaveraceae, 56
Papilionaceae, 172, 183, 212, 229, 304, 379, 421
Pedaliaceae, 125, 219
Phyllanthaceae, 306
Pinaceae, 288, 376
Piperaceae, 61, 63, 377
Plantaginaceae, 164, 254
Poaceae, 82, 92, 95, 100, 128, 247, 352, 391
Polygalaceae, 220
Polygonaceae, 177, 186, 222, 318
Polypodiaceae, 141, 222
Pteridaceae, 141, 276
Punicaceae, 312

Q

Quillajaceae, 224

R

Ranunculaceae, 12, 36, 406

Rhamnaceae, 162, 184, 326
Rosaceae, 122, 178, 180, 181, 224, 232, 256, 382, 464
Rubiaceae, 25, 27, 30, 52, 188
Rutaceae, 44, 59, 85, 145, 190, 202, 244, 347

S

Salicaceae, 191, 319
Santalaceae, 384
Sapotaceae, 398
Scitamineae, 338
Scrophulariaceae, 164, 176
Smilacaceae, 192
Solanaceae, 17, 37, 48, 51, 54, 67, 97
Sterculiaceae, 241
Styracaceae, 198
Symplocaceae, 198

T

Taxaceae, 420
Theaceae, 21

U

Umbelliferae, 34, 275, 278, 279, 280, 340, 341, 349, 351, 356, 374, 401

V

Valerianaceae, 423, 425
Violaceae, 393
Vitaceae, 102

Z

Zingiberaceae, 263, 272, 338, 353
Zygophyllaceae, 57, 227

NOTES

NOTES